Fun Love with Food

ISBN: 978-1-7352759-0-1

Fun Love with Food

A Cross-Cultural Celebration of
Food, Fantasy, and Other Erotic Obsessions

by Dominique Beriniki

PROLOGUE

Umm my! Delicate ... light ... creamy ... and crispy! Last night's dinner and my date were simply mouthwatering. Tender medallions of crispy veal scaloppine topped with tangy strings of fresh mozzarella cheese and bathed in an aromatic cream sauce and the eggplant Parmesan immersed in that fragrant tomato sauce were simply amazing. Best in show, though, was that orgasmic chocolate mandarin mousse parfait. It really got my love juices flowing. It was so silky and sexy, I just wanted to lick it off his delicious lips. But I had to restrain myself before we got kicked out of the restaurant.

"Anais! Anais are you listening to me?" Saturn shouted at me. I had dazed off into a daydream while waiting for her to get into the car after visiting her daughter at a foster home. "I'm sorry! I was just thinking about something. What were you saying?" I quipped while thinking to myself that I'd have to test the recipes for those delicious delicacies and add them to my catering menu.

Growing up in New York I, Anais Alexandre, was always known as a culinary prodigy, and I was certain I'd become one of the best chefs the world had ever known. However, shortly before finishing high school reality set in, and my loving parents had a different plan for my life. They regarded my culinary aspirations as more of a hobby and mandated that I finish a college degree before pursuing my "hobby." According to them, I'd have to be able to pay the bills, and after slaving as menially paid cooks in my uncle's restaurant for years before they landed government jobs, my parents didn't feel cooking was a viable career option for their beloved daughter.

Fast-forward to four years after high school graduation, and there I was—now a beautiful, hip, and sexy 23-year-old social worker, with awe-striking bluish-gray eyes, golden brown skin, and a cast of suitors. Armed with a newly minted college degree in social work and years of experience in the culinary arts, I accepted a job at a girls' shelter and continued to indulge myself with my passion for cooking by moonlighting as a romantic caterer.

From the throngs of seedy confessions to the immensely painful encounters I witnessed through the eyes of children who professed to be in love with the unlovable, captivated with their captors, and betrayed by the persons they least expected, I'd been thrust into a world unlike any I'd ever known. These were just some of the unwelcoming situations I endured daily as a social worker in that emergency shelter for girls— a completely different career path from what I'd expected to be on.

Cooking, however, remained my love language. I believe that being able to cook is a precious gift that lavishes the sensual, sporadically brushes the erotic, and often aspires to accentuate the exotic. To heighten the pleasure of each culinary experience, I also believe that good food should not only stimulate the appetite but all of the body's senses. I've always had an unyielding ambition to satiate even the most discriminating appetite with my culinary prowess—and there's never been a shortage of takers.

Fun Love with Food is a sensual, often erotic, and always dramatic love story and memoir. It introduces Anais Alexandre shortly after she graduates from college, where she started her catering career by hosting intimate parties for clients, her controversial "College Crew," and a colorful cast of suitors. It juxtaposes Anais' love of all things food, and her life-long goal of becoming a restaurateur, with the often daunting and life-changing experiences she encounters while working in the girls' shelter.

Her alluring culinary adventures serve as a welcoming contrast to the breathtaking stories of pride and prejudice manifested throughout her personal life, as well as her work in the shelter. She uses a variety of culinary events and foodie adventures as a catharsis for coping with the oft-unthinkable encounters she endures during a year of employment at the girls' shelter—the tragedies of human trafficking, kidnapping, abandonment, and ultimately murder.

Anais' perseverance and persistence eventually lead her out of the shelter and into a global adventure as a culinary emissary. There she continues her quest for true love and the pursuit of her life-long goals. It is ultimately her burning desire to share her culinary genius with others that drives an enigmatic global love affair with food, people, and fun.

A complimentary electronic Cookbook and Entertainment Guide for each of the featured events mentioned in the novel is available online. Register at www.FunLoveWithFood.com to download.

KEY CHARACTERS

Alona: Young Asian American client and temporary resident at the girls' shelter.

Anais Alexandre (main character): African American from New York City; recent college graduate from the University of Pittsburgh; social worker and counselor. Anais moonlights as a romantic caterer. She is an aspiring food writer and restaurateur, a founding College Crew member, a creative chef, menu designer, and caterer for the College Crew's monthly events.

Ashtley: Young biracial client and a temporary resident at the girls' shelter.

Chantelle: A graduate from the University of Pittsburgh, Chantelle is a hospital administrator, Anais' good friend, and a founding College Crew member.

Charise: A graduate from the University of Pittsburgh, Charise is a law student. A new College Crew member, she is a good friend of Anais and Chantelle and a love interest of Henri.

Chris: A graduate from the University of Pittsburgh, Chris is a newly wealthy Lebanese American and a founding College Crew member. Chris is also a narcissistic love interest of Anais and a best friend of Rafi.

The College Crew: An oft-times controversial, multicultural social group started by a group of good friends and recent graduates from the University of Pittsburgh who meet up monthly for an intercultural celebration of love, life, and fun love with food orchestrated by founding member Anais Alexandre. New members are almost always welcomed to join after attending an event with a founding member.

Corrine: Young African American client and temporary resident at the girls' shelter; Darlese is Corrine's sister.

Corry: Young African American client and temporary resident at the boys' shelter.

Darlese: Young African American client from an unsettled family and a temporary resident at the girls' shelter. Darlese is Corrine's sister.

Diamond Damon: International businessman and Chantelle's Black Nigerian love interest.

Mr. Doug: The girls' shelter's maintenance man.

Dwayne: African American graduate from Point Park University; a probation officer, social worker, and counselor at the girls' shelter; Dwayne is a love interest of Regina.

Eastman: African American parent of shelter clients Darlese and Corrine, Eastman has a violent history.

Ed: Afro-Mexican American male counselor at the girls' shelter.

Evelyn: Jewish American psychologist at the girls' shelter.

Greg: White Italian American graduate from the University of Pittsburgh and friend of Mark B and Rafi; Greg is an honorary College Crew member.

Henri: A Black Congolese musician, Henri is a College Crew member and love interest of Charise.

Ingela: Swedish masseuse at Walter's spas.

JB: African American master musician, teacher, and saxophone player; a graduate from Carnegie Mellon University and a graduate student at the University of Pittsburgh School of Music; JB is a friend and colleague of Penny and a new College Crew member.

Jacque: Tariq's little brother.

Javier: First chair Spanish violinist with the Global Symphony Orchestra and music professor, Javier is one of Anais' favorite catering clients.

Jill: African American catering assistant to Anais.

Joe: Croatian American bartender for Anais' catering.

Julio: Endocrinologist at New York University's medical center, Julio is Javier's baby brother. He is also a philanthropic director and board member of Doctors Working Borders (DWB), a medical missions charity.

Khady: Young Black African Muslim girl from Rwanda, a client and temporary resident at the girls' shelter.

Lauren: White Polish American supervisor of the girls' shelter.

Laverne: Anais' older sister.

Leila: Long-time Malawian friend of Anais; graduate from the University of Pittsburgh; social worker and counselor; Leila is a founding member of the College Crew.

Mari: Spa butler in San Francisco.

Mark B: A University of Pittsburgh graduate, Mark B is a White German Italian American, a social worker and counselor, co-worker of Anais, and a founding College Crew member. He is a brother-like protector of Anais and best friends with Rafi.

Monica: White Italian American supervisor in the Global Cloud University's music department.

Naila: Black Egyptian love interest of Pierre.

Ms. Nellie: African American cook at the shelter and mentor to Anais.

Ollie: Chris's oldest brother, Ollie heads the family's financial planning and investment firm where Chris works.

Patty Jo: White German American female counselor at the girls' shelter.

Penny: Kenyan College Crew member; graduate student of music at the University of Pittsburgh. A member of Pierre's dance troupe, she has a long-term affair with him.

Pierre: Congolese master musician; College Crew member; love interest of Leila, Penny, and Naila.

Rafi: A graduate from the University of Pittsburgh, Rafi is a Black British Ghanaian, a founding College Crew member, a brother-like protector of Anais, best friends with Chris and Mark B, and infatuated with Chantelle.

Regina: African American co-worker of Anais, Regina is a recent graduate from the University of Pittsburgh. A social worker and counselor, Regina is a new College Crew member.

Saturn: Young Puerto Rican client and temporary resident at the girls' shelter, Saturn is a victim of sex trafficking.

Sheila: A graduate from the University of Pittsburgh, Sheila is a White Irish American, a registered nurse, a founding College Crew member, and infatuated with Rafi.

Shirley Santos: A Filipino American, Shirley is a long-time love interest of Chris.

Tariq: Anais' Lebanese love interest from Paris; she meets him while driving down a street in Pittsburgh. A graduate from Carnegie Mellon University, Tariq is an aspiring graduate student.

Trina: Young African American client and temporary resident at the girls' shelter.

Walter: Chris's older brother who owns the Happy Endings Spa chain.

Zee: Young African American client and temporary resident at the girls' shelter.

Fun Love with Food

A Cross-Cultural Celebration of
Food, Fantasy, and Other Erotic Obsessions

1

"Phew! Another day done in the jungle," I said to myself.

It was a beautiful early summer day in the city, and I was finally free to paint the town. I was on the way home from another day of work as a social worker and counselor at a safety net shelter for troubled girls, and I was thanking my momma and daddy for protecting me and helping me get through my teenage years. The stress I felt on a daily basis from the results of trying to deal with young girls who've been faced with the tragic results of human trafficking, kidnapping, endemic prejudice, and abandonment, was daunting.

Every time I left that job I would drive down the Parkway and daydream about my real passion. This day was no exception. It was a cathartic ritual I'd use to protect myself from the crazy atmosphere from which I had just disembarked.

As I moseyed down the Parkway, my head was swimming with imaginations of myself living in Paris while studying French cooking. Suddenly a crazy truck driver started bobbing back and forth, and in and out of both lanes. He finally just settled for straddling the lanes while blocking anyone from passing on either side.

Caught up in my fantasy, I thought to myself, "It would be a true blessing if I could just get to Paris and study cooking with the experts. Maybe then I could get someone to help me open my restaurant. Then I could leave this miserable job and not have to drive this route anymore."

Wishful thinking or not, I was sure it was going to happen one day. I had been catering parties for small groups and romantic couples as a side hustle for the past four years. At this point, I was ready to move to the next level—opening my own bistro and lounge.

I began to visualize myself in my opulent chef's kitchen, fully stocked with all the latest culinary toys. Jumbo lobster tails and butterflied filet mignon drenched in a sultry garlic and tarragon butter sizzle under the stainless steel salamander. Succulent crab bisque carefully crafted with lumps of flavor-packed meat from freshly cracked king crab legs deliciously perfuming the air through the plumes streaming from the steam table. And the double-sided glass door refrigerators beautifully dressed with coiffed salads and jumbo glasses of inviting shrimp cocktails on one side and mouth-watering parfaits and cake bombes on the other. Just as I got to the part where I began to greet the fully packed house of adoring diners, the jerk in the truck cut me off from the passing lane, again!

Good or bad, I'm a little cocky and extremely intolerant when assholes cut me off in traffic. I truly get pissed off when people drive like dangerous maniacs, and I couldn't believe this jerk in a big ole truck was so irresponsible. I decided he needed to be informed that he'd almost killed me, and I was determined to let him know.

Although his truck dwarfed my little Honda Accord, when I finally got an opening, I sped up just enough to reach the driver's window. I began to yell at him.

"Sir, do you know that you're cutting people off in traffic? Are you trying to kill someone?" I yelled out my passenger window.

It quickly became clear to me that he wasn't paying attention to what he'd been doing. Blaringly loud country music poured out from his open windows while he clumsily chatted with someone back and forth with a walkie-talkie in one hand and juggled food and the steering wheel in the other. When he heard me yelling, he got pissed off because I had the audacity to challenge him.

His neck was beet red, his eyes were blazing, and he had no front teeth. He scared the hell out of me!

Then, he picked up a bottle and started threatening me with profanity, while gesturing like he was going to throw the bottle at my windshield. I'm cocky, but not stupid! I slowly retreated as I realized this idiot wasn't playing with a full deck.

I was right! He subsequently slowed down to wait for me while flailing that glass bottle in his hand out the window. At that very moment, I jumped off the Parkway one exit early and moseyed along a less familiar route.

"I'm cocky, but not invincible!" I thought. "And I know how to choose my battles, and when to leave them alone."

Anyway, it was a very beautiful, sunny day, and since the weather had been kind of contemptuous the past few days, this day seemed magical. I was feeling quite nice and I didn't want anything to spoil my joy.

I rolled the windows down, pumped up my music, and jammed my way down the street as I sang at the top of my lungs. All of a sudden I noticed these guys driving alongside and gazing at me while trying to get my attention.

Pretending not to notice the two guys, in two different cars, vying for my attention while attempting to navigate the road, I stared away in shyness. The guy in the first car pulled up beside me at the light for a second time before I finally acknowledged him with a quick glance. At the third light, he made it through. But I didn't, and neither did the guy in the second car who quickly rolled his window down to chat.

"Can I have YOU name and YOU phone number?" he shouted.

I giggled at his broken accent. I couldn't believe he was so bold as to not even say hello first. He just got right to the point and asked for my phone number.

"Why don't you give me your number and maybe I'll call you?" I said. I wasn't in the habit of giving my phone number to just anybody I met while driving down the road.

"Okay!" he said with excitement. And he did! I continued the drive home in disbelief.

When I got home, I'd almost forgotten about the encounter until I received a call an hour or so later from Regina—another counselor and friend at the shelter. She wanted an update on how the family visit went for one of the new girls earlier in the day.

The shelter is a 24 hour, 7 days a week emergency care facility that operates in three shifts. As counselors, we always had to update each other on the status of the girls in the house when we left so that the next shift wouldn't go in blinded by situations that might negatively affect the demeanor of the house. It made for a smoother transition between shifts.

Regina was late that day and as soon as she walked in, the younger girls began to complain and an argument ensued. They questioned why the new girl—Saturn, didn't have to attend school that day. Regina didn't know how to respond to them and called me for the answer. I informed her that Saturn was absent because she had a family visit with her daughter. Although it doesn't take much to get the girls riled up, they often get especially difficult after a family visit. She was no exception.

A majority of the girls—usually preteens and teenagers—are from unstable homes. Most are remanded to foster care and/or the shelter by the juvenile courts very early in their fragile lives. However a number of them are placed in the shelter because their parents no longer want to put up with their shenanigans of running away, staying out late, and not listening to reason. We affectionately referred to them as the "I know knows" because they typically think they know everything.

When they repeatedly get into legal trouble because they clearly don't know everything, the parents eventually decide to temporarily relinquish custody to the juvenile court system as a wakeup call. The judges remand them to the shelter and ultimately to a long-term group home if they're not successfully reunified with their parents after six months.

Sadly, a majority are pseudo-abandoned girls who are there because their parents had either lost custody or abandoned them to the state foster care system—and they were no longer allowed to stay in a foster home. They typically grow up in the foster care system from very young ages, and as a result, they have very poor attitudes and low self-esteem. However they are usually fully informed of their legal rights and well versed in how to use them to manipulate the counselors and the system. Many of those who end up in the safety net shelter lack proper discipline and often act out without severe consequences. Why? Because they inherently know that there isn't much that the counselors and their sworn protectors can do to penalize them—a tough job by anyone's standards. I often felt like raw meat entering the lion's den each time I went to work.

As social workers and ostensibly what's called in loco parentis—parents in place of a legal and/or biological parent—our job was to amicably help them get through the oft-perceived rejection from their families. We were also charged with trying to give them a familial experience in the shelter before they were either reunited with their families, put into a long-term group home, or placed in a permanent foster home, which was very rare.

As for me, I just happened to be one of the lucky recent college graduates who decided that it was in good taste to give back to the community through working with needy youth. Besides, I had student loans up the wazoo and really needed a job to survive.

So there I was, one of the newest youth counselors or should I say "fresh meat" on the block. When I first started, the girls and the seasoned counselors seemed to approach me as if I were just another gullible, wet behind the ears, college grad that wanted to change the world in ninety days. What they didn't know was that I am a "sistergirl" from the heart of New York City, and I grew up with people like them all around me.

I, however, was more fortunate. Although they divorced when I was very young, I was lucky to have very strong, compassionate, and supportive parents who raised me well and taught me that giving back for the betterment of the community was the right thing to do. I also have three older sisters and three brothers who taught me how to be tough but tender, and to always make smart choices. As I saw it, these people were in for a rude awakening.

After I updated Regina, I decided to tell her about my crazy encounter while driving home. I told her what happened, how handsome he was, and how I thought that the guy was Arabic or Lebanese.

She quickly replied, "Girl, you know those Arabs will treat you like a queen. I used to date one and he always took me to the finest places, and the sex was A-MAZING!" she said.

"Well where is he now?" I asked.

"He went back to wherever he was from!" she said in a humorous rant. "Just know one thing, don't marry him, or you'll be his slave. Or should I say, just another one of his many wives," she followed.

"You're crazy!" I replied as we both laughed hysterically.

"First of all, why would you stereotype people? And second, if you think I'm going to marry some man I don't even know anything about, you have certainly lost your mind," I said. "Besides, can you imagine me bringing home an Arab guy to my dad, the great Rev. Emanuel Gibson Alexandre, leader of the National Baptist EVERYBODY and EVERYTHING Convention? I'm not sure he'd take that too well!" I said as we both continued to laugh hysterically.

"Yeah, well, give the man a call and have fun. You're young and you ain't got nothing to lose," she replied. Then she went further and said, "I have an idea, how about we make it a double date in case he's a maniac?"

Regina was always on the hunt for a man, and I was sure it would be a disaster if she were with me. So I quickly replied, "No, ... that's okay! I'll just meet him in a public place where there are lots of people. You might run him off," I joked. We both laughed again and said our goodbyes.

Later that evening, I decided to call him. He immediately answered the phone and spoke with a very thick but sexy accent. I couldn't really make out its origins, so it was the first thing I asked.

"Where are you from?" I asked.

He laughed a bit and said, "Well how about we start with my name?" I was a little embarrassed. I guess he perceived my angst.

"Oh, I'm sorry, please excuse my manners," I said. "My name is Anais. What's your name?" I followed. He chuckled.

"Your name is just as beautiful as you are!" he said. "I couldn't stop thinking about you, and I was hoping that you would call," he followed.

Then he told me his name is Tariq, and that he'd never forget my name. He was from Paris, France, via Beirut, Lebanon.

"Now what are the chances of this happening?" I thought to myself.

He said I should never forget his name either because he was named after the famous leader of the Moors, Tāriq ibn Ziyād, the renowned conqueror who brought Spain under Muslim rule in the eighth century, and subsequently gave his name to the Rock of Gibraltar—which translates to *mountain of Tāriq* in Spanish.

My first impression was that he's an intellectual, and I had to put my thinking cap on. Then I finally realized what he was referencing.

Wow! My great, great grandfather was a Moor. The Moors were black Africans. No wonder he likes black women I thought to myself in a snicker. He'd taken me by surprise and impressed me at the same time.

"Very interesting," I said. "So what brings you to Pittsburgh?" I asked.

He said he graduated from Carnegie Mellon University a week earlier with a degree in electrical engineering and was awaiting a decision on his admission into the graduate program in robotics. In the meantime his father was working to get him an internship with a friend's company here in the U.S. He had a little downtime to relax until either he heard something from the graduate school or the internship came through. Then he asked me if he could take me to dinner to get to know me a little better.

I was a bit hesitant. "But I don't know you," I said.

With his strong, sexy accent he quickly responded. "Well I don't know you either, but that's why I want to take you to dinner and talk a little more. You can meet me somewhere if you'd like."

He was right, so I thought if I suggested a place that I liked and met him there, it should be filled with enough people to protect me. I suggested my favorite jazz spot. I love jazz, and I'm a big time foodie. The Balcony in Pittsburgh had some of the best crab bisque I'd ever tasted, the best jazz in town, and the ambiance was fantastic.

"Okay, how about I meet you at the Balcony in Shadyside at 6:00 p.m. tomorrow?" I said. He agreed and we hung up the phone.

All night I couldn't help but wonder if he was going to be nice or a nut. After all, I'd never met anyone driving down the street before, let alone taken anyone's phone number for a date while driving down the street. But being the adventure-seeking romantic I am, I was up for the challenge and couldn't wait to see what lay ahead.

I decided to prepare my clothes ahead of time so I wouldn't be late. My shift at the shelter didn't end until 4:00 p.m. and it usually took me at least a half hour to get home.

Excited but apprehensive about what to expect, I wanted to be ready for anything. I chose a sassy blue silk swing dress that fit ever so nicely around my shapely hips and complimented my bluish gray eyes; matched it with corset sandals with two-inch heels that graced my mocha cream skin; and complemented the outfit with emerald-cut blue sapphire pendant earrings with a matching necklace that my mom gifted me for graduation. I was all set and ready to indulge in a new adventure.

2

Tariq: The First Date

I slept well the night before and woke up early to be sure to get to work at the shelter on time. I wanted to leave as soon as the clock struck 4:00 p.m. As usual, work seemed to drag on forever. After breaking up two fights, reprimanding three wanna be gangbangers for harassing the new girl, and sitting through two hours of what was supposed to be alternative school, I was finally free to go home and doll up.

I drove home and proceeded with my beautification ritual. First I drank my special hibiscus yoni love teatox elixir to "perfume my juices" like the French say. Then I took a sensual bath while sipping more of the elixir to cleanse myself on both the inside and outside. At the same time, I gave myself a quick shave to make sure everything was clean below the belly button, and followed that with one of my delicious natural scrubs to lacquer my skin with fragrant essential oils—chocolate-covered strawberry seemed just right for this occasion.

After fixing my hair, I put on my beautiful outfit, a little makeup, a splash of "love dew," and I was out the door. I wanted to make a good first impression, so I didn't want to be late.

I actually arrived before Tariq and decided to wait for him at the bar near the jazz band. Shortly after I sat down, the bartender asked me what I'd like to drink. I informed him that I was waiting for someone for dinner and didn't care for anything. But he insisted.

"A band member has already purchased you a drink and asked me to deliver it. He just wants you to order what you'd like," he said.

"Oh!" I exclaimed. I was a bit taken by surprise.

"That was sweet of him. Please tell him I said thank you," I responded.

I ordered a pomegranate martini, but I didn't have time to really digest what had just happened. Just as I turned to thank the mysterious band member for the drink, the saxophone player began his announcement.

"This next tune titled 'This One's for You' is dedicated to the beautiful lady in blue at the bar. Cheers!" he said, as he raised his glass to me.

Mystery solved! I thought. I was flattered to say the least. I blew a kiss and whispered "Thank you!"

Suddenly a hand gently touched my shoulder and whispered my name. It was Tariq. I looked up and he was so handsome he nearly took my breath away.

"I'm sorry I'm late. A friend borrowed my car and returned a bit late which held me up," he said.

"No problem," I said. "I've been well taken care of as you see."

He smiled and brushed it off as if he hadn't seen what had just happened at the bar. I didn't think anything of it either, so I took the drink off the bar and we headed for the main dining room.

When we got to the table, he immediately pulled the chair out for me to sit down before taking his seat. Then he told the waiter to give him the same thing I was drinking. I think he did that to blow smoke in the saxophone player's face because he had walked off with me. But he wouldn't stop gazing at me with his beautiful chestnut brown eyes. I felt obliged to ask, "Why are you staring at me like that?"

"Because you're even more beautiful from head to toe," he said.

"Now what does that mean?" I followed. My defenses began to get the best of me. But he quickly cleaned it up.

"No, no, no! I just mean that I only saw your face in the car, and I really didn't know how the rest of you would look. But I was right, you are as beautiful as I'd expected. All of you! I'm having a hard time taking my eyes off of you!" he said.

We both laughed. Then he asked if he could order for me as a way of guessing about my personality. "After all, you picked the restaurant, so I'm sure you like the food." He said this as a matter of fact.

I was a bit hesitant. I'd never had anyone ask to order for me, but I eventually relented. It was actually a bit of a turn-on.

"Okay, let's see if you can figure out my favorites," I said.

The Balcony was one of Pittsburgh's most notable jazz spots. Each time I visited the famous restaurant, I would have to order the Kickin' Crab Bisque. But I refused to give Tariq a hint of what my favorites were just to test his wit. Surprisingly he did a great job.

He started out by ordering: "The Kickin' Crab Bisque for the lady and shrimp cocktail for me, and a bottle of pinot grigio to compliment the seafood. The lady will follow with the flame-broiled lobster tail with a twice-baked potato, followed by a fresh salad. I will have a New York strip steak prepared rare with the same accompaniments. We'll save dessert for later, if we have room," he finished. Then he thanked the waitress.

"Okay, so how well did I do?" he said.

"You did pretty good," I said. "You lucked out and ordered two of my very favorite dishes. However, I don't drink a lot of wine, and I never eat dessert because I never have room. But I'll have a couple of sips of the wine with my lobster."

"Very good?" he said with a confident but cocky smile.

"Very good!" I replied—I was quickly becoming more attracted to his brilliance.

The service was wonderful, the conversation was very stimulating, and dinner was magical. After the delicious dinner laced by the sultry sounds of that mysterious saxophone player, I was almost swept off my feet.

The crab bisque was exquisite! Giant lumps of fresh-picked king crab bathed in a velvety cream sauce with a kick of picante, and served with homemade crackers. The tender lobster tail was broiled to perfection with an herbal butter glaze and a side of heated butter and lemon wedges. His filet mignon was grilled to perfection with just the right amount of pink on the inside, and the twice-baked potatoes and refreshing salads were like eye candy—not only delicious to look at, but truly upheld the Balcony's four-star reputation.

Tariq applauded my choice of restaurant. During the conversation, I told him that I'm a foodie who loves to cook and shared my dream of studying cooking in Paris and opening a restaurant. He said his mother's also a foodie, and he too cooks a bit. To entice him, I promised to make him dinner one day—if he deserved it.

"So what are the criteria for deserving the honor of you preparing a meal for me?" he said.

"I'm not quite sure yet, but I'll let you know," I replied.

After dinner, I went to the restroom and attempted to thank the saxophone player for the drink. But I only managed to wave goodbye. He winked at me while playing his sax, and waved back.

Tariq and I left the restaurant and decided to take a walk before saying goodnight. I thanked him for dinner with a warm hug and said he could choose the restaurant next time.

"Can next time be tomorrow? Please?" he said.

At first I was taken aback that he wanted to meet again so soon. But I was enamored with his beautiful smile, his gentleness, and most of all his intellectual and stimulating conversation. I was excited to be able to see him again. The word just fell out of my mouth.

"Okay!" I said.

"Great!" he replied with enthusiasm.

"Can I pick you up at seven?" he asked. "That way I won't keep you waiting again so some musician can try to move in on my girl." He snickered. I thought he hadn't caught on to the saxophone player's move, but clearly he had. But I just took note just like he did.

"Your girl huh?" I questioned as I chuckled and wrote my address and phone number on a card for him.

"Yup, you'll see. You'll be mine soon," he said with unabashed confidence. We both laughed and I gave him the card.

"I'll see you tomorrow at 7:00 p.m., and I hope you choose a good restaurant," I said jokingly.

He laughed and assured me I'd enjoy it. We wished each other good night and off we went.

Menu

Join Us for a Surf & Turf Dinner for Two
featuring

APPETIZERS

Kickin' Crab Bisque

Shrimp Cocktail

⁓

DINNER

Herb-Roasted Filet Mignon

Lobster Tails

Twice-Baked Potatoes

Fresh Buttercrunch Salad

⁓

BEVERAGES

Pomegranate Martinis

Pinot Grigio Wine

⁓

BEAUTY RITUAL

Hibiscus yoni love teatox elixir. Bodacious body chocolate-covered strawberry body treatment and "love dew."

3

"What a wonderful guy he is! I just may have to treat him to some of my culinary skills. But we'll see how this next date goes, and I'll decide from there," I thought to myself as I drifted off to sleep in content. It was one of the few times I was truly impressed with someone after the first date.

The Shelter: The New Girl

The next day at work was beastly as usual. I had to take the new girl, Saturn, on another family visit to see her daughter, and decided to conduct my mandatory daily individual counseling session with her. It was a perfect time because we were alone and none of the other girls were around to interrupt us.

It turned out to be one of the most unusually disturbing sessions I'd experienced while working at the shelter. She told me her stepfather had been molesting her since she was eight years old. I had not yet gotten an opportunity to read her file, but she shared with me that it was the real reason she was in the shelter.

Saturn was only sixteen years old, but one of the oldest girls in the shelter. To make matters worse, she explained that the baby I had just taken her to visit at another foster home was the love child of she and her stepfather. He was now in jail for beating and molesting her and her mother in the middle of the street.

From listening to her talk, it became apparent to me that the beatings in the street had been a regular occurrence for years. But these were ignored because they lived in a dangerous neighborhood, and the neighbors assumed they were prostitutes and he was their pimp. Unfortunately nobody reported the public beatings, and they lived in obscurity for quite some time until a new neighbor finally got fed up and turned the stepfather in. So there she was in the shelter—away from her family, and she was not happy.

After talking with Saturn more at length, my gut feeling was that the stepfather had forced her and her mother into prostitution. Even worse, she seemed empathetic toward her stepfather, and spoke as if she was in love with him. But it didn't stop there; she really didn't understand why Child Protective Services took her and the child from her mother.

My parents consistently reminded me that we are all charged with making the world a better place. My job at the shelter was part of that charge. As such, I always had to remind myself that I had to help the girls to understand why things happen the way they do—even if it's not always fair. But most times, that's easier said than done. These kinds of situations were just the beginning of the real drama I had to reconcile every day. When it was quitting time, it was like thank God it's Friday over and over again—a true relief.

Four o'clock quickly came after we got back to the shelter, and I was free to go home and get ready for my second date with Tariq. I felt like a kid on the way to a candy store. On the drive home I couldn't stop thinking about him.

"He is soooo handsome. A five foot, eleven inch tall, clean cut, slim, debonair French gentleman, who certainly knows how to treat a lady," I said to myself.

He made me feel so special, and I couldn't wait to see him again. I was overwhelmed with excitement.

Tariq: A Titillating Surprise

I got home at 4:30 p.m., finished my beauty ritual, and was almost dressed when the doorbell rang at 6:30 p.m. It was Tariq. I wasn't quite ready so I invited him in.

When he walked past my kitchen and dining room, he noticed all of the utensils and serving items. "What kind of work do you do?" he said with heightened curiosity. I explained to him that I'm a social worker, but I moonlight as a romantic caterer. "And like I said last night, if you're nice to me, I might let you try the goods one day," I playfully reminded him.

"If you cook for me, I'll reciprocate and make you a delicious French meal," he quickly replied.

Now my curiosity was elevated. He already knew about my desire to learn about French food, so I was certain he was using it to his advantage. The first thing I thought about was my desire to take cooking classes in France. I began to get a little excited about the possibility of tasting that homemade, rich French cuisine that I had so longed to learn more about. But then I caught myself before I shared too much information. First I had to make a determination of whether he had good taste in restaurants before I would even cook for him and then trust him to cook for me.

"I'm sure you'll enjoy it!" he said confidently.

"We'll see," I replied, and we left to go to the restaurant.

The quick ride in the car was filled with relaxing music and playful conversation about living in Pittsburgh. After about a ten-minute ride, he turned the car into a somewhat empty parking lot across from the Foodland grocery store, and touted, "We're here!" The outside of the building was rather generic—just a simple red sign mounted on the front of the building that read Asian Fusion.

"This is interesting," I thought. He opened my door and escorted me into the restaurant.

The first entrance was a somewhat bland foyer, with a few posters in Mandarin and a beautiful assortment of porcelain masks hanging all over the walls. He opened the second door, and it was breathtaking. It was an incredible Japanese-inspired indoor village. I felt as if I had been transported to another country. The walls were covered in what looked like ancient silk scrolls. Multitudes of bonsai trees in all sizes flanked beautiful cherry trees in full bloom throughout the space. Traditional Japanese string music played softly in the background and perfectly complemented the ambiance.

A beautiful sushi bar loaded with people enjoying fresh sushi being prepared by four different sushi chefs (aka *itamae*) wrapped around the entire front wall. Just across from the sushi bar stood an intricately carved, fifty-foot wide wooden bar with matching bar stools. It was complemented by at least three hundred different bottles of liquor on mirrored walls behind it and ten-foot high wine refrigerators on either side.

The hostess greeted us, and led us to another part of the restaurant. We walked over a small bridge atop a huge pond filled with hundreds of beautiful multicolored koi fish. The pond was fed from a massive waterfall on an intricately carved rock wall. Upon exiting the bridge, we began to pass a series of private dining coves.

"Your private *ryoutei* is just to your right Mr. Tariq," she said. He thanked her, and we entered one of the most intimate places I'd ever seen.

It was a cozy and elegantly decorated hidden enclave. The walls were draped in red and gold silk cords that surrounded an ornate framed picture of a Japanese geisha. The chairs were a combination of black stained teak wood with black silk cushions intricately woven with huge pink and red chrysanthemums. When I sat down it was so soft I felt like I was sitting on a cloud.

But the table was the *pièce de résistance*. It was already staged with a beautiful bottle of still water, crystal glasses, cloth napkins, and porcelain chopsticks supported by small porcelain knife stands to prevent them from touching the table.

The polished yet rustic table was cut from a single wood block and had a petite barbecue grill built in the center. A strategically hidden ventilation hood was suspended from the ceiling to quickly rid the room of the smoke from the grill. I had never seen anything like it before, and my curiosity was at an all time high.

I leaned over the table to ask Tariq how he found this little gem in Pittsburgh. But before he could answer, the waitress came and asked for our drink orders, and if we would be having hibachi.

"Yes, but I think we'd like to start with a few appetizers, and maybe a couple of sushi rolls," Tariq responded. "Can we take a quick look at the menu?" he followed.

We ordered drinks while she handed us menus. I didn't recognize anything—it listed a variety of Korean and Japanese dishes, but they were all foreign to me. I'd never eaten Japanese or Korean food before, and certainly didn't know what to order. I relented.

"You picked the restaurant, so I'm at your mercy for the food selection again," I said.

We both chuckled. "I'm sure you'll enjoy the food," he said.

First, the sushi—he ordered a California roll, a dragon roll, two pieces of seared tuna *nigiri*, and two pieces of *unagi nigiri* sushi. "We'll have the assorted bulgoki for dinner," he said. Off the waitress went, and shortly thereafter the parade of beautiful food began its arrival.

The first waitress arrived with our drinks. For me, a frozen piña colada served in a hurricane glass and garnished with a whipped cream topping, a cherry, and a side skewer of fresh pineapple topped off with chunks of sugared coconut. For Tariq, an Oral Sex on the Beach—first time I'd ever heard of that drink. I couldn't wait to see it, and it did not disappoint. A beautifully and colorfully layered drink with red brandy on the bottom, a shot of blue curaçao liqueur in the middle, a garnish of fresh pineapple and peach slices, and a cherry skewered on top, it was a carefully crafted piece of art in a small brandy snifter that clearly articulated the skills of the bartender.

The drinks definitely began to set the mood for an interesting evening. Before I could even begin to process that message, another waiter arrived with a beautiful two-foot bamboo boat–shaped serving dish filled with sushi. It too was an explosion of colors and textures—small dishes of pickled ginger and wasabi occupied the bow; the stern held the ponzu sauce for dipping; and the sushi stood out in the middle of the boat like a series of perfectly wrapped little edible gifts of differing shapes. It was my first real shot at trying sushi—it was a home run! The choices were impeccable—a perfect balance of savory, sweet, and salty, with a wonderful umami finish. I couldn't wait to see what the bulgoki was going to taste like after the delicious appetizers.

"Did you enjoy the sushi?" Tariq asked.

"It was incredible, and it was my first time trying it. Thank you for introducing me to something new," I said.

"Great! So how am I doing for restaurant choices?" he said.

"Well you hit first base when you opened the door and I saw this magnificent place. Then you made it to second base when we were seated in this very intimate and private *ryoutei*. You're on third base now," I said.

"That's promising," he said as he picked up his drink for a toast and suddenly kissed me. I felt like I was struck by lightning—it was an extremely titillating sensation. Chills ran up and down my spine, and a stream of moisture promptly lubricated my love canal. I couldn't even respond quickly enough. I just kind of looked at him with a stunted glimmer.

Luckily I didn't have to respond because again the waitress interjected by taking the empty sushi boat away and lighting the hibachi. After she finished, two other waiters followed. The first delivered platters of raw chicken, beef, and shrimp that had been marinated and prepared for the grill. The second waiter followed with steamed rice, condiments, and an assortment of fresh and pickled vegetables, and put the first round of shrimp on the grill.

The bulgoki was even more amazing than the drinks and appetizers. The explosion of flavors from the searing hot shrimp bursting with hints of garlic and ginger commingled perfectly with the fragrant steamed rice and crunchy pickled vegetables. Then Tariq taught me how to wrap the rice and all of those delicate morsels in the fresh green lettuce leaves that came with the sides, and to eat them like a wrap. My whole body reveled in the delicious combinations while my taste buds leaped with the precision of a perfect solo executed by a prima ballerina.

"Umh, umh, umh ... home run!" I exclaimed with excitement. "You've impressed me for sure!" I said.

The delicious and beautiful food, the amazing ambiance of the restaurant, and another great intellectual conversation made for a second magical evening. I felt compelled to invite him to dinner at my place. Then he confessed that his group of college friends had just celebrated graduation at the restaurant and he really enjoyed it. He thought I'd enjoy it, too.

He was right! So I had to pay up. But I informed him that it would have to wait for a couple of days because my plate was full on Friday and Saturday. I already had plans for girls' night out on Friday and my monthly Saturday Night Live party with my college crew. So I invited him to Sunday brunch.

"That's perfect!" he said. Then he put down his chopsticks and started kissing me so passionately I couldn't catch my breath. When he started nibbling at the sensitive spot on my neck, I knew I had to stop him.

"Oh my God!" I said. "We shouldn't do this here."

"You're right. But I just can't seem to stay away from you. You're making me crazy! ... But I know it's inappropriate, so I'll be good," he said with the emotion of a child who had been told to stay out of the cookie jar.

I, however, was enchanted with him, and his attraction to me. I was glowing from the inside out. We finished the amazing dinner and decided to drive downtown and take a walk to the Point Park fountain. It was a beautiful backdrop for closing out the romantic evening.

We walked and talked about what he wanted to do in the future, and I continued to be amazed by his brilliance. We even jokingly agreed to disagree that Michael Jackson was a musical genius. But the tension from kissing at dinner was like a giant gorilla in the room—hot and heavily weighing on us the entire time we walked.

"I can't take it anymore! Can I please kiss you?" he said with angst. Overwhelmed with emotion and feeling extremely good, I kissed him, and he stole my breath again. He held my face ever so gently. There was a fierce passion in the way his tongue thrust past my teeth. It was like he was starved for the taste of me ... like he couldn't get enough ... and I was the most wanted woman in the world.

Just as he realized I was losing my ability to breath, he gently moved to my neck again. This time he started biting me with a passionate pressure that I went nuts over. I started going crazy inside, and I couldn't control myself.

"Oh God! You feel so good," I said.

"You smell so good! I just want to eat you!" he said as he continued to devour my neck and work his way down to my breast.

I knew I had to stop him. I pulled his face to mine and planted a big kiss on him.

"I think we should go now. I have a long day of work tomorrow and don't want to be exhausted," I said as I pulled myself together.

The first thing on my mind was that I didn't want him to think that I was a cock teaser. But I hardly knew him well enough to let him into my personal space so quickly—or my *boudoir* as the French call it. We ended the night with another long passionate kiss goodbye from his car and confirmed our date for Sunday brunch at 2:00 p.m.

Menu

Join Us for an Asian Odyssey for Two
featuring

APPETIZERS

SUSHI SURPRISE

California Roll: cucumber, imitation crab, and avocado

Dragon Roll: fried shrimp, cucumber, and avocado

Seared Tuna Nigiri

Unagi Nigiri Sushi: eel and rice

DINNER

ASSORTED BULGOKI

Korean beef, chicken, and shrimp barbecue

PICKLED VEGGIES

STEAMED RICE

BEVERAGES

ROYAL PIÑA COLADA

ORAL SEX ON THE BEACH

4

F riday at the jungle, the shelter that is, and I was prepared for the drama. All I could think about was the fun-filled weekend I had planned.

First of all, I couldn't wait to share my excitement about Tariq with the girls at girls' night out after work. It was also the weekend of our monthly Saturday Night Live celebration with my College Crew, which was always special.

I came up with the idea after we did something similar while struggling to get through college. I figured that if we could make a party on almost nothing while in college, it should be a blast when everybody really had something to contribute. Saturday Night Live, aka "SNL," was a monthly event started by a group of us who stayed in Pittsburgh after graduation. It would help us to stay in touch, support each other, and catch up with each other's lives while having a blast. The great thing is that we all agreed to set aside time and support each other through life.

There were seven original members, but it quickly grew to fifteen plus over the year after graduation. Each month we'd plan a different theme and everyone contributed. I designed the menus while everyone else chipped in on planning the activities. Rafi, who is like a little brother to me, was responsible for invitations and making sure everyone knew the time, date, place, and theme. Sheila, our resident nurse, and Leila, who's like a sister to me, helped coordinate what everyone needed to bring or send to make things go smoothly. We rotated the hosting every month so that everyone shared the expense and the responsibilities, but all of us always helped out as needed.

The rules of attendance suggested that we could invite other people whenever we wanted. Everyone just had to do his or her best to inform me, as the chef, along with whoever was hosting, early enough to prepare properly. It was always a great time for catching up with the guys and girls, having a blast while we let our hair down, meeting new people, and even talking about things that might not always be comfortable—which was always the highlight of the evening.

The best thing was that we always felt secure enough with each other to get through the good and the bad conversations without being disgruntled for too long. It helped all of us to mature in ways we didn't even think possible.

The College Crew: Leila

June's theme for SNL was a salute to the beginning of summer, and was being hosted by Leila. I was looking forward to the celebration but was sure we were in for a bit of drama. Leila has been a family friend and like a sister to me from the day I stepped foot in Pittsburgh to go to college. Her older sister went to college with my aunt and hooked me into the family immediately so I'd always have somewhere to go when I couldn't be with my family. Leila also helped me get the job at the girls' shelter—so we always shared horror stories because she worked at the boys' shelter for the same company.

Leila is still a true confidant to me. I love her dearly, but sometimes the relationship is very challenging. She never allows herself to be vulnerable, which often causes me a lot of angst. The worst part is that she often lies about what's going on in her life to avoid reality or opening up to people. Unfortunately those lies often catch up with her, and always at the wrong time.

About six months before she was scheduled to host SNL, she'd got into a situation with the leader of her dance troupe, Pierre. We affectionately called him "the Congo Casanova." Everybody knew his reputation for being a ladies man, including Leila. However, she first introduced him to the group as her so-called "brother." That wasn't true.

The College Crew: Pierre

Pierre is a suave, handsome, and debonair five-foot, ten-inch French African from the Congo, with silky smooth dark chocolate skin and a slim but muscular build. Keeping with the Congolese tradition for style, he's always dressed to perfection, smells good all the time, and treats women like gold—most of the time that is. To top it off, he's a master musician and performer.

He was well sought-after internationally in the early days of his career. However, when he discovered he could fare better in America with citizenship, at the ripe old age of 23 he naively married the first woman who agreed to help him out. The biggest problem with what he called his "marriage of convenience" manifested itself through a conflict with his devout Christianity—which mandates that he be committed physically and emotionally only to his wife. However, he wasn't physically or emotionally attracted to her, and never hesitated to make it well known to anyone who inquired. As almost a matter of fact, he'd eloquently explain that at the blooming age of 53, she was old enough to be his mother. It clearly bothered him.

Shortly after taking his vows, he started having affairs with his dancers.

Leila, his so-called "little sister," was always in the background helping to clean up the carnage. The girls would fight, leave the group, and warn her to spare herself from ever getting trapped by his physical and sexual enticements. The last warning came from Penny, the Kenyan.

The College Crew: Penny

Penny is a pianist, dancer, and African music scholar. Leila introduced Penny to the College Crew after the two met while dancing with Pierre's dance troupe. She joined the group while still in undergrad and was a good friend to Leila.

The girls never trusted Penny because she started sleeping with Pierre while he was married for citizenship, and was often the cause of the controversies with the other dancers. However, she also became Pierre's go to administrative assistant—which caused her to have favor with him.

After Penny's first year of graduate school, she accepted a one-year music performance residency in South Africa. Even though she was leaving, she continually made it well known to everyone that she was deeply in love with Pierre, had no intentions of ending their relationship, and would continue to claim her man. She specifically implored Leila not to sleep with Pierre as she suspected them of being too close.

But to Leila, Penny's warning was more of an invitation to seek out Pierre for herself. As soon as Penny started traveling back and forth to South Africa, she quickly replaced Penny as Pierre's right-hand girl, and started hanging out with him more and more. As predicted, it ultimately led to a clandestine relationship that neither one would admit to at first. He clearly had other ideas. But so did Leila.

To make matters worse, after a five-year marriage of convenience, Pierre got his green card shortly after Penny's initial departure and immediately divorced himself from the marriage. For him it meant he now had the freedom to be with whomever he wanted, and he took great strides to find the right one. He immediately flew to South Africa to visit Penny for two weeks.

Leila, however, continued lingering in the background like his flunky. Whenever he needed money, or transportation, or even a booty call, we'd later learn she was right there for him. He essentially had the best of both worlds.

We also learned that shortly after Penny's departure, she started sending tickets for Pierre to travel to South Africa to service her sexual needs under the guise that he was coming to make music. In the meantime, Leila continued to take care of his financial needs in Pittsburgh. When he wasn't traveling to see Penny, or going back and forth to New York to facilitate a drumming residency he picked up at the Brooklyn Museum of African Art, he was hanging with Leila all the time.

The gig at the Brooklyn Museum was another added layer to his complicated life. While completing his so-called drumming residency in New York, which was now moving into year two, he'd often borrow Leila's car to make the six-hour journey to New York from Pittsburgh. Every now and then Leila would join him. That, too, became less frequent and Pierre again began to capitalize on his freedom.

During the residency, Naila—one of the volunteers at the museum—was really inspired by his music and befriended both Pierre and Leila. Naila was a young, beautiful Afro-Egyptian American, who had a cushy job as an assistant editor for one of the top Black magazines in the world. She became a dear friend and resource to Pierre and Leila, and after hanging out with them several times after the workshops and concerts, she invited them to sleep in her guest room when they came to New York. Her generosity saved them the expense of hotel stays.

However, soon thereafter, Pierre refused to allow Leila to travel to New York with him, and he began renting cars instead of borrowing hers so that he didn't have to explain where he was going. Leila didn't think anything of it and assumed he was just handling business as usual.

About eight months after the guest room invitation, out of the blue, Leila got an unexpected phone call from Naila. She was in tears. She said she was in Pittsburgh at Pierre's house and asked if she could spend the night at Leila's. Leila didn't quite understand what was going on. But when Naila tried to explain, her explanation was incoherent due to her crying, so Leila finally resorted to going to Pierre's house to pick her up.

When she pulled into the driveway, Naila was sitting on the steps. She had calmed down a bit and began to explain.

While attempting to make a surprise visit to see Pierre, she didn't receive the warm welcome she was expecting. She flew in from New York, took a taxi to his house, and knocked on the door. She said she'd confirmed with him that he'd be home, but it took a long time for anyone to answer the door. Finally his roommate answered, but it threw her off because it was a woman and he'd never mentioned her. She was invited in and asked if Pierre was available. But she said the woman didn't speak good English and simply pointed to his room. When she knocked on the door, she could hear people scurrying, so she opened the door.

Pierre looked at her in shock. He was in the bed with another woman and Naila went ballistic! She tore into him, tore up the house, and destroyed anything that was in her way. He was so taken aback that he told his roommate to take her outside, and not to let her back in the house.

Furious now, she tried to push her way back into the house to confront him again. But no one would open the door. She started crying again and Leila suggested they go to her house.

They got in Leila's car, went to her house, and the shit hit the fan. This time the shit flying was hitting everybody.

Naila went on to tell Leila that Pierre had recently asked her to marry him after courting her for the past eight months. He wined and dined her, and she really fell in love with him. But she became suspicious because she couldn't always account for his whereabouts, so she told him she'd think about it.

Feeling somewhat insecure about the idea of giving up her life in New York to move to Pittsburgh with him, she said she needed to be sure. To feel more comfortable with making a decision about whether or not to accept his offer, she decided to make a surprise visit.

"Is he really single? And, is he truly ready for me?" she said. Those were the questions she said she kept asking herself. Unfortunately her uneasy feeling was now validated, and she was devastated.

Now it was Leila's turn to get in on the action. She told Naila that she had no idea about the two of them. According to Leila, she and Pierre had been dating for the past ten months.

Both stood silent. Facing each other with their mouths open and hearts broken, the tears fell relentlessly. They were caught up in a devastating but awakening moment in time. Not knowing what else to do, they decided to go back to Pierre's house and confront him.

Leila banged on the door and shouted, "Pierre, you are a liar and a cheater! Why didn't you tell Naila that we're together?"

After about two hours of shouting and banging on the door, Pierre finally opened it. He humbly apologized to Naila for what she saw, and then began angrily shouting at Leila.

"Why are you lying?! Huh!? We were *never* in a relationship! I *don't love you like that*," he shouted as he scolded her for seemingly ruining a relationship with Naila.

Again he turned to Naila and asked for forgiveness. But Naila was not only heartbroken from catching him in the bed with another woman, but from the fact that he could be so mean and indifferent to Leila. She decided to leave with Leila and talk about what had just happened.

The next day Naila returned to New York heartbroken, and Leila called me every day for two weeks to lament about how badly he treated her. Not only was she heartbroken, but also even more devastated because he had "borrowed" more than $10,000 from her savings, and she wasn't sure if he'd pay it back. But to be honest, she was fully aware that one of his flaws was that he had a habit of not paying back loans. Against her better judgment, she'd loaned him money she'd set aside to help her widowed mom buy a house for the family thinking that he would never renege on his commitment to her.

I'd never seen her so vulnerable. I tried to assure her that things would get better, but she had to insist that he return the money. However, it was clear to me that he didn't have good intentions with her heart. So I advised her to get her money, and to not get intimate with him again because he would only hurt her again.

But a true Casanova doesn't give up so easily—and neither did Pierre. It didn't take long before he laid the moves on Leila again, and she willingly jumped right back in his trap. This time he was in for a rude awakening.

During their rants, both Leila and Naila proudly shared their status as virgins. I guessed it was probably why Pierre was so attracted to them. Even though she knew he wasn't in love with her, and betrayed her, Leila decided to get the upper hand. She offered her virginity to him. Sure enough, she ended up pregnant after the first month. Two weeks after he found out, he left on a plane to visit Penny in South Africa. Again Leila was heartbroken, but she hid it from all of us for three months.

The real truth was that she not only betrayed herself and her friends Penny and Naila, but Pierre, too. She'd decided to conceive a child without his permission, and later confessed that she couldn't imagine herself having a baby with anyone else. So she intentionally got pregnant.

I'd been having great difficulty with the situation, but just as a friend would do, I tried to stick by her the best I could. Now the fireworks and fallout were increasing as she entered her fourth month of pregnancy. However, on a more positive note, despite all the drama, she was still prepared to host the great Saturday Night Live as a salute to the summer solstice, and I was at her disposal.

5

We planned to do a variety of grilled fish, ribs, vegetables, and steaks to celebrate the summer solstice and opening of the summer partying season. I wanted to test a new shrimp ceviche I'd been working on for an upcoming catering event, and added it to the list. Leila also suggested that I make my infamous strawberry and chocolate ganache tarts as gifts for everyone to take home. Since she was hosting the event, I went to her house to prep the food for the main courses but agreed to make the dessert at home.

The activities crew planned for us to play volleyball and Spades, but Leila and I decided to spice things up a bit. We hid a sack of water guns near the water hose, and individual ones all over the backyard for backup. Right after dessert we would give the cue so everyone could join in the water fight.

Our plan was in place and I couldn't wait for the festivities to begin. All I had to do was get through the last workday of the week at the shelter and a weekend of excitement awaited.

Girls' Night Out: A Smooth Touch

Every other Friday night some of the girls from the College Crew and I meet up to have our special girls' night out. A nice club or restaurant, sexy food and drinks, and lots of fun are our mottos. It allows us to catch up with each other's lives in between the larger monthly SNL celebrations, while decompressing from the crazy workweek.

After wrapping up the last arduous workday of the week, I was ready to turn up the volume for fun. I left work and went home with the intent of planning for brunch with Tariq and making the strawberry and chocolate ganache tarts before going out with the girls. Time was running short before I had to meet everyone, so I didn't have enough time to make the tarts. No one ever wants to be late for girls' night out, or we'd risk missing something important—like the good gossip, so I pushed making the tarts to Saturday morning. But before I set out, I needed to cleanse my mind and body of all the week's stress.

I indulged in one of my beauty rituals: a double portion of my hibiscus and orange yoni teatox love elixir, a deep soak with my favorite bath salts—risqué rose this time—and a healthy dose of the complementary body splash. I finished my makeup and put on a sleek red jumpsuit and black stilettos, then complemented my outfit with an assortment of gold earrings, necklaces, and bangles. I grabbed my keys and out the door I went to pick up Chantelle, Sheila, and Regina.

Strangely enough, this week's girls' night out took on a whole new meaning. We weren't really enjoying the club, so I suggested we go to the Balcony for dancing and dinner. Once again I ran into that sultry saxophone player, and once again he sent me a complimentary drink. No conversation, just an announcement once again.

"To the beautiful lady who was dressed in blue the other night, and burning up the dance floor in that sassy red jumpsuit tonight, this one's for you!" he said as he lifted his drink up and greeted me. The waitress delivered me a complimentary pomegranate martini, and my friends looked at me like I was crazy.

"Wow that was smooth! What's going on with you and the sax player?! And what happened to Tariq?" Chantelle quipped.

I reluctantly updated them on what happened with the sax player and the drink when I was on the date with Tariq. Regina abruptly responded, "Oh so you have a twofer huh?"

"What the heck is a twofer Regina?" I said.

Chantelle laughed hysterically and said, "That's when you have two men, and Regina wants you to pass one over to her!"

We all laughed, and I quickly informed them that I'd never even talked to the saxophone player. So as far as I was concerned, he was fair game if he wasn't already taken.

I couldn't stop thinking about my upcoming date with Tariq on Sunday. After indulging in more good food and sexy drinks, we closed out the evening with more dancing and intriguing conversation about topics of interest to bring up at Saturday Night Live with everyone else. At the end of the evening, the sax man was nowhere to be found. I was unable to thank him or say goodbye, but it didn't really bother me.

When I got home I decided to plan a light but tasty meal for Sunday brunch with Tariq. I wanted to make sure the food was delicate and delicious. After all, I had a lot to live up to after the delicious meals we'd already shared together. It only took a few minutes to plan the brunch, and about forty-five minutes to make the delicious tarts, but they were pretty simple. I set two aside for Tariq and me to enjoy after Sunday brunch, and went off to bed.

The College Crew: Chris

The next morning I was pumped up for Saturday Night Live, but I knew there was another little mess to clean up. I had to figure out how to best fight off the enticements of my dear friend Chris, aka "Mr. Narcissistic Nuevo Riche."

Chris was my on-again, off-again love interest who consistently wanted his cake and all of the fixings from me. He was also one of the College Crew and was successfully managing his brother's highly profitable financial planning business, and he flaunted every bit of his newfound independent wealth.

I'd decided a couple of months earlier that I was done with his indecisiveness and feeling like I was just another booty call. I nearly fell in love with him, but we had too many problems with his family's cultural expectations for his life. After a nearly two year tumultuous relationship, I refused to continue taking a back seat in his life, and broke it off.

A second generation Lebanese American, Chris was a somewhat egotistical recent college graduate who failed to get accepted into dental school. He didn't want to leave Pittsburgh, so his plan B was to go into the high-powered world of selling annuities and life insurance with his millionaire brother's firm.

Unfortunately, he was also a typical playboy who loved ethnic women, but felt pressured by his four brothers and five sisters to assimilate into white culture. He also had difficulty reconciling himself to the kind of person he wanted to be with, versus who his family thought he should be with.

Chris loves to drive expensive cars and always wears top-of-the-line designer everything. He especially prides himself on wearing tailor-made suits that accentuate every beautiful, masculine curve of his muscle-clad body, and this drives me crazy.

His biggest downfall is that he's a very self-assured narcissist. He loved to brag about his financial wealth to other friends who went on to graduate school—mainly because he envied them. On a more positive note, he really knows how to treat his women—when he's with you that is. More importantly, although he doesn't pack the biggest wrench in the toolbox, he knew how to work his tools like an expert craftsman in the bed. He'd wine, dine, and sixty-nine you to make sure all of your physical needs were met, but that's where he'd leave it.

Interestingly enough, he was good at attempting to offer me a great sense of security while giving me everything but himself. However, my second sense always gave me the feeling that he had another woman, or a booty call in the wings. As a result, I had a difficult time trusting him.

I'd met Chris in our junior year of college. I was selling Valentine's cakes, and Rafi sent him to my house to buy one of my cakes for his so-called girlfriend at the time. Chris came to pick up the cake and after inadvertently tasting it, jokingly told me that he was in love with me, and the cake.

"I'm serious Anais! I can't take my eyes off of you," he said with heartfelt emotion. "Can I take you to dinner?" he asked.

Even though I called him out for having a girlfriend, he said we could just be friends like Rafi and I. But that didn't last for long—the attraction was too heavy. Shortly thereafter he told me he'd broken up with his girlfriend, and I fell right into his trap.

In the early stages of our relationship, Chris really taught me how a man is supposed to treat a woman—he really was a consummate gentleman. But for whatever reason, we always had a torrid love affair. He consistently wanted to have his cake and eat it too.

After nearly two years of ups and downs, I was fed up with his indecisiveness and inability to love me the way I need to be loved. So about three months before the summer solstice SNL, I cut him off. He wasn't very happy, nor accepting of my decision.

He'd been on my case at every Saturday Night Live since. Constantly trying to shower me with all kinds of gifts, he consistently made claims that he couldn't get my scent out of his mind. I, on the other hand, knew better. I refused to take his gifts or fall for his bullshit anymore. The real truth for me though was that he's always a lot of fun, so I tried to make the best of the situation when he was around.

Menu

Join Us for a Salute to the Summer Solstice
featuring

APPETIZERS

SHRIMP CEVICHE

YUCCA CHIPS WITH SEA SALT

JUMBO NACHOS
with fresh cucumber and heirloom tomato salsa

DINNER

GRILLED TILAPIA FARCI
stuffed with garlic and fresh herbs

ARGENTINIAN BARBECUED PORTERHOUSE STEAKS

CURED BARBECUED PORK RIBS

GRILLED VEGETABLES

DESSERT

FRESH FRUIT ASSORTMENT

STRAWBERRY & CHOCOLATE GANACHE TARTS

BEAUTY RITUAL

Hibiscus and orange yoni love teatox elixir. Bodacious Body collection
of risqué rose bath salts and body splash.

ENTERTAINMENT

Group talk roundtable; volleyball; Spades tournament;
water gun fight.

6

woke up early Saturday morning to go to Leila's house and help prepare for the evening's activities. Chantelle arrived shortly thereafter and brought Charise with her. Charise graduated from college with us too, but she went straight to law school. We met Charise during a freshman year sorority rush, and we've all been friends ever since. Although Charise pretty much knew the rest of the College Crew, she'd never spent time with us after graduating from college, and this was her first time participating in SNL. It was Chantelle's attempt at bringing Charise back into the fold during her summer recess. However, another truth was that Chantelle, who was always cooking up some kind of business scheme, was trying to pick Charise's legal brain about some business idea she had and inadvertently invited her to attend the event. A founding member of the College Crew, Chantelle has always been an interesting case study.

The College Crew: Chantelle

The person who almost always brings her unique, albeit sometimes corrupt, spark to girls' night out and SNL is Chantelle. She and I became friends during freshman year when we worked on a fashion show for the student government board together. Although we didn't really socialize much outside of that, we remained cordial friends throughout the school year.

In the summer between my junior and senior years, I decided to move out of the dorms and into an apartment. I was only in the apartment for a week when I ran into Chantelle, and she asked if she could live with me for a little while. She said her grandmother had kicked her out of the house because her grandmother's very old-fashioned and wouldn't permit Chantelle to stay out past 11:00 p.m. Although she'd made plans to get her own place, she needed somewhere to stay for a few days until she found one. My heart wouldn't allow me to say no, and I let her move in the next day. I later learned that it probably wasn't the staying out late that her grandmother didn't approve of, it was more than likely the company she keeps.

During her short stay at my place, I had the displeasure of learning early on that she truly lives a controversial life, filled with crooked people. She had a crazy habit of getting herself into compromising situations that for most people would have been life changing. Not Chantelle though. She also had an uncanny ability to get herself out of those same situations either by luck, her charming personality, or her wit.

An even sadder truth was that she'd always try to live the high life off someone else's money—legally or illegally. While pretending to be a naïve young college graduate, she often kept the company of drug dealers pretending to be wealthy businessmen, and identity thieves who presented themselves as royalty from Africa to support her shopping addiction. But just like a lifetime criminal mastermind, she always managed to keep her hands clean while leaving a trail of carnage. As long as she looked pretty, and played dumb, she felt like she didn't have to get her hands dirty. I was certain that one day this, too, would catch up with her.

Game On! Let's Party!

Rafi, Sheila, and Mark B carpooled and brought the booze and beer as usual. Shortly after their arrival, somebody started ringing the doorbell relentlessly, like they didn't have the sense they were born with. It was clear to everyone who it was, the obnoxious but playful Chris. He was carrying a beautifully wrapped present in one hand, and a bottle of Dom Pérignon in the other.

Leila answered the door and immediately greeted him. "What are you up to now Chris? And who's the gift for?" she said with a giggle. She loved Chris, and was always tolerant of anything he did. He kissed her and politely handed her the bottle of Dom Pérignon.

"This is for you and the crew tonight. The gift is for Ms. Anais, who doesn't love me anymore. I want her to know she still drives me *crazy!*" he shouted while gazing into my eyes. He, too, undeniably had some of the most beautiful and sparkling chestnut brown eyes I'd ever seen, and could always get me going because he's so handsome.

I, however, was determined I was done with his antics. As I said before, he wanted to wine, dine, and sixty-nine me, but I was never good enough to meet his family. It was clear to me that he only wanted me in his life when it was convenient for him. I never knew where he was, or whom he was with when he wasn't with me—which was very often. The ongoing excuse was always, "I'm working Babe!" But I knew better.

"I'm too good for you Chris," I snarled. "And I keep telling you I don't want your gifts," I quipped.

Thank goodness Rafi caught on to my frustration and grabbed him.

"Come on buddy, let's help with the barbecue and have some drinks," he said as he pulled Chris out of the kitchen.

We all had a wonderful time with great jokes, delicious food, a heated volleyball game, a few rounds of Spades, and even some dirty dancing. More important, dinner and the water gun fight were both big hits.

Dinner started with the refreshing and tasty shrimp ceviche, fried yucca chips with sea salt, and jumbo nachos with fresh cucumber and heirloom tomato salsa. The feedback was all positive. Everyone enjoyed the ceviche and even suggested a variety of other seafood items that could potentially be prepared in the same way. The grilled whole tilapia stuffed with garlic and herbs and the Argentinian barbecued beef and pork ribs were showstoppers. For dessert, I strategically wrapped the strawberry and chocolate ganache tarts in pastel heart-shaped gift boxes with matching ribbons—they were a pleasant surprise for everyone.

The biggest highlight of the evening, however, was at the dinner table when everyone started to share updates on their individual lives. I took the opportunity to talk about Tariq, and informed everyone that I'd probably be inviting him to the next Saturday Night Live fiesta. As expected, Chris went ballistic.

"You can't do that to me Anais!" he yelled as he jumped out of his seat.

The room got so quiet that you could hear a pin drop. I simply sat there in silence and looked at him like he was crazy. But I didn't have to do or say anything. I guess Rafi felt my angst and was frustrated with Chris's antics too. He promptly interjected.

"Sit down Chris! You should either shit, or get off the pot!" Rafi said calmly.

"Oh shit!" Mark B exclaimed with disbelief. I, however, felt like Rafi's statement was very befitting for the situation.

"What the hell does that mean!" Chris shouted. "She can't do that to me!" he fervently reiterated.

The room was still very silent. Everyone seemed to pause so that Chris could finish throwing his tantrum. I decided to let the conversation play out to see where it was going.

"*Do ... what?*" Rafi exclaimed while slowly exaggerating his words. "She doesn't have to put up with your playboy bullshit while you try to figure out whether or not you want to be with a black woman," he said with a calm fervor.

I could hear everyone taking deep swallows as they tried to suppress their sighs of disbelief. It was like a sleeping giant had awoken in Rafi. Even Chris was taken aback. And although we were all shocked that Rafi was so blatant with his thoughts, everyone else sort of just put their heads down—they clearly didn't want to get into the argument. As for me, I wanted to make it clear that I agreed with Rafi.

Breaking the deafening silence, I decided to let him know. "My dearest Chris, I will always love you as my dear friend. But you cannot have me anymore. *You* made that choice!" I exclaimed fervently.

Chris, however, doesn't take rejection well, and he was on the hot seat now. First he looked at me like he was in shock, and then without even responding, he took his dessert, grabbed his keys, and stormed out the door with a quick shout out. "I'll see you guys next month." He always had a tough time accepting it when someone pointed out his faults.

As Chris was leaving, Pierre was making his entrance even later than usual. "Why are you leaving Chris?" Pierre said as he greeted him with a hug.

"I just have somewhere to be now. I'll see you next time," Chris said.

"Yeah I know that routine myself, hang in there," Pierre responded.

Rafi, on the other hand, decided he needed to talk to Chris a little more about what had just happened, so he ran outside briefly. When he came back, I asked him what happened.

He politely informed me that as my "little brother," he didn't like how my relationship with Chris had developed. He asked me if Chris and I had made a secret marriage pact or something, because he had never seen him so obsessed with someone. But he didn't think it was fair that Chris wouldn't commit himself to me, and felt he needed to make it known to everyone. When he went outside, he said he shared with Chris a few words that his father taught him when he was growing up. "A good man apologizes for his mistakes of the past, but a great man corrects them!" he said.

He thought that if he left Chris with that advice, he'd better understand why he needed to apologize to me. After clearly digesting what he said, I assured him that Chris and I hadn't made any kind of pact. I just knew I deserved better, and appreciated him standing up for me. He shrugged it off. "It is what it is!" he said. We left it there and enjoyed the rest of the evening.

7

After hours of eating great food and enjoying a great time with friends, we ended the Saturday Night Live celebration with a reminder to everyone that next month's shindig would be at my place. While having dinner, we decided that that month's SNL would celebrate the bold, fresh flavors and cultures of Spain and Latin American.

To highlight the evening, we'd dance salsa and merengue, while Pierre and Leila's crew entertained us with conga drumming. I just had to design a wonderful menu and give everyone his or her assignments.

I, however, was somewhat preoccupied during the planning. My mind kept drifting to what I needed to do to prepare for a wonderful brunch date with Tariq. Although the pressure was a little high, I was very excited. I also felt like I had everything under control because it was only brunch, and not too complicated.

Tariq: A Soft Caress

On Sunday morning, I woke up early and attended the eight-thirty church service. Afterward, I went to the grocery store to pick up a few items for brunch, including flowers to brighten up the table and perfume the air.

I decided to serve a delicate dark chocolate–stuffed French toast with a fresh raspberry coulis sauce and a sidecar of warm maple syrup, thick sliced maple chipotle bacon, and eggs. For drinks—sparkling water and raspberry-lime Bellinis made with fresh raspberries and Prosecco. It was a light, artisanal, and refreshing combination.

The table was decorated with fresh peonies, white porcelain plates, and crystal stemware filled with orange twists and fresh raspberries. Then I put a bottle of sparkling water, some fresh limes and raspberries, and the remainder of the Prosecco on ice in a small wine bucket for additional Bellinis. It was a beautiful presentation for the gastronomic feast to come.

After I finished setting up, I still had about two hours before Tariq's arrival. Everything was ready to go, except for me. This was a great time to unwind, indulge in a quick beauty ritual, and to make sure I was just as scrumptious as the brunch I'd prepared.

I started with a warm cup of hibiscus yoni love teatox elixir while lighting an essential-oil diffuser filled with my special combination of floral and grapefruit essential oils to perfume the air while complementing the peonies. Using my fragrant hibiscus sunrise body mask powder, I whipped up a quick batch and slathered it all over my body for a perfect polish and shine. The aroma was alluring, and the complementary hydrating grapefruit body refresher perfumed my skin like fine silk.

After my beauty ritual, I lightly brushed my entire body with my favorite shimmery powder, fixed my hair, and gently slipped into a soft lavender and pearl button-down dress with spaghetti straps and matching slippers. I wanted to feel beautiful yet comfortable, and I did.

When Tariq arrived, it was a picture perfect moment for me. The aroma in my apartment was amazing. The allure of fresh, sweet peonies was complemented by tender hints of sensuous grapefruit and florals from the diffuser. Smooth jazz played softly throughout, and I was looking and feeling good.

When I opened the door, he was standing there with a bottle of wine, a giant bouquet of flowers, Belgian chocolate, and oh yeah, he looked extremely handsome. I had to hold myself back again. I didn't want him to get the wrong idea. I hugged him, and he gently kissed the back of my neck.

"You're always more beautiful each time I see you," he said.

"Well you've only seen me twice, how would you know if I always look like this?" I said jokingly.

"I've seen you three times now, and each time you're more and more beautiful," he quickly responded. It was almost like he knew just what to say to make me blush and crave him more.

At five feet, eleven inches, he's a well-groomed vision of loveliness. Smooth, taut skin the color of lightly toasted almonds; a perfectly trimmed mustache; not too muscular but just enough to give you that strong, but gentle, manly hug that all women need; and of course, chestnut brown eyes so gorgeous they'd make you fall for anything if you looked into them too long. More important, he was both very romantic and down to earth. All of that wonderfulness wrapped up with a deep, sultry French accent made my heart drop every time he spoke.

What more could I ask for? I thought to myself. Then I quickly reminded myself not to get too caught up in the moment.

"Well don't just stand there," I said. "Come in and have a seat. Would you like to start with a Bellini or a glass of your wine?" I asked. He opted for Bellinis and brunch, so we indulged.

As a professional caterer, I prepare everything I serve with the idea that people eat with their eyes first. Therefore, a beautiful presentation of the food is just as important as the taste—my goal was to impress him with both. I think it met his approval.

"Wow! You did all of this for me? It's beautiful!" he said with excitement.

"I wanted to properly thank you for two amazing dinners, and for getting lucky and ordering my favorites. This time I decided to take a stab at what I thought you'd enjoy from my kitchen," I said.

I went on to describe the menu and to prepare his eggs. He hugged me and thanked me for going to all of the trouble. But he kept caressing me and rubbing my legs throughout the entire meal—which turned my juices on and started to become distracting.

Brunch, however, was a wonderful success. He loved everything, and I thoroughly enjoyed his company. But things began to get a bit complicated. Again he kept staring at me, and gently caressing me. He'd already gotten me excited. At some point my underwear was so wet, I thought I was going to have to change it. Then he stood up. I didn't realize what he was doing, but he looked so delicious that I couldn't focus on anything but him.

"Can I properly thank you for the magnificent brunch?" he asked.

"Sure! But you didn't have to stand up for that," I responded. He walked over to me and gently pulled me out of my chair.

"I need to thank you with a traditional French kiss, so we have to stand up," he said. Every ounce of my being wanted him to kiss me, but I was afraid of where it might lead us. My heart spoke before I could process anything my mind was telling me to say.

"Okay." I said.

He moved in to kiss me on both cheeks in the traditional French manner, but when he started to move to the second cheek, he gently caressed my face with one of his hands, looked directly into my eyes, and with his beautiful French accent whispered, "Ummh ... I need you!"

At that point I was toast. All my thoughts about how I was supposed to react had simply abandoned me. Even though I wasn't sure what he meant at that point, I was so enthralled that I decided to just go with the flow, as long as it didn't get uncomfortable for me.

"Really?" I said as I giggled with heightened curiosity.

"Yes really! I just touch you, and I lose control," he said. "To make matters worse, I think I'm getting addicted to your smell," he whispered as he softly grazed my face with his nose.

I slowly began to visualize myself melting into him. I was speechless. I watched his lips the entire time he was talking. The sweet seductive aroma of his cologne, his gentle touch, and the way he looked at me got me extremely excited. My heart started racing. I couldn't take it anymore. I went in for the kill and started kissing him first.

He kissed me so passionately, I again felt the thrust of his tongue down my throat. I tried to get myself together, to think rationally. But he quickly lured me into his lair.

I could feel his rock-hard penis bulging from his pants, rubbing against me. The sensuality of his cologne drove me crazy. I started to lose control and my body began to betray my convictions.

My nipples were just as hard as his penis now, and a new surge of moisture dampened my inner thighs. I didn't know how to stop it. Hell, I didn't want to stop it.

"I, oh! We should stop ... Oh God, you feel so good," I said as I tried not to lose control. But I couldn't let go of him.

We stumbled onto the couch, and he started to bite my neck with the force of a vampire about to get his first feeding. My whole body convulsed with joyful pain. I couldn't help myself. I had to let go. I became putty in his hands as I moaned passionately for more.

"Harder! ... Harder!" I cried—I was enthralled with passion. My cries increased as he methodically grazed on each part of my neck. With one hand on my lower back, he slowly began to loosen my dress with his free hand, one button at a time. Each time he loosened a button, my body quivered more and more until my breasts were fully exposed.

My nipples began to tighten like pebbles. They were so sensitive that my dress felt like sandpaper. They were starving for a release. All at once he filled his mouth with my breast, and tantalized me as he alternated between sucking and gently nibbling on it.

My body began to crave him. I had to bite my lip to control my thirst for his delicious flavor. My mind was racing back and forth, as my entire body trembled with desire. I was in a mental battle with my hunger for him to touch me, and the right thing to do. This was only my third time seeing him, but my body sent a clear and constant message that I really needed him to touch me ... to kiss me.

The message was coming from my lips up top, and my hips down below. My underwear began to overflow with my juices. I felt like a horny bitch in heat that sees the first male dog on the street and allows him to jump on her ass and hump like there's no tomorrow. I was in heat and common sense had left the building.

"Your body feels like warm silk," he said in a soft and gentle voice. My entire body quivered with excitement.

"God, I can't get enough of your smell. I just want to bury myself inside you!" he whispered as he buried his head in my belly, and started licking my stomach just above my pelvis. I purred as my juices gushed down my love canal with every stroke of his tongue.

"Ummh! ... You're amazing! I just want a taste ... Can I please taste you?" he pleaded. I wanted him to taste me too. It felt so good when he was kissing my stomach that I really needed him to quench my thirst for him just as much as he wanted to taste me. My body was so tense I could have exploded at any moment.

"Can I just have a taste?" he pleaded again.

I couldn't control myself. He kissed my sex, and I wrapped my legs around his head. He lifted me up and gently pulled my underwear off with his teeth as he kissed my inner thighs. Then he just dove in and began to devour me.

The soft caress of his tongue was warm, and juicy. Savoring every inch of my sex, he knew all the right places. Stroke after stroke, swirl after swirl, he skillfully increased my pleasure until my hips took on a life of their own. Suddenly he hit just the right spot on my clitoris, and I lost it!

My whole body quivered with intense emotional and physical pleasure. The faster he caressed that beautiful spot with his soft, warm tongue, the more the incredible sensation intensified.

"Oh my God! You, you! ... Oh yeah! Right there!" I moaned with euphoria as my hips began to thrust back and forth like I was riding a wild bull at a rodeo. He followed every move as I got closer and closer to my climax.

"I'M CUMMING! I'M CUMMING!" I shouted.

I finally exploded. I began to see stars, and my entire body convulsed with overt pleasure. I gripped his head between my legs so tight that I almost smothered him. He, however, was perfectly content. He just continued to gently kiss my thighs, then laid his head on my sex when I was finished.

"I could lay here forever. I think I'm addicted to you" he said.

I wasn't sure how to respond to him. Even though my mind was telling me that I shouldn't have been intimate with him yet, I knew I needed more of him. It was a sensuous yet somewhat intimidating end to a beautiful and refreshing brunch.

Menu

Join Us for a First-class Brunch for Two
featuring

MAIN COURSE

Dark Chocolate–Stuffed French Toast
with a raspberry coulis sauce and a sidecar of warm maple syrup

Thick-Sliced Maple Chipotle Bacon

Eggs

BEVERAGES

Raspberry-Lime Bellinis
made with fresh raspberries, Prosecco, simple syrup, and freshly
squeezed lime juice

Sparkling Water

BEAUTY RITUAL

Hibiscus yoni love teatox elixir. Floral and grapefruit essential oil
diffuser. Bodacious Body hibiscus sunrise body mask treatment
and "love dew."

8

My weekend activities were more often than not the antithesis of my workweek activities at the shelter. The weekend that had just passed was no different. I had partied with my girls, hung out with my College Crew, and brought the weekend full circle with an intimate and exhilarating third date with Tariq. Not only was I rejuvenated from the last workweek, I was full of energy and ready to tackle the week ahead.

The Shelter: Something Stinky's Brewing!

Monday mornings at the shelter were always difficult. This one was no exception. As soon as I walked in the door, the girls were dying to bring on the crazy. Two of them had run away over the weekend, and the others tried to test my patience when I greeted them at breakfast—they didn't get a chance though. I walked in the office to sign in, and the supervisor told me that the replacements for the girls that had run away were waiting at the intake center, and it was my duty to go and pick up the new girls.

It was the first time I'd be going to the intake center, so it was a bit intimidating. But I didn't have to deal with the drama in the house for a little while, so I was happy to be going.

When I arrived at the intake center the first person I saw was Mark B. He was standing in a corner with a young boy.

"Hey Mark B, what's up?" I said with excitement.

"You beautiful!" he replied with a smile as usual. He always knew how to make a girl feel special. Perhaps that's why Regina was so crazy about him.

"By the way, this is Corry," he said.

"What's up sis?!" Corry quickly responded as he began to gaze into my eyes.

"Back off Corry," Mark B said as he quickly intercepted him. "She's already spoken for, and you wouldn't want Chris to come after you," he said as he laughed at me.

"You're nuts Mark B!" I exclaimed. "You know the real deal. So what's up with Mr. Corry here?" I responded with shyness.

"Well apparently he ran away on Friday night with two of your girls. Now he's seen the light. He came back to the intake center to turn himself in, and they asked me to pick him up so he could come back to the boys' shelter," he said. In the meantime, Corry sat quietly with a somewhat worried, but relieved look on his face.

"That's interesting. I'm here to pick up two new girls to replace the ones who ran away," I said as my interest began to peak.

"Hey Corry, where are my two girls?" I asked. He perked up and proceeded to give us an earful of drama.

He said that the two girls had robbed one of their grandmother's houses of money and jewels, hooked up with two other boys from his shelter, and took a bus to Florida. He said he left them when they got on the bus to go to Florida.

"Well that explains why they aren't back," Mark B said. "Why didn't you go with them Corry?" he inquired.

"Cause I just wanted to see my girl. She was supposed to be at the shelter with those girls, and nobody would let me see her. One of my boys told me she's pregnant, and I wanted to see her, so I left," he said fervently.

"Pregnant!" Mark B exclaimed.

"Yep! And I want to know if the baby is mines," Corry responded.

"Well, did you find out?" Mark B asked.

"I don't think it's mines," Corry declared as if he was somewhat disappointed but relieved.

"Why not? If you do the crime, you gotta do the time my man!" Mark B said emphatically.

Corry went on to explain that he'd hooked up with Darlese while they were at the intake center, which is coed and centrally located in downtown Pittsburgh. They dated for three months. When they were placed in our longer term facilities, they got separated into the boys' and girls' shelters, which are located on opposite sides of the city and more than 40 miles apart by car. Even worse, they weren't allowed to communicate with each other, and he felt like he was unfairly left in the dark.

He wasn't allowed to see or talk to her for four months. Then, one of the other boys at the shelter was at a court hearing and saw her. That's when he found out she was pregnant, and told Corry.

Corry didn't think it was fair that no one would take him to see her even though he knew it wasn't allowed. So when he found out where she had been placed, he ran away to get to her and find out if it was his baby. He said Darlese wasn't sure, but he didn't think it was his baby.

Mark B was surprised by what he was hearing, but he wasn't the least bit restrained with his responses. "Why don't you think it's your baby Corry? You slept with her, and you said she was your girl?" he quipped with the disciplinarian voice of a father figure.

"Because she's a hoe!" Corry quickly replied.

"Whoa! That's a pretty strong word for somebody you considered 'your girl!'" Mark B said with disgust. "Why do you say that?" he followed.

"Cause I found out I wasn't the only one she was sleeping with. Apparently she slept with both of my boys, and a bunch of other people too! Then she told them they had to pay her, or she was gonna get her brothers to hurt them," Corry said as he defended himself.

I felt like a fly on the wall. Mark B seemed to assume the position of father figure in the situation, and I had nothing to lend to the conversation. But I learned a lot about Darlese that wasn't reflected in her file. It gave me more insight into how to better interact with her.

Corry started going into more detail with Mark B about why he didn't believe he was the father of the baby, but I was called away to pick up my new girls and couldn't finish listening. I said my goodbyes and told Mark B I would confirm a date for dancing with him later in the week.

The College Crew: Mark B

Mark B is a handsome, athletic type, who trains all year for marathons and works out every day. He's another cutie—a five foot, eleven inch, sky-blue eyed, German and Italian American, from a small town in central Pennsylvania.

When I found out where he was from, I was amazed that he was so comfortable working at the shelter with rough inner-city kids. But he loved it. In fact, he was always one of the more successful counselors with the kids. I guess he had something I didn't see initially, but I was happy he was just as willing as I to give back and help the kids.

He also loves to dance as much as I do, and we go dancing whenever the fever hits us—which is usually when neither of us have other plans. However, Mark B has always been an interesting mystery when it comes to his personal life.

Funny thing, when I saw how he interacted with Corry in that situation, I realized that it was a side of him that I'd never seen before. He loved hanging out with the crew, but we never saw him get intimate or emotional with anyone. Whenever drama surrounded any of our relationships, he very rarely had anything to say.

He'd always talk about girls he dated in high school, and we all knew how girls from college would swoon over him all the time, because he's very handsome and self-assured. But we never got any read from him on an intimate relationship, and Regina's almost obsessive affection for him seemed to be going nowhere fast.

I met Mark B through Rafi at one of our parties when we were juniors in college. Rafi, Chris, and Mark B all met in biology class and became hanging buddies in freshman year. But Chris never really cared for Mark B because he felt that he was too possessive of Rafi, and could never understand why Mark B wouldn't even try to get a girlfriend. Despite his personal life, Mark B was a great and reliable friend. Best of all, he was a fabulous dance partner, and I always looked forward to our dance outings.

By the time I finished processing the two new girls, Mark B and Corry were gone. We inherited a twelve- and a thirteen-year-old as our new residents, and I was charged with transporting them and getting them acquainted with their new home.

While they were getting in the van, it broke my heart to hear them say they were more afraid than ever, because they didn't know what to expect. They'd come from two different foster homes and met at the intake center where they became best friends. Being able to place them in the shelter together was a stroke of luck; typically we'd only get one bed open at a time. But they lucked out because both of the girls that ran away weren't eligible to come back.

Due to the shelter system being extremely congested, sometimes the kids had to stay at the intake center for months until they were either placed in a longer-term shelter like ours, moved to a group home, or their families were allowed to take them back after agreeing to a counseling program. Unfortunately, these two girls didn't fit well in foster care, and their families weren't legally cleared to take them back. So off they were on a new adventure to live in a new type of facility—a medium-term shelter—with six other girls they'd probably never met.

The ride back to the shelter was long and quiet, but I had been told that the cook, Ms. Nellie, was whipping up a special welcome surprise for the new girls upon their arrival. Ms. Nellie was like a warm and fuzzy teddy bear, who gave everyone the love and nurturing of a grandmother through her heartwarming food and warm advice. From the delicious meals she prepared every evening, to the wonderful birthday celebrations and even tasty cold remedies she prepared ad hoc, she was the main ingredient in helping the girls and the staff feel at home.

The shelters are located in the eastern and western suburbs of Pittsburgh, thirty minutes from the downtown intake center. The idea behind locating them so far away was to take the troubled youth away from the convenience of the center city so they wouldn't be tempted to flee, or in some cases to discourage them from continuing whatever disruptive behaviors were responsible for them being in a shelter in the first place. However, every weekend at least one or two of the girls would get anxious and inevitably run away, or at the very least make a feeble attempt at it.

When we arrived, the other girls were at school. The supervisor timed it so we could get the girls settled into their rooms, set up their files for the other counselors to read, and introduce them to their new, albeit temporary home before the other girls returned.

I got them settled in and then took them to meet Ms. Nellie to share their favorite, and least favorite foods, allergies, etc. Afterward, she explained her special surprise to welcome them to their new home, and invited them to help her make cupcakes.

She'd prepared an evening of do-it-yourself tacos with chicken, beef, vegetables, and an assortment of fixings, accompanied by homemade strawberry lemonade, and watermelon-lime juice. For dessert, she prepared what she described as "Garbage Dump Cupcakes."

Before the girls helped her make the cupcakes, she prepared several small bowls filled with all sorts of small candies, dried fruits, and nuts. Two larger bowls were filled with chocolate and vanilla frosting. She said they were called Garbage Dump Cupcakes because everyone could put whatever they preferred on top of the cupcakes, and nobody had the right to say if it was good or bad.

"Very creative Ms. Nellie!" I exclaimed.

"Well, I think it gives the girls a sense of independence and a little control. They get to do it on their own without anyone telling them that they have to do it this way or do it that way," she said while defiantly waving her always-handy wooden spoon from side to side.

"It's especially important for the new girls, because it helps them feel like they have a little more freedom," she followed.

"I love it and you Ms. Nellie!" I replied as I hugged her. I left the girls with her, and went into the office to finish my paperwork before the other girls returned from school.

Menu

Join Us for a Do-it-yourself Quick Dinner
featuring

DINNER

Tacos
chicken, beef, vegetables, and an assortment of fixings

BEVERAGES

Homemade Strawberry Lemonade

Watermelon-Lime Juice

DESSERT

Garbage Dump Cupcakes

ENTERTAINMENT

Group talk roundtable

9

Making My Money

While driving home from work that evening, I decided I needed to slow things down a bit with Tariq. Even though he made me feel so good, our relationship seemed to be getting too hot and heavy, too fast, and I was afraid of potentially going through the same heartache I went through with Chris. He tried to call several times, but I was working and couldn't answer the phone.

I had a full week of work and catering on both Friday and Saturday nights and knew I'd be exhausted. In my mind, it was going to be a week of peaceful preparation for the upcoming weekend. I did intend to touch base with Tariq later, however my desire for a peaceful week turned out to be wishful thinking and was preempted.

It was the week before the Fourth of July holiday weekend, and two more girls ran away from the shelter on Tuesday night. When I got to work on Wednesday morning, all hell was breaking loose.

A majority of the girls at the shelter were sent by a court order from a Child Protective Services judge after becoming wards of the state. More often than not this was caused by their parents' inability to take care of them. Sometimes, but very rarely, we'd get children whose parents were unable to control their child's behavior, and when they'd get into legal trouble, the judge would send them to the shelter at the parents' expense for the girls to get themselves together. It was designed to be an intermittent step to avoid sending them directly to the juvenile detention center.

The parents of one of the girls that ran away were wealthy construction company owners who couldn't deal with their daughter's disrespect. She'd gotten in trouble for smoking weed and skipping school regularly. In an attempt to teach her a lesson, they agreed with the judge's decision to put her into the shelter temporarily as a scare tactic. But she ran away, and we had the unfortunate task of alerting them, and the judge, that she was gone.

They weren't surprised. But we had loads of paperwork and phone calls to make to release her and the girl she ran away with from the shelter system. We had to return her custody to her parents and the judge. Returning custody to the judge meant the girl was violating the original agreement she'd made with him or her, and she would either be sent home, or more likely be remanded to the county juvenile detention center. I wasn't sure who we were releasing her to, but the paperwork was very stressful and consumed the entire shift.

As a result, I needed to blow off some steam, and cooking is like a catharsis for me. So I was happy to be going home that evening to continue preparation for the two parties I booked for Friday and Saturday evenings.

Saturday's party was booked by one of my favorite clients—Javier Torres, the first chair violinist with the city's Global Symphony Orchestra. I'd hosted several parties for him and his friends, and he liked my style. He asked me to put together a fun and delicious barbecue for him and fourteen of his closest friends, and I was happy to oblige.

He's also an avid fan and supporter of the University of Pittsburgh's football team and planned his event to be an after party following a preseason scrimmage/Fourth of July celebration. It was going to be a backyard shindig so he selected one of my infamous High Top Grilling party menus. He had a big, beautiful house and an even bigger backyard, with an outdoor kitchen and all the fixings. As long as I planned it well, I was sure it would be perfectly executed.

Javier was also pretty generous and chose a menu that amounted to $200 per person. After expenses and paying my assistant Jill and Joe the bartender, I would net at least $1,800. It was almost twice my monthly salary from the shelter. Not a bad payday, but lots of prep work, so I needed to manage my time well.

Each time Javier attended one of my casual events he went nuts over my Wild and Crazy Buffalo Wings Collection. He insisted we include them as part of the starters, along with one of his favorite dishes, shrimp ceviche—which is why I had wanted to test the recipe at the last SNL celebration. The High Top Grill menu also includes fresh vegetable crudités served with lemony hummus and seven seas dip and assorted sourdough rolls with a variety of seasoned butters, plus a selection of fresh fruit mocktails and cocktails. The bountiful collection of appetizers is designed to prohibit the guests from being hungry while we collect and prepare the individual grill orders for the main course.

The main course included a choice of marinated and grilled jumbo shrimp kebabs, herb-roasted tilapia fillets in parchment paper, triple-thick hand-cut marinated pork chops with the bone in, marinated and grilled portobello mushrooms and cauliflower steaks, and prime cut porterhouse steaks. Each main course was accompanied by a baked potato and grilled vegetable assortment.

Dessert included a collection of fresh fruit, and the often irresistible grilled piña coladas. It's one of my signature desserts. Made with fresh pineapple slices macerated in rum and lightly grilled, the pineapple slices are served on top of coconut ice cream, sandwiched between homemade coconut rum galettes, and topped with my homemade sour cherry topping.

To make the evening even more memorable, I would prepare gift packs for each attendee with pairs of delicate white and dark chocolate truffles, and attach my card to advertise. While prepping, I was certain I had everything under control for Javier's party, but Friday night's party was a different story.

Although I was comfortable with the food to be catered, the real mystery was the girl who booked the party. She said she'd found my brochure with the Valentine's cake her boyfriend had purchased for her more than a year prior. She said she'd wanted to book a romantic dinner for months, but found it difficult to plan because she lived with her parents. She went on to say that after dating for five years, she was recently at the mall with her boyfriend and they started looking at engagement rings. As a result, she was positive he was going to propose to her soon, and thought that a romantic dinner would be the perfect way to give him incentive.

I've hosted many pre-engagement parties, so this type of request wasn't unusual. I suggested she rent a suite at the Omni hotel with a kitchen and dining area. She agreed and said it was the best way to facilitate the evening without having to inconvenience her parents. I knew the staff from hosting other events, and it was my go-to destination for people in her situation. I was also confident that my security wouldn't be compromised.

After the initial formalities, I walked her through the menu selections over the phone, and she chose a delicious Asian-inspired seafood menu with Silky Royal Mandarin Chocolate Almond Galettes for dessert. It was a simple, yet elegant menu that was relatively easy to prepare.

For starters, a fresh buttercrunch salad, topped with lightly seasoned jumbo scallops sautéed in an herb-infused butter, and served with warm sourdough rolls. The main course featured wild-caught, red sockeye salmon fillets baked in banana leaves, and dressed with a sweet teriyaki sauce, served with seasoned sticky rice and a refreshing crunchy kale salad.

After a light palate cleanser of lemon sorbet, dessert followed with orange pekoe tea lattes to accompany my signature mandarin chocolate galettes. But the mystery of who she was continued to haunt me.

I'd sold more than 150 cakes during the previous year's Valentine's campaign, but for some unknown reason, I didn't feel comfortable asking her boyfriend's name. I brushed it off, and moved on with my preparations. My plate was too full to be worrying about something like that. "Oh well, I'll find out soon enough," I thought.

As part of my routine, I'd complete most of what the French call *mise en place*, or prep work, at home and finish the meals on-site. This gave my clients the feeling that they had their own personal chef serving them, and allowed the food to be served like it was coming straight out of a restaurant kitchen.

Another underlying secret to all my cuisine is to source all-natural whole foods, and to make as many things from scratch as time and money permit. I find that more often than not, time makes up for the money. The more time I have in advance of an event, the less expensive it is to make a beautiful collection of food that's wholesome, fresh, and delicious. It's why my clients and my family love my food. Therefore I always try to plan my time accordingly.

Wednesday and Thursday evenings were always my big prep days. Luckily I was able to take comp time off from work for Friday. It allowed me to drop off some of the food at Javier's house early, and then set up for the mystery girl's party.

Wednesdays were also the only days my food supplier stayed open late, so I usually went right after work. It was the best time to shop for the fresh food, marinade the meats, and prepare the sauces and desserts. By the time I finished organizing the items for each event, I was exhausted and called it quits around 11:00 p.m.

Unrequited Love

Just as I jumped in the shower, the phone rang and I jumped out to answer it. All I could hear was Chris babbling about something I could hardly understand. But what I did make out was that he was on the way to my house. Before I could stop him, he hung up the phone. Five minutes later the doorbell rang.

I reluctantly buzzed him in the security door, and two minutes later he was knocking on my apartment door. I opened it, and he was standing there with two beautifully wrapped gift boxes, his tie loosened, and his head hung down.

"Please Anais!" he said as he quickly brushed past me and entered my apartment. "I need to talk to you. I'm so confused. But I don't want to lose you," he said.

I let him talk because I was too tired to say anything. He wouldn't have listened to me anyway.

"Please reconsider being with this other guy. I just need a little time. I can't bear to see you with someone else," he followed.

Before I could remind him I was no longer available to him, he put the gifts on the table, and started kissing me, and rubbing my sex. I had just gotten out of the shower and the only thing I had on was a silk robe.

He, on the other hand, had come to my house straight from work and was dressed to the nines as usual. A tailored pin-stripe suit, crisp white shirt with a matching Ferragamo necktie, and black leather Berluti mules. It was almost a uniform for him. I get magnetized by men who know how to dress, and to make matters worse I was addicted to his Armani cologne.

Even though I was exhausted, he always knew how to push my buttons. After a long day of working both jobs, my body needed to loosen up a bit. But I kept telling myself I had to make him leave. That, however, was easier said than done.

He was irresistible. I found myself addicted to his smell again. It was so intoxicating ... so sensual ... and dammit, sexy as hell! It drew me in like a moth to a flame.

Chis always knew just how and where to touch me. I'd had my first real orgasm with him, and my body quickly began to crave his prowess. I tried to gather myself, to push him away. But every part of me ached for him.

He bit the back of my neck, and the words just dropped out of my mouth before my mind could process them. "Ummmmh ... I need you!" I purred.

I began to tear his clothes off as we swallowed each other with passion. "Eat baby! ... Eat!" I commanded as he began to devour my neck and breasts.

I pushed his head down to my sex and he began to feast like a lion getting first dibs at a fresh kill. Savoring every drop of my warm, tender, and fragrant juices, he couldn't get enough of me.

"I can't get you out of my mind Anais!" he said over and over again.

His tongue stroked my clitoris faster and faster until my body began to convulse. Quivering and bursting with overwhelming pleasure, I exploded in ecstasy. He kissed his way back up to my breasts and began to nibble them ever so slightly.

"I'm fucked up Anais! I don't know how to stay away from you. I think I'm addicted to you," he said.

I'd heard that before, but my endorphins had me in a trance. I was still swimming in the overwhelming pleasure from the intense orgasm. I couldn't even respond to him. But when he stood up, he was mouthwatering.

His body was perfect. His delicious butterscotch skin glowed like silk riding on top of a firm six pack. I got one look at his rock-hard erection, and a burst of warmth rained down my love tunnel. He put on a condom and I quickly grabbed him into me.

Lifting one leg with his arm while bearing his weight on the other, he pushed into me. Inch by inch he stretched me ... filling me ... until the pain overshadowed the pleasure. I felt an amazing emotional connection to him. I didn't know how to tell him, or if I should tell him.

Then he whispered, "I love you ... Oh God! ... I need you so much Anais!" He drove into me faster and faster ... deeper and deeper. I could see the tension spanning his delicious, rock-hard body. Beads of sweat trickled down his jaw as he pinched his eyes shut. I was completely under his control—the emotional connection I felt with him at that moment pervaded my whole being.

Suddenly I felt like lightning struck and fused us together in perfect love-making harmony. I couldn't let go of him. He felt so incredibly good that I dug my nails into his back and held on for the ride.

I quickly began to lose myself in his lust. He abruptly began to draw back slowly. Fighting for control, he turned me over and entered from behind. He drove into me hard ... burying himself deeper and deeper into my psyche. I went crazy!

"Harder! ... Harder!" I cried.

I could feel him deep in my womb, like he was touching my soul. Then he stood me up on the wall, held the other leg up, and shifted his weight. When he entered me, his pelvis was rubbing my clitoris as he moved faster and faster. I exploded, again.

"I'm, I'm, Oh God Chris! I'm CUMMING!" I screamed like a teakettle that had reached its boiling point.

"Oh baby! I love you so much!" he shouted while pounding me with the force of a jackhammer. Then, he exploded.

He was the only one that ever made me feel that way. It was the most intense feeling of connection to a person I'd ever had.

We lay in each other's arms all night, and talked until we fell asleep. He talked about his family's expectations for how he was supposed to live his life. I talked about my family's desire for me to find true happiness. Then he said he was in love with me, but he didn't know how to share that with his family without what he described as "severe consequences."

I didn't quite know how to interpret his statement. However, it surprised and disappointed me to learn that this proud, outspoken, and overly confident man, was afraid to share his love for me with his family. He was always so protective of me and attentive to anything I needed, and he ensured that all of our friends were fully cognizant of our relationship. But it seemed like he worked just as hard to hide it from his family.

He blamed it on fear of rejection if he didn't adhere to their cultural expectations for his life. I wasn't sure how to respond to him. I'd never seen him so confused, nor had I ever felt so loved and so rejected at the same time.

He kept telling me how much he needed me, and wanted me. I was very confounded. I felt myself getting more and more emotionally attached to him, but I quickly realized I needed to keep things in perspective. I didn't want to get hurt again. So I eventually decided to just let him talk.

The next morning we made love again in the shower, and treated each other to one of my beauty rituals like we did in the past. Chris always loved for us to indulge in one of my full body treatments, while sipping on my yoni love teatox elixir. It always rejuvenated us and prepared us for incredible nights of lovemaking.

But we had to get through a day of work, so I started with a gentle avocado caramel mask for our faces, which we playfully licked off each other. To invigorate us for the day ahead, I chose a coffee and mandarin scrub with essential oils to polish our skin. Not only is the aroma of the mandarin oil scintillating and refreshing, the pungent smell of the coffee is quite stimulating. The scrubs gave our skin a natural glow, and the delicious aroma of the refreshing skin toner and moisturizer increased the pleasure when making love.

"Is this why your juices always drive me crazy?" he said.

I smiled and continued to rub his body with the luxurious scrub. I explained to him how it would keep his beautiful skin glowing naturally, relieve tension, and make him smell delicious. I also shared with him how the love elixir works on the inside to perfume the juices and cleanse the body naturally, while the body polishes and scrubs work to keep the outside beautiful and balanced.

"Together they create a harmonious symphony of deliciously erotic and healthy body aromas," I said.

"So that's your secret!" he said jokingly.

"I'll never tell!" I responded.

He started to get dressed and continued to explain why he was so confused about our relationship. I didn't buy it. I felt like he was basically telling me I wasn't good enough for him to take a risk for with his family. I was torn up inside all over again, and even more angry with myself for letting him into my personal space, again.

As he walked toward the door, I began to feel that deep depression of missing him and feeling like I wasn't good enough again. My heart was filled with a heavy sense of loneliness and abandon. But I had promised myself I wasn't going to let him do that to me anymore. I was tired of being tired—but it hurt like hell!

"You can't have me anymore!" I shouted as he began his exit. I had an over-whelming feeling that I needed to protect my pride.

"The gifts are for you Anais! Open them this time," he said with an uneasy snicker. "They'll help you when I'm not around. And stay away from that ass-hole!" he shouted as he left.

I closed the door and dropped to the floor in emotional agony over him once again. I began to think that I had no one to blame but myself for letting him in again, and cried like a baby. The tears invaded my hiding place and left a residual of overwhelming despair. Loneliness and abandon had reared their ugly heads, and replaced love once again.

knew I had to pull myself together quickly for the long day ahead. I put on my big girl panties, tucked my emotions away, and went about my day.

Work started out surprisingly pleasant. The girls had gone hiking for a school field trip and I got to stay at the house with Saturn, who was constantly nagged by strep throat.

I had a little down time while she slept, so I decided to help Ms. Nellie prepare dinner. I also needed to get my little rendezvous with Chris off of my mind. To do so, I asked her to help me plan a wonderful meal for my next date with Tariq. She loved the idea of a romantic date with a French gentleman and suggested I do something delicate, but delicious.

"I wouldn't try to do french food if you haven't been to France!" she said jokingly. We both laughed.

"You know I never back down from a challenge, right?" I responded.

Ms. Nellie knew about my catering business, and I always gossiped with her about how most of my parties were booked by women who wanted to have romantic dinners with their husbands or boyfriends. She was also fully aware that I was under complete control of how to create a romantic ambiance—I just wanted suggestions on exactly what to cook.

"It's about time you get to make one of those fancy dinners for yourself my dear," Ms. Nellie chided as she giggled.

I'd told her about our incredible dates, my special brunch, and how I wanted to treat him to one of my special catered dinners. The only problem was, I was usually the host, chef, and server. This time I was going to be the guest as well, so I needed a little advice from her on a special dinner menu that was easy to execute.

My biggest challenge was to impress Tariq without the first-class service I'd provided to other couples. But again, I was up for the challenge. After all, I had a reputation to uphold for creating fantasies that combined adventurous flavors and fun love with food! I was determined that this date would live up to that same expectation.

Ms. Nellie was also like a mother to the staff as well as the girls. Whenever we needed help or weren't feeling well, she always had a remedy. Even if the remedy was as simple as a hug, or quick words of encouragement when you're down. Today was no exception.

The Shelter: Saturn

While I was in the kitchen picking Ms. Nellie's brain, Saturn came in and asked for something to soothe her lingering sore throat. I suggested she start by gargling with warm salt water. Afterward, Ms. Nellie made her a warm apple cider vinegar and honey tea to sip on. I made myself a cup of coffee, and suggested Saturn and I take advantage of the beautiful day and sit on the porch.

I asked her how long she'd had the sore throat.

"Seems like forever," she exclaimed as if she was just fed up with it. "I know I've had it on and off for at least six months," she followed.

"How do you think it started?" I asked.

"Who knows!" she exclaimed. "My mom and dad had me laid up with all kinds of people. As long as they had money to pay, they were allowed to play … with me!" she said with exasperation and a sad sense of regret.

Again I was totally taken by surprise. I almost couldn't believe what I was hearing. Given our earlier conversations about her being molested by her stepfather and my suspicions of her and her parents' involvement in prostitution, I was certain that this was what she was alluding to. But I needed to confirm it. On the other hand, I didn't want her to think that I'd treat her any differently. It became a delicate balance of walking on eggshells while letting her vent and tell her story.

We sat quietly for about fifteen minutes. Although she was mired in deep thought, it seemed like she was itching to talk. I said nothing, and just waited it out. I feared that if I said anything, it would breach her sense of trust while talking to me. Suddenly, at the top of her lungs, she began to shout.

"THAT BITCH! She let that mother fucker pimp me for years to feed her drug habit!" She just belted it out and started crying. I didn't want to touch her. I wasn't sure where her emotions were going. However, I did try to reassure her that she was safe now.

"I'm here for you. You can talk about it if you want to, or not at all. Just know that you're safe now," I said.

Once she got herself together, she started talking like someone who was flushing the garbage out of her consciousness. She began by telling me that she wished she had stayed with her grandmother, but her mom told her she needed her.

Mom said they were now going to be a family with her new husband. She loved her mother, and missed her when she would go away. She thought it was going to be a great life, and agreed to leave her grandmother's house to live with her mom and stepfather when she was eight years old.

"I have regretted it ever since," she lamented.

Saturn explained that the sexual molestation started at the ripe old age of eight—shortly after she left her grandmother's house. Her stepfather would bring her into the bedroom to sleep with him and her mother while they watched porn movies together. Then he and her mother would start having sex.

"In front of you?" I asked with surprise.

"In front of me!" she replied while shaking her head.

By this time she was rocking as if she was trying to find peace, and needed comforting. I still didn't want to invade her space, so I allowed her to continue talking unencumbered.

She said after about two weeks of watching her mother and stepfather have sex, he coaxed her into touching his penis. That led to her sucking it before he had sex with her mother.

The first place my mind went was to how she may have gotten the persistent sore throat, but I didn't want to jump to conclusions because it was so long ago. I let her continue to vent.

"Can you believe that my virginity was sold for five hundred dollars?!" she exclaimed as she looked at me in what seemed like her own disbelief. "Sold me to some old ass black businessman," she said with disgust and spit on the ground.

"My stepdad came up with the great idea to sell my virginity to that old geezer, then he took over from there," she lamented.

My heart was breaking for her stolen youth. But I didn't want to stop her from talking. I did, however, reassure her that none of it was her fault.

I began to think about how her accusations would strengthen the court's case for child abuse against her stepfather. But she had only just begun to talk.

She gave detailed accounts of how her mother and stepfather would set up tricks almost every day and night, vividly describing memories of how she and her mother had become specialists in having threesomes and would service men together—including her stepfather. Then she clearly recounted a time when two white guys paid extra money to pretend to be her slave masters while they recorded their fantasy. Her mother operated the video camera while they sodomized her and spit on her and called her a ghetto bitch.

"I had a dick in every hole, including my mouth. And all my mother could say to me was 'Why are you crying baby? You're gonna get some new shoes after this one.'" She recalled it as if it had just happened.

They violated every part of her body and her mind. She said she had continuous nightmares of the guys calling her a slut, and a bitch, and slapping her in the face. Afraid of getting pregnant, she said when they finally finished penetrating every hole in her body, she asked if one of them was still wearing a condom.

The other guy responded. "Of course he is! We wouldn't want any more like you running around," she recounted. Then she broke down crying again.

It took all my strength to hold back my tears. Again I drew strength from my mother's statement to me when I told her I was taking the job at the shelter. She reminded me that we are all responsible for making the world a better place. It helped me to more appropriately put things into perspective.

I reassured Saturn that the reason Child Protective Services stepped in was to prevent anything like that from happening to her baby and to her again. After I finally got her calmed down, she decided to go to her room again.

I wrote up a report in her file and discussed what happened with my supervisor, Lauren, who was appalled, but not surprised by what she'd heard. She instructed me to make an appointment to speak with Saturn's mother to see if she confirmed any of the accusations without bringing Saturn into it. Then we could inform the judge about what she said at her next court hearing. I made the appointment for the following week and signed out after another unbelievable day at the shelter.

I was mentally spent and very happy that I'd made the decision to use my earned comp time from working tons of overtime to take Friday off. I needed the time to prepare for the long weekend ahead. As part of my last-minute request, I also traded my Friday appointments with Regina, but I had to take her on-call duties for the shelter on Sunday night in case there was an emergency.

11

An Impromptu Dinner

After a disturbing ending to a day that started perfectly good at the shelter, I fully intended to go straight home, finish preparations for the weekend's catering events, and rest. I rested well, but not without a few surprises.

When I got home, I decided to unwind with a nice bath, my favorite sweet grapefruit aromatherapy oil in the diffuser, and some light jazz. I was emotionally spent. Between Chris juggling my emotions like balls in a bingo game, and Saturn's shocking revelation of being sexually trafficked, I really needed emotional healing. But I had to finish the desserts for the weekend parties, including Friday night's mystery couple—which intrinsically continued to haunt me.

The mystery woman ordered Silky Royal Mandarin Chocolate Almond Galettes, and for Javier's party of fifteen, grilled piña coladas, which required coconut rum galettes as a base. I quickly baked off the galettes and set them aside to cool while I made the toppings and fillings.

Galettes are a cross between a cake and a cookie. The best part is that I can prepare the dough and freeze it until I need it. This allows me to quickly make several varieties of desserts without taking too much time to make the base.

While making the desserts, I kept thinking about the mystery woman's dinner. I tried to rack my mind to figure out who it could be, but that just began to add to the stress. I decided to forget about it and managed to convince myself that it was just another party. Then Chris's gifts caught my eye.

I'd made a decision earlier not to take any more gifts from him because it just kept me emotionally invested. But I felt like I deserved to at least see what was in the boxes after all that I'd gone through—they were so beautifully wrapped, I couldn't resist the temptation. One was the size of a box you'd wrap a robe in at Christmas, and the other was about half its size. They were draped in black-and-white striped linen paper and dressed with two beautiful neon green silk bows.

I wasn't sure what to expect. Chris always loved to buy me beautiful lingerie and expensive perfume, but I had a hard time figuring out why he thought it would keep me away from Tariq. I started to open the box and the phone rang. I dropped them back in the corner and ran to answer the phone.

It was Mark B calling to set up a dancing date for the following Wednesday. While I was talking to him, Tariq's call clicked in, and I felt obligated to answer it. He'd been calling me for two days and I hadn't had a chance to call him back. I quickly confirmed a dancing date with Mark B for after work, and took Tariq's call.

Tariq's voice was filled with excitement. He asked if he could pick me up for a quick bite to eat because he had some news to share with me. I agreed, and he picked me up at my house and took me to a little French bistro in Shadyside.

"My friends love this place," he boasted. "Even though I don't think it's the greatest French food, it's pretty good. I think you'll enjoy it," he said.

He was right, again! I thoroughly enjoyed it. The food was delicate and small, but very light, fresh, and tasty.

For starters, *escargots à la Bourguignon* (snails in garlic, parsley, and herb butter); for the main entrées, quiche lorraine for him and mushroom risotto for me. And for dessert, we shared a flaming crêpes suzette. He took me off guard when he insisted that I try the *escargots*.

"You want me to try *snails*?" I said. "No way!" I exclaimed with trepidation.

"Yes, because if you are going to travel to France, you must at least try the national dish so you can tell people you know something about the culture," he said with a very convincing yet reassuring voice.

Needless to say, I tried one, and it was actually very good. Unfortunately I couldn't get past that first one. I kept thinking about the slugs that sometimes leave trails of slime in my driveway. He laughed at my excuse and we finished the next two courses with great conversation and a beautiful tableside flambé presentation of crêpes suzette bathed in Grand Marnier, served with lightly sweetened whipped cream and charred caramelized oranges.

"So what makes you think I'll be going to France anytime soon?" I said.

"Because I'll be there, and I'd like to invite you to visit me and my family," he said very warmly.

At that moment, I felt a loving sensation overcome my whole being. He had touched me emotionally and mentally. The fact that he felt comfortable enough to invite me into his world, and to visit his home and his parents in Paris, really touched me. After all, I had wanted Chris to invite me into his world for so long without success. Tariq never even hesitated.

He never said anything about cultural differences, or problems of any sort, and he was Lebanese just like Chris. In fact, he was a first-generation Lebanese and was raised in Lebanon until he was fourteen years old. He never talked or even hinted about there being a problem with dating someone from a different race or culture. I began to value our relationship as the beginning of what could be a great friendship.

I gained a lot of respect for Tariq at that very moment, and this further validated my decision to disconnect myself from Chris emotionally and physically. But I still wasn't sure if I was ready to travel to France with him.

During dinner, Tariq also shared that he hadn't gotten accepted into the graduate program at Carnegie Mellon. Therefore he was scheduled to leave in a couple of weeks to go home to Paris for a couple of weeks. Upon his return to the U.S., he'd be moving away from Pittsburgh to San Francisco where his father had arranged for him to take a paid internship with a friend's company. He wanted to know if I would visit him.

"I'd love for you to come with me to Paris," he said.

I wasn't surprised. But I was a little disappointed. However, he had it all figured out. He said if I came with him to visit Paris for two weeks, he would return to Pittsburgh with me and stay with his brother for a week before making his way out to San Francisco to complete the internship for the year. After the internship, he planned to go to graduate school in Atlanta where we could still visit each other.

"After all, if you love to cook like you say you do, and I know that you cook well, why not come to Paris and take a short cooking class?" he said.

I was overwhelmed with excitement, but I couldn't really respond. After a very pregnant pause, I replied, "Well ... I'll think about it."

"While you're making up your mind, how about I make dinner for you tomorrow night," he said with a smile.

"Can you cook?" I said jokingly with a bit of skepticism.

"You'll know after tomorrow. I'll pick up the groceries and meet you at your place around six if that's okay," he said.

I reminded him of my busy weekend of catering events, and we agreed on Sunday night instead. He drove me home, kissed me as I got out of the car, and I finally went to bed.

Menu

Join Us for a French Bistro Dinner for Two

featuring

APPETIZERS

ESCARGOTS À LA BOURGUIGNONNE

snails roasted in garlic butter

DINNER

CREAMY MUSHROOM RISOTTO

QUICHE LORRAINE

DESSERT

CRÊPES SUZETTE

*bathed in Grand Marnier, served with fresh whipped cream
and charred caramelized oranges*

The Surreal

After tossing and turning for most of the night while thinking about Tariq's invitation to Paris, Chris's games, and the mystery woman's dinner, I finally dragged myself out of the bed at eight in the morning. I got dressed and picked up my assistant, Jill, before heading to the Strip District to pick up fresh fruit and flowers. The hotel is just five minutes away. After a quick ride in the car, we were on our way to set up another romantic and luxurious evening for two.

"Hey Anais! Making another love connection tonight?" Those were the famous words of Joel, the concierge, every time he saw me.

"It's supposed to be a pre-engagement party. They're first timers this evening, and I don't really know the couple. But it's a good chance," I replied.

"It's the penthouse suite this time Anais. Must be a pretty special evening," he said while handing me the service keys. He was familiar with my work from several other private parties I'd catered in the past and was always kind.

Jill and I transformed the quintessentially antiseptic hotel suite into a romantic den of passion. Starting at the entrance, we stationed electric candles and sprinkled rose petals throughout the entire suite. The table was set with gold placemats, beautiful porcelain china, and crystal glasses that came with the suite. I wrapped the silverware in red and gold cloth napkins, and placed them on top of the plates. Finally, Jill created a trail of red and yellow rose petals starting from the candle-lined walkway that stretched from the door, to the dining table, and ultimately led to a giant heart in the middle of the bed.

Music is always a key part of setting the mood for our romantic parties. The mystery woman told us they both liked romantic rock music. In response, I made a tailored playlist to set the mood. It included some traditional love songs like "Open Arms," "Faithfully," "When You Love a Woman," and "Don't Stop Believin'" from the group Journey. I also interspersed a mix of songs from my favorite romantics, including John Legend, Brian McKnight, and of course, the ever-erotic Prince, to add variety.

I lit an aromatherapy clay pot filled with my special rose oil mixture in the living room, set up a crisp bottle of white wine in an ice bucket with glasses for toasting on the dining table, topped off the living room coffee table with a plate of my chocolate and vanilla almond truffles, and placed a beautiful gift pack with samples of chocolate-covered strawberry body polish and massage oil on the bedroom nightstand. We put the finishing touches on the room and retreated to the kitchen. After the food was prepared and ready to serve, Jill took off before the mystery woman arrived.

At five-thirty I heard the front door to the suite open. "Hi! It's Shirley Santos. I'm hosting the dinner here this evening," she said as she announced her arrival and began to rave about how beautifully the suite was decorated. "Wow! This is much more than I expected," she said with a nervous glow.

"You asked for my top-of-the-line romantic special, and that's what we tried to provide," I said with an appreciative smile. "I hope it's all you want it to be," I followed.

After I gave her the tour, she said her boyfriend would be arriving around 6:00 p.m. I informed her that I'd be leaving after dessert, and they would have the rest of the evening to enjoy the suite, including our special gift pack. She paid her balance, thanked me, and went into the bedroom to freshen up.

Shirley was a polished, well-dressed, pretty little Filipino girl, who looked to be around my age. It seemed to me that she was dressed rather conservatively for a romantic dinner with her boyfriend. She wore a dark-blue maxi dress, dark blue stockings, and pumps that matched the dress—almost like a flight attendant. Her hair was cut into a consummate conservative blunt bob, and she had a silk Prada scarf tied around her neck, and a Prada bag on her arm.

She came out of the bedroom without the silk scarf and bag, and took off her shoes, but she seemed quite nervous as the clock moved closer to 6:00 p.m. It was clear she was unsettled about something. After about ten minutes of watching her restlessly pace from one end of the room to the other, I asked if she was okay. Unfortunately, it was like opening Pandora's box.

Apprehensive at first, she kept racking her mind, and seemed unsure about whether or not to tell me what was going on. After going back and forth for another two to three minutes, she finally let it out. She smacked herself in the forehead, and then started talking like she had diarrhea of the mouth.

As a devout Catholic, she was nervous because she'd promised to save her virginity for marriage and felt like she might be betraying her own convictions. Although she was pretty confident he was going to propose soon, she set up the romantic evening in an attempt to expedite the proposal. They'd been dating since freshman year of college, and she thought she was ready to fully commit herself to him. It was clear to me, however, she may not have been ready to have sex with him yet. Although she was pretty confident he was going to propose to her, it was the chastity vow that haunted her. She fought back and forth with her inner convictions.

"What if he doesn't ask me to marry him? Worse, what if I give myself to him, and he doesn't propose?" she questioned her objective.

Before we knew it, the clock moved past 6:15 p.m. "This doesn't surprise me," she said abruptly. "He's always late. But I'm sure he won't let me down."

The biggest part of my job is to listen to my clients and to provide reassurance that everything is going to be okay. My job as a social worker often came in handy in these situations. I reassured her that everything would be just fine. Then I returned to the kitchen and left her in the living room to wait.

A knock at the door came five minutes later—it was her boyfriend. I was in the kitchen so I couldn't see him come in, but my curiosity got the best of me.

I desperately wanted to see which of my clients was her boyfriend. I also knew I had to be professional, so I waited until they came to the dining table—which would indicate to me that they were ready for service.

After listening to their ten-minute greeting and discussion about how beautiful the room looked, I got a nagging feeling that the voice was too familiar. Shirley finally invited him to the dinner table. When he walked into the dining room, my mouth dropped open. His mouth dropped open, too. Shirley's back was turned to me as she was trying to gage his reaction to the beautiful tablescape, so she didn't see my face. She seemed to assume his reaction was to the table, so he quickly gathered himself.

"It ... it's amazing! How did you manage to arrange something like this Shirley?" he stuttered as he pulled her chair out and put his head down in embarrassment.

She told him how she got the idea from the card that came with the Valentine's Day cake he'd given to her two years ago. The mystery client was Chris! *Yes*, it was my Chris. He dropped his head and tried to act surprised.

I, on the other hand, was pissed off! He had just left my bed less than 48 hours earlier where we made the most incredible love, and he professed his so-called true love for me. Now he was at a table with his so-called girlfriend that I was under the impression he broke up with more than a year and a half earlier. To make matters worse, there she was expecting him to propose to her.

I began to panic. I decided I couldn't stay and watch him put another dagger through my heart. But I knew I had to get myself together for the sake of my business if nothing else.

I told myself this was another perfect excuse for finally giving him up. For the sake of finally letting him go as reality bashed me in the face, I decided to stay and finish out my contractual obligations.

I detached myself from the situation and treated them as any other couple. I walked them through each course, explained which foods were aphrodisiacs and how they were prepared from scratch. However, I tried to stay in the kitchen as much as possible.

Each time I talked, he'd gaze into my eyes. I knew he wanted to talk to me. But he never said a word.

At the end of the evening, I had taken all of my supplies to the car and was finishing the last of the cleaning when Shirley came into the kitchen to thank me. She gave me a $50 tip, and said she was still nervous. That's when my claws came out.

"He might want to let those scratches heal on his back before he jumps in the sack with you!" I shouted curtly as I grabbed the last of my supplies and prepared to leave.

She just walked away in total confusion. But I wasn't finished. I needed

Chris to feel my wrath. I went to the door and before I exited, I dug in deeper. "Oh yeah Chris, you might want to show her the scratches I put on your back the other night while we fucked until the next morning. Better yet, maybe you can give her a demonstration of how you polished every inch of my body with the chocolate and strawberries polish that you've been licking off my ass for the past year and a half!" I shouted. Then I left.

I felt a little vindicated, but again I was torn up inside emotionally. The rejection seemed more realistic than ever, especially if what Shirley believed about their engagement was true.

In the past he'd told me his family really liked her—which I now questioned because she was neither white nor Lebanese. He also told me that after more than three years together the relationship had run its course, and they supposedly broke up shortly before we started dating.

Things really began to come into focus for me now. I began to put the puzzle together as to when I couldn't find him, and why he was so confused about our so-called relationship. The one good thing was her confirmation that he wasn't sleeping with both of us at the same time. But at this point he had ripped a hole the size of Texas in my heart.

I made it home in one piece, but there was no one to lament to. Everyone was out, including Tariq who'd gone to hang out with some of his college buddies. I was left alone to really think about what had just happened. I had to think about how I was going to react the next time I saw Chris.

Reaching the conclusion that there was no way I could ever be with him again, I committed to investing my time and energy into building my relationship with Tariq. Even though he was leaving Pittsburgh, it didn't mean I wouldn't be able to visit him wherever he was located. After all, I rationalized that if he invited me to Paris, I was sure I could visit him anywhere. So I decided to take one day at a time.

Menu

Join Us for a Romantic Pre-Engagement Soiree for Two
featuring

APPETIZERS

FRESH BUTTERCRUNCH SALAD
topped with lightly seasoned jumbo scallops sautéed in herb butter

WARM SOURDOUGH ROLLS

JUMBO SCALLOPS
sautéed in black pepper and thyme butter

DINNER

RED SOCKEYE SALMON FILLETS
baked in banana leaves, dressed with a sweet teriyaki sauce

SEASONED STICKY RICE • CRUNCHY KALE SALAD

PALATE CLEANSER

LEMON SORBET

BEVERAGES

ORANGE PEKOE TEA LATTES

DESSERT

SILKY ROYAL MANDARIN CHOCOLATE ALMOND GALETTES

BEAUTY RITUAL

Bodacious body chocolate-covered strawberry body polish and massage oil
scrub and love splash.

GIFT PACK

Chocolate Truffles; Vanilla Almond Truffles

12

S aturday morning's wakeup call came even quicker than Friday's after another sleepless night. All I kept thinking about was Chris marrying Shirley ... how rejected and betrayed I felt. My emotional connection to him kept bringing me back to the intense lovemaking we'd just shared. I couldn't shake the feeling of connection I'd had with him for nearly two years. I was sure he shared the same feelings. But then again, Shirley was sure he was going to propose to her. I didn't know what to think.

Reality struck and I quickly realized I had to pull myself together and prepare for Javier's shindig. Once again I had to tuck away my pain and push forward.

Patiently awaiting my arrival, Jill jumped in the car around 8:00 a.m., and again we made our way to the Strip District to pick up the fresh fish, fruit, and flowers. We returned to my place to finish last minute preparations, packed the car, and headed to Javier's house in Shadyside to set up for the High Top Grill. Joe, the bartender, was also patiently waiting in front of the house when we arrived—I hated making him wait on us, so I knew I had to pull myself together.

Javier is hot, but a little old for my taste. His brother Julio, however, is another story altogether. Five years younger than Javier, Julio is an endocrinologist at New York University's medical center. He was visiting for his birthday weekend and Javier had planned a special celebration in his honor.

Five feet nine inches tall and about 190 pounds, Julio is a slim, strong, muscular, well-dressed Spanish man, with green eyes, dark brown hair, and skin the color of Madagascar cinnamon. He's as kind and gentle as he is beautiful, which makes him even more enticing—a simply scrumptious specimen of a man.

"Umh, umh, umh! Tempting!" I thought. However, I didn't need any more complications with men in my life. Besides, I needed to maintain my professional integrity. So I stayed in my lane, and decided not to let anyone cross the lines of intimacy.

Javier planned to have most of the activities in his beautiful backyard. The evening's entertainment highlights were a contemporary jazz trio that played during dinner on the backyard patio and some of my crowd-pleaser games in the living room afterward.

The backyard was a magnificent piece of eye candy—amazingly grand and secluded. It could easily accommodate up to fifty people with a fair amount of room to spare—yet it was very intimate.

Three huge retractable French doors lead to the backyard from the living room, and one from the kitchen. The backyard is laid out on a grid, with an enclosed stamped and stained concrete patio that extends for about 70 yards across and 50 yards deep into the sprawling backyard—a rare find in the heart of the city.

The entire area is lined with perfectly groomed 30-foot pencil shaped cypress trees, anchored at the bases with floodlights. A generous herb garden sits on the right side, and pink English rose and peony patches are perfectly appointed throughout the entire yard. About five yards from the entry doors to the living room is a 75-foot heated saltwater lap pool, with an elevated spa and fireplace. It spans nearly the whole width of the yard and juts off to the far right corner.

To the left there's an entire outdoor kitchen and bar with seating for at least twenty people, and a fully equipped barbecue pit sits off to the left of the bar and directly in front of the kitchen door. The entire backyard is lavishly furnished with teakwood seating and lounging chairs, and Tuscan-inspired dining chairs and bar stools on the patio and around the water areas.

But the *pièce de résistance* is the intimate seating area situated just in front of the herb garden. Two huge round loungers with closing sun protectors are dressed with matching pillows and blankets. A complementary table and cooler filled with an assortment of beverages and snacks is placed between the loungers. The loungers are more like outdoor beds and are clearly designed for the relaxation of one or even up to four people at a time.

Truth or Lies

When the guests began to arrive, Javier and Julio were still upstairs getting dressed and we needed a finalized guest list. I ran upstairs to call for them and inadvertently ran into Julio coming out of the shower. He had nothing on but a towel—I had to pull myself together. He is simply gorgeous. I quickly turned around, excused myself and asked for the guest list.

"*No pasa nada bella dama!*" Julio responded.

I'd studied Spanish for several years, but I'd never heard anyone speak so beautifully. Perhaps I was a little startled by his beautiful body, or his startling marble-green eyes, but I knew it roughly translated to "No problem beautiful lady," and I started to blush.

"I'm honored to meet you!" he said. "What's your name?"

"Oh hi! I'm Anais, the caterer," I replied.

"I've heard a lot about you," he quickly responded. Javier walked out of his room upon hearing my voice and kissed me on both cheeks.

"Here it is Anais. Sorry about the delay, and thanks for helping me make this event special. By the way, don't forget we're also celebrating my baby brother Julio's twenty-eighth birthday. I have a special surprise planned for him too," he said.

"*Feliz cumpleaños* Julio!" I chanted. "Hope we can help make your day special, too," I said with a smile. He thanked me and finished getting dressed.

The guest list was rather diverse, yet interesting. It included a group from the symphony, a few university professors and administrators from around the city, and the guest of honor—Javier's brother Julio. Most of the group appeared to be single. Some people were coupled-up, but my first thought was, "This is going to be an interesting evening."

Javier, a Spanish native, is rather attractive and an accomplished violinist and music professor. But at thirty-two, like I said earlier, he was a bit too old for me. On the other hand, his brother Julio was on fire! The downside, according to Javier, Julio's a workaholic. Most admirably, he's a prominent researcher and practitioner searching for a cure for juvenile diabetes. Javier also boasted about how he often volunteers to take missionary trips to Africa with a team of medical professionals from Pittsburgh to perform surgery in remote villages. I was thoroughly impressed.

Javier said Julio's too dedicated to his work and needed to come up for air. So he obliged Julio to take a break and come to Pittsburgh for his birthday, hence the celebration.

I later learned that Julio had a twin brother named Jorge who passed away from complications with juvenile diabetes when they were six years old. It's what inspired him to become a doctor, and to search for a cure while reaching out to the less fortunate.

Smart, principled, and gorgeous—he's a great catch for anyone. "I really have to restrain myself," I thought as I licked my lips with delight and continued with my work.

Grilled Perfection

Javier greeted the guests as they arrived while Jill checked off the guest list and took dinner orders for the grill. She also handed out game packs with questionnaires for the icebreaker and Dirty Bingo Trivia games.

In the meantime, I started putting the food on the grill. The whole time I was cooking, I couldn't get Julio out of my mind. His beautiful body and alluring smile pervaded my rational thinking—the way his sun-kissed skin gently glided over his firm, taut muscles while his fine-tuned chest perfectly complimented his broad shoulders and prominent six-pack. As soon as the cooking began to command all of my attention, he walked over to the grill and started chatting me up.

"Oh Lord! Why is he teasing me?!" I thought to myself.

Needless to say, he turned me on with his intellectual conversation and beautiful personality. Yep! He sucked me right in. But I had everything under control. At least I thought I did.

Julio was casually dressed in a white polo shirt, dark blue plaid polo shorts that prominently revealed his sun-starved legs, and dark blue leather saddle sandals. His hair was still wet, and little bits of water were glistening on his face, but he smelled of a deliciously familiar aftershave. When he smiled, the water drizzled down his face ever so slightly caressing the soft crevices of the enticing dimples that kissed his cheeks.

He looked so good I thought about licking the water off, but I handed him a paper towel instead. He smiled as he wiped the water away, which revealed his pearly white teeth. Again I was tempted to go after him, but I restrained myself as he thanked me and moved on to greet some of the other guests.

"Oh well! It's back to cooking for me," I said to myself. I'd finally received all of the dinner orders, which meant everyone had arrived, and we could get started with the festivities.

After the dinner service is finished, I like to start each of our parties with a crowd-pleasing icebreaker to warm everyone up. Today's icebreaker was the game Two Truths and a Tale. The game packs Jill handed out to the guests upon their arrival included trivia cards for the dirty bingo game and questionnaires that required everyone to complete them by telling two truths and a tale about themselves to allow everyone to get to know each other better.

During the game, the host gives everyone a chance to blindly select one of the completed questionnaires, read it aloud, and take the first guess on who's answers they thought it was. There were a couple of surprise truths, but the ones that interested and took everyone aback were that Julio is pretty shy, and Javier is heavy into sex games. At that point I knew things were going to get interesting—I started to question just how far Javier was going to push the envelope.

Javier had attended at least four other parties I catered in the past, and not once had I seen him exhibit anything that would indicate he was a little freaky. I guess he really decided he'd let his hair down at his party.

Dirty, Dirty Bingo

During the party, Julio asked my staff and I if we wanted to play Dirty Bingo Trivia after we finished dinner cleanup. Joe, my bartender, and Jill opted to just watch. However, I insisted on helping Javier facilitate the game since he had only played once before.

The Dirty Bingo Trivia game is an added trivia twist to the original Dirty Bingo game, which is designed to be a surprise for everyone except the host. The host wraps a collection of useful and/or gag gifts and is the only one who really knows what's in the boxes. During the game, participants are allowed to choose gifts, and at the end of the game they reveal what's in the boxes. Javier relished the opportunity presented by obscuring the identity of the gifts. It later defined a lot about his hidden personality.

He insisted on buying and wrapping the gifts himself, and had them ready for us to set up upon arrival. They were beautiful—it was very evident that he'd spent a lot of time and thought into choosing and wrapping the gifts. He also had one specific gift set aside for his brother in honor of his birthday. I had no idea what was in the gift boxes and was just as intrigued as everyone else when the game began.

Before the Dirty Bingo Trivia game starts, all participants are given three raffle tickets and for bonuses, they are invited to fill in slots on a Jeopardy-like game board. The board is made up of twenty-five trivia questions. Whoever gets the correct answer first receives additional numbers based on the difficulty of the question.

After the question and answer period, the fun begins. Participants are told that when any of your ticket numbers are called, you're allowed to choose anything from the table of wrapped gifts. The catch is that the gifts cannot be opened until *all* of the numbers have been called. Then, the host throws all of the matching bingo numbers into a large box, and begins to call the numbers. When the participant's bingo number is called, that person is allowed to choose a gift. However, there are only enough gifts for half of the numbers called. When the gifts run out on the table, the next person whose number is called is allowed to take whatever gift they want from anyone who already has a gift. This cycle continues until all the numbers are exhausted. Even though we don't share this until the end of the game, we make sure that anyone who doesn't have a gift is either given a gag gift, or one of our Bodacious Body sampler gift packs after the fun is over.

The game was hilarious! Everyone fought over the largest and most beautifully wrapped gift as expected. It went around the room at least four times. Some people even tried to hide gifts so that no one would potentially take them. But that's why we put them on display early—so that everyone would remember what was available even though they couldn't touch or see what was inside.

At the end of the game, we asked everyone to stand up and open their gifts one at a time to share the spoils with the crowd. I had no idea what Javier put in the boxes, which made it more fun for me. But I was truly shocked when everyone started opening the gifts.

The first person to volunteer was Monica, a music department administrative assistant. She was very comfortable with everyone because she interacted with them daily and took care of all the musicians' schedules. She volunteered to go first to break the ice.

She ended up with one of the smaller rectangular boxes. When she opened it, on top there was a note with a $5 bill taped to it. It read: "May your life be as long and useful as this roll of toilet paper."

Everyone giggled. However, the more interesting part of the gift was the roll of toilet paper she pulled out of the box after reading the note. It was covered with a variety of sexual positions from the *Kama Sutra*. I was flabbergasted! The chatter grew louder about what others thought might be in their boxes.

"Well I can see how this evening is going to turn out," I whispered to Jill. She snickered with skepticism.

Next, a fellow symphony member decided to open one of the biggest and prettiest boxes. He removed the top, and the gift was very neatly covered with tissue paper. It too had a note on top that read: "For those long, lonely days on the road, when your **** is engorged like a toad, here's a little something to help you drop a load."

He pulled back the tissue paper, and it somehow triggered a blow up sex doll to pop out of the box, and reveal herself. That was just the beginning. A thirteen-inch dildo, along with three different flavored lubricants stuffed in cutouts on the sides of the box accompanied her. Needless to say, everyone's jaws dropped. However, this guy seemed to be eternally thankful, and tightly embraced his newfound friend. I was speechless.

The fun didn't stop there. The music department's chairman opened a box of edible undies and a "touch me erotica" massage game. Another woman opened a happy penis massage cream, another vibrator, and jelly pleasure mitts. Gift after gift was filled with erotic sex toys and games.

"No wonder he wanted to wrap the gifts himself!" I thought to myself. But his friends didn't seem fazed by anything. In fact, they were delighted by his thoughtfulness.

"This Dirty Bingo Trivia game has taken on a whole new meaning. Javier seems to have taken the word *dirty* and redefined it for his own purposes," I told Jill as we both laughed in amazement.

Jill reminded me that during the Two Truths and a Tale icebreaker, Javier wrote that he was single, a freak, and didn't want action tonight. I guess the last one was the lie, because by the time this game was over, the sexual tension in the room was so thick it started oozing out of everyone.

The telling moment came when a frisky clarinet player opened a box with a Sex on the Beach drink mix, a strip game, and a supersize vibrator. Poor Joe was getting overwhelmed because everyone started ordering up the drinks to release some of the tension. Jill and I started helping, and the next thing you know, all I heard from one of the ladies was "It's getting hot in here!" and the clothes began to fly off.

Then Mr. Frisky—the clarinet player—started running around and zapping everyone in his or her private areas with the vibrator. At that point, I abruptly suggested to Jill and Joe that it was time for us to pack up and give them privacy. I guess Julio felt the same way. He left his unopened gift and followed me to the kitchen and offered to help carry my things to the car.

We finished cleaning and left a self-service setup on the bar for drinks, my signature thank you truffles for a snack, and leftover appetizers. I'm sure the extra snacks came in handy sometime later on in the evening.

On the way out, Julio and I inadvertently passed Javier's guest room while stacking the boxes near the door. The door was slightly cracked open, and I could hear Monica struggling to suppress her moans of pleasure. Apparently Javier had gotten ahold of one of the vibrators and went to town on her. When she could no longer suppress the moans, she shouted,

"Fuck me Javier! Please fuck me now! I want you inside of me RIGHT NOW!" she screamed.

Beneath what seemed to be the alternating sound of the vibrator, Javier said in a deep and sultry voice, "I'm gonna fuck you just like you need it, long ... hard ... and deep. And I'm gonna make you cum over and over again."

Julio blushed as he looked at me. We both laughed and he said with amusement, "I guess she's having a good time." Then he mistakenly dropped one of the boxes.

Javier abruptly came to the door. He nervously brushed his disheveled hair out of his face—which was now red from his head being buried in Monica's sex.

"Where are you going Julio?" he said. Julio explained that he was helping us pack up. Javier insisted on helping too.

After excusing himself from Monica, he came out and thanked us for a beautiful and entertaining evening, and confirmed a booking for the symphony's fall season opener after-party. Along with the booking came a big fat three-hundred-dollar tip. For me that was the biggest compliment of all.

I said goodbye to Julio. "I hope to see you again soon Anais," he said as he kissed me on both cheeks. Blushing on the inside, I flirted a little. "I hope to see you again soon too! Don't work too hard," I said.

Although smitten by his attention, I was exhausted—mentally and physically. I dropped Jill off and went straight home to take a shower.

When I finally got out of the shower, I lay on the couch to watch a little TV and got a glimpse of Chris's gifts staring at me. It was time to open them. I had every intention of burning them and sending the ashes to his office with a dirty note.

I started with the large box. I popped the top off to discover a long, hot pink, velvet and satin sleeveless robe, accompanied by a matching iridescent leather strapped bondage teddy with no crotch, and matching pink, three-inch heels with gladiator straps that wrapped all the way up to the knee.

"Clearly Chris was fantasizing when he selected these gifts," I thought.

I moved to the small box, and things escalated.

A crisp set of pink leather handcuffs with a soft leather whip, a ten-inch marble hot pink vibrator, and a hot pink velvet blindfold were packaged neatly like a perfect matching set of trinkets. I couldn't even believe I was in the midst of sex toys again. I wasn't quite sure how to process everything in my mind. I packed it all back up, threw it back in the corner, and went to my bed to sleep.

Menu

Join Us for High Top Grilling
featuring

APPETIZERS

WILD & CRAZY BUFFALO WINGS COLLECTION

SHRIMP CEVICHE

FRESH VEGETABLE CRUDITÉS
served with lemony hummus and seven seas dip

ASSORTED WARM SOURDOUGH ROLLS
with seasoned butter selections

DINNER

MARINATED GRILLED SHRIMP KEBABS

HERB-ROASTED TILAPIA FILLETS
in parchment paper

BONE-IN PORK CHOPS
hand-cut triple-thick and marinated

PORTOBELLO MUSHROOMS & CAULIFLOWER STEAKS
marinated and grilled

PORTERHOUSE STEAKS
prime cut and aged

menu continues …

Menu

BEVERAGES

FRESH FRUIT MOCKTAILS & COCKTAILS

DESSERT

GRILLED PIÑA COLADAS

fresh pineapple slices macerated in rum on top of coconut ice cream sandwiched between homemade coconut rum galettes and topped with sour cherry topping

FRESH FRUIT COLLECTION

GIFT PACK

white and dark chocolate truffles

ENTERTAINMENT

Jazz trio; icebreaker: Two Truths and a Tale; Dirty Bingo Trivia.

13

Too Close for Comfort

Although it ended in what seemed like a big orgy, Javier's party was an amazing hit. He had graciously expressed his satisfaction with that hefty three-hundred dollar tip. I didn't realize it until I got home, but Julio's card was in the middle of the money with his phone number, and a note for me to call him for a drink tomorrow. I was flattered, but I'd already had plans with Tariq.

After a nonstop beginning to the long weekend, I slept in on Sunday, went to the late service at church, and prepared for Tariq to make dinner at 6:00 p.m. But once again, Chris tried to throw a wrench in my plans.

He called five times in a row, but I refused to answer the phone. Then he decided to leave a message on my machine. He seemed to be obsessed with controlling my life, and refused to take no for an answer. I finally picked up the phone and entertained his phone call for all of five minutes.

"I'm coming over there now!" he insisted.

"No!" I said emphatically. "I won't be here, I'm going out with friends," I quipped.

With a very sentimental and sincere whisper, he pleaded, "Please Anais, please don't leave. ... I need to see you. I have to talk to you, and I'll just be there for a few minutes. I'm up the street and I'm coming now."

I never understood why he was always "just up the street." Sometimes it felt like he was stalking me. He hung the phone up before I could further refuse. Five minutes later the doorbell rang. It was already 5:05 p.m., and Tariq was due to arrive at 6:00 p.m.

By this time I was sweating bullets. I didn't want either of them to run into each other. My apartment was on the bottom floor and everyone coming in the building had to pass by my door after being buzzed into the security door.

Although I pontificated about allowing Chris to suffer the same pain I felt while watching him dine with his so-called ex-girlfriend, I didn't want to hurt

Tariq. It was too late though. I had to rely on the fact that if they ran into each other, they wouldn't realize they were both visiting me. I just had to get rid of Chris as fast as I could.

As was his usual approach these days, Chris came rushing in, ranting about how sorry he was for the so-called misunderstanding, how much he'd missed me, and how good I looked. I told him I was meeting some friends and he had to leave. After unsuccessfully trying to kiss me, he finally agreed to leave at around 5:55 p.m. Just as he went through the security door, my doorbell rang again.

Yep! It was Tariq. I prayed he didn't suspect anything, and he didn't. I later learned that Chris did see him. Since I'd told him that I was on the way out, he didn't think anyone was coming to see me—the joke was on him.

French Kissed

Tariq came in, rolled up his sleeves, and poured me a glass of wine. He jumped right in to dinner preparation.

"It's your turn to be spoiled," he said as he gently rubbed a heated sauté pan with a clove of garlic while pretending to seduce me with his technique. Then he put a pat of butter in the pan followed by two tender scallops of veal. Caressing my nose with the sumptuous scents from the garlic and butter, he began reciting the menu: "Veal scaloppine, *pommes frites,* and sautéed broccoli for the main course; a delicate chocolate mousse parfait layered with mandarin chocolate cake, chocolate ganache, and fresh slices of strawberries and cream for the dessert. And I thought we'd have a little port wine I purchased on my last trip to Portugal with dessert," he said like he was singing the menu.

"Wow, now I'm impressed!" I said with a feeling of relief that he didn't run into Chris. I felt like I could now exhale, relax, and enjoy this opportunity for someone to spoil me.

Dinner was absolutely magnificent. Of course I was already sold by the seduction of smells, and the sensuous preparation techniques, but the taste was even more amazing. Everything was light and creamy, but savory—truly mouthwatering. I wasn't accustomed to eating meat and not having a feeling of heaviness afterward, so this meal was truly a treat.

"You're a very good cook too!" I said. I was truly impressed.

He said his mother is also a great cook. Given that they lived in the food capital of the world, she made every effort to teach both him and his brother how to cook, too.

After dinner, Tariq invited me to visit him in San Francisco if I couldn't make it to Paris. He would only be in Paris for a couple of weeks and then return to Pittsburgh before heading to San Francisco. Again I told him I'd think about it—that sounded more promising since I didn't have to leave the country. Then we played backgammon and talked for a couple of hours until the phone rang.

Surprise! Surprise! It was the shelter calling. I had traded an on-call shift with Regina in order to have Friday off, and they made sure to interrupt my weekend.

The shelter was unable to locate Saturn and needed me to come in to file a police report and help with the other girls. My never-ending weekend wouldn't have been the same without a crazy adventure at the shelter to round things out.

I said my goodbyes to Tariq and headed to the shelter. Just as I pulled into the driveway, I spotted a car running in the parking lot, and Saturn walking up the stairs with a man. It was dark, so I wasn't quite sure who he was. But I was startled to see her walking up to the house with a man in the middle of the night.

I parked my car and headed inside where I found Saturn accompanied by one of our male counselors, Ed. Ed said he lived close and was driving by when he saw her hitchhiking in the middle of the remote road. He said he picked her up and convinced her to return to the shelter so she wouldn't get in trouble. He didn't have access to a phone to call, so he just brought her directly to the shelter.

"Phew! Crisis averted," I said to Patty Jo. She was working the overnight shift and had just arrived. She was just as relieved as I was. None of us wanted to deal with the daunting paperwork, nor the consequences Saturn would suffer.

Not only would Saturn have lost the privileges she acquired as an older girl at our shelter, she would not have been able to visit her daughter as often. In addition, all of her counseling would have had to start over with another crew. It would have been a very costly setback for her. She was, however, facing in-house restrictions as a result of leaving the shelter unescorted and without permission.

I was very happy I didn't have to go through all of the protocols. I bid everyone goodnight and took my happy behind home to prepare for the wrath that was to follow the next morning at the shelter.

I got home, jumped in the tub, and lavished myself with one of my stress relief bath bombs. Afterward, I finished up the lovely dessert Tariq prepared before retiring to bed and sleeping quite peacefully.

The Shelter: Deception

The next morning, the details of Ed picking up Saturn on the road began to get a bit muddy. It seemed they didn't have their stories in sync. However, she'd made it back to the shelter before the four-hour deadline after which the courts would have required her to be declared a runaway. Therefore we weren't able to push harder about the situation without Saturn pushing back. The therapist reluctantly suggested we let Saturn bring out what really happened when she was ready.

In a shelter, the drama wheel of fortune never stops turning. It was only twenty minutes into our morning discussion when Saturn's spotlight was quickly overshadowed by what had now become Darlese's drama.

She was the pregnant girlfriend of Corry who was upset because she'd heard he allegedly called her a whore. To retaliate, she decided she was going to get her brothers to jump him, and teach him a lesson. Everyone tried to reassure her that it wasn't a big deal, and that she shouldn't promote violence. As fate would have it, she is the offspring of a very vindictive and violent family. She refused to let it go without revenge.

I decided I'd already had my hands full with Saturn's case. I tried to get as far removed from Darlese's situation as possible. However, later that evening, Regina asked me to call Mark B to find out if he knew anything about the situation, and he didn't.

But he did reconfirm our dancing date on Wednesday. He also informed me that Rafi invited us to go for massages and dinner at a friend's house before dancing. One of his friends owned a group of day spas and needed volunteers to try out some new products. I thought it was a great opportunity to unwind, so I welcomed the invitation.

The Shelter: Saturn

After a truly mentally unstable weekend filled with too many highs and lows to count, and returning to the madness at the shelter again on Monday morning, the invitation to just relax sounded magical. As expected, the weekend left a residual of problems. At the top of the list—unresolved runaways, like Saturn, and disgruntled girls who didn't have an opportunity for a family visit—mainly because there was no one to visit, or they weren't allowed to visit them. There was also an entire schedule of appointments for each girl that had to be completed with the counselors as chaperones.

I, however, was scheduled to visit Saturn's mother to investigate the child sex trafficking allegations. I was a bit on edge because I didn't know how to best begin the discussion. My supervisor, Lauren, who was in foster care as a child and had worked for Child Protective Services for over twenty-five years, was very reassuring.

She instructed me to begin by updating Saturn's mother on the health and welfare of Saturn and the baby. Then to just proceed in normal conversation as we were trained to do during a normal home visit. She assured me that at some point, the conversation would move to where it needed to be, and I should just be calm and not allow anyone to get upset. She was right!

The conversation with Saturn's mother kept me intrigued and flabbergasted—but not in a good way. The visit lasted eight hours, during which time her mother shared incredible and oftentimes disturbing stories about her being trafficked herself since the age of thirteen.

She elaborated on her travels throughout the United States with numerous pimps and groups of women she referred to as her "wife-in-laws" to service clients. Bruised by the memories, she cried while recounting her brushes with sexually transmitted diseases, unwanted pregnancies, and a more recent battle with epilepsy.

Disturbingly, she told horror stories of servicing her least pleasant clients, and then getting beaten up and being left for dead in alleys because they didn't want to pay for her services. Not only did her clients beat her, she'd also get beaten by her pimps for not delivering their cut of the money from "pulling the trick" as she described it.

While recounting her experiences as part of a traveling prostitution ring for eleven years, she disclosed how she got pregnant with Saturn. When she realized she was pregnant, she called her mom and begged to come home, and promised to live a normal life—but old habits die hard.

Two weeks after she had the baby, she went out against her mother's advice and inadvertently didn't contact her mother for three months. She tried to find her old crew, but they had already moved on to the next unannounced city. So she hooked up with Saturn's stepfather because she needed someone to protect her while she did her work on the streets.

Although Saturn lived with her grandmother for the first seven years of her life, her mother maintained legal custody. Shortly after Saturn's eighth birthday, her mother married the new stepfather in what she described as an effort to create a stable environment for Saturn. She assured her mom that Saturn would be safe now—they were going to be a happy family with the new stepfather. He, however, was on a totally different chapter in the book of family; evidently his book didn't describe a "happy family."

Saturn's mother inadvertently began to confirm the accusations made against her and the stepfather, and I didn't have to say a word. She said the stepfather was nice and accepting at first. But after a while, when she wanted to get high, he began using the drugs as leverage to start messing with Saturn.

She confirmed the stories about how he broke Saturn in by forcing her to give him blowjobs, and then making her sleep with both of them. Most striking to me was when she recounted how they scored what was supposed to be big payouts a couple of times. It was just as Saturn recounted—the first was by selling Saturn's virginity, and another later on by recording her in a threesome with two white boys. I began to cringe in my seat. My heart sank with every breaking word.

She said they were on a drug rant when her husband sold Saturn to some old black businessman who thought she would make him young again. From that point on, she and Saturn would have private parties with all kinds of men—most of whom were white guys who wanted threesomes, or to gang bang them.

I asked her how they set them up. She said her husband took care of those details. She didn't really know. "What I do know, is that it was the best thing since hot water corn bread!" she quipped with excitement. I found it incredible that she was comparing a child's innocence to a delicious piece of bread. But it became clear to me that selling her child in the sex trade was somehow good for her, and she relished in it.

"Saturn could go to school during the day and at night make the M-O-N-E-Y!" she chuckled. "And nobody knew what was going on. As a matter of fact, as long as she showed up to school on time, and kept her mouth shut, nobody cared what was going on. We liked it that way, and my husband did everything to keep it that way. Until everything got fucked up," she quipped with an eerie disappointment.

I was taken aback. I could only think about the many kids under the radar who may be suffering the same fate.

According to her, the benefit to having the private parties was that they no longer had to go on the street to get clients. As long as everyone kept the secret, they could pull as many tricks as they wanted without being harassed by the police, or even her mother. She claimed this helped her protect Saturn.

"And anyway, it was nobody else's business what went on in our house!" she shouted with a drunken air of cockiness.

I couldn't help but think to myself, "This is too easy." She was rattling off stories that horrified me not only for Saturn, but for her too. I began to realize she was either high or medicated, and she didn't really know how to restrain her tongue.

I also got the impression that it was somewhat cathartic for her to get some of that craziness off her chest. So I decided to ask her about Saturn's accusation of sleeping with her stepfather. Her response was consistent—jaw dropping!

"We all slept together from time to time. But everyone understood the lines," she quipped.

I was so taken aback this time that I couldn't stop myself. The words fell right out of my mouth. "Where were the lines when he made you strip and he beat the crap out of both of you in public while you were naked?" I inquired of her in a somewhat timid but horrified voice.

She took a long, pregnant pause. Then she replied in a more subdued voice. "Well ..." She paused for three long minutes as if she had to carefully measure the next words coming out of her mouth. Then she continued in a somewhat slow and sad cadence. "That ... wasn't ... all ... the time," she reticently exclaimed. "I told Saturn not to cry when she was making that last video with those white guys. But she wouldn't stop. My husband said they wouldn't be able to use the video because people would think those guys raped her, so they only gave him half the money. He was pissed off, and he beat both of us," she said in a somewhat remorseful voice.

"Then one of our nosey neighbors saw us outside and called the police. Now my man's in jail, and they took Saturn and the baby." She started crying. "And

I'm here all alone, and I have epilepsy." She finished the statement as if she had been violated by the state and didn't understand what the real problem was. Needless to say, I was dumbfounded—but I managed to keep my composure.

I encouraged her to take care of herself and to work hard to reestablish her household as a suitable place for the return of Saturn and the baby. I also implored her to work with the courts and seek counseling for the abuse she'd suffered and as a victim of sex trafficking.

After carefully documenting the resources with phone numbers and addresses, I handed her a list of contacts and told her she could probably get free help as an epileptic. I also highly recommended that she investigate Social Security as a possible source of income so she wasn't tempted to return to that life. With that I left her and returned to the shelter to record the interview in Saturn's case file.

Menu

Join Us for a Little Taste of Paris!

featuring

DINNER

VEAL SCALOPPINE

POMMES FRITES
hand-cut, twice-cooked potatoes

SAUTÉED BROCCOLI
with roasted garlic

BEVERAGE

PORT WINE

DESSERT

CHOCOLATE MOUSSE PARFAIT
*layered with Grand Marnier chocolate cake, chocolate
ganache, fresh strawberry slices, and whipped cream*

14

Wednesday night couldn't come soon enough. Free massages, dinner, and dancing with my favorite dance partner, what more could I ask for in the middle of the week? Rafi put the icing on the cake with his offer of door-to-door pick-up and drop-off service, and I was more than ready for some welcomed stress relief.

After work, I took a quick shower and slipped into a comfortable yet sexy mocha chocolate jumpsuit with long silky straps that wrapped around my trim waist and accentuated my bodacious booty. Rafi, Sheila, and Mark B were waiting in the parking lot at 6:00 p.m. sharp. Ready for a great evening of food, fun, dancing, and relaxation, I put on a pair of black patent leather spaghetti strapped platforms—my favorite sexy but comfortable dancing shoes, and headed out the door.

The Familiar Stranger

We crossed two bridges, drove through two tunnels, and traveled up an incredibly long hill to arrive at a rather obscure house built in the side of a cliff. The house was ultra modern and comfortably couched at the end of a long driveway set back about fifteen hundred feet from the main road.

Rafi parked the car, and his friend, Walter, greeted us. He was joined by a coed team of four masseuses, all dressed in the same red uniforms with the words *Happy Endings Spa* embroidered over the left chest pocket. It kind of surprised me—the name was so blatantly sexual. My first thought was to demand an explanation from Mark B. Rafi abruptly interjected before I could say anything and insisted that we should all just relax and trust him. I hoped it wasn't anything crazy and decided to let it play itself out. After all, I was kind of at his mercy since he was the designated driver for the night.

Walter welcomed us, and explained that he's the owner of the spas and needed to test a new line of elixirs and massage products before introducing them to his clients, hence the invitation. After we signed waivers and made our choices from six different aromatherapy blends, he suggested we start with a relaxing elixir tea, enjoy our massages, and have dinner before going dancing. Then he instructed his team to lead each of us to a private bedroom.

A middle-aged woman named Ingela escorted me to my room—she was a vivacious, tall and slender, natural blond, with a pronounced accent. I felt obliged to ask her where she was from. She proudly explained her Swedish roots and championed her role as director of product development for Walter's spas.

The room was rather large and luxurious. Upon entering, the first thing I spotted was a small dining table set up with a beautiful fine porcelain tea service and flanked by two big red velvet wing chairs. The air was perfumed by a cornucopia of lighted candles that filled the room with the sensuous smells of sweet orange, honeysuckle, and lotus blossoms. Piped-in music played the soft sounds of nature, and the floor to ceiling windows overlooked the entire city. Most strikingly, the dazzling water fountain marking where Pittsburgh's three rivers meet at Point State Park served as a picturesque focal point.

An oversize massage table draped with bright white cotton sheets cradling a bright red satin robe, sat boldly in the middle of the floor. I began to wonder if everyone's room was like mine, and how did I get so lucky?

Ingela seemed very nice, which helped me to let my guard down a little. She walked me through each of my product selections, and reassured me that all of the products being used were all-natural, hypoallergenic, had not been animal tested, and were safe.

She invited me to start with a cup of elixir tea—I chose the lotus flower bomb collection of products and went with the same tea. It was designed to relax me by bringing down my blood pressure while eliminating toxins.

"The best part is that it leaves a sweet flavoring of your juices—it's sort of like an aphrodisiac," she said with a chuckle. Having a little experience in that area myself, I was quite familiar with that notion and very excited to try it.

The base of the elixir was lotus leaf. It was scented with rose petals, chamomile, orange peels, green tea, and honey—a very delicious combination! The brightness of the sweet orange peel juxtaposed quite nicely with the woodsy flavor of the lotus leaves, and the touch of sweet from the chamomile and honey perfectly accented the flavor and smell.

Ingela prepared the towels and turned up the heat on the massage table while I drank the elixir. Afterward, she instructed me to lay face down on the heated table under the sheet until she knocked on the door to reenter. Then she stepped out so I could undress.

I opted for a deep tissue massage with the scintillating lotus flower bomb oil infused with hibiscus, rosemary, mandarin, and black pepper. Part of the collection, it was designed to gently reduce inflammation, but intensely loosen up the multitude of tight muscles that pervaded my body from the stressful weekend.

She also suggested I put on a cooling eye gel mask to relax my sinuses.

I took one last sip of the elixir, quickly stripped down to my birthday suit, slipped on the eye mask, and buried myself in the warm, cozy white cotton sheets. I nearly fell asleep before she knocked at the door.

After reconfirming my selection of oils, she asked what part of my body needed the most attention. As I was explaining, she abruptly informed me that she had to step out for a minute, and that I should feel free to relax and nap. Everything was so comfortable—I quickly became intoxicated with the soft music and calming scents. I fell asleep.

I was suddenly awakened by someone standing over my head and caressing my neck with deeply penetrating and intentional strokes. Thumbs firmly penetrated each ripple on either side of my neck as they glided boldly over the smooth yet scintillating oil that lubricated every nook and crevice.

The person was standing over my head and I had the eye mask on, so I couldn't really see who it was. However, I was certain it was a man just by his touch. One thing for sure, I knew it wasn't the woman I'd walked in with. Another thing, those strong yet tender hands seemed familiar, but I thought I was being a bit paranoid, so I just brushed it off.

The warm, invigorating touch of his hands sent soft convulsions throughout my body. He started with my neck, moved to my shoulders where he used his knuckles and deep, penetrating strokes from the top of my neck to the end of my shoulders to tenderize the relentless knots. Then he started again at the nape of my neck—using his knuckles and that silky, scintillating massage oil with just the right amount of pressure, he intensively kneaded the muscles again from the nape, around each shoulder blade, and back to the nape for ten straight minutes. All of the knots were melted into a perfectly relaxed symphony of happiness.

Without a word, he moved to the right side of my now alert, but semi relaxed body. He rolled the sheets up to expose only the right side of my fully naked body, but made sure to keep my private areas private. Still silent, he generously ladled his muscular hands with more of that delicious oil and dove in.

Starting with my arm, he used the palms of his hands, pads of his fingers, and his thumbs to intensively massage and slowly macerate each muscle. Moving on to the top of my right shoulder, he gradually moved down the right side until he reached the small of my back. Rhythmically stroking each muscle, inch by inch, he moved outward from the middle of my spine to the side of my torso, and finished each section with a gentle stroke of my breast.

The *pièce de resistance*—my legs and feet—it was a virtual party of pleasure. He started with long, deep, tender strokes from the top of my buttocks, to the tip of each foot. It only got progressively better and more intimate. My feet began to feel like clouds! He rubbed and kneaded every muscle and tendon, and rolled each toe between his fingers to release all of the tension. His knuckles glided like buttered balls, up and down my arches as they melted every cramp and replaced the aches with sheer joy. It stimulated pleasure points throughout my entire body.

With every stroke, he pushed further and further into my psyche. He awakened incredible nerve endings that I didn't even know existed. Then I nearly lost it when he finished the other side and returned to my booty. He began to vigorously knead his way into paradise. As he approached my inner thighs, he got closer and closer to my sex. At that point I started thinking that he seemed a little too familiar with my body. I got so excited I wanted to see who it was, and where I could sign up for weekly massages. I quickly removed the eye mask.

"Oh my goodness!" I exclaimed. "You bastards set me up! I should have known it was too good to be true," I shouted.

I couldn't believe my eyes. It was Chris! Again. He had surreptitiously replaced the original masseuse. The worst part—I didn't think he had anything to do with our evening's activities—he hates to dance.

"Please Anais! Please forgive me. I begged Rafi and Mark B to help me set this whole thing up because I need you! I need to be near you. I'm going crazy without you!" he pleaded as he kissed my behind. I thought he had lost his mind.

"When my brother told me he needed people to test his new products, I knew you loved this type of thing. I saw a great opportunity and asked Rafi and Mark B to help me to talk you into coming. I knew if I'd asked you, you would have refused, and I miss you," he followed.

"YOUR BROTHER!?" I shouted. I was livid to say the least. I couldn't believe he had the audacity to even touch me again. And I was appalled that he thought it was okay to trick me for his brother's purposes when he didn't even want to introduce me to him in the past.

"Chris, this is really *so* unfair! I'm guessing you didn't share with Rafi and Mark B that you are soon to be wed to Shirley, correct?!" I screamed in anguish. Tears streamed down my face. I felt like every muscle in my body had seized up and the pain started all over again.

"What the fuck do you mean soon to be wed!?" he exclaimed.

I painfully shared the conversation Shirley and I had about the two of them ring shopping, and how she believed he was going to propose to her. He reacted as if he'd had an awakening. After some thought, he remorsefully responded.

"I broke up with Shirley for good that night. She tried to give herself to me for the first time, and we talked about marriage. But I knew she wasn't the right fit for me and refused to do that to her," he said calmly with what appeared to be a heavy heart.

I didn't believe him. I'd heard the breakup story before. My heart was still in my stomach, and the tears streamed relentlessly.

"It didn't look like that to me. You couldn't even look me in the face. And to make matters worse, it seemed to me that you were enjoying the ride," I quickly responded.

He tried to console me by asking how we ended up in the situation with Shirley in the first place. Then he questioned me about why I stayed and then lashed out at him upon leaving. "I nearly lost my mind when I saw you in that hotel suite. I didn't know what to do! When you left, the first thing Shirley asked was how well did I really know you, and why were you so mad at me?" he lamented.

"I had to come clean. She had already said she'd gotten your information from the cake I brought from you. When you abruptly left, she immediately asked to see my back," he said with a snicker as if he knew he was busted—but it was almost like he felt a sense of relief.

"Another broken heart on your trail of tears, right Chris!" I snarked.

At that point I knew I needed to get up and get dressed or I'd get into trouble with him once again. I was determined not to let that happen. I looked around to find the robe, but Ingela had placed it on one of the chairs, which was out of my reach. Chris took advantage and just as I tried to get up, he passionately kissed me.

I shoved his face away and tried to get off the table to grab the robe. But he pulled me back into him.

"I'm so sorry you had to go through that. I promise to do better," he said while gently kissing my tear-stained face. Anytime he touched me I felt like my body glowed from the inside out. This time was no different, except it was accompanied by the guilt I felt from betraying my emotional self. He started gently massaging my sex with soft, silky, circular stokes. I tried to stop him, but the feeling betrayed me again.

My whole body immediately relaxed. The stimulation of his undulating fingers to my clitoris took me to a heightened level of sensitivity. I began to melt in his arms—again. But something kept nagging at me on the inside.

"Oh God Chris! Why do you keep torturing me?" I pleaded for him to stop as I moaned with pleasure.

Suddenly he bit into my neck with unrelenting force. My whole body shivered with delight, and again it betrayed my rational mind.

"Harder ... Harder!" I cried.

He thrust his fingers into my sex and devoured my neck. I fell back onto the massage table as he plunged them into me harder and harder. Then he went in for the kill. Sucking and licking his way down to my rock-hard breast, he nibbled just enough to cause small but erotic convulsions.

"Please Chris, Please stop! I can't take it!" I cried willingly.

"I love you Anais! And I have to have you!" he groaned with a deep sense of passion. He gently kissed my stomach and filled his mouth with my sex.

"I need you! All of you!" he repeated over and over again.

He licked one finger and gently slid it into my ass while he stroked my clitoris with an unwavering rhythm. It took my body over the top.

"Oh! ... Oh No!" I cried. "I can't ... Oh God! You feel soooo good!" I was consumed with the feeling.

"Chris! ... Shit! ... Please Stop!" I begged. But I couldn't push him away. The physical and emotional connections I felt with him were in a tug-of-war—the physical won the battle.

My body quickly became addicted to the sensation. Just as I began to climax, he ripped his finger out of my ass, pulled me to the end of the table, and ripped off his pants.

"What are you doing Chris? You need a condom!" I shouted. He was clearly immersed in overwhelming pleasure. He got distracted and didn't hear or care about a word I said.

My heart was beating hard—for him. I could barely speak. He kept biting my nipples while skillfully removing his pants.

He lowered himself as his rock-hard cock grazed over my tender and now super juicy sex. I could feel the head nudging at my entrance as he grabbed my ass, and lifted me up off the table. I grabbed a hold of his neck and he impaled me with his love muscle.

"Ay! Ohhh! Ooh! Ooh!" I moaned with sheer pleasure. Inch by inch, he slid into position. Stretching my warm, tender sex until it molded to him like a silicone glove, I moaned and he groaned—I had clearly gotten distracted too.

"Anais! Anais! Fuck! Oh my God! No one makes me feel this way but you," he quipped with what seemed like disbelief. "I can't explain it, but damn! I'm going crazy!" he shouted as he began to thrust his cock in and out like a fine craftsman.

The smooth flesh felt like silk, tickling every inch of my body with each long, deep thrust. I could feel our hearts beating in sync.

I needed to see his eyes. I opened my eyes and he was staring at me—as if he needed to see my eyes too. I could see his soul through those piercing brown eyes. In that instant, again our two souls became one. It was a brief yet intense emotional connection, but it scared me this time. It was almost like I could literally feel him taking a piece of my soul. Then he kissed me, and shifted his thrust into high gear.

"I love you! ... I LOVE YOU!" he shouted over and over again. My heart was beating so fast, my body erupted.

I screamed, "Awh! Awh! Oh God Chris, I'm cumming. I'm CUMMING!

He screamed, "AWH BABY YEAH! I know you like it ... I told you this is my pussy!" And he began to thrust harder and faster. It was crazy as hell. My body convulsed over and over again with extreme pleasure—but he wasn't finished.

He pulled his cock out and gently licked my sex to savor the juices. Then, with a reassuring nudge, I turned over as he climbed onto the massage table and entered me from behind.

Slowly, his methodical thrusts filled my joy. He gently slipped a finger in my ass and again the feeling took me over the top.

"Come on baby, fuck me!" I exclaimed with a soft yet firm voice. "I need it, I need you!" I boldly exclaimed.

He took his finger out of my ass and rode me like a bull at a rodeo. His long ... hard ... deep thrusts touched the very tip of my soul. I needed more of him.

It felt incredible! Although my body betrayed my convictions, the more he gave, the more I wanted. Then he hit it. He slapped my ass and the explosion came like a tidal wave. I squeezed my ass as hard as I could and he screamed with pure pleasure.

"ANAIS! FUCK! HOW ... DO ... YOU ... DO ... THIS ... TO ... ME!" he shouted with long pauses between each word. He pounded so hard it felt like he was trying to reach the very tip of my soul. Again my body convulsed help-lessly as he began to empty himself inside me. I experienced the most intense organism ever.

He quickly pulled out and came all over me. Then he rubbed it all over my ass like it was some kind of a lubricant.

"Umm!" he chanted. "I'm marking my territory," he said with confidence as he lowered himself beside me.

"Like a dog does his bitch, right?" I facetiously responded.

"No! Like a man who's in love," he quickly replied.

I fell silent. Honestly, no one ever made me feel as good as he could, inside and out. But I no longer took his words seriously. I no longer trusted him. Again I simply said nothing.

We lay silent for ten long minutes. Then came a knock at the door. It was a call from Ingela to let us know that dinner would be served in thirty minutes. Chris jumped up and opened a door that seemed to appear out of nowhere.

"Come on Anais. I have another surprise for you!" he said with excitement.

I wasn't sure what to expect. I still had that uneasy nagging feeling about ev-erything that was happening. Chris's constant declarations of love had messed up my mind at this point. I couldn't understand how he could so boldly profess his love for me while still knowing that we could never be together. My heart began to hurt again. But before I could vocalize it, he abruptly grabbed my hand and pulled me through the hidden door.

"Check this out!" he exclaimed.

Behind the door was an amazing ensuite bathroom. The first thing I spot-ted was the round sunken Jacuzzi tub in the middle of the room filled with voluminous bubbles. The same scintillating candles that perfumed the other room surrounded it, and a dainty little crystal chandelier hung from the ceiling complimenting the Jacuzzi and beautiful deck covered in mosaic tile. It, too, sat in front of a wall of windows overlooking the city.

The view was magical. It appeared that Chris was obviously secure with his ability to get me to go along with his plan, and I must admit, he planned it well.

A sparkling crystal ice bucket filled with Champagne was skillfully placed on one side of the Jacuzzi deck along with two long crystal Champagne flutes. A serving dish filled with fresh strawberries and chocolate sauce accompanied it. On the other side of the Jacuzzi deck sat bottles of alkalizing mineral bath beads, two sisal body brushes, and a body wash that complimented the lotus flower bomb teatox elixir and massage oil I'd chosen earlier.

The bathroom itself was a mosaic and marble–filled palace that appeared to jump off the pages of a high-end decorator's magazine. A heated towel rack stacked with two plush white body towels mounted the wall between two bottom lit rock crystal sinks. Two bottles of Evian and a beautiful gift basket filled with a plethora of body products adorned the sink on the left. The floor was heated travertine marble and felt just as comfortable as walking on a luxurious carpet. It was extremely enticing, however I continued to remind myself to proceed with caution.

"This time I get to treat you to something special," Chris exclaimed with excitement.

We slid into the Jacuzzi and he layered one of the sisal brushes with the lotus flower bomb body wash. Then he went to work on my back. At that point I decided to relax and just enjoy the ride. After all he'd put me through, I felt at the very least I deserved an apology. This wonderful evening was a good start, I thought to myself.

He gently brushed every inch of my body, from the back of my neck to the very tips of each and every toe. Afterward, he took the hand sprayer and vigorously washed the soap off—my skin glistened like silk.

Apparently the allure of the lotus flower bomb collection is that it's made with a rare beauty oil from the Amazon. It made my skin feel like butter without irritating my lady parts—it was a whole other orgasmic experience.

In the meantime, I felt obliged to reciprocate at least some of his kindness. Believe me, it was very easy. His tawny and taut body tempted me all over again. I dove right in.

I took the sprayer out of his hand and gently washed him everywhere. Then I lathered up the other sisal brush and went to work on his beautiful six-pack. Out of the blue came an interruption. His cock jumped up like it had a mind of its own. I was so turned on that I abruptly dropped the brush and began to devour him.

The sensuous combination of the oils mixed with his enticing body drew me to him like that proverbial moth to a flame. I had to taste him—every bit of him.

I worked my way down to his engorged cock slowly as his body melted like caramel in my mouth, and he moaned with anticipation. Suddenly I could feel my tongue sliding over the smooth skin of his cock. He groaned with extreme pleasure. I'd never done that before and he was pleasantly surprised.

I pressed forward until my big, juicy lips enveloped his entire steely cock. The tip hit the back of my throat and I gagged a bit, but I was determined to taste him—all of him. I needed to experience him feeling pleasure from me just as he'd pleased me.

I gently fondled his balls and stroked his perineum to intensify the pleasure with one hand, and thrust his cock in and out of my mouth with a progressively increasing rhythm with the other hand. Small, sensuous eruptions shook his entire body as he groaned with intense pleasure. It turned me on!

"Shit! You … You never did that to me before! Oh God! Why Anais?! Why are you fucking me up?!" he whimpered while trying to restrain his ejaculation.

He grabbed my face, pulled it to his, and kissed me so hard I almost lost my breath. While placing one of my legs over his shoulder, he lifted me up onto the deck of the Jacuzzi and pulled himself close to me. I could feel his warm breath on my neck—it sent chills throughout my entire body. Then with one thrust, he plunged into me again.

"Hold onto me," he whispered.

I held onto his neck for dear life as he lifted the other leg and fucked me so hard I begged him to cum. "Oh God baby, please cum!" I whispered.

But it seemed like he was ready to start all over again. My body was almost numb from the euphoria of intense pleasure. On the other hand, I loved watching him lose control. Voluminous beads of sweat rolled down his face as the roar of the Jacuzzi muted his intense moans. I could feel every muscle in his body tense up.

Boom! He suddenly exploded and pounded every bit of himself inside me. We had simultaneous orgasms from another dimension. My head fell onto his shoulder. I was wiped out.

Gently kissing my head, again he reiterated his earlier claim. "I really love you Anais! I don't know what to do without you," he said calmly.

It was one of the most confounding experiences I'd ever had. I didn't know how to respond. At that moment I took a deep breath and his forehead fell onto my shoulder. We both fell back into the Jacuzzi and briefly fell asleep in each other's arms.

Ten minutes later we were quickly awakened by another knock at the door alerting us that it was time to eat. Unsure of what to expect from all of the others who awaited our arrival for dinner, we decided to take our time anyway. We basked in the afterglow for just a few minutes more. Then we showered, dressed quickly, and met everyone else in the dining room for dinner and drinks.

Gastronomic Zen

There was another beautiful surprise at dinner—a true Zen-like experience of decadent food. The light and airy delicacies brought my relaxation full circle.

Upon our arrival at dinner, the first thing I spotted was the amazing table. It was artistically landscaped like a petite Japanese garden. Three miniature bonsai plants separated by two light-filled ice bowls overflowing with fruit and punch served as the centerpieces. Each of the ten place settings was marked by bamboo place mats topped with triangular plates, and was flanked by porcelain chopsticks on the left side and an origami folded napkin holding a knife, fork, and spoon on the right. Crystal water and wine glasses, small heated porcelain pitchers hosting warm sake with tiny cups on top, and personal condiment trays with three slots filled with pickled radishes and peppers, crunchy bean sprouts, and sweet soy sauce put the finishing touches on each setting. We were treated to an awesome collection of tasty, light, and delicious eye candy! It was another great gastronomic feast.

Dinner featured marinated and seared *nigiri*-style hake steaks, perfectly sliced and beautifully layered on top of seasoned sushi rice decorated with julienne carrots, cucumbers, and pickled ginger, and drizzled with sweet soy sauce and roasted sesame seeds. Dessert quickly followed with a neatly packaged dainty little duo of green tea and chocolate *mochi* ice cream balls.

The seared hake *nigiri* was amazing! According to Walter's chef, he marinated it overnight and seared the steaks whole to add char. Charring the fish brought out another dimension of flavor to the dense and meaty fish. I'm not a big fan of raw fish, so this was the perfect sushi for me.

Others requested rare pieces, but everyone enjoyed the unforgettable flavor. The accompaniments and the sake were a perfect balance and set the stage for the light and interesting dessert.

New to my food repertoire, *mochi* balls are small, round dessert balls with a pounded sticky rice cake on the outside—this is called *mochi*—and an ice cream filling on the inside. We had green tea ice cream filling in one and chocolate ice cream in the other. The *mochi* balls are light, chewy, and just enough after a flavor-packed meal—a perfect complement.

After dinner, Walter invited everyone to join him in the sunken living room for drinks and dancing. Chris didn't dance, however he did take the opportunity to introduce me to his brother as a very special friend who means a lot to him. I was pretty sure by this time Walter already knew that, but he was very kind. However, I was not impressed by Chris's attempted candor.

I didn't dance much either. I was so sore from Chris's so-called tantric massage, as he so aptly referred to it, and three hours of truly amazing sex, I ended up sitting down more than dancing.

The downtime worked to my benefit. It gave me an opportunity to get to know Walter better, and learn a bit more about his products. I learned a great deal about how to move a product from conception to the public market place— I was hoping to do the same with my food one day.

Chris, however, was deceptively quiet. I could only imagine that he was processing the deeply emotional tryst we'd just finished. He seemed pretty happy with being able to successfully execute his plan, but I don't think he thought about what would happen afterward. On the other hand, he may have been afraid of what would happen afterward.

It was very difficult emotionally for me, too. But I had already made up my mind not to invest my emotions in him anymore. Although I was really in love with him, it was too complicated, too painful. I asked Rafi to take me home.

Given that Chris didn't offer to take me home as usual, my first thought was that he was probably just as exhausted as I was, and not sure how to process my interactions with his big brother. But he passionately kissed me goodnight while Walter thanked everyone and said his goodbyes. I wasn't sure what to make of the situation. I began to realize that my attempts at divesting in Chris emotionally would continue to be very difficult. I'd hoped it was just the sex talking.

I loved the way he made me feel when he was with me, but I had to keep promising myself that I wouldn't allow him to hurt me again. Deep down inside, I felt like it was too late. Again I revisited the pain I felt when he left my house that last time we were together. How lonely and abandoned I felt. Then the last strike was the disaster with Shirley at the hotel.

I'd made a promise that I would never allow myself to feel that way again. Regrettably, it appeared I was right back where I started, and it was somewhat through no fault of my own. Knowing it would be easier said than done, I finally convinced myself that I just had to let him go. I jumped in the car with Rafi and the others, and left to go home.

Salt in the Wounds

The ride home started with Mark B apologizing to me for what was clearly a set up on his part. Sheila had no clue of what was going on—she was too busy with her head up Rafi's ass, literally.

"Anais, you mean you didn't know Chris was going to be there? Walter's his brother!" she quipped.

Again Rafi interjected before I could respond. He went into a long soliloquy. "Fuck no! She didn't know because she would never have agreed to come. The poor guy was crying his heart out to me about how much he's in love with her, and how she doesn't want to be bothered with him. I felt responsible because I introduced them to each other, and now Chris keeps raggin' my fuckin' balls about needing to see her," he shouted as if he was tired of the whole situation. Then Mark B kindly reminded him that Chris was not exactly honest with me about ending his relationship with Shirley.

"He assured me he broke up with Shirley for good and he really wants to do the right thing by Anais. So I made an executive decision and decided I would help him try to get another chance," Rafi responded. "Every fuckin' body deserves a second chance!" he shouted.

"Anyway, I figured if Anais didn't want to be bothered, we could just leave and go dancing in Station Square as originally planned. But it appears it didn't go *too* bad," he said and started laughing as he glanced around at me.

All kinds of emotions were running through my mind at this point. I kept telling myself I need to always be true to me. Although I had an amazing evening, and I was madly in love with him, I had to be honest with myself, because I knew he was unavailable. It was a daunting realization, but one I was confronted with each time I saw him.

In the end, I refused to let my guard down with Chris because he hurt me deeply. I absolutely no longer trusted him. I also didn't want Rafi to give Chris the idea that he'd won, so I decided to respond.

"Well you could say I had a wonderful evening with friends. I still don't trust Chris and I'll never let him burn me again," I said reluctantly.

"That's not what it sounded like coming from that massage room!" Mark B quipped, and they all laughed hysterically.

I began to blush and quickly joked it off. "Well you know, I had a few knots that needed to be worked out, and he's pretty good at untying them. So we got a little animated," I said while laughing and blushing in a bit of embarrassment.

Sheila quickly piped in to rub salt in the wounds, "In that case, I've got a few knots that need untying too!" she said while trying to hint to Rafi. But he wasn't buying what she was selling and simply ignored her.

We finally got back into the city at the close of the long evening and Rafi kindly dropped me home first. I had one of the best night's sleep in a long time, but I paid for it the next day.

I was so sore I could barely walk. Every time the pain hit me, I forced myself to reflect on that amazing evening—it helped me get through the day a lot easier. But my maniacal relationship with Chris continued to haunt me. I finally told myself that the only thing I could do was to try to put it behind me and focus on my friendship with Tariq.

Menu

Join Us for a Celebration of Japanese-Inspired Gastronomic Zen

featuring

DINNER

Seared Nigiri-Style Hake Steaks

sliced and layered on top of seasoned sushi rice decorated with julienne carrots, cucumbers, and pickled ginger and drizzled with sweet soy sauce and roasted sesame seeds

BEVERAGES

Warm Sake

Sake Punch

Still & Sparkling Water

DESSERT

Green Tea & Chocolate Mochi Ice Cream Balls

BEAUTY RITUAL

Lotus flower elixir tea. Bodacious body Collection lotus flower bomb massage oil, body wash, and love splash.

ENTERTAINMENT

Tantric massage; dancing.

15

The following Friday, the events coordinator for all of the shelters organized a roller skating party for all one hundred kids in the system. Every counselor from the eight shelters had to work except those who covered the overnight shifts. That meant working with Leila and Mark B. I was truly very happy about getting paid to hang out with my friends.

But as usual, the drama wheel was certain to rear its ugly head in an attempt to spoil a wonderful evening. The winner this time—Darlese and Corry's drama, all over again.

Darlese was now six months pregnant and wasn't allowed to skate, however she was allowed to attend the party, and therefore stir up trouble. Shortly after we got settled in and everyone started enjoying themselves, she made her way over to Corry. She started yelling at him to assure him she'd get back at him for calling her a whore.

Most of the counselors were either skating or preparing to serve dinner. Mark B, Leila, and I were monitoring the kids on the skating floor across the room from them. Suddenly, all of the kids began to run toward where Darlese and Corry were apparently arguing. As we started to make our way over to see what was happening, Darlese was screaming at Corry extremely loudly.

"Don't worry you little dick fucker, I'll fix you for spreading rumors about me. I've already told my dad, so expect a visit from my brothers. They're ready for your little scrawny ass!" she said as she threatened Corry. His pride wasn't going to let her have the last word when all of his friends were watching them go at it. So he came right back at her.

"You just a freak! A fuckin' prostitute!" he shouted in front of everybody. "How you gonna sleep with me and say you my girl, and then suck *all* my boys dicks for money!? Even worse, you gonna try and blame the baby on me!?" he angrily shouted with disbelief.

That's when things really got out of hand. She threw her drink at him and promised to have him "fucked up!" Unfortunately, because she was a minor, we couldn't take her words verbatim. Corry just brushed her off and told her to kiss his ass.

At that point Mark B decided it was best to remove Corry from the situation. He took Corry for a walk and a long talk in the van. We would all learn later that there was a lot more to Darlese's words than just idle teenage threats.

It was no secret that Corry had a difficult life. This situation simply added more fuel to the fire. According to Corry, Darlese's threats couldn't just be brushed off, and he admitted that he was really scared. He said he still couldn't let her punk him in front of everybody when he knew she was in the wrong. However, according to Mark B, Corry did seem to get a bit traumatized anytime someone asked about his relationship with Darlese's father, also known as Eastman.

During their conversation in the van, Mark B asked Corry if he thought Eastman would really send her brothers to potentially hurt him. With tightly pursed lips, Corry defiantly shook his head from left to right, as if he really didn't want to answer the question. He reluctantly responded, "I don't know!"

Weeks later, while driving to a counseling session with his mother at the intake center, Corry confessed to Mark B that while he was on the run he needed money to survive. Eastman offered to take him to the loading docks in the Strip District to help unload the produce trucks as a day laborer. He thought it was a great opportunity to earn quick money without having to do anything illegal. It would also have allowed him to give Darlese's mother a few dollars for allowing him to stay at their house. He ended the conversation by saying he'll never be the same from the experience.

Darlese's father, Eastman, was no stranger to the law. We were all fully briefed about the family's reputation for violence. He had just completed eight of a fifteen-year sentence for racketeering and attempted murder, and was released early for good behavior—even though he was known to be ruthless and just as cruel while in jail.

According to him, he was a reformed man trying to walk the straight and narrow in a concerted effort to stay out of jail. He successfully convinced the parole board of his sincerity to accomplish his goals. Corry said Eastman bragged about being successful because he convinced them that he would fight to achieve his goal of family reunification.

"My main goal is to reestablish my family and to be there for my children. Black children need their fathers in their lives, not in jail cells," he told the parole board.

Strangely enough though, eight of his ten children were either in foster care, a shelter, or group homes. The other two had grown up in the foster care system, and both had served time in jail and juvenile detention. He clearly knew how to successfully work the parole system to his advantage.

Eastman was originally convicted on a racketeering charge as the head of an illegal sports betting ring. He was accused of coercing an organized group of young boys into collecting and distributing money to and from corrupt college athletes for him. He used young boys from local high school football and basketball teams to deliver steroids and bribes, and to collect bets. He was also accused of paying off countless college athletes to throw games so bets would pay off.

He got busted when a young college football player who'd been taking bribes from him for four years publicly identified him as the ringleader of a steroids ring targeting local college athletes. When the corrupt football player was no longer eligible to play and didn't make it to the pros, he was no longer of use to Eastman and couldn't deliver the goods. Eastman cut him off at the same time he left college. He had no income, no job, and a bad reputation because everyone knew he was dirty and on the take.

The young man got depressed and attempted to kill himself by jumping off a bridge. But death eluded him, and fate took over. He became paralyzed from his waist down. He said he felt like he'd been dealt a bad hand again.

Now permanently confined to a wheelchair, he sought comfort in his religion, and decided to repent for his sins. In so doing, he had to purge himself of his bad thoughts—which included confessing that he felt as if everyone who made him feel like he was going to be a great football player had betrayed him. Feeling like he had nothing else to lose, he squealed like a bleeding pig!

During his recovery he decided to come clean. He wanted to help other athletes avoid the same mistakes that landed him in his current situation, and decided to tell as much as he could. "Fear is what kept all of us from telling the truth. I no longer fear anyone. They will no longer control me," he confessed during an interview with the local news reporter. He said he didn't care if someone tried to kill him and he told everything. Eastman was the one who took the biggest hit as the ringleader.

Eastman also faced charges for corruption of minors—but they didn't stick. None of the young boys he used to deliver and collect the goods would testify against him. Basically, he really wasn't the one to piss off. He'd been in and out of jail all his life, had a terrible temper, and a sense of privilege that made him believe he was superior to everyone else. From what we could surmise, his children were no different.

Just like the other boys, Corry wouldn't really elaborate on his direct experience with Eastman when asked. Instead, he would just put his head down and shake it in opposition—as if to indicate that he too would never betray him.

At one point, the shelter's psychologist thought Eastman had sexually abused Corry because of the way he described his affection for him. Mark B also thought maybe this was why Corry wouldn't talk about it and didn't want to pressure him. He decided to let Corry talk about it whenever he got the urge, like he did on the way to the counseling session. The hope was that eventually he'd come to terms with his true relationship with Eastman. In the meantime, the plan at the shelter was to keep Darlese and Corry as far apart as possible at least until the paternity of the baby was established.

16

The emotionally draining work at the shelter weighed heavily on my spirit. It was starting to take a bigger toll on me. My catharsis, I finally told myself, would be that I'd have to leave that work at the shelter.

But every time I tried to get away from it, something crazy would happen. Then it would haunt me until either they called me while I was on-call, or I got back to work to make certain the kids were okay.

I soon realized that in order to improve my emotional well-being, I would need to work harder at compartmentalizing my life. I came to the conclusion that I really needed to let my hair down, so I was very excited about the weekend's Saturday Night Live celebration at my house. I'd also decided to take Tariq up on his invitation to visit him in San Francisco and couldn't wait to tell him.

Saturday Night Live: A Celebration of Latin Fusion

We had an amazing evening planned for July's Saturday Night Live celebration. The month's theme was Latin American Carnivale with conga drumming, Afro-Latino salsa and merengue dancing, and lots of glorious food.

I designed the menu to be a feast for even the pickiest of diners. For starters: fried yucca sticks with coarse sea salt, jumbo nachos with fresh cucumber and tomato salsa, and fresh guacamole topped with shrimp. For dinner: slow-roasted *cochinita* pork served in banana leaves for juicy carnitas with all the fixings; a tabletop hibachi for grilling shrimp, beef, and a roasted vegetable medley to make fajitas; Costa Rican *arroz con pollo* (chicken and rice); Brazilian collard greens; and *gallo pinto* (Costa Rican black beans and rice). For dessert: Spanish flan; mock Tovallo Fresco—my version of a Spanish goat's milk cheese—topped with creamed honey; Amazon Lemon Crunch Cake with lemon mousse; and fresh tropical fruit with coconut ice cream. The drinks: fruity margaritas; Key lime and mint mojitos; fresh watermelon and lime juice with or without vodka; Spanish hot chocolate with Kahlúa; fresh brewed Columbian coffee creams; and Spanish Cava for toasting.

We were expecting fifteen people and clearly had an ambitious menu to prepare. Leila and Regina helped me prep all of the main courses earlier in the week and came by early to help finish cooking everything. Rafi and Mark B were in charge of the drinks, and Regina came over after work on Friday to help finish the desserts.

Instead of meeting at our favorite watering hole on Friday after work, Regina followed me home. We virtually inhaled some of the pork carnitas I cooked the night before, and then got to work on the desserts. The meat was so tender and flavorful, we had to force ourselves to stop eating so there'd be enough for Saturday. The desserts were easy to make and left lots of room for good conversation.

Although we tried to leave work at work, the conversation continued to drift back to all of the unbelievable things we'd encountered on a daily basis. "So much for my catharsis!" I thought.

First of all, we couldn't believe what was going on with Darlese and Corry. I dreaded the outcome of that situation and worried about Corry every day.

Regina was more concerned about Saturn. She said every time she'd work the evening shift, Saturn would disappear for long stretches. Then she'd reappear out of nowhere when everyone had begun to frantically call for her.

"It's like she's hiding in the walls, and all of a sudden she appears out of nowhere when we get frantic," Regina exclaimed.

"I think we probably need to keep a closer eye on her," I responded. "She's got an interesting history. A couple of weeks ago when I covered your on-call duty, they called me in because they thought she'd run away. When I arrived, Ed was bringing her back to the shelter," I said.

"Yeah, we probably need to put a tighter leash on her," Regina responded. Then she went on to recount some of her childhood memories and some of the unwelcomed situations she'd found herself in because she wasn't well monitored.

Regina and her younger sister have different fathers. Her mother raised both girls alone, and her sister is eleven years younger. Growing up was made even more difficult because neither she nor her little sister had relationships with their fathers. She said it initially made her interactions with men very difficult.

Before her sister was born, her mom worked all the time, and Regina would most often spend her evenings at her aunt's house. Given that she never really knew her father, to fill the void she said she always found herself searching for a father figure. Her aunt's boyfriend conveniently honed in on her needs, and ingratiated himself with Regina.

She recounted how one day at the ripe old age of ten, her aunt's boyfriend cornered her when they were alone. He said if she'd let him "lick her pussy," he'd give her five dollars. She recalled it as if it happened yesterday.

"At that time five dollars was like fifty dollars, and I was a hustler. I didn't really understand what he meant, but I figured as long as he wasn't going to hurt me, it should be fine," she said.

"He told me to sit on the chair and he took my undies off. I asked what he was doing and he said he just wanted to smell it," she recounted.

"He opened my legs and stuck his head in my couchie! I thought he was nuts and pushed his head back. He stopped," she said.

"Did you run away?" I asked.

"No! Because he reassured me he wouldn't hurt me," she responded. "He put his head back down there and put his tongue on my puetty tang. I didn't know what to do. I knew I shouldn't be letting him touch me there, but it felt good and I wanted that money," she said with what appeared to be a naïve disappointment in herself.

"How old was this man? More importantly, where the hell was your aunt?" I inquired with disgust.

"She was always at work when I got home from school. But he worked overnight. So he was always there when I got to their house," she said. She continued to recount her experience.

"I had never felt anything like that before. His tongue felt like a warm massage. It sent tingles all over my little body. Then he started licking more and more. The more he licked, the better it felt. I grabbed on to his head and at some point it felt so good, I shook like crazy. Then he pushed my legs open wider and licked my entire couchie. I didn't understand it at the time, but I think that was my first orgasm," she confessed.

I sat quietly. She seemed to be in a daze and I didn't want to encroach on her memory. I realized she wanted to get it off her chest. So I just let her talk. I felt like I was back at work all over again.

"He knew what he was doing, but I didn't understand why it made me feel so good. But somehow I did know it was wrong. I felt dirty after he gave me the five dollars and vowed I'd never tell anyone. Even after *he* made me promise not to tell anyone, he decided to torment me every time he saw me, even when my aunt was around," she said with remorse. Then she said something that kind of creeped me out.

"Whenever he thought nobody was looking, he'd wink at me and stick his tongue out to mimic how he licked my pussy. I think he was trying to entice me into letting him do it again. I absolutely despised him after that. I felt like he was blackmailing me. I even resisted going to my aunt's house if I knew he was going to be there," she said.

"But didn't you have to go there after school?" I asked.

"Yeah! But shortly after that happened, my little sister was born. My mom was on maternity leave and I used the excuse that I had to help her so I didn't have to go over there anymore.

"I didn't feel safe until the day they told me he died in a car crash. That's when I hoped the secret died with him and I could finally be in peace," she said with a sense of relief in her voice.

"The sad part of the whole story is I think I sought that same feeling from older men unsuccessfully for years. I learned that from talking to Evelyn, the shelter's psychologist," she said.

"When older men have sex with young girls they sexualize them. You know what they say—once you know how, you never forget that feeling. For some it's like a drug. A lot of times it's how the young girls end up pregnant too early," I said.

"I think that's why I masturbate so much," she said.

"Damn girl! You just be puttin' all your business out there," I quipped. I was a little shocked.

"I saw my mother struggle every day of my life. Although I wasn't promiscuous, I never forgot that feeling. But I surely didn't want to risk getting pregnant. Sometimes I think if I didn't have my toys, I'd be a nympho," she said callously. I was still dumbfounded by her boldness.

"Like you said, having been sexualized at the ripe old age of ten coupled with not having a relationship with my father probably could have made me a ticking time bomb," she followed.

"I believe that's why it's so important that we're able to encourage and strengthen the girls' and guys' self-esteem. My hope is that those who have young or absent parents will not solely rely on someone else for their happiness or trying to buy their prized possessions," I said. "I think if we taught boys how to respect themselves and honor their bodies the same way we try to teach the girls, we most likely could have very different outcomes," I followed.

"I really hope the guys are being taught how to love themselves too. I often questioned why my aunt's boyfriend preyed on me," she said with deepening sadness.

She could no longer hold back her tears. Slightly whimpering, she went on to say that's why she wanted to work with troubled youth. Given that she never felt comfortable sharing that experience in the past, she described Evelyn as a Godsend for her emotional healing. After spending time with Evelyn while working on the girls' cases, she said she was beginning to feel a strong spiritual connection to her.

That moment was a turning point in my understanding of who Regina really is. My heart broke for her. I was sure my response was probably one she had needed to hear for many years.

"Regina, it isn't and never was your fault. You've been carrying that shame around for years and it's completely unwarranted. He was one of the people who should have protected you. Nobody, and I mean nobody, has the right to treat you like that. He not only physically abused you, but he mentally abused you and probably your aunt, too. Typically it doesn't start and end with one person," I said.

Many of my questions about why Regina was always throwing herself at men began to be answered. She seemed to have an unyielding desire to be loved and feel loved.

"Hopefully soon you'll find someone who'll truly help you to understand how you're supposed to be loved," I said.

The conversation had started getting a little too heavy. I didn't want to get bogged down and not be able to finish the desserts. I told her to be careful and that we should talk about something fun. That's when I decided to tell her about Tariq's invitation to visit him in San Francisco after his return from Paris, and my decision to accept as part of my emotional healing.

"Didn't I tell you those Arabs take care of you?! When do you leave? Does Chris know?" she exclaimed with excitement and concern as she shot off a series of questions all at once.

"He'll be in Pittsburgh for the weekend and then leave on Sunday, and I'm going to visit him for Labor Day weekend," I said. "And why would you ask me if Chris knows? I don't care whether he knows or not. Besides, he's probably dating someone else by now," I said fervently.

"What! Who is he dating *now*? ... It won't last. He's obsessed with you. Anyway, where are you staying in San Francisco?" she rallied off those words like she had diarrhea of the mouth.

Although Tariq asked me to stay with him, I booked a room at the Marriott in Union Square. He was going to have a roommate and I didn't want to be at his house. I didn't really know him or the roommate very well. "A hotel is neutral and the best way to enjoy myself without any expectations," I assured her.

"You're right!" she quipped. "But if Tariq is coming to SNL tomorrow, it's gonna be a rather interesting evening. And, if Chris finds out about San Francisco, I *know* that won't sit well with him. I hope you didn't tell Mark B or Rafi because you know they'll automatically tell Chris," she said with trepidation as she grabbed her coat to leave.

I did mention my potential trip to Mark B, but he and Chris don't normally get along well. I doubted he would bother to mention it to Rafi. But I didn't want to share that with Regina because I didn't want it to become an issue at SNL. Regina said her goodbyes and I headed to bed.

It's Party Time!

Bright and early Saturday morning and my internal alarm clock woke me up at 7:30 a.m. sharp. I decided to pick up the fresh foods from the strip and head back home to meet the girls around noon at my place.

Twelve noon and Regina rang the doorbell right on time. Leila was a bit late after suffering a bout of morning sickness. But she was fine once she got up and got moving.

We set up a self-serve minibar for drinks and an appetizer table near the entrance for munching and socializing upon entering the apartment. One area of the living room was set up as a makeshift lighted stage with enough room for drumming and dancing. The dining area was set up like a Moroccan *medina* interior—where everyone sits on low-lying couches with lots of cushions and large, comfortable pillows on the floor, surrounding a long table.

I'd found two old bifold closet doors in my basement that worked well as the table. I cleaned them up and stacked them on some old crates. We covered them with white tablecloths and created a runner with beautifully stenciled red and yellow paper place mats—colors typical of Latin America. We created dining seating for each of our fifteen expected guests with large pouf pillows covered in sun-drenched yellow, silklike polyester pillowcases I'd purchased from Ikea. Then we set up individual place settings from the same place mats used to make the runners.

Each place setting was simple yet elegant—individual place mats layered with simple white, round dinner plates, topped by appetizer plates and handwashing bowls filled with red cloth napkins folded in triangles. Hibachi prongs and gold utensils perfectly matched the red and gold wine glasses and water goblets. We sprinkled red and yellow rose petals all over the table and strategically placed beautiful bottles of sparkling water and a variety of homemade and bottled condiments for a touch of sweet and spice between every other place setting.

Finally, after putting the side dishes and condiments around the table, we arranged three smokeless hibachi grills surrounded by seasoned shrimp, beef, and vegetables to make fajitas. Three large Crock-Pots with the simmering *cochinita* pork surrounded by all the fresh fixings and sauces for carnitas rested between every five place settings.

I wanted to make certain that everyone felt comfortable and relaxed, so next we tackled the ambiance. The soothing sounds of Brazilian bossa nova, Carlos Santana, and a mélange of Spanish guitarists piped throughout. Finally, I lit up two aroma diffusers with the sweet smells of a calming calendula essential oil blend—the mood in the room was intoxicating, and I was happy.

I also decided to do an icebreaker to add an extra level of excitement. I thought the Two Truths and a Tale game would be a great way to loosen everyone up—in hindsight, I probably should have thought more about the potential consequences. I printed the questions on cards and set them up on the appetizer table for people to fill out and place in the accompanying box while they poured drinks and munched on appetizers.

We finished setting up early and had a good amount of time to glamourize for the evening. Regina joined me in drinking my customary beauty elixir hoping she would finally garner the attention of Mark B. Leila enjoyed a luxurious hibiscus sunrise fragrant bath and lavished herself with the complementary body refresher and oil. I followed with the relaxing and calming calendula body collection, and Regina chose to refresh herself with the scintillating risqué rose body collection.

We felt amazing, and smelled delicious. Everyone wanted to eat well, drum like the masters, and dance all night while maintaining our glamour, so we dressed elegant but comfortable.

Being pregnant and planning to dance, to maintain her comfort, Leila wore a vintage lightweight embroidered Mexican tunic, and she complemented her outfit with a traditional fez hat. She claimed it was only to be worn while she was drumming—as if it had some kind of magical powers to take her into a trance that made her perform better. Regina wore a multicolored, embroidered, off-the-shoulder Mexican dress, with a matching red headband. I slipped on a beautiful red Mexican flyaway gauze dress accented with yellow satin ribbons, and tied my hair with matching ribbons. We were all beautifully coiffed, relaxed from the soothing scents and delicious bath and body treatments, and ready for a great evening.

The College Crew

Excited about seeing everyone and raring to go, we were off to a running start at five-thirty sharp. We greeted everyone upon their arrival with little Mexican sombreros to wear, a tray of drinks, and cards for the icebreaker.

Pierre and his fellow drummer Henri arrived first to set up the instruments and sound system. We asked everyone to leave their shoes in the bedroom so we could dance without ruining the carpets and making too much noise. Although some of the guys pouted about having to take off their shoes, it worked out great because it made them more relaxed.

We enjoyed the appetizers while everyone filled out the icebreaker cards, got settled, and waited for the stragglers to arrive. I hadn't seen Chris for nearly a month after he lured me into his so-called tantric massage lair. It was getting late and I began to think he wasn't going to show up. Fortunately for me, Tariq arrived before Chris—which made it a little easier. Chris didn't have a chance to feel Tariq out and to start grilling him with stupid questions (I worried that could've potentially caused problems due to Chris's temper). Even better, Tariq seemed to be getting along well with everyone. It was just what I'd hoped for.

True to form, Chris was an hour late. He arrived with his usual fanfare and joined the party with everyone else. In the beginning he wasn't saying much to me, but he quickly began to make himself at home. He began greeting and serving everyone as if he were a co-host—I guess he wanted to make it known that he'd already marked his turf.

The big surprise came when Penny arrived with JB, the sax man, who was tastefully accompanied by his beautiful alto saxophone. My mouth dropped open when he walked in. Fortunately, no one really knew what was going on between the two of us—maybe Tariq did, I thought. But I didn't get the feeling that Tariq had caught on.

Penny had informed us at the last gathering that she would be bringing an old friend from graduate school, but she didn't mention who it was. Things quickly began to get a bit awkward for me. Once Chris arrived, I was faced with the reality of three men, at three different stages of a personal relationship with me, all of whom were partying in my house at the same time. What a trip! I thought to myself. But eventually I decided I wouldn't panic, and instead enjoy the party we'd worked so hard for.

Tariq stuck close to me during dinner. It was apparent he wasn't quite sure how things were going to transpire. He played it safe until everyone started mingling and dancing in between courses.

As for JB, every time he tried to pin me down to talk, Penny would intentionally make her way over to interrupt us. The only time he was able to have a decent conversation with me was when Pierre called her over to review the dances he wanted her to lead. This also made for an interesting evening.

Before dinner, we played the icebreaker—Two Truths and a Tale. As expected, it was very intriguing and often controversial. It was similar to Javier's party but not as erotic.

After everyone had completed a card, they were mixed in a box. The game starts with a pair of dice thrown to see who gets the highest number. Whoever wins gets to pull and read the first card from the box. After reading the card aloud, everyone tries to guess whose story it is. Whoever figures it out first gets to pull and read the next card. If no one figures it out, the person has to reveal his or herself, and that person gets to pull the next card.

Sheila had the highest number and read the first card. Immediately after Sheila read the card, Leila linked the story to Penny. Her two truths were that she'd accepted an internship in South Africa and would be leaving in August and that she was in love with the one man who kept eluding her—everyone knew it was Pierre. Her so-called lie was that she would take anyone out who got in the way of her love for Pierre. It too may have been a truth, but it would have to wait.

As fate would have it, the timing was controversial. Leila pulled and read her own card and everyone learned about her and Pierre's pregnancy. Even though we joked that it could be the lie, Leila's protruding stomach was clear enough evidence that it was a truth. Penny tried to put a big girl face on, but the tears in her eyes were ever-present representatives of her disappointment and hurt.

To calm the waters a bit, Regina quickly professed her unrequited love for Mark B who simply blushed and joked it off. I don't think she took too kindly to how he responded, but it wasn't the first time he'd failed to respond to her advances. She too joked it off and as usual he pacified her saying "You know you're always gonna be my G!"

We all laughed it off. It seemed there wasn't ever going to be anything intimate going on there. However the fun had only just begun.

After Leila's shocking pregnancy revelation that Regina correctly linked to her, Regina pulled and read my card. My truths were that I love children and I love to travel … my lie was that I despised cooking. Everyone immediately pointed to me because they all know that cooking is my passion.

The game is always loads of fun although sometimes controversial and very revealing. But it is usually a great way to loosen people up by allowing them to share only as much about themselves as they are comfortable with sharing.

All three of my "would be suitors" shared very interesting information about themselves. Chris shared his distrust of his brother Ollie, who heads the family financial planning business, and his disappointment in himself for his inability to react to his emotions the way he wanted. What he was alluding to wasn't very clear to everyone else, however I clearly understood the significance.

When Chris first arrived, I'd introduced him to Tariq. Tariq, who recognized Chris's nationality, introduced himself in Lebanese. I didn't understand what he said, but immediately recognized a sudden disappointment in Chris's face. I asked Tariq what he said, and he translated it for me.

"I'm Anais' boyfriend!" he said.

I guess this was Tariq's way of marking his territory. I didn't quite know what to say. I just smiled and went back to what I was doing.

Chris's disappointment with the relationship between Tariq and me became clearer when Chantelle selected and read Tariq's card. I didn't want to rub salt in Chris's wounds, but the facts simply spoke for themselves—he was now face to face with his own ridiculous reality.

The first statement was apparently Tariq's lie. He said he was afraid he'd never graduate from college. Everyone in the room had already graduated but because no one knew Tariq, they didn't catch on. Chantelle went on to read the next statement.

"I'm in a new relationship with a beautiful and talented woman and I really hope it will continue to flourish so she'll visit me in Paris," it read. Immediately everyone turned to me and started with the oohs and ahs.

Although it was very flattering, I found myself a little embarrassed by the attention. Chris, however, decided it was too much for him to handle. He simply put his head into his hands as if he were about to cry. To spare me from being put on the spot, Chantelle calmed everyone down so she could finish reading.

Tariq's remaining truthful statement came as no surprise to me, but seemed to be highly applauded by Chris and JB alike. He shared with everyone that he'd be relocating to San Francisco the next day. Chris breathed a sigh of relief. JB with his coolest jazz improvisation voice said, "Alright, alright! You're making progress my brother. San Francisco is a very nice city."

Everyone chuckled as if they were all privy to an inside joke and then congratulated Tariq. Everyone except for JB and Chantelle's date knew about the relationship between Chris and me, hence the chuckles. Then everyone, except for Chris, told Tariq they'd hoped he'd come back and hang out with us again. It seemed he was easily making a mark for himself.

Tariq's upbeat personality added to the excitement of the evening, while JB's cool demeanor and kind words were soothing to everyone. Both brought a breath of fresh air to the group dynamic.

Tariq ended up reading JB's card on which he revealed his love of music and traveling. His tale was that he's a mean person. Everyone immediately identified him. His kind and gentle personality clearly discounted the "mean person" statement as the lie.

At the end of the icebreaker, we indulged in the Latin feast and continued into an amazing evening. The delicious food, unique drinks, and our makeshift Spanish and Moroccan fusion dining setup was adored by everyone. After dinner, we cleared the tables and Pierre immediately summoned everyone to dance with a magnificent drum call.

Henri and Leila joined him on the drums. JB pulled out his saxophone and the party shifted into another gear. The drumming and dancing created a magical evening with some of my favorite people, favorite foods, and fabulous fun. Even Chris tried to dance a little bit. He eventually gave up, sat back, and simply observed everyone else.

Tariq, on the other hand, had the time of his life. He danced and sang with everyone, and even participated in Pierre's traditional welcome ritual for both him and JB.

Things began to get a little awkward for me though. Tariq is a very affectionate Frenchman, so he wouldn't keep his lips, nor his hips off of me all night. I wasn't accustomed to such public displays of affection around my crew.

He kissed me every time he got a chance and kept grinding on me while we danced. I began to get a little embarrassed.

Strangely enough, this meant nothing to JB who clearly ignored Tariq and continued to flirt and wink at me while playing his saxophone. Chris, on the other hand, refused to look at me. Whenever I tried to catch his eye, he would call Rafi or anyone else over to talk to him. I couldn't help but to question whether it was because he was uncomfortable with the attention I garnered from Tariq … if he was disappointed in himself … or if he had finally given up on me. Either way, I decided I wasn't going to let him impact my evening. Both Tariq and JB did a fine job of helping me to refocus my thoughts.

JB is a little older than everyone else, but he has one of the most youthful personalities. The way he tickled the keys of his saxophone during the concert really got my motor running.

He's a five-foot-eleven, well-groomed, statuesque mocha chocolate gentleman with a little meat on his bones, and absolutely no hair on his head. On top of all of that goodness, he just had a joy for life that made him sexy as hell.

I tried not to show too much interest so I wouldn't offend Tariq, nor get Chris riled up. But every time he blew the saxophone during the dancing and drumming, he kept winking at me. Again I was flattered. However, I knew it wasn't appropriate to respond. I continued to immerse myself in being a great hostess.

Menu

Join Us for a Celebration of Latin American Carnivale
featuring

APPETIZERS

FRIED YUCCA (CASSAVA) STICKS
with coarse sea salt

JUMBO NACHOS
fresh cucumber and tomato salsa

FRESH GUACAMOLE
topped with grilled shrimp

DINNER

SLOW-ROASTED COCHINITA PORK
served in banana leaves for carnitas with all the fixings

TABLETOP HIBACHI
for grilling shrimp, beef, and zucchini, eggplant, and parsnip fajitas

COSTA RICAN ARROZ CON POLLO
chicken and rice

BRAZILIAN COLLARD GREENS

GALLO PINTO
Costa Rican black beans and rice

Menu

BEVERAGES

FRUITY MARGARITAS • KEY LIME & MINT MOJITOS

FRESH WATERMELON & LIME JUICE
with or without vodka

SPANISH HOT CHOCOLATE WITH KAHLÚA

FRESH BREWED COLUMBIAN COFFEE CREAMS

SPANISH CAVA
for toasting

DESSERT

SPANISH FLAN

MOCK TOVALLO FRESCO
a "Spanish" sweet goat's milk cheese, topped with creamed honey

AMAZON LEMON CRUNCH CAKE
with lemon mousse topping

FRESH TROPICAL FRUIT
with coconut ice cream

BEAUTY RITUAL

Bodacious body calming calendula bath, body, and essential oil blends. Luxurious hibiscus sunrise bath and body collection. Scintillating risqué rose bath and body collection.

ENTERTAINMENT

Icebreaker: Two Truths and a Tale; conga drumming; Afro-Latino dancing.

C H A P T E R

17

Beaties Brunch

The final musician's break was around three o'clock in the morning. JB cornered me in the kitchen while Tariq received a drumming and dance lesson from Penny and Pierre. He finally made his move.

"So do I need to send you another martini before I can take you out to dinner?" he said with a sultry grin.

Initially I was taken aback. I didn't know how to respond in the moment. I simply laughed it off. I thought it was a pretty clever way of asking someone on a date. I was also surprised by his boldness given Tariq's somewhat possessive behavior all night. However I felt obliged to give some kind of response.

"Oh yeah! Thanks for the drinks and the shout outs," I responded. "But this might not be such a great time," I said while glancing over at Tariq.

He was somewhat relentless and didn't seem to care. He clearly had the solution to that problem and quickly replied.

"Yeah but ya boy Tariq is leaving tomorrow. So I figured this is my chance to get to know you a little better. After all, I've been chasing you for the last three months. When I arrived here for the party and saw that you were hosting it, I figured it was either karma or God has a great sense of humor," he said as we both laughed.

Before I could respond, Penny walked in the kitchen, grabbed his arm, and insisted he immediately come join the other musicians. She'd been keeping a tight leash on him all night—even though she claimed he was only like a brother to her. I'd heard that one before.

To me it seemed like she was trying to take license of him and to control his every move. But I chalked it up to her just trying to cock block because she now knew about my situation with both Chris and Tariq. Again I just pushed the situation to the back burner and decided to continue enjoying my guests.

We sang, ate, and danced into the wee hours of the morning. Chris gave up and left around 2:30 a.m. Chantelle's date started getting frisky, so they left at around 3:30 a.m. At about 6:00 a.m., Regina and I decided it was only appropriate to serve breakfast.

I love to keep quick breads and cakes in the pantry. I had just purchased a variety box of all-natural Just Add Water Happy Cake mixes that included a wonderful variety of delicious toppings. I immediately whipped up three varieties and baked them in silicone molds. They were so easy to make and ready in just a quick ten minutes.

I used the Barcelona Beatnik Banana Bread mix to make soft and moist banana nut bars topped with a silky walnut toffee glaze included in the mix. They were easy, delicious, and beautiful.

The Amazon Lemon Crunch mix is one of my favorites. It's a delicious combination of zesty lemon cake topped with a tangy lemon glaze and chunks of Brazil nuts couched in a crunchy oatmeal streusel topping. I made mini muffins and topped them with the candied lemons that came with the cake mix.

Finally, I used the Mandarin Chocolate and Almond mix to make little dome-shaped cake bombes and topped them with the chocolate ganache frosting, chopped almonds, and candied oranges that were included in the mix. All three Happy Cakes made for a lovely presentation of what turned out to be a quick and delicious assortment of beautiful breakfast treats in a variety of shapes and sizes.

To get breakfast started, we served the cakes with fresh coffee, thick and rich Spanish hot chocolate, and refreshing Hibiscus Sunrise Sparklers. We used a leftover bottle of Cava to make the sparklers, and I made the hot chocolate with chunks of semisweet chocolate, light cream, vanilla, and cinnamon. This allowed everyone to warm up or cool down, and to nibble a little while we finished preparing the main course.

Rafi and Charise reset the tables while Leila and I cooked. We used the leftover shrimp to make fluffy frittatas, the leftover *cochinita* pork to make delicious huevos rancheros, and added potatoes to the leftover vegetables to make savory home fries. Sheila warmed a bunch of the remaining flour and corn tortillas on the electric tabletop griddle and placed them in two warming baskets on either side of the table.

In the meantime, I instructed Rafi on how to whip up a batch of rich and delicious traditional Costa Rican coffee for service during brunch. He placed it in a hot pot and set it up with hot water and an assortment of teas in the middle of the drink table for self-service. Then he placed glasses of iced water accented with refreshing leaves of lemon balm at each place setting on the dining table. I also placed the electric tabletop griddle in the middle of the table. It was for eggs to be made at the table any way people liked and eaten with the warm tortillas.

Breakfast was a hit too! Easy prep, and a relatively short cooking process—

given the group effort—resulted in another delicious feast. It's what I always strive for. This entire meal hit every mark. Even though only a few people chose to make their own eggs, not only was it quick, but it was a welcomed personal touch. They got to have nice, hot eggs and/or egg whites prepared tableside.

After breakfast Tariq said his goodbyes to everyone. He had to finish packing and catch his flight to San Francisco. I walked with him to his car and after confirming my travel arrangements to visit him for Labor Day, we kissed goodbye. I knew I'd miss him, but I was excited about being able to visit him in a new city.

Upon my return, JB decided to press forward a little harder for an answer to his request for a dinner date. He apparently wasn't deterred by Penny's attempts at keeping him away from me. Strangely enough though, after I returned Penny announced she'd be getting a ride home with Pierre and Henri. I guess Pierre's invitation took precedence.

JB immediately offered to stay behind to help with the cleanup, which took Penny off-guard. But that's when things got a bit more interesting.

As a result of worrying about my three would be suitors, and making sure everyone was having a good time, I was quite tense after the party. JB tuned in to it. While everyone was leaving, he strategically offered to take the garbage out and to make sure everything was put away.

When we finally finished cleaning, I was exhausted and plopped face down on the couch. Suddenly I could feel these strong, muscular hands penetrating every tense muscle in my shoulders and neck. Deep, intentional rubbing and stroking was interrupted every five or six minutes by him touching pressure points on my head, shoulders, stomach, and feet.

"What are you doing?" I asked.

He explained that he was monitoring the pressure points to determine where to release the tension in my muscles—he reassured me that he wouldn't try anything inappropriate. Then he insisted I relax for the full effect.

After assessing my nervous system, he went on to massage the muscles of my shoulders again while alternating down my arms to the very tip of each finger. My head went right back to Chris's massage. I tried to get him out of my head, to take JB at his word. But it was a challenge.

He moved on to my head and used his thumbs to release the tension in my sinuses and jaws. Then he performed an amazing reflexology technique on both my feet and hands. Those amazing hands not only burned up the saxophone, but made JB an amazing masseuse as well.

I complimented him on the technique and then he shared with me that as a classically trained musician, he learned a variety of techniques for relaxation of the whole body through kinetics. It's basically an intensive method for monitoring his nervous system to improve his ability to hold notes longer, and to be a more versatile musician. He called it kinesiology and claimed it as his secret to fine tuning his playing. I, however, called it Amazing!

He finished working on my hands, feet, and scalp and began a whole body-tingling massage. Suddenly the doorbell rang. I ignored it at first. It was shortly after noon on a Sunday morning. Most of my neighbors were either sleeping or in church. More important, I wasn't expecting anyone.

Whoever it was began to ring the doorbell relentlessly until one of the neighbors let them in the security door. Their next move was to start banging on my front door like crazy. It scared the hell out of me.

I went to the door to look out the peephole. Whoever it was had the audacity to cover it up so that I couldn't see who they were. So I refused to open the door.

JB offered to answer the door, but I refused to allow it. I knew it had to be someone playing a trick or something, and I didn't have the energy to play games. After thirty straight minutes of constant knocking, whoever it was finally left. I breathed a sigh of relief, but I was still pissed off.

JB suggested we move to the back patio to enjoy the beautiful weather. He promised to continue the great massage while enjoying each other's company as friends. I was enjoying it and didn't want to be interrupted again. I figured that if it were someone who needed me bad enough they would have had enough manners to call me on the phone first.

Menu

Join Us for a Besties Bistro Brunch

featuring

STARTERS

BARCELONA BEATNIK BANANA NUT BARS
with a walnut toffee glaze topping

AMAZON LEMON CRUNCH MINI MUFFINS
topped with candied lemons and crunchy Brazil nut streusel

MANDARIN CHOCOLATE CAKE BOMBES
*topped with chocolate ganache, chopped almonds,
and candied oranges*

BRUNCH

FLUFFY SHRIMP FRITTATAS

HUEVOS RANCHEROS WITH COCHINITA PORK

SAVORY HOME FRIES

SELF-SERVICE EGGS

WARM CORN & FLOUR TORTILLAS

BEVERAGES

SPANISH HOT CHOCOLATE

HIBISCUS SUNRISE SPARKLERS

COSTA RICAN COFFEE & HOT TEA

ICED WATER
accented with lemon balm leaves

Lunch Alfresco

By the time we got set up on the porch the excitement of my wonderful kine-siology massage had been rudely interrupted. I couldn't get back into it. I decided it was time to make lunch and invited JB to join me. He happily accepted.

In keeping with the Latin-inspired cuisine, I raided the fridge and whipped up some delicious grilled Spanish torpedo sandwiches. I had a couple of small baguettes in the freezer from the brunch I'd prepared for Tariq. I warmed them in the oven and stuffed them with the last of the grilled beef and some feta cheese, pickled red onions, shredded cabbage, steamed lentils, lettuce, and tomatoes. For the finishing touch, I topped them off with a refreshing cucumber and Greek oregano yogurt sauce. It was a quick and tasty way to use the leftovers.

JB had made his love of iced tea well known at dinner. To oblige him, I made a light and delicate iced mandarin tea latte topped with whipped foam and sweet chai spices. We sat out on the patio, ate, and enjoyed the beautiful summer afternoon.

JB flirted quite a bit, but he was a consummate gentleman. He continued to remind me that he wanted to spend more time with me, but I insisted that it wouldn't be fair to Tariq if I went out on a date with him. He agreed it wouldn't be fair and settled for just hanging out.

"No strings attached, right?" I insisted.

"Fair enough, I'll be good," he said. "For now!" he followed with a smile. Then he invited me to join him as his guest at an upcoming performance at the arts festival on the following Friday. He was invited to be the featured guest art-ist with a reggae group that was headlining. He said he needed all the support he could get.

"Wow! That sounds exciting. I'd love to come," I said with intrigue. I already knew he was a great musician but it seemed things were looking up for him. I was delighted to offer my support.

After nearly 24 hours together, around five in the evening he said he prob-ably should be getting home and set out to leave. I agreed to meet him at the gig and we hugged goodbye.

I was finally free to try to get a little sleep before having to get ready for another crazy Monday morning at the shelter. I started with what I thought would be a nice long bath. This time the phone ringing interrupted it. Now I really started to get aggravated.

Initially I wasn't going to answer it for fear it would be the same jackass that was ringing my doorbell earlier. But then I relented and jumped out of the tub to answer.

Good thing I did. It was Tariq who had just arrived in San Francisco. He had already gotten settled into his apartment and began to miss Pittsburgh. I put him on the speaker phone, jumped back into the tub, and decided to chat with him to keep him company.

He said he really enjoyed the party and that he couldn't wait for me to meet him in San Francisco. Deep into the conversation, I could hear him purring as if he were touching himself. He said he missed my scent and started reminding me of how he made me feel when he came over for brunch.

"I can't get your smell out of my head, Anais," he whispered. "I wish you were here so you could wrap your legs around my head. Just like you did at brunch. Ummh! I want, no I need to taste you!" he said while moaning. I couldn't resist touching my sex too.

His voice was deep, sultry, and sexy. He made me horny as hell.

"I want to shove my face deep into your delicious pussy and lick your ass-hole," he whispered with a soft sultry groan.

My imagination started getting the best of me. I started to climax, moaning with him. "Oh yeah!" I purred. "And then what?" I said.

"Then I want to lick your pussy with long, juicy, soft strokes until you can't take it anymore. You'll shove my head deeper into that beautiful place ... and wrap your legs around me so hard ... I won't be able to breathe. And you'll go crazy as you CUM!"

He got louder and exploded ... then I exploded.

"Oh my God Anais! ... You don't even have to be near me and I go crazy. What are you doing to me!?" he said with a shouting whisper.

After listening to him talk us both into an orgasm, I was super relaxed now. I fell asleep in the tub and only woke up when he yelled my name.

Now he was relaxed, and clearly I was relaxed. We confirmed my travel plans to visit him, said our goodbyes, and went to bed.

Menu

Join Us for an Intimate Lunch

featuring

LUNCH

GRILLED SPANISH TORPEDO SANDWICHES

*French bread stuffed with marinated beef, feta cheese,
pickled red onions, shredded cabbage, steamed lentils,
lettuce and tomatoes, and a cucumber
and Greek oregano yogurt sauce*

BEVERAGES

ICED MANDARIN TEA LATTES

18

Monday morning's drive to work was uneventful, but I couldn't stop reminiscing about the great weekend and even better, my upcoming trip to see Tariq in San Francisco. We had made plans to visit Fisherman's Wharf for lunch, tour the Ghirardelli Chocolate factory, have dim sum in Chinatown, and to take a tour of wine country. I was also looking forward to a quick stop in Monterey to visit Cannery Row for a little shopping.

It was the first time I'd be visiting San Francisco and I was very excited. Tariq seemed to be just the right person to tour the city with. We seemed to enjoy a lot of the same things, loved trying new foods, and loved traveling. Plus he was a very patient and laid-back yet adventurous person, and it would be his first time visiting many of the places, too.

Good thing I enjoyed my drive to work because as soon as I walked in the door there was an awkward buzzing in the office. Everyone seemed a little upset. I finally cornered Regina and asked what was going on.

She informed me that Darlese somehow found out that Corry had left his shelter after implicating her father in a crime. She threw a tantrum in the middle of the night and the psychologist, family therapist, and director were all called in. Apparently, the overnight counselor couldn't calm her down.

To make matters worse, Darlese started tearing up the house. The counselors were afraid to touch her because she was six months pregnant, and the tantrum went on for six hours. By the time the morning shift arrived, everyone was exhausted. That was what all the buzzing was about.

In order to calm Darlese down and get her away from the other girls, the psychologist made arrangements to have her transferred to a shelter for pregnant girls. She'd have a little more freedom, but it would come at a price.

Since she was already seventeen years old now, she could come and go with limited supervision. It was unlike our shelter where the girls are supervised all the time. But she would also lose the protections the shelter system provided. My motherly antennae immediately went up—I wasn't sure if this was a good or a bad thing, especially for Corry.

When I first entered the office, I could hear Darlese repeatedly saying that she was going to "fuck Corry up!" She insisted that he'd sold her and her father out, and that she would "get him back."

What she meant was quite clear. But the psychologist still felt that because she was pregnant, she posed little risk to Corry. She allowed the transfer without taking any of the other counselors' concerns into consideration.

Regina and I both were dismayed about the decision to let her move on without addressing the consistent threats she'd made against Corry. However we weren't allowed to enter our objections on the record once the final decision was made.

After work, Regina and I went to our usual watering hole to have a drink, let off some steam, and reminisce about how much fun we had at the SNL celebration. That's when Regina filled me in on what was really going on.

Following four months of his refusal to talk honestly about the situation with Darlese's father, Eastman, Corry finally got the court ordered paternity test results. He wasn't the father of Darlese's baby. The revelation seemed to relieve the pressure he felt to protect his relationship with Eastman, and he finally decided to talk.

Corry filled the shelter's family therapist in on all of the events of his last runaway when he was hiding at Darlese's parents house. He finally explained to the therapist why he told Mark B that he'd never be the same, and it was a jaw-dropper.

Again he shared how Eastman took him to the loading dock to earn quick money. But this time he elaborated. He went on to say that in order for them to get to the loading dock on time, they needed to be up by 4:00 a.m. to arrive by 4:30 a.m. Eastman informed him that it was imperative to be the first up for the work or there could be trouble.

As fate would have it, they were running late and didn't arrive until 4:45 a.m. He recounted that there was a guy that Eastman didn't recognize ahead of them. Eastman attempted to explain to the guy that he'd been a regular for the past nine months, and that he usually gets there early but he was trying to help a friend. He tried to plead with the guy to understand that this was his lifeline and he really needed the money. But the guy continuously ignored him.

Then Eastman tried to reassure the guy that there should be enough work to go around. When he felt like he wasn't getting through to the guy, he began to emphatically insist that he should get first dibs because he was there all the time.

According to Corry, the guy pretty much turned a blind eye to Eastman. He wouldn't even entertain anything he had to say.

When the truck arrived, the guy insisted on helping himself to the first and what turned out to be the only opportunity offered to unload it. He even got a little obnoxious with Eastman. With a broken English accent, he indignantly stated that he was going to get first choice at the work and he didn't care who didn't like it. In the end neither Eastman nor Corry were able to work because there wasn't enough to go around. Eastman was not happy.

They stood in disbelief that the guy could be so indifferent to them. When the guy finished unloading the truck and it left, he went in a back alley and started counting his money. Eastman confronted him and the guy reached in his pocket as if he was going to pull something out.

Eastman abruptly punched him in the face and proceeded to stab him to death with his own knife while Corry watched. He took the guy's money and gave Corry fifty dollars.

"I'm a man of my word! Here's your wages for the day," he told Corry. Then he told Corry to help him dispose of the body and threatened to kill him too if he ever talked about what he'd seen.

It was later discovered that they had thrown the body into the Allegheny River. It washed up several days later and was identified as that of a homeless Mexican immigrant with no known family connections in the area.

For six months Corry was afraid to tell anyone about what he'd seen. He feared that Eastman would make good on his threat to kill him too.

As he again began to feel more protected in the shelter environment due to their strict rules and heightened security, this normally extroverted kid could no longer hide his fear. He decided that if he told the therapist at the shelter about the incident, it would be confidential as with all of his personal records. Unfortunately, after Corry told the therapist, it was mandatorily reported to the police, and Eastman was immediately arrested. He didn't take it so well and vowed to get revenge.

When the therapist told Corry she was obliged to report the crime, he left the shelter because he no longer felt safe. That's when Darlese found out about everything and vowed to get revenge. Corry ran away and went into hiding.

Regina and I were both dumbfounded by the gravity of the situation. Even worse, we had to embrace the sad reality that there wasn't much we could do. We were compelled to call Mark B immediately after finding out.

He confirmed what happened, and that Corry had run away. He, too, was worried about Corry's safety, but he had already come to terms with the fact that there wasn't much he could do to help either. It also bothered him that he didn't have a clue about where Corry was hiding, nor what he could do to keep him safe.

After hanging up the phone with Mark B, I decided to lighten up the situation and share my plans for travel to San Francisco to visit Tariq. Regina insisted that I take lots of photos so she could replicate the trip with one of her soon to be lovers. I found her remarks quite strange.

"I want to do everything you do, just like you do it!" she insisted. I felt like she was being a bit presumptive and was a little uncomfortable with her reaction—it seemed to be a bit covetous to me. Then I started thinking that perhaps I was overreacting. I reluctantly responded.

"I'll keep notes on those things that are worth visiting. Just remember, what goes on in San Francisco, stays in San Francisco!" I quipped. We both laughed. Then we joked about the fun we had and what we learned about each other at the SNL party before finishing our drinks and parting ways.

19

fter surviving three weeks of nonstop drama at work and in my personal life, I was finally leaving for San Francisco the next morning. I desperately needed a vacation. I braided my hair so I wouldn't have to fuss with it and packed a treasure trove of beautiful clothing for what I'd hoped would be a magical experience. But as with everything else in my life, I couldn't just ride off into the sunset, the demons of my past always had to rear their ugly heads and refused to let me go in peace—by that I mean Chris. Yes, the ever present, always confused yet relentless, Chris!

Again he showed up at my apartment with very little notice and went into another one of his jealous rages. The difference this time was that I knew I was done with the relationship. It didn't really matter what he had to say. I had made up my mind to simply let him talk and not to succumb to any of his advances ever again.

True to form, he started again with his profession of love for me—it didn't work. This time I was truly done with him. I let him know that I would not and could no longer entertain his advances, professions of love, gifts, or anything else. He noticed my luggage and began to get upset while pressing me to find out where I was going.

"That's none of your business Chris!" I said very calmly.

But he was persistent. He kept trying to convince me to tell him where I was going while emphasizing that he hoped I wasn't going to see Tariq. At that point I got frustrated and decided to try to reason with him.

"Look Chris, we both already know this is not going to work out between us." I pointed to the two of us to drive the point home. "After all, we're not getting any younger, and you can't commit to love me the way that I need to be loved," I said, to be sincere, but forceful. "I don't want what you have to offer me anymore. So let's agree to love each other from afar as friends and move on with our lives," I finished in a calm but assertive voice.

I think I shocked him. He was clearly taken aback and didn't really know how to respond. His mouth dropped open. He abruptly stopped talking and dropped his head in defeat.

There was a deafening silence for what seemed like six straight minutes. Then he closed his mouth, lifted his head and responded in a strained, raspy, and somewhat relenting voice. "I love you. I've loved you from the first day I met you," he said as he looked me dead in the eyes and began moving closer to me.

Even though I knew I was done with the relationship, I was happy with myself for having the courage to truly end it ... to tell him how I really felt. It was neither easy nor painless.

But I didn't want things to turn on a dime, so I moved away from him and sat at the dining room table. I was hoping this would create a less intimate atmosphere. He followed me, pulled up a chair in front of me, and touched my face as he attempted to get me to look at him. Then he continued.

"Even worse, I have a physical and mental connection with you that I've never felt with anyone else. I don't know how to process that," he said.

I couldn't look at him. It was a bittersweet moment for me. I felt somewhat better in hearing that he, too, didn't know how to process his feelings. I was shaking like a leaf.

I really loved him, but I had felt the sting of his empty pledges and indecisiveness one too many times. I no longer trusted nor desired him in that way—it was like I'd had an epiphany.

At that very moment I realized that I was no longer emotionally bound to him. I just stared at him in silence. Even though there were a million things running through my mind, I didn't say a word for fear that it would cause me to let my guard down again. So I let him continue to speak.

"Out of respect for you, I won't bother you, and I will grant you the wish of loving you from afar. But I will continue to tell you to STAY AWAY FROM THAT ASSHOLE!" he shouted with disgust.

We both laughed nervously and that was my cue to be certain not to tell him I was going to visit Tariq. In fact, I managed not to tell him whom I was going to visit before rushing him out the door. I used the excuse that I had an early flight and needed to get some rest.

San Francisco: A Proper Welcome

I had a great flight directly from Pittsburgh to San Francisco and landed at 12:30 in the afternoon. Tariq was waiting at the arrivals gate with a beautiful bouquet of exotic ginger flowers, Ghirardelli Chocolate bars, and a big sign with my name on it, as if he were my chauffeur. I felt like a little princess. Things got even better.

After a warm embrace, he gently caressed my face and planted a deliciously long kiss on me in the middle of the airport. I was a little embarrassed by the attention of everyone in the airport—but it did make me feel very special.

On the way to the hotel he took me on a quick tour of San Francisco and gave me a little overview of the plans he'd made for our long weekend together. I felt wonderful, and the city was beautiful. I love being by the water, and the Bay was simply magical.

We arrived at the hotel where the royal treatment continued. After the valet parked the car, I walked into the huge lobby. It was a beautiful showcase of contemporary artwork and featured three floor-to-ceiling walls of leaded glass windows that framed the San Francisco Bay with a glimpse of the Golden Gate Bridge and Twin Peaks on the left side and an open view of the street in front of the hotel on the right side. The front was flanked by a sprawling seating and outside dining area for people watching in one of the hotel's four restaurants.

Just as I began to marvel at how beautiful the hotel was, the concierge walked up and asked to check us in. I was a member of the hotel's rewards club so he made registration quick and easy and sent my suitcase upstairs ahead of me.

I was excited but exhausted. I needed to unwind and relax, so we went straight up to my room. A ride on the elevator to the third floor, and a stroll down a picturesque hallway, led to me opening the door to a beautifully equipped haven for relaxation:

A well-appointed, king-size bed gracefully topped with a crisp, white, fluffy duvet and a cornucopia of pillows; a beautiful chaise lounge well-positioned in front of the picturesque window overlooking the Golden Gate Bridge; and the *pièce de résistance,* a five piece bathroom featuring a separate Jacuzzi tub and steam shower all greeted me upon my initial room inspection. I knew the hotel was nice when I booked it, but the room was much nicer than I even anticipated. I was very impressed with the amenities. I thought they had given me the wrong room.

I walked farther into the room and was greeted by a huge gift basket atop a lavish white velvet robe, and a beautiful and unique floral bouquet resting atop the bed. The gift basket was filled with a variety of snacks, San Francisco keepsakes, bath and body products, and even a sample of a lotus leaf yoni teatox elixir. The bouquet was a beautiful arrangement of tulips accented by fresh green, purple, and white asparagus stalks tied with a large purple silk bow and a card.

I was in awe—I couldn't believe my eyes. I asked Tariq if he was responsible for any of this. He quickly confessed that he'd upgraded my room and had the gifts brought up so I'd be surprised. Then he insisted that I open the card.

It was a hand-painted card with a beautiful picture of the Golden Gate Bridge on the outside and a handwritten note on the inside. The note was a heartwarming thank you and invitation to enjoy an amazing weekend.

To my beautiful Anais who has so graciously come to visit me in this daz-
zling city, I want to make your visit just as magical as you make me feel every
time I see you. The honor of your presence is requested for the following:

A visit to Fisherman's Wharf for dinner and a tour of the Ghirardelli
Chocolate factory,

A driving tour of California's wine country for lunch and wine tasting,

Dim sum in Chinatown,

And, a picnic at Monterey Beach and a visit to Cannery Row.

However, I would really like to ensure that you have an ultimately
relaxing vacation, so I'd like to begin with dinner tonight and a couple of
spa visits at the hotel starting at 9:00 a.m. tomorrow morning.

Please say yes?!

Your Hairy Arab Prince Tariq!

I was flabbergasted! He had really thought the whole trip out and it sounded
amazing! I offered him my sincerest thank-you and confirmed all of the plans—
but the jet lag coupled with my fatigue began to get the best of me.

Tariq picked up on it and suggested I take a little nap while he went home
to freshen up—he planned to return at 6:00 p.m. to take me to dinner. As soon
as the door closed behind him, I dove into the beautiful basket and passed out
in the middle of the cozy and ultra-comfortable bed. I could have slept all night
but the hunger pains woke me out of my sleep at around 4:30 p.m. and forced
me to get dressed for dinner.

Dinner by the Bay

Tariq knocked at the door at 6:00 p.m. sharp. Although I had already indulged in a few of the snacks from the delicious gift basket, I was hungry and
ready to go upon his arrival. I had even had time to indulge in my favorite
beauty rituals.

I adorned myself in a slinky little cream-colored Chantilly lace dress that
landed at the top of my knees and had lace platform sandals to match. The
creamy lace complemented my beautifully polished mocha chocolate skin that
ever so discreetly peeked through the microscopic holes in the embroidered
trim. The dress was just short enough to allow my sumptuous long legs to take
center stage, and the platform shoes allowed me to accentuate the strength of
my legs while continuing the effects of the lace with the shoes at the bottom. A
little shimmer powder to make everything glow and I felt beautiful!

When I opened the door, Tariq looked and smelled scrumptious enough to
eat—and I'm sure I would have been pleasantly satisfied. However, I knew I had

to control myself ... to be sure to maintain boundaries so I didn't get myself into something I wasn't ready for.

Oddly enough, he unwittingly complimented my outfit with a cream-colored light Armani sweater, matching tan pants, and mahogany sandals. His cologne was absolutely hypnotizing. I asked what he was wearing because I nearly melted in his arms when I smelled him. I can't remember his answer but the combination of the cologne mixed with his testosterone made my hormones go crazy—my love juices started rushing down my love canal.

I quickly composed myself after a long, sultry kiss, and insisted that we'd better go before we didn't make it to dinner. He just smiled and held the door open for me.

We decided to visit the Mission District, which was highly recommended by his roommate. Neither of us had ever been there and didn't have any idea of what or where to eat. So we decided to ask the hotel concierge for a restaurant recommendation.

Following his recommendation, we walked for about thirty minutes until we came upon a quaint little restaurant called Rusty's. Couched between two towering office buildings, it was very well appointed with a front showcasing contemporary black-and-white furnishings and an enclosed patio with heaters to warm the evening's chill. It was also very intimate. The mood was cozy and romantic, and we were lucky enough to arrive just in time for the Friday night jazz set.

We were greeted by what I would call a bohemian-dressed waiter whose claim to fame was that he was one of the few "native San Franciscans." Although he seemed a bit quirky, he was very nice and informative.

I suggested that Tariq order for me as a gesture to signify my trust in him and he was honored by my request. Upon the recommendation of the waiter, he started with garlicky clams casino and what was listed as a Sauntering Shrimp Cocktail for appetizers. For dinner we agreed to share a chargrilled grouper fillet for me and what was listed as *escabeche mezclado* for him.

The appetizers started the evening off just right. They were well appointed and dazzled our eyes and taste buds. The garlicky clams casino were presented in a wooden bowl in extra-large clamshells. The clamshells were stuffed with a tasty combination of bacon, leeks, bread crumbs, and chopped clams, baked to a golden brown, and then topped with a steamed baby clam drenched in a savory garlic herb sauce. They were absolutely delicious. The stuffing was packed with flavor and the clams were tender and savory. I would have settled for them as a main course, however I was too excited about what was coming next.

I was very curious to find out why they labeled the dish "The Sauntering Shrimp Cocktail." When it arrived, it too was well appointed and presented in a wide mouth glass dish with a tall bottom like a margarita glass, except the rim of the glass was extra wide and dotted with holes that held the skewered chilled shrimp in place. There was a well in the middle of the glass that was filled with thick, long twirls of carrot and celery strips, and between the center and the rim was what looked like a river of sauce for dipping—it was an arousing and captivating presentation of culinary gastronomy.

I asked the waiter why the dish was called Sauntering Shrimp Cocktail. He said it was named in honor of World Sauntering Day—a day designed to get people to slow down and do as little as possible. Apparently the dish was designed to get people to take their time and to enjoy the food at the restaurant. The shrimp was very fresh, tender, and succulent—the sauce was an interesting combination of horseradish, fresh lime juice, honey, and vinegar, infused with fresh cilantro—a very different yet delicious twist on traditional cocktail sauce. It was an interesting dish with an even more interesting history.

Between the appetizers and the main course, we managed to get a little talking and a lot of kissing in—I felt like a princess on a first date. Tariq was so kind and gracious and I loved kissing him because he always sent tingles down my spine, especially when he caressed my face and nibbled at my neck. Despite the allure of his sensuality, his most attractive asset quickly became his love of good food just like me. I began to increasingly trust his culinary judgment and couldn't wait for the next course. It too was spot on.

The chargrilled grouper fillet was very light and delicately topped with an herb infused panko and garlic butter coating. The fish sat atop a deliciously light and flavorful fresh tomato pan juice accented by green capers. It was accompanied by a San Francisco–style wild rice pilaf and grilled local asparagus. Although the fish was beautifully and tastefully presented, it was the rice pilaf that drew a good amount of my attention.

An interesting combination of long-grain black rice, also known as forbidden rice, a warm, aromatic red rice called Wehani, and a fluffy brown rice, complemented with brown lentils, dried cranberries, white currants, and roasted pine nuts, it was very complex yet simple and delicious. It was also my first experience with this type of wild rice pilaf and the tender young asparagus was a perfect complement.

The "best in show" for the evening, however, was Tariq's *escabeche mezclado*—a magical mixture and creative presentation of thin-sliced, marinated fish and poached seafood fresh from the Pacific. A delicately balanced, chilled plate made of steel was filled with thinly sliced layers of marinated ahi tuna, abalone, giant clams, octopus, and snow crab claws that sat atop a sweet and tangy shredded lettuce, red cabbage, and carrot slaw. The center of the steel plate was elevated and filled with smoking dry ice that mimicked a sort of flowing volcano, and there was a glass cauldron of the marinade for drinking and dipping that sat in the midst of the dry ice. The beautiful eye-catching presentation of the fish surprised us both.

I was not accustomed to eating what initially appeared to be raw fish, but I was told that the marinade contains lemon juice and the enzymes from the lemon juice literally cook the fish during the marinating process. It was very light and naturally crunchy, and it allowed for the unadulterated sweetness of each type of fish to come shining through on my taste buds. It was simply delicious!

After a Michelin star worthy and very satisfying dinner, we took the waiter's advice and moved out to the patio for fresh air and after-dinner tea, which the waiter explained was designed to aid in our digestion. It was a lovely 71 degree night and we could see a glimpse of the beautifully lit Golden Gate Bridge. We sat, relaxed, and enjoyed the music and the tea.

After about thirty minutes, the waiter came to check on us and said that we shouldn't miss the decadent desserts they offered. Then he brought out the sample plate and neither one of us could resist. We agreed to share a Mild Mocha Red Velvet Cake Bombe filled with dark chocolate crème fraîche, and draped with a thick ribbon of sweet cream cheese frosting accented by chopped salted pecans.

It was elegantly presented on a petite covered crystal cake stand. We were both very impressed with the presentation. The cake melted in my mouth like butter. It was a tender, moist, and flavorful combination of fruity vanilla and cocoa complemented by the earthy, sweet, and nutritious flavors of buttermilk. However, there was a deeper flavor I couldn't quite figure out. I asked the waiter what it was and he described it as fresh beets added to the mixture. It gives the cake a dense, rich texture, he said.

Apparently the beets were used to not only add richness to the cake, but also to replace red dye in an effort to keep the cake all-natural and healthy. To finish it off, the airy cream cheese topping dotted with lightly roasted and salted pecans added a perfect balance of sweet, tangy, and salty—so, so delicious!

We were both amazed by the consistent high quality of the food, the relaxing atmosphere, and the wonderful service. It was a great start to my vacation.

Menu

Join Us for a Seafood Celebration
Down by the Bay in San Francisco

featuring

APPETIZERS

GARLICKY CLAMS CASINO

SAUNTERING SHRIMP COCKTAIL

DINNER

CHARGRILLED GROUPER FILLET
with an herb-infused panko and garlic butter coating,
served on top of a fresh tomato pan juice and green capers

ESCABECHE MEZCLADO
poached seafood melange

SAN FRANCISCO–STYLE WILD RICE PILAF

GRILLED ASPARAGUS

DESSERT

MILD MOCHA RED VELVET CAKE BOMBE
draped with a thick ribbon of sweet cream cheese frosting,
accented by salted pecans

20

We held hands and teased our way back to the hotel through the cool yet invigoratingly breezy San Francisco evening. Tariq was a perfect gentleman and respected my wishes to end the evening with a kiss in the lobby before he went home. After agreeing to meet him after my spa treatment in the morning, I worked my way up to my room and began to explore the gifts in the basket.

Delicious, long-stemmed strawberries dipped in silky Ghirardelli Chocolate and a lovely giant chocolate, almond, and fruit bar took center stage of the basket. I began to dig deeper and surprise, surprise, I discovered a delicious and beautifully appointed collection of bath and body products—a theme was evolving here I guess. Ironically, the collection included bubbling bath oil, body polish, and massage oil that were also chocolate-covered strawberry flavored. They smelled incredible! I started to briefly question why I was so lucky on this trip—but that was just brief. I decided to enjoy the treatment and the sweet, musky, and fruity scents of the bath products drew me right in.

I filled the tub and dropped some of the bubbling bath oil into the running water. A sensual and warm infusion of smells permeated the entire bathroom and eventually worked its way into the bedroom. I turned on the Jacuzzi motor and the bubbles went everywhere. It was hilarious! There I was preparing to enjoy a luxurious bubble bath but the bubbles ended up in my hair, all over the floor, the walls, everywhere!

"Wow! That's some potent stuff," I thought.

I finished my bath, rubbed the body polish all over my skin, and got in the shower to rinse off. Then I drenched myself with the silky body oil, which seduced me into a deep sleep. The smell was so alluring and relaxing I fell asleep right on top of the covers.

I woke up around 6:00 a.m. with a bit of a chill from sleeping on top of the covers, but I felt and smelt great. I'd usually wake up at 7:00 a.m. at home, which would be 4:00 a.m. west coast time. I guess I was so relaxed that my body took advantage of the opportunity to get a couple more hours of rest without interruption.

I was still ahead of the day because it was early, so I went to the gym to get a good workout on the elliptical machine, and had a nice light breakfast in the executive lounge. Ironically the amazing views of the Bay from the executive lounge offered a familiar feeling of comfort.

The relaxation was real. I had a true sense of clarity and freedom to think and feel like I'd never been able to feel at home. I didn't have any appointments to prepare for, a beeper to be on call twenty-four seven, nor a need for a cell phone in case of an emergency at the shelter. I felt great!

After breakfast, I headed to the spa to indulge in one of the treatments Tariq had arranged for me. I was assigned my very own personal butler named Mari who was responsible for making sure I'd have a wonderful and relaxing experience. "What more could I ask for," I thought.

The spa featured a very special collection of the same Bodacious Bodies and BB's Fresh Face products I'd found in my basket. I quickly began to fall in love with them after Mari informed me that the products are designed to keep the skin naturally clean with food-based products.

"Everything is edible!" she exclaimed.

Wow! I can feed the inside and outside of my body all at once!" I joked with Mari.

She laughed and touted how wonderful the products have made many of her clients feel and how the products have natural antibacterial and healing properties to keep free radicals away from the skin. I dove right into the testers.

"Something bold and something new!" I said with intrigue. "How refreshing! I'm excited to try them and to hopefully take a new concept back to Pittsburgh with me," I said before telling her how the alluring smell of the chocolate-covered strawberries collection cradled me right to sleep. Then she prompted me to test the products before making my final selection to use for the treatment.

I chose to have a soothing seaweed body wrap and facial. It was marketed as a muscle detox and moisturizing treatment to brighten and clarify sensitive skin. The treatment included a selection of spa rinses, so I chose the cucumber and honeysuckle rinse, which was designed to clarify and close the pores of your skin while sealing in the glow.

"It all sounds magnificent to me," I quipped to Mari with excitement.

"Trust me! You'll enjoy every moment of it. Not only is the treatment a detox to release poisons pent up in your muscles from the lack of oxygen, but it also leaves a beautiful glow to your skin. The Vichy water massage with the Bodacious Body rinse is akin to an aromatherapy session. It's true candy for the body and mind!"

Upon completion of the obligatory health status paperwork and the selection of my treatments for the next two days, Mari led me to the locker room. She instructed me to remove all of my clothing, cover myself with the luxurious spa robe and sandals, and to relax in the waiting room until the technician called me. I didn't exactly feel comfortable without underwear so she gave me two pairs of disposable thongs to wear during the treatment. Ironically, my mind immediately reverted back to the time that Chris tricked me into a tantric massage at his brother's house and seduced me. I almost forgot I wasn't in Pittsburgh.

Crazy thoughts began to race through my mind. After all, Tariq offered me the treatments just like Rafi did for Chris. I began to wonder if he was trying to pull the same kind of stunt. I wasn't ready to go there with him yet and I was having such a nice time that I didn't want to ruin it. I didn't know what to think. Then I quickly realized that I was in a major hotel chain. If they pulled a stunt like that, I could sue them. I convinced myself that I was sure they wouldn't allow anything like that.

"Phew! I almost talked myself out of what seems to be an amazing experience," I thought to myself.

I eventually shared what happened at Chris's brother's house with Mari and she assured me that I was safe and didn't have to worry about something like that happening there. First of all, they wouldn't allow anything like that to happen on their property, and second all staff have to sign "no fraternizing and/ or intimate contact agreements" as part of their contracts. She assured me I had nothing to worry about unless I wanted to include someone in a treatment. I thanked her and made a mental note of the conversation before moving on to the waiting room.

Immediately upon entering the room I was greeted by the same amazing wall of windows from the lobby that overlooked the San Francisco Bay. The remaining walls were covered in vibrant sea blue crystal tiles, which elucidated a feeling of being surrounded by tropical blue seawater. However, I was quickly drawn in by an appealing scent that reminded me of the lovely honeysuckle trees that lined my backyard as a kid. The waiting room was an extra-special sensory experience unto itself.

It was filled with plush wingback chairs with matching ottomans, magazines of all kinds, a variety of fruit, drinks and dainty little cakes shaped like French madeleines labeled Sweet Potato Sweeties, Carrot Cake Cuties, and Banana Bread Bliss. They were not only delicious but also very healthy as indicated on the labels. The excitement didn't end there. To my surprise, I also found a pineapple version of the yoni teatox love elixir tea that was in my gift basket and decided to give it a try while waiting for the technician.

A warm infusion of jasmine flowers, rose petals, pineapples, and juniper berries glided across my mouth almost like a pineapple-infused gin and juice without the alcohol. The delicate but familiar flavor of the love elixir surprised me. Its tag line indicated that the gourmet and rotund elixir delivers a very good sensation while flavoring the body juices—it was right up my alley.

I enjoyed the waiting room and all of the delicious and interesting accoutrements for thirty minutes before the technician led me into the treatment room. It was a large, cozy room covered in iridescent brown and white glass tile throughout, with a stationary massage table situated in the middle, a shower room with head to toe water jets on one side, and what appeared to be five or six long handheld shower hoses with a variety of spray nozzles mounted on the wall next to a door that led to a supply closet.

I was instructed to hang up my robe and to lie face down on the table to begin the treatment. It was the start of a wonderful relationship between me, the amazing way that water can penetrate sore muscles in the body, and the sensual feeling of euphoria I experienced with my newfound Bodacious Body blends.

The treatment started with the technician using the different shower hoses to cleanse and open up my pores with alternating applications of warm and cool water supplied from the nearby mineral springs. After the fifteen minute water treatment, she placed a foil blanket under me and proceeded to generously paint my entire body with the seaweed body mask. Then she wrapped me in the foil and plastic followed by applying warm, wet blankets on top to allow the treatment to infuse in my skin. I felt like a butterfly in a cocoon. I couldn't move and was totally at her mercy. But she assured me I would love the results while she proceeded to give me a facial.

The facial was pure and delicious. She started with a refreshing cucumber and honeysuckle facial cleanser made by the same Bodacious Body line but called BB's Fresh Face. She used a buff puff with the cleanser to gently exfoliate my face, wiped it clean with a warm cloth, and applied the BB's Fresh Face seaweed mask.

I asked her what the difference was between BB's Fresh Face and Bodacious Body products and she explained that it's the same company founded by two sisters who are both cosmetic chemists. One specializes in developing natural products for the face, including cosmetics and makeup, and the other is a medical doctor who specializes in developing products that heal and accentuate the body from the inside and outside.

What attracted me to the products is that they're all edible and they only supply small batches so that the products are always fresh. It's the most effective way to avoid bacteria and harm to the skin caused by free radicals, pollution, and too much sun exposure, Mari explained.

"I'm impressed already," I exclaimed. "I can't wait to see how they work on my skin so I can bring something new to my friends in Pittsburgh."

She assured me that if I was like most of her other clients, I would be very happy with the experience and the convenience of the company's recurrent subscription service that automatically sends fresh products every six weeks. I was excited about the possibilities.

After she finished applying the facemask, she left me to relax for another fifteen minutes while everything dried. Once the mask dried, she again used the buff puff to gently brush off the mask and rinsed my face again with a warm washcloth.

The time to release the butterfly from the cocoon had come. She took off all of the wraps and sent me to the shower with instructions to rinse my entire body, including my face, with the cucumber and honeysuckle body wash. It was organically designed to cleanse without drying the skin or leaving an oily residue as with most other soaps—it too was incredible.

I finished showering with the multitude of shower jets that drenched my body to a spotless clean. My skin was soft, silky, and had a remarkable glow. I dried off, put on the second pair of disposable underwear, and laid back on the table, which was now draped with soft white satin sheets.

Supple droplets of pure joy enveloped my body from head to toe as the technician sprayed my face and entire body with a clarifying toner. She said it was designed to remove any of the residues from the masks while shrinking my pores. It too smelled amazing!

The massage followed—she rubbed my entire body with the complementary cucumber honeysuckle serum and wrapped me in the satin sheets one last time to allow it to penetrate my skin. Then she moved to my face again, but this time she pulled out a steam machine.

The steam machine was equipped with a magnifying glass. She used a special tool to remove blackheads and wiped off any residue that may have been left on my skin. It wasn't the most pleasant experience because she had to dig into my skin with the tool to remove the blackheads—it felt more like torture. But the results were worth it.

She finished by cleansing my skin again with the clarifying toner, put a couple of cold cucumbers and an ice-cold washcloth over my face for five minutes while she unwrapped the satin sheets to allow my entire body to cool down. After finishing my face with an anti-aging serum that nicely calmed the inflamed areas, my skin was vibrant, felt revived, and more importantly my whole body including my face was radiant. I was thoroughly impressed.

The spa treatment was exhilarating but intense—my body needed to rest at least one day before the next one. I attempted to reschedule what I thought was going to be just a regular massage for Monday. To my surprise, Mari informed me that Tariq had reserved the hammam for my massage. I wasn't quite sure what she meant, but she went on to suggest that if I were comfortable I could probably invite him to join me.

"It's an open Turkish bath and there could be two specialists working on the two of you," she said. I'd never heard of it.

"It's a lovely experience for couples," she exclaimed.

I didn't want to miss any part of the treat. I decided to check it out and scheduled the appointment. I told her I would let her know later on if it would be one or two of us. Then I picked up a collection of the Bodacious Body and BB's Fresh Face products before retreating to my room to lavish in the experience with another quick nap. I was exhausted from being pampered—imagine that.

Adventures in Wine Country

Tariq picked me up at noon for a drive down to Monterey Beach and a visit to Cannery Row. He'd made plans to meet up with some of his friends from college. They lived in the area and had planned a nice Saturday picnic, snorkeling, and observing the sea lions. I was thrilled. Not only would it give me a chance to see more of northern California but it also would be an opportunity to meet some of his co-workers and friends.

We traveled south from San Francisco for about ninety minutes and crawled our way through the sprawling vistas of the Pacific Coast Highway. The beautiful drive was dotted with a variety of concessions from wine vineyards and fruit farmers. During the photographic drive, we stopped twice to purchase grapes and wine—each vending stand sold different varieties. I was surprised at how the fragrant Concord grapes perfumed the air in the car throughout the journey. They tasted just as good as they smelled.

Once we got close to Monterey, we could see the sea lions on the public pier, and pelicans and seals roosting on the rocks and cavorting through the water. The sky was a magical blue, the sun shined brilliantly over the ocean, and the sand dunes perfectly complemented the picturesque views of Monterey Beach.

After working our way to the end of the pier, we parked and found Tariq's friends. They had set up a small dining tent on the beach with an assortment of interesting and delightful Lebanese specialties.

The tables hosted a cornucopia of matching platters filled with a tantalizing assortment of dishes I'd never tasted—I began to salivate. I was already hungry and they looked like little edible gifts and smelled incredible.

Fresh yogurt cheese topped with an herbal sesame spice mixture called za'atar, giant olives stuffed with feta cheese and soaking in olive oil, lemony chickpea hummus, and a cold green bean and tomato dish called *lubiah* were all plated with fresh pita bread. Grape leaves stuffed with ground lamb, rice, and roasted pine nuts were mounded on another platter. Mounds of sliced lamb from a spit centered a platter with all the fixings for gyros. A fresh fruit platter, and a platter filled with perfectly formed petite pieces of baklava shaped to look like cigarettes stood out as dessert along with thermoses of piping hot Arabic coffee.

The second table showcased a variety of specialty wines, crafty bottles of a refreshing pomegranate, rose water, and lime drink, and a case of mineral water all immersed in an ice bath. It was very well apportioned and a generous treat for a beautiful day at the beach.

I spread blankets on the sand while Tariq put on a wet suit to join his friends for snorkeling and windsurfing. The water was very cold, which precluded me from swimming. I was content with sunbathing, people watching, and eating the delectable morsels.

My entertainment came from watching the guys first wrestle with the cold water while snorkeling, and then with the wind while trying to get the surfing sails moving. The water was so cold that they had to drink several cups of the thick Arabic coffee every hour on the hour to keep themselves warm.

Adventurous yet optimistic at best, somehow they tried to impress themselves with the windsurfing. They fell off the surfboard at least twenty-five times. It was hilarious! They only managed to get the proper wind in the sails after about forty-five minutes of trying. It was very clear that none of them were well versed in windsurfing.

It was a hilarious case of the blind leading the blind—funny as heck. I must say though, it was funny and frustrating for them too, but they didn't give up until they were successful at least once.

We packed up and left the beach around 3:00 p.m. to head toward Cannery Row—a renowned tourist location that formerly housed a group of fish canneries. Situated along the bustling shoreline of the mighty Pacific Ocean, it's now host to an array of tourist shops, restaurants, and a magnificent aquarium.

Luckily the aquarium didn't close until 7:00 p.m., so we got a chance to see an amazing show with a killer whale. It seemed more docile than dangerous. Following the visit to the aquarium we did a little souvenir shopping and we were amazed at the multitude of things that can be and were canned. They contained almost any kind of fish you could and would not imagine.

After collecting a variety of souvenirs, we settled for a light dinner of fried fish and chips and headed back to San Francisco before nightfall. I fell asleep and didn't wake up until we were back at the hotel. I'd never felt so relaxed and comfortable with a gentleman friend. He quickly began to not only gain my respect, but more importantly my trust.

I invited Tariq to shower in my room so he wouldn't have to go home first. Then we relaxed on the patio and ordered a nightcap. While sitting on the patio, we could hear music and laughter. It was Saturday night and dancing at the hotel's rooftop nightclub appeared to be the thing to do. We could see hoards of people coming from the parking lot dressed in their finery.

He knows I love to dance and asked if I wanted to go to the nightclub. I was stoked. I threw on a sweet rust-colored velvet swing dress, black strapped stiletto heels, and a collection of gold necklaces and bracelets. Then I pulled my hair up into a high messy bun and off we went to the club.

The vibe was rather different than I was accustomed to, but everyone seemed to be enjoying themselves. The nightclub was just as beautiful as the rest of the hotel. The most notable standout was the wall that held the stained-glass window, which housed a huge rack filled with every kind of alcohol you could imagine. It was rather impressive.

The music was a mix of house and electronic disco. I just love to dance, so it didn't matter what kind of music was playing. I simply enjoyed it. We danced, drank, and laughed until one in the morning before retreating back to my room and sat on the terrace again.

He stayed the night upon my invitation, but only after agreeing that we wouldn't have sex. It probably wasn't what he wanted to hear at the time, but I also felt compelled to tell him about my relationship with Chris—the whole, long, complicated drama. I wasn't quite sure if it was the right time. However, I felt comfortable and thought I could trust him with my emotions.

Chris was my first lover and I explained how I was heartbroken by the relationship because he couldn't commit to me. I explained it as the reason I didn't want to rush into another physical relationship. I needed Tariq to understand why.

When Tariq learned that Chris was afraid to commit to me because of my race, he was taken aback and offended. "I thought he was a nice guy. He's just as racist and prejudiced as his family!" Tariq exclaimed.

I'd never thought about it that way. It was almost like I had an awakening. I didn't quite know how to process that. My mind began to wander erratically.

I'd never felt like Chris was prejudiced, although his ongoing references to his family's objection to our relationship were clearly indicative of their preju-dice. I began to think. Then I came back to the fact that Shirley wasn't white or Lebanese and he claimed his family liked her. I really began to get disturbed and began to think that perhaps I didn't really know how to define him.

After some quick but deep introspection, I came to the realization that although Chris may not be a racist, clearly he and his family are prejudiced against who I am. "That's just as bad," I thought to myself.

Then I began to question why it felt like we were so in love, but couldn't make it work. "Was it really his family manipulating him or was it something he was doing by his own volition?" I asked myself.

Incredibly I actually attempted to defend Chris in my mind. But I quickly caught myself. I realized that if I rationalized his behavior, I would be condon-ing his treatment of me and that I was not willing to do.

I knew Chris couldn't nor wouldn't give me what I needed. After nearly two years of riding an emotional rollercoaster with him, it hurt to think that I was in love with a potential racist, or at the very least, someone who was prejudiced against me.

I came to one conclusion—it was very clear, he valued his family's money more than our love. I was now forced to confront that reality and reluctantly responded, "I've never looked at it like that because our group is very diversified, and he was always professing his undying love for me. On the other hand, he has always been reluctant to introduce me to his family as his girlfriend," I said in confusion. I felt myself letting my guard down again. But it was very painful to admit the real truth.

"Although he often downplays it, everyone in the group knows his family expects him to marry either a white or Lebanese girl. He often voices his concern that they'll disown him if he doesn't comply with their wishes. So perhaps you're right—the truth is that it's his own prejudice that destroyed our relationship. Honestly I'm happy to have discovered it before I truly committed myself to someone who doesn't really love me just for who I am—a strong, black, beautiful woman," I concluded with bold affirmation.

"His loss is my gain," Tariq quickly responded.

"I agree!" I said as I playfully kissed him. But the pain cut me deep.

I didn't want to spoil the amazing experience I was having with Tariq so I decided to move on quickly. I began feeling even more comfortable with him and made my decision to spend more quality time with him.

I poured two glasses of wine and invited him to join me for the upcoming massage in the hammam. He happily accepted and we lounged on the terrace and played backgammon until the chill of the San Francisco evening forced us back inside the room where we fell asleep in each other's arms.

Menu

Join Us for a Lebanese-Inspired Beach Party in Monterey

featuring

LUNCH

FRESH YOGURT CHEESE
topped with za'atar

FETA-STUFFED OLIVES IN OLIVE OIL

LEMONY HUMMUS • PITA BREAD • GYROS

LUBIAH
chilled green beans and tomatoes

GRAPE LEAVES
stuffed with ground lamb, rice, and roasted pine nuts

BEVERAGES

SPECIALTY WINES

A POMEGRANATE, ROSE WATER, & LIME DRINK

ARABIC COFFEE • MINERAL WATER

DESSERT

BAKLAVA • FRESH FRUIT PLATTER

ENTERTAINMENT

Beachside picnic; snorkeling; windsurfing; aquarium visit.

21

Tariq loves gospel music and he knew I didn't like to miss church on Sundays. He surprised me and found a beautiful Baptist church for us to attend. The sermon was inspiring, but the choir was so soulful and uplifting that even Tariq was dancing and shouting. It was hilarious to see a young, debonair Lebanese man with no rhythm dancing and clapping his hands—albeit off beat—to gospel music in a Baptist church and surrounded by mostly black people. "God surely has an amazing sense of humor!" I thought as I cracked up laughing.

After church we were scheduled to go for a visit to San Francisco's famed Chinatown. Tariq wanted to take me to experience dim sum for the first time. He likened it to a traditional American Sunday brunch, but a bit different. I was eager with anticipation. Although I had never experienced dim sum, ever since I was a young girl growing up in New York, Chinatown has always been my favorite place to celebrate my birthday. It was truly a treat to be able to visit one in another city.

The streetcar dropped us off at Stockton Street. My excitement became his passion, and our quest to find what we thought would be the city's best restaurant to have traditional dim sum began. It was an often wacky but fun adventure.

First of all, every touristy restaurant we encountered only had the dim sum menus in Chinese. We couldn't read a thing. Every time he attempted to ask someone how to translate the menu, they would act like they didn't speak English. He started speaking French, then Spanish, and finally Arabic to see if he could get their attention. They still ignored him. I tried not to let him see it, but I was laughing my ass off.

After this happened three times in a row, we finally spotted a bunch of Chinese people waiting on a staircase to enter a dim sum restaurant located off the beaten path. We decided to join the line and to take our chances.

"When in doubt, always follow the natives," I advised.

"They'll typically only eat the good stuff. So I think we're on the right track," Tariq replied while we both laughed cautiously.

"Let's hope it's not something we'll both regret! But on a more positive note, nothing ventured, nothing gained I believe," I exclaimed.

While waiting in line for the restaurant to open, Tariq said he'd often go to dim sum in Paris with his friends on Sundays after early morning tennis matches. He explained the difference between a traditional American Sunday brunch and Chinese dim sum is comparable to visiting a buffet and helping yourself to the food verses servers bringing the selections to you to make your choices from the prepared foods.

I learned that in a traditional dim sum hall, you find yourself a seat at one of the long tables and make your selections from the series of servers who parade around the room offering up to a hundred different small plates of traditional Chinese delicacies. You pick and choose which plates look interesting to you and the waiter enters it as a purchase on your check. When you get full and want to leave, you simply take your check to the register and pay the bill.

When the doors opened we filed in with everyone else, found seats at a long table with everyone else, and the parade of food carts began immediately. The delicacies included notable items like steamed pork buns and not so notable boiled chicken feet. The food was hot, fresh, and delicious. And I mean really fresh.

So fresh that some of the dishes were still moving—like the live octopus we saw a waiter pull from a tank and simply sprinkle with lemon juice before cutting it up and serving it to our neighbors. And, stewed chicken feet that looked like they'd just been hacked off the chickens' legs—Tariq enjoyed every bit of them. I loved watching everyone enjoy the food just as much as I did. It was like being in foodie heaven.

Our selections were well appointed and very tasty, even though I did have to pass on the chicken feet appetizer. Tariq also ordered a variety of steamed dishes including shrimp dumplings, steamed buns filled with three different items—barbecued pork, teriyaki beef, and sweet bean paste, steamy bowls of tasty garlic pork cubes with sticky rice, and an array of steamed desserts and custards. It was an interesting cultural and culinary experience, especially since we appeared to be the only non-Asians in a room filled with about three hundred people sipping and slurping all kinds of dishes.

Plate after plate, our neighbors devoured at least four plates of the freshly killed octopus and Tariq fell in love with the steamed chicken feet. It was a new and exciting experience that I enjoyed even more than the food.

We ordered about twelve different dim sum appetizers, finished eating, and left the restaurant to do a little sightseeing. The next adventure on our itinerary was to find the infamous "crookedest street in the world," also known as Lombard Street, located on Russian Hill.

The hotel concierge suggested we take the cable car to the top and catch a cab to experience the joy ride down the hill. It was absolutely bonkers! I felt like beef jerky being pulled back and forth with every sudden and abrupt turn the taxi made down the winding street. Dotted with landscaped islands stationed in the middle of the road every hundred feet or so, it was obligatory to continuously turn left, then right, then left, then right constantly while going downhill for about a mile. When we finally made it to the bottom of the hill, we asked the driver to take us back to the hotel so we could head south for a garlic and wine tasting festival. I was so dizzy that I couldn't even think about walking back to the hotel.

Menu

Join Us for a
Traditional Chinese Dim Sum Brunch
in The City by the Bay

featuring

DIM SUM

SHRIMP DUMPLINGS

STEAMED BUNS
filled with barbecued pork, teriyaki, beef, or sweet bean paste

GARLIC PORK CUBES WITH STICKY RICE

DESSERT

STEAMED EGG & RED BEAN CUSTARDS

Swept Away

We breezed along stretches of flat, never-ending roads dotted by brief peeks of the the Pacific Coast before highway signs for San Jose, Sunnyvale, and Santa Clara captured my attention early on in the journey to the Gilroy garlic and wine tasting festival. About an hour into the ride, the roads became more rugged and as we got closer to Gilroy, the roads were lined on either side with miles and miles of beautiful purple and green artichoke bushes as far as the eye could see. After a quick stop for a wine tasting, we finally started seeing the signs for Gilroy and the festival.

As soon as we hit the gate, we were greeted with a tasty fried garlic and Asiago cheese appetizer and what looked like communion cups with a very dry white and a sweet red wine on offer. The appetizer was scrumptious, but the dry white wine threw me off. Tariq enjoyed everything and laughed at my distaste for the very dry wine.

We doted over the hundreds of varieties of garlic and wine, and the often eccentric dishes people made with them. One of the most notable for me was the garlic ice cream with chunks of roasted garlic in a sweet, creamy vanilla ice cream. The ice cream was well churned but I found it difficult to get my taste buds to juxtapose the sweet and savory flavors of the garlic—I just didn't like it.

I did, however, find my happy place at dinner. The appetizer was fire-roasted artichoke hearts and asparagus tips in a garlic béchamel sauce. It was a tender juxtaposition of the citrusy essence from the artichokes with the umami of the asparagus tips all complimented by the sweet creamy flavor of the char from roasting the artichokes and the béchamel sauce.

The main course was an exquisitely prepared garlic teriyaki duck breast. It was thinly sliced and served atop a garlic sesame rice with chanterelle mushrooms and water chestnuts. At the waiter's suggestion, we paired dinner with a local white grenache wine.

I'm not typically a big fan of duck but this dish really piqued my curiosity. My investigatory antennae went up. I had to know how the dish was prepared. We summoned the chef who just so happened to also be the owner. He graciously shared the preparation techniques, the most memorable of which was to get fresh duck breast and brine the meat before marinating. I was very happy to be adding another exciting feather to my culinary hat.

After dinner, we visited a few more booths at the festival, purchased a few bottles of a delicious garlic chili oil and sauce to take home, and made the decision to enjoy dessert back at the hotel. Again I slept on the way back and Tariq was a perfect gentleman. He put on his favorite French and Arabic music playlist and before I knew it, we were pulling up to the hotel's valet.

We went back to the room and rested for a few hours before visiting the hotel's flagship restaurant for dessert. We ordered the chocolate fondue and it was one for the record books.

The waiter arrived with a bubbling cauldron of hot Ghirardelli Chocolate sauce with a sidecar of Grand Marnier surrounded by an assortment of fresh fruit, dried nut cakes, cookies, and pretzels. They even surprised us with a flower made from steamed artichoke leaves to dip and eat in the chocolate. Apparently it was also the height of artichoke harvesting season and this was a perfect use of the excess leaves.

We were instructed to pour the Grand Marnier into the chocolate first to get the full effect and then to just go for it. It was orgasmic! The creamy, decadent chocolate sauce kissed with the seductive citrusy orange flavor of the Grand Marnier sent my taste buds into a dance recital. I tried everything and each item was a perfect complement of sweet, salty, bitter, and even a well-balanced savory taste from the tender artichoke leaves that offered the final bow.

Our bellies overflowed with the decadent chocolate. We ate until our hearts were content and not another drop would fit into our mouths. I was so full that I suggested we take a walk to burn off some of the sugar and let the food settle in our stomachs.

After a nice evening stroll, we worked our way back to the hotel room to close out the relaxing evening. We watched a few old movies and prepared for our couple's treatment in the hammam the next day.

My body's internal alarm clock was ever faithful and woke me just as the bright morning sun peeked through the curtains. "Early to bed, early to rise!" I touted in an attempt to awaken Tariq. But he was knocked out and didn't seem to want to move. I guessed the comfortable bed had gotten the best of him, too.

I got up and took a nice hot shower with a new flavor of my now favorite Bodacious Body blend—the collection featured another variety of the same lotus flower bomb scent I'd tried at Walter's spa. I also ordered room service for breakfast. Tariq finally woke up at 8:30 a.m., took a shower, and finished dressing just as breakfast arrived.

It was Labor Day Monday and despite being a holiday, the hotel continued to uphold its five-star reputation and treated us like gold. It was also the last full day of my long weekend and I was excited for what was on tap for the day—breakfast in bed, a visit to the Ghirardelli Chocolate factory with lunch by the bay, and the long awaited hammam spa treatment, and I had every intention of enjoying every minute of the last few hours of my much-needed vacation. I wanted to get the ball rolling and that started with the breakfast order.

I'd been eyeing the highly recommended smoked Alaskan salmon tray all weekend and finally had an opportunity to indulge. I ordered a light collection of mini bagels, the hotel's highly recommended heat-smoked Alaskan salmon tray served with cream cheese, capers, chopped red onions, and heirloom tomatoes, a plate of fresh fruit, and fresh coffee.

Breakfast was delivered on the terrace with white-glove service. It was light, delicate, and afforded us the opportunity to taste the famed salmon, which is dry rubbed, cured, and heat smoked to create a succulent masterpiece.

I really enjoyed the smoked salmon breakfast and was quickly becoming very fond of the San Francisco food scene. Its reputation had preceded it and did not disappoint—it was just what we needed to kick start our ambitious agenda for the last full day of my vacation.

Well-nourished and inspired by the delicious salmon, we set out to visit the famed Fisherman's Wharf to purchase some to take home. Following that we planned to visit the nearby Ghirardelli Chocolate factory to learn how the beautiful chocolates in my gift basket were created. We hailed a taxi and made our way over to Fisherman's Wharf.

Unfortunately we were unable to purchase the salmon—it was all sold out. Disappointed but inspired, we took the opportunity to walk to the chocolate factory and loaded up on a variety of delicate and meticulously created chocolate cordials to take back as gifts.

To avoid getting sleepy and feeling heavy during our long awaited hammam spa treatment, we wanted to eat a light lunch. While venturing along the pier, we found a discrete Chinese restaurant tucked in a little corner of the wharf. Again I asked Tariq to order—after all, he'd done such an amazing job of it at every meal, I didn't want to chance spoiling my culinary fortune. He hit jackpot again. But I suspected he'd had some insight on what to order from his frequent visits to Chinatown in Paris.

For starters we had sizzling rice soup with roasted pork, shrimp, and fragrant herbs. The main course was called moo shu pork and was made of a delicately smoked and candied pork that's shredded and stir-fried with a variety of vegetables then served with thin pancakes for wrapping. Along with the wraps we indulged in a variety of sauces and other accompaniments.

The sizzling rice soup was presented in a large soup bowl and heated rice cakes were dropped into the broth tableside to create the sizzling effect—it's a full-throttle experience that stimulates all the body's senses, including tasting very good. Similar to the beef bulgoki we ate on our second date, the moo shu pork was served on elevated metal bowls filled with a variety of stir-fried shredded vegetables. There were thin rice pancakes for wrapping and a trilogy of dipping sauces. The flavors were mouthwatering, well balanced, and the dish was surprisingly light but filling.

The soup and moo shu pork were both new dishes to me and again I thoroughly enjoyed them. After we were well satiated, Tariq paid the bill and we went back to the hotel to prepare for our adventure in the hammam.

We changed into robes and slippers provided by the hotel and made our way up to the spa. The entrance to the hammam was inside the spa and was located up a full flight of stairs that led to a room situated at the very top of the hotel.

Also known as a Turkish bath, a hammam is the Middle Eastern variant of a steam bath or wet sauna, where technicians scrub and cleanse your entire body with special bath mitts and soaps. In this case the hammam was designed with a huge, round marble stone table in the middle of the very hot, humid room in order to facilitate a couple's mud masks and massage treatments. According to the technician, it was akin to the more ornate Moroccan hammams.

Tariq was the go-to person on the hammam ritual and explained that although our treatments would be more complex, typically the experience is rather simple but does involve several common steps. He fervently emphasized how each step is aimed at cleansing and relaxing the body and the mind.

Typical of his generosity and kindness, he selected the more expensive Moroccan-style mud mask treatment for both of us. Highlights of the treatment included the use of soap derived from black olives to cleanse the skin and a Mediterranean clay mask from Morocco for the full-body treatment. "Wow! This is another way to have fun love with food," I thought to myself.

The full body treatment was rather intense. Along with the body scrub with black olive soap and the warm mud mask treatment, it included a hair wash, condition, and scalp massage. I only opted for the scalp massage so my hair wouldn't get messed up. It was another invigorating experience.

We were instructed to remove our robes, put on the disposable undies if we wanted to, and then lay face down on the huge hot stone slab. I had a male technician and Tariq had a female. They started with a dry brushing followed by scrubbing our entire bodies with a mitt and the black olive oil soap.

The full body scrub with the black soap initially took me off guard—it kind of hurt. I kept thinking to myself, "Please don't let these mitts leave scars on my skin!" The scrubbing mitts are called kessa mitts and they're designed to deep clean the outer layer of the skin. But they felt like sandpaper, and the technicians scrubbed every inch of our bodies with them. When they finished I was somewhat relieved. After the scrubbing came a quick rinse off with alternating temperatures of warm and cool water, and then they proceeded with the warm Mediterranean clay mask application, which invigorated me by cooling down my skin from the vigorous scrub.

They painted the warm, silky mud all over the front and back of our bodies and allowed us to marinate for twenty minutes to let the minerals soak in our skin. There was a wonderful aura of peace and tranquility that accompanied the stillness. Then came another intermittent rinse of hot and cold water before they used a variety of pressure hoses as a water treatment. We were then instructed to shower and lay back down on the stone.

We showered individually, dried off, and put on another pair of disposable undies before lying back on the hot stone. That's when the real fun began.

Each of us got to watch the other's technician massage the other, and we flirted with each other—it was a whole other level of erotic stimulation. I even started to get a little jealous when the technician got too close to Tariq's jewels—she couldn't help it though. His cock was so big it spilled out of the disposable undies. With every massaging stroke of his legs, it became more and more engorged as he stared into my eyes.

I'm sure my technician also sensed how stimulated I was. I made numerous attempts to suppress it as he poured ladles of the warm, silky oil all over my body and meticulously stroked and rubbed it into every muscle. Tariq continuously joked about licking it off and our conversation began to get rather hot and steamy. It was almost like a cue for the technicians because shortly after they finished the massages, they left us in the room alone to relax and enjoy each other.

As soon as the door closed, Tariq poured his whole bucket of oil over my booty. I tried to get up, but with each attempt I'd slip and fall back onto the marble slab—we both laughed hysterically.

I retaliated by dumping my bucket of oil all over his head. When I finally was able to get off the table, I took one of the high-pressure water hoses and sprayed him off the table. He kept trying to catch me to stop the water but continuously slipped from the oil on the floor and the water I sprayed to keep him away. When he finally caught me, he quickly grabbed the hose and shut the water off—it was hilarious! After the amazing body treatment and the invigorating water fight, we dried off, dressed, and went back to the hotel room.

We ordered room service and enjoyed each other in our spa robes while playing backgammon. I had a 6:00 a.m. flight to catch, Tariq had to be at work the next morning, and we'd already had a full day—I thoroughly enjoyed my entire vacation. Couple that with the amazing hammam treatment and all the fun we had, all I wanted to do was relax and have a good dinner on the beautiful terrace—that's exactly what we did.

We finished a light dinner of club sandwiches, chips, and slaw, and played one last game of backgammon. Then we slept like babies. The next morning I caught the early flight back to Pittsburgh and my dream vacation was over.

Menu

Join Us in Celebrating the
Gilroy Garlic and Wine Festival

featuring

APPETIZERS

Fire-Roasted Artichoke Hearts
& Asparagus Tips
in a garlic béchamel sauce

***

DINNER

Garlic Teriyaki Duck Breast
thinly sliced and served atop garlic sesame rice with chanterelle
mushrooms and water chestnuts

***

BEVERAGE

White Grenache Wine

***

DESSERT

Grand Marnier Chocolate Fondue

***

ENTERTAINMENT

Movies

Menu

*Join Us for Moo Shu at the Market
on Fisherman's Wharf*

featuring

APPETIZERS

SIZZLING RICE SOUP
with roasted red pork, shrimp, and fragrant herbs

LUNCH

MOO SHU PORK
with a vegetable medley and rice pancakes

SPA TREATMENT

*The hamman treatment; black olive oil soap scrub; warm
Mediterranean mud body wraps; seaweed and cucumber body
refresher and facials; massages.*

22

landed early off the flight directly to Pittsburgh from San Francisco. Fortunately, I'd left my car at the airport, which made for an easy ride home. I managed to make it home in less than thirty minutes and had the rest of the day to myself.

I prepared myself for work the next day, checked in with my parents, and closed out my final evening of rest with a long and sensuous bubble bath and conversation with Tariq. We reminisced about all the fun we had while visiting wine country, and he joked about hoping I would've gotten drunk from the wine so he could've convinced me to let him make love to me.

Attempting to divert his attention, I talked about the fun we had while looking for a place to enjoy dim sum and then watching everyone eat bizarre foods like freshly harvested octopus being eaten while still moving, and soup made from pig's blood. He assured me that it just seemed strange to me because I wasn't accustomed to food of that sort. We both agreed it was both a funny and exciting learning experience. Our relationship was blooming and I assured him I was happy to have shared the vacation with him.

The highlights of the trip for both of us were the amazing San Francisco food scene and, of course, the amazing massage and water fight we had in the hammam. Not only was it one of the most sensual and gratifying massages I'd ever experienced, but we both agreed the water fight was a lot of fun.

I began to revisit the quiet sensuality and potency of Tariq's presence during the hammam experience. Suddenly the narcotic power of his voice began to overtake my emotions as he shared his desire to indulge while he watched the masseuse gripping and kneading my body.

"It drew an onslaught of raw physical desire to make love to you," he said. "I was dying to touch your heart-shaped ass, but all I could do was watch while another man enjoyed my prowess. That was very difficult," he lamented as his husky voice began to whisper want and need.

My juices started revving up and the water began to feel like warm honey between my legs. I could hear him panting and strongly stroking himself. My eyes shut in ecstasy as he begged me to just let him smell my sweet juices again—to just let his tongue touch the tip of my love canal.

The blood started bumbling in my sex. I trembled with the thought of him burying his hot, juicy tongue in my sweet heat while shock waves of pleasure began to sizzle throughout my body. I could hear him coming to climax. With one stroke of my hand I fell apart. Water was flying everywhere. I exploded with spasms of pure, unadulterated joy.

"Wow! I'm amazed how your voice transcends physical pleasure and made me cum like that," I said.

He thought about it for a minute while he finished cleaning himself up. Then he made me feel like a goddess.

"There's a narcotic power in your voice that activates your hypnotic scent in my mind, and I simply can't control my thoughts about you. I crave you all the time," he said.

I didn't quite know how to respond, so I said nothing for about two minutes. I already knew that there was an aching sexual tension building between us, but I wasn't ready to go there with him yet. I knew I had to change the topic of conversation, so I decided to talk about my upcoming birthday.

After such a great trip, I thought it would have been nice to spend it with him in San Francisco. He asked if I wanted to come out again, but I wouldn't have had enough vacation time, so I passed. He followed with a suggestion that if I traveled home with him at Christmas, although it would be belated, we could celebrate my birthday in Paris and that would be his gift to me if I accepted.

His offer tempted me. But it would be the holiday season and my family expected me to come home to visit and greet our relatives. So it was difficult to say yes to his invitation. But I had been longing to visit Paris nearly my entire life and I couldn't imagine just passing up the invitation. I agreed to think about it.

"Don't worry! I may not be there and I'll miss you for your birthday, but I know you have a great group of friends that'll make sure you won't miss me too much," Tariq assured me. With that he told me to kiss my finger and rub it on my love canal to remember him through the night and we said goodnight.

The Shelter

Surprisingly, when I returned to work the next day, the girls all jumped on me and told me how happy they were that I'd returned. Sadly, they also told me Saturn was gone, but they didn't know why she'd left. Nobody was talking to them, not even Saturn. They said she simply packed her bags and was escorted out of the shelter by the psychologist without saying a word—again I was astonished by how the psychologist abruptly dismissed the girls. I had to quickly gather myself and find out what happened before passing judgement.

Apparently Ms. Nellie was glad to see me too because she decided to do a celebration in honor of my return. "Cake Pop Party!" she exclaimed with excitement as she went into a personal commercial about her newfound culinary treat.

"You know, ever since I found these delicious and simple Just Add Water Happy Cake kits, it's been easier to please everyone for breakfast, lunch, and dinner. I can make eight different kinds of muffins for breakfast, loaf cakes for lunch or dinner, and if it's someone's birthday, all I have to do is select their favorite flavor, bake it in a cake pan, and apply all of the fixings already included in the kit. And they're very nutritious! I simply love them," she professed.

"Now let's all eat cake shall we!" she exclaimed with laughter.

Ms. Nellie took the girls into the dining room to make the cake pops, so I went into the office to read the logs and find out what was going on in the house. Evelyn, the psychologist, was already in the office meeting with Lauren, so they pulled me in to update me on Saturn's situation.

Ostensibly, the situation I'd encountered earlier in the month with Ed and Saturn wasn't as innocent as it was made to appear. Ed was working the Sunday shift with Regina, Patty Jo, and Dwayne, and was supposed to be out in the yard playing volleyball with the rest of the group. Ms. Nellie didn't work on the weekends so the counselors had to cook the meals for the girls. Regina was cooking lunch and needed something from the pantry in the basement. As she was going down the stairs, she heard what appeared to be a man's voice moaning and a slurping noise in the distance. It startled her.

She ran upstairs and asked Patty Jo to come back down the stairs with her to further investigate the situation. Upon their return, she heard Saturn and Ed in a heated exchange.

"Fuck me you motherfucker! Fuck my brains out! You know this yo' pussy!" she exclaimed according to Regina. They were so engaged that they didn't hear Regina and Patty Jo on the stairs.

Unsure of what to do at that moment, they went back upstairs and waited until Saturn and Ed emerged from the basement. In the meantime, Patty Jo had already called Lauren to report the incident and ask what they should do.

Lauren immediately called Evelyn, and they both came to the shelter. Evelyn had a brief but stern conversation with Saturn before escorting her upstairs to the bedroom to gather her personal belongings and taking her back to the intake center. Saturn was ultimately registered for placement in a home for single parents and was to receive intense counseling for victims of sex trafficking.

As a child advocate, Lauren was obliged by the law to mandatorily report any violations that occurred with the girls under her supervision, and she called the police to file a report. Ed was immediately arrested for child molestation and statutory rape. In an effort to avoid disturbing the other girls, the police managed to get Ed out of the house without anyone else seeing him in handcuffs. That was why the girls didn't say anything about him and didn't know what happened.

Lauren and Evelyn asked for more details about my interview with Saturn's mother. Regina walked in a few minutes later and Lauren instructed us to have a roundtable discussion with the girls that evening to make sure no others had been molested by Ed or Saturn. I knew it had to be done because sometimes abused children victimize other children, but all I could think to myself was that I had just enjoyed five days of bliss only to come back to another major crisis at work.

It was starting to get the best of me. I began to think more and more about other options, including wanting to study in Paris and open a restaurant. But I knew I had to put my personal feelings aside and focus on the girls.

They were at such fragile stages in their young lives that it would have been easy for someone to manipulate them and ruin them forever. I thought that at least if we could catch it early, we could address it appropriately and hope to avoid the potential long-term effects of the abuse. I feared this could be the situation with Saturn, especially if she didn't receive intensive therapy soon.

The roundtable and cake pops idea was a great inroad to opening the girls up to talk freely while not feeling like they were being interviewed or that anyone had any expectations of them. They mashed up sheet cake, mixed it with frosting, nuts, and dried fruit and formed it into balls with molds that held the sticks. Then they rolled the balls in nuts, flavored sugar crystals, dried fruit, and melted chocolate to create their own masterpieces while revealing some not so wonderful stories about their childhood.

One of the youngest girls vividly recalled how one time she had walked away from her mother while shopping at a farmers' market and a man walked up to her and said he'd lost his puppy. After trying to help him locate the puppy, he lured her away from the market and inside an old abandoned house. She was only five years old and didn't suspect he would do anything to her, so she went inside the house. When she looked up, there were hundreds of bottles of what looked like urine that lined the walls.

It was frightening to her, so she turned around to leave but he was covering the exit. He tried to reassure her that everything would be okay, so she wouldn't panic. But as soon as he moved away from the door, she jetted out and ran into her mother's arms. Her mother had thankfully been looking for her and unknowingly followed the same trail that led to the abandoned house. She spoke as if it had just happened and began to tear up. Fortunately, the cake pops helped to suppress some of the sadness.

Another girl wanted to talk about why so many girls can go missing after just walking down the street. Everyone had advice on how to try to avoid predators, however the new girl, Ashtley, alarmed everyone when she said it's not always possible to avoid them. It wasn't quite clear what she was trying to say, but it was a startling response.

Neither Regina nor I had gotten the time to read Ashtley's file. She was Saturn's replacement and had only been in the house for one day. As usual, Ashtley came with her own issues and they were massive. Her case would later become a turning point for me.

She was a fourteen-year-old runaway from Cleveland, Ohio, with a would-be boyfriend who was seventeen years old. According to her, the boyfriend encouraged her to perform unscrupulous acts with guys on the street to earn money so they could eat while they were on the run. When her father finally found her, he moved her to Pittsburgh with his family to get her away from the boyfriend. But for some reason she didn't want to stay with her father, so she arranged for the boyfriend to meet her in Pittsburgh, stole her grandfather's car, and attempted to go back to Cleveland with the boyfriend.

Her father heard the car engine and proceeded to chase them down the Parkway. Not knowing how to drive the car, the boyfriend ended up crashing it on the side of the Parkway, and they both ended up in the emergency room. Both were arrested at the hospital for car theft. When they ran Ashtley's fingerprints, they matched those of a baby girl who'd been abducted from Missouri thirteen years earlier.

Ashtley didn't know what was going on. Her father insisted that they had the wrong identity, but the police didn't buy his story. The boyfriend went to jail and Ashtley was obliged to wait in a court-ordered shelter for more extensive testing to determine if she was the missing child. It was later determined that she was indeed the missing child and the police arrested her father for child abduction. We were now charged with working not only to find and inform her mother, but to reunite them.

"Another day of unprecedented drama at the shelter," I thought to myself.

I had returned from my amazing vacation to a lovely welcome by Ms. Nellie and the girls only to be stopped in my tracks by Saturn and Ed's freak fest. Then I learned that we were working with a child who had been abducted as a baby and needed tremendous support to be properly reconnected with the mother she believed gave up on her so long ago. Although I was passionate about advocating for children, I really began to feel the quagmires of burnout.

Another glorious adventure in the shelter ended at midnight and as usual Regina invited me to have cocktails and hot wings at one of our favorite restaurants. She also wanted to debrief me about my trip to San Francisco.

Regina grilled me about the trip for nearly two hours. She wanted to know everything we'd done, including and especially about whether or not I'd made love to Tariq. I assured her it wasn't time because I didn't want to rush into a physical relationship with another guy after such a long and tumultuous affair with Chris.

She reluctantly agreed that it was the best decision. Then after ogling over my description of how Tariq upgraded my room to a suite, and my enjoyment of the amazing spa treatments, she abruptly commented, "I want to do everything you did, just like you did it!"

Again I was taken aback. But I finally figured out how to tell her that she wasn't welcome to indulge in information pertaining to my personal life without outright telling her to mind her business.

"Remember, what happens in San Francisco, stays in San Francisco!" I said. We both laughed. She didn't contest my statement but I was certain she'd gotten the message.

Before we got in our cars to go home, I assured her I'd give her a list of the places we visited if she decided to go to San Francisco. But that would be the extent of the details.

"No kiss and tell!" I insisted. I'm never comfortable discussing my intimate life outside of my relationships, and I wasn't about to start now.

When I finally got home, I started thinking again about Regina's comment that she wanted to do everything like I did it. It felt a little creepy to me. I decided from that point on I would have to censor some of my experiences and downplay them when talking to her. My mind continued to wonder. I ended the night by calling Tariq to calm me down.

As usual he was a calming voice in the midst of the storm and always knew the right things to say to make me feel better. He reiterated his invitation to go to Paris for Christmas and assured me that I wouldn't regret it. The offer became more and more enticing. However Christmas seemed like a long time away, so I filed it in the back of my mind.

Menu

Join Us for a Cake Pop Party

featuring

CAKE POPS À LA CARTE

CARROT CAKE & CREAM CHEESE
covered with toasted walnuts

RED VELVET CREAM CHEESE
covered with toasted pecans

LEMON LUSH
with candied lemon and Brazil nuts covered in powdered sugar

MANDARIN CHOCOLATE
with candied oranges covered in chocolate ganache and almonds

VANILLA SPICE
with white chocolate and walnuts

ENTERTAINMENT

Roundtable discussion.

t was early September and after a topsy-turvy summer of romantic and not so romantic adventures, I was excited about my upcoming twenty-fourth birthday. I didn't have any specific plans, but just about every weekend in September was filled with work, fun events, and/or parties to cater, which I loved.

I'd even had a special request from my favorite client, Javier, to deliver trays of desserts to his friend's condo complex for a symphony event—hence I was also excited to be making new business connections. He told me he was responsible for dessert, always loved my cakes, and wanted to share them with his colleagues for an annual planning meeting.

He ordered an assortment of one hundred gourmet mini cake bombes and tortes. After taking a note from Ms. Nellie's cooking philosophy for quick cooks, I used the Just Add Water Happy Cake kits as the base for the desserts. They were simple to make but required a few hours to fill and decorate individually.

Javier told me he would just be arriving from a gig and needed them delivered to the location before 6:00 p.m. when everyone would be arriving for the meeting. I had the day off so I tried to deliver them a little early.

When I arrived, I noticed it was the same building Sheila lived in, but I chalked it up as just a coincidence. I got in the elevator and went up to the rooftop delivery room after being buzzed in by the security guard. When I got off the elevator, I asked the security guard where to deliver the baked goods and he pointed to the rooftop terrace and pool area. As I proceeded to make my way over to the dining area, all of my friends jumped from behind a series of moving walls and screamed "Surprise!" and then started singing happy birthday to me. I was in complete shock.

"What in the world is going on!" I shouted with elation.

I was honored they did such a wonderful thing for me, but I couldn't figure out how they managed to get my client to help them arrange a surprise party for me. I was totally confused.

I asked Sheila if there was another event that was supposed to be in the same location. I didn't want to be late delivering the cakes. Then Julio came out of nowhere, gave me a kiss on the cheek while wishing me happy birthday, and handed me a check for $500.

"Happy Birthday Anais! The cakes are for you. We wanted you to enjoy your birthday cake and we couldn't think of a better way than to have you make it yourself. By the way, please remind me to catch up with you later on in the evening, I have something I'd like to ask you about," he said.

When I asked how they arranged for Javier to order the cakes and Julio to accept them, Jill said she knew I would respond to Javier's request because he was one of my favorite clients. Javier loves me so he happily participated. He, however, was at a gig in Norway and asked Julio to attend the party in his place. They both offered to pay for the cakes as a gift. I was truly overwhelmed with their heartwarming gesture and even more elated about having such a valuable client think so highly of my work and me.

Then there was the party—It was off the hook! Not only did they convince one of my favorite clients to pay for the cakes, somehow they persuaded JB to invite the reggae band he freelanced with to provide the entertainment. To my astonishment, Chris commissioned the chef from my favorite Jamaican restaurant to cater the party on-site and to cook fresh food on the grill. Chris was sure to boast about it while letting me know that he'll always love me and only wants the best for me.

The rooftop party room was a contemporary masterpiece that rivaled any modern nightclub. It was well dressed for the occasion, too. Sheila and the girls decorated each of the ten round tables with chic floral arrangements filled with some of my favorite exotic flowers—wild ginger, birds of paradise, and assorted calla lilies. Each place setting was elegantly appointed in full regalia and accented by petite heart-shaped tin keepsakes that held a variety of butter mints and a message of *Happy Birthday Anais* printed on the outside. I couldn't figure out how they managed to get that done or even how long they'd been planning the party right under my nose.

Sliding glass doors opened onto a huge wooden deck for dancing and socializing, and a heated saltwater swimming pool was flanked by Jacuzzis on either side that jetted into the pool. I was gobsmacked! I didn't know what to say and simply stood in awe.

The girls quickly grabbed me and led me to the temporary boudoir they'd set up for me. "We want you to change clothes so come in the bathroom, we have a surprise for you," Chantelle said. I followed them to the bathroom and they kept insisting that I go in first. When I opened the door, Tariq was standing there with a handful of gifts, flowers, and my favorite chocolates.

I lost it and broke down in tears. I was so happy to see him that I just jumped in his arms and held on to him for a good five minutes while trying to stop crying. The girls left us in the bathroom so I could properly greet him and change my clothes. When I finally let him go, he insisted that I open the gifts.

They had figured everything out. Upon the recommendation of Chantelle, he bought me a sexy two-piece bathing suit with a matching cover-up, blinged out beach shoes, and a travel size collection of my new favorite BB's Fresh Face makeup and Bodacious Body care kits. He was always so thoughtful and attentive to me and increasingly earned my respect and admiration. I quickly changed clothes, kissed him for five more minutes, and we departed the bathroom to enjoy the party.

Ras Furry, the lead singer of the Reggae band, hosted the entertainment portion. He kept everyone thoroughly entertained. We danced traditional and dance hall reggae, and even did the limbo. I must say, Tariq was the life of this party—he won the limbo contest by getting under the pole when it was only a foot and a half from the ground.

Ras Furry and the band did an amazing job of keeping everyone engaged. Shortly after the limbo contest, he directed everyone to jump in the pool for a chicken fight using a bunch of three-foot foam noodles already floating in the pool. Everyone doubled up, with most of the girls finding a guy's shoulders on which to position herself.

We hammered each other with the noodles while the band played upbeat reggae and funk music. In the meantime, Ras Furry eliminated people one by one after they'd gotten knocked down until the last two teams were standing—ironically these were Chris and Chantelle, and Tariq and me.

The music stopped. Ras Furry sent us to opposite sides of the pool, gave us a ten second countdown, and yelled "Charge!"

We had a blast! It was an interesting battle of Chris and Tariq trying to hold Chantelle and me while we poked, prodded, and slapped the heck out of each other with the foam noodles. After ten long minutes of going at each other, Chris tripped and Chantelle fell into the pool. Tariq and I were the last ones standing and appropriately crowned the champions.

After our victory, Sheila quickly jumped in the pool and set up the volleyball net and then we all randomly chose sides. After two highly competitive games, my team lost. I think it was because we were mesmerized by the food chef Benjamin was preparing on the grill. As soon as the second game was over he called us out of the pool to eat and we happily complied.

He spoiled us with an amazing variety of traditional Jamaican delicacies with customized levels of spiciness. Allowing everyone to select their grill selections cleverly customized each person's dish and spiciness levels from the dinner menu order sheets given to them to fill out when they arrived. The sheets were then sent to chef Benjamin at the grill where he prepared each individual order. The food was fresh, delicious, and piping hot right off the grill—precisely how I like it.

The menu was composed of my favorite Jamaican foods—mini beef patties with coco bread, fried plantains, and codfish cakes for starters. Dinner's selections included escovitched red snapper; mesquite wood-smoked jerked chicken; red peas and rice; fried dumplings; and callaloo with ackee and salted codfish.

The food was to die for! The fish was moist and crisp with a light vinegary sauce and just the right amount of spice. The chicken was tender, flavor filled, and smoked just enough to allow the sweetness of the pimento to shine through the crisp skin, and the side dishes were perfect accompaniments.

For dessert, chef Benjamin and his staff skillfully rearranged the assortment of mini Happy Cake bombes and tortes on a platter in the shape of a beautiful tower surrounded by homemade coconut macaroons and a tropical fruit collection. He topped the amazing presentation off with thin, long-stemmed candles, and everyone sang happy birthday to me. I was in heavenly bliss.

Although dinner was mesmerizing, dessert was the showstopper. The Happy Cake bombes were filled with either chocolate mousse or vanilla pastry cream and covered with chocolate ganache, orange, or raspberry fruit glazes. They looked like little jewels. The tortes were layered with cream cheese and covered with roasted almonds, toffee walnuts, and/or shaved coconut and perfectly framed the cake bombes along with the coconut macaroons and the fresh fruit prepared by chef Benjamin.

After everyone indulged in the gluttonous feast, we all rested by the pool on the luxurious loungers and chatted for a while. That's when I finally got a chance to talk to Julio. He reminded me of his role as an active board member of Doctors Working Borders, aka DWB, an international charity based in Pittsburgh, and said that he'd been selected to serve as the chairman of the annual fundraiser. He wanted to know if I could help him plan this. The committee had tentatively scheduled the fundraiser to take place in February since they were scheduled for a mission trip later on in the year, so he thought something surrounding Valentines Day would be great. After a bit of chatting back and forth, I told him that I was honored for him to consider me for the job and agreed to help. Shortly thereafter he said his goodbyes to his newfound friends and left to catch an early flight back to New York.

I finished thanking all the other guests for coming and we closed out the evening with a game of dodgeball in the pool. However the evening was not without impending drama.

Chris was not happy to see Tariq. He confronted him and asked what he really wanted with me. But Tariq didn't back down. He suggested that Chris should have handled his business with me properly when he had the chance.

"She's an amazing woman and I *will* love her like she deserves to be loved," he said calmly. Even though I was extremely disturbed by Chris making a scene again, I was very impressed with Tariq for standing up to him in my honor.

However his bold response appeared to piss Chris off and he took a swing at Tariq. But Tariq grabbed his fist and told him he wouldn't dignify his attempts to hurt me anymore with his antics. He made Chris look and feel like an idiot.

Initially Chris walked away, but as soon as he saw Tariq turn his back, he turned back and attempted to jump on him and grab his neck. Tariq quickly moved out of the way and Chris fell to the floor. As he began to get up I offered a hand to help and he pushed me out of the way—which really pissed me off. At that point Rafi intervened and asked Chris to leave because he was letting his temper get the best of him. I couldn't believe Chris had the audacity to push me. Now I was really angry. After he grabbed his things to leave, I kicked him in the middle of his ass as hard as I could before slamming the door.

"Don't ever put your hands on me!" I shouted.

I pulled myself together and returned my attention to the remaining guests to thank everyone for all the hard work and the amazing surprise. And even though Chris tried to make a scene in the end, I'd had an unforgettable experience.

I was also very impressed and honored by Tariq's surprise visit. My trust and heartfelt emotion grew deeper and stronger for him. He protected my honor and me, and I began to feel more secure than ever about our relationship.

After almost everyone had left, I decided to invite Tariq to come home with me for a private after-party. I thought it was only appropriate as he had proven himself not only to be valiant, but strong and secure with whom he is. We said our thank-yous and goodbyes to those still present and headed to my place.

My Boudoir

I devoured another one of my mini birthday cakes along with a glass of wine and excused myself to freshen up. Upon my return Tariq decided to get playful and pretended he was going to feed me more of the leftover cake, but he tricked me. Instead of putting it in my mouth, he rubbed the cream on my face and swiftly started licking it off and nibbling at my neck.

I was already horny after watching him stand up to Chris, so it didn't take much to pull the trigger—my juices began to rev up like a junky. Then he looked me straight in the eyes and began tantalizing me with his kisses while professing his so-called obsession with the idea of me.

"I'm falling in love with your soul." *Mwah!* He kissed my forehead. "Your beautiful mouth." *Mwah!* He gently kissed my lips. "Your beautiful eyes." *Mwah!* He kissed my eyes. "And this little dimple right here on your face." *Mwah!* He kissed my dimple while gently touching my face.

I began to get more and more excited. My emotions took a hold of the situation and true feelings of warmth and security overtook me. I felt safe with him, especially after he stood up to Chris the way he did.

Tariq was always attentive to my needs, treated me like a queen during my visit to San Francisco, and he really earned points by surprising me for my birthday. More important, even though our relationship started with a fiery passion, he always respected my desire to refrain from having intercourse and I really appreciated it. Cause he is truly a skilled craftsman at eating pussy, and he could have tempted me at any given time.

By now all kinds of thoughts ran through my mind. He'd been a beam of light in my life for the past four months even though I hadn't fully committed myself to him. Praying that I was making the right decision and that my body wasn't again betraying my convictions, in that split-second I made what I felt was a full evaluation of our relationship. I decided it was now okay to share myself with him and to enjoy every bit of him.

I excused myself again and went to my room to change into something more comfortable. That's when I got the brilliant idea that it was the right time to try out some of the toys Chris had given me. I figured it would be something new for both of us.

I quickly washed off and spritzed with a delicious shimmering body spray. Adopting the persona of a dominatrix, I put on the beautiful hot pink crotchless leather teddy, strapped the gladiator heels all the way up to my knees, and laid out the vibrator, the whip, and the pink velvet blindfold and cuffs on the nightstand.

When I returned to get him, Tariq was eager with anticipation. His face lit up like a Christmas tree when he saw me.

"Always more beautiful every time I see you!" he said with excitement.

I invited him to come into the bedroom and he made a quick detour to the bathroom to wash up while I prepared the room. I picked up the whip, met him at the bathroom door, then used it to guide him to the bedroom and presented him with a distinct set of instructions.

"First, when you enter my boudoir, I love to play. So in here I'm your master, and you, my humble slave, agreed?!" I softly quipped. "Absolutely!" he shouted with extreme excitement.

"Second, no one violates the sleeping area with street clothes, so you must remove your clothes immediately," I implored, insisting that he lay his clothes on the chaise lounge. He happily complied with my demand.

"Now ... sit on the bed and tonight your name will be Nuli Ana Tariq, which means Tariq the slave of Anais. When I call you Nuli, you must follow my command. You are only allowed to call me Mistress. If you're not comfortable, your safe word will be Ting which means stop. Do you understand?" I asked. He just shook his head up and down.

"What's the safe word?" I asked.

"Ting! Ting! Ting!" he shouted with elation. "But I'm sure I won't be needing it," he joked with excitement.

I tantalized him with the whip and slowly nibbled at his neck and upper body. It drove him mad. He couldn't contain himself and began to move his hips while trying to position his love muscle into my vagina. My body was just as excited as he was and began to mimic the rhythm of his rocking motion. I felt an overwhelming sense of freedom to let go ... but I wanted to play a bit more.

I kissed him while gently draping the velvet blindfold over his eyes. "Can I play?" I whispered softly in his ear.

"Of course!" he exclaimed with the excitement of a virgin teenage boy who's garnered the attention of a supermodel. I was fully aroused, and I wanted to explore more of his beautiful body.

I guided him into the middle of the bed where he lay completely naked with a fully erect cock. I drooled with anticipation. I wanted and now needed to feel his hot, steely cock penetrating my love canal. But it was only appropriate that I make every effort to reciprocate the amazing orgasm he'd given me months earlier. Plus I wanted to get him worked up a bit more to intensify our first full experience together.

I playfully nibbled my way through the erogenous zones on his face and his chest. And then I dove into his neck like a vampire thirsting for a feed. He went nuts. He kept trying to grab at me for penetration.

"No! No! No! You're being naughty!" I whispered. "I'll need to restrain you!" I said while tying his hands to the headboard with the leather wrist cuffs.

"Now ... can I continue exploring in your playground?" I said while biting his nipples.

He began to beg. "Please! ... Please! ... I'll do anything. I need you! All of you!" he pleaded.

"In due time," I responded softly while stroking his love muscle ever so slightly with the whip.

He was going crazy with excitement from the stimulation ... the anticipation of what was next. I knew I was in control. It felt great. I took the whip and gently stroked his entire body to amplify his anticipation. It sent chills all over his body and then I went in for the kill.

While filling my mouth with his big, beautiful cock, I used the vibrator on his perineum to intensify the effect. Nearly reaching climax, he begged me to let him touch me ... to free his hands ... to let him see me. It was like I had unleashed a wild animal in both of us.

Agreeing to release him, I took the cuffs and blindfold off. He immediately took the vibrator, flipped me onto my back, and planted himself on top of me.

"My turn to play with you now!" he exclaimed with a boyish excitement as he kissed my body passionately.

He nibbled and sucked my breast while tickling and teasing my sex with the vibrator. The feeling was slowly but deliciously intensifying. Chills rippled up and down my entire body. My hips synchronized with the melodic rhythm of the vibrator.

"Uhmmm! I want to taste you," he purred. "I've waited four long months to enjoy this beautiful flavor again," he exclaimed.

He nibbled my thighs inch by inch ... the closer he got to my sex, the more I hungered for his touch. My whole body quivered. Then he buried his head in my sex. I was enamored as he softly caressed my clitoris with deep, long strokes from his delicious and juicy tongue. I now wanted and needed more of him. It was very clear that he needed me too.

He strategically began licking my asshole and rubbing my sex. After gently sliding his finger inside my ass, he went to town on my clit. At first I was almost embarrassed by how good it felt, then he took the vibrator and gently inserted the end of it into my sex. I exploded!

Again I gripped his head so tight with my legs that I almost smothered him. But he enjoyed every bit of me while mopping up my juices with his tongue. As for me, the pleasure was only beginning.

He put a condom on, slid me down to the edge of the bed, and lifted my legs up. His greedy mouth took sole possession of my love canal with his tender, hot, delicious lips. Already in a state of euphoria, I was enamored with the musky scent of his sweat and pleasantly startled when he slid his huge cock into my drenched love hole.

"Ohhhh! Ohhhh God! It's so big!" I screamed with joy. I couldn't take it all at once. Inch by inch, the deeply penetrating sensation of his cock filling me elicited passionate cries of pleasure.

"It ... it feels soooo good!" I purred with unwavering joy. The deeper he penetrated, the more I wanted to feel all of him.

"More! ... I want ALL of it!" I cried.

That unbelievable feeling of euphoria overtook me. He fucked my brains out! I was speechless and pleasantly surprised. But he wasn't finished.

"Only two orgasms, I can do better than that!" he bragged while turning me over and lifting my ass cheeks up with both hands.

He rammed his huge cock into my love tunnel, lifted one leg up, and penetrated me so deeply it felt like he was touching the top of my stomach. The sensation was a cross between intense pleasure and wanton pain. His cock was so huge; I feared and reveled in it at the same time. But the pain won out. I began to beg for a little relief. I couldn't take it all in that position. Suddenly he shifted his hips, withdrew just enough, and hit a spot that made me go wild.

"Oh God Tariq! Fuck me baby! Fuck me fast and hard!" I exclaimed.

"I'M CUMMING AGAIN!" I screamed at the top of my lungs. He happily obliged and fucked me so fast and hard that we both came together and passed out in each other's arms. There was a soft coziness of passion's aftermath that endured. I felt safe ... I felt loved.

Menu

Join Us for a Jammin' Jamaican Surprise
Birthday Celebration

featuring

APPETIZERS

MINI BEEF PATTIES WITH COCO BREAD

FRIED PLANTAINS • CODFISH CAKES

DINNER

ESCOVITCH RED SNAPPER

JERK CHICKEN

RED PEAS & RICE • FRIED DUMPLINGS

CALLALOO WITH ACKEE & SALTED CODFISH

DESSERT

ASSORTED MINI CAKE BOMBES & TORTES

COCONUT MACAROONS

FRESH EXOTIC FRUIT PLATTER

BEAUTY RITUAL

Bodacious Body collection of love elixirs and body treatments.

ENTERTAINMENT

Limbo contest; pool party: couples chicken fight, water volleyball,
and dodgeball.

24

A Proper Farewell

Tariq returned to San Francisco on a Sunday evening flight. Before he left, I wanted to make sure he had a wonderful send off. I was still feeling so much love from his impromptu visit that I decided to wake up early and make a nice picnic lunch before his departure. We packed the car and then set our blankets, grill, and picnic baskets at one of our favorite hidden spots in Schenley Park that overlooked downtown Pittsburgh. Things got so hot and heavy that we did everything but eat!

He loves Mediterranean food and I wanted to surprise him, so I prepared a light but filling rendition of his favorites. I quickly chopped, marinated, and skewered a couple of chicken breasts and thighs, and chopped up zucchini and an assortment of mushrooms to make chicken and vegetable kebabs to cook on my portable hibachi. Then I filled two bento boxes with a fresh herb and garlic chickpea salad topped with black beans, feta cheese, and wild rice to accompany the kebabs. I folded a few pieces of pita bread and wrapped them with plastic wrap on top of the boxes. For dessert I made four of Tariq's favorite mandarin chocolate cake pops with a crunchy almond topping and accompanied them with fresh mandarin orange slices and a bottle of chilled white moscato.

After we set up the picnic area we immediately put the kebabs on the grill to cook. Tariq inadvertently discovered the cake pops and couldn't stop nibbling on them. Then he started playfully feeding me the fruit and eating the cake off of my breasts. One thing led to another and he drew me in again. I couldn't resist him.

We quickly removed the food from the grill, pulled the blankets on top of us, and fucked like rabbits. We were encapsulated with an amazing feeling of joy and sensuality. Even though we had to keep ourselves covered, Tariq was very strategic in how he sat me on his lap to keep me comfortable while plunging his huge cock into my love canal.

Ripples of pleasure began to overtake my entire body. I couldn't contain my excitement. Need began to defy reason and our sultry mews grew louder and louder. Faster and faster, I matched his rhythm, then he gently slid a finger in my ass and I lost it again.

Molten waves of pleasure engulfed reason and forbade me from suppressing my cries of joy. He kissed me voraciously to suppress my screams as I convulsed with an intense orgasm.

"Oh God! I'm cumming!" he said in a whispering scream. He quickly pulled out and ejaculated so strong his semen shot up my belly, hit my breasts, and landed on my lips. I rubbed it all over my face and body and smiled.

"The best moisturizer in the world!" I quipped.

He laughed, kissed my breast, and playfully replied, "The best nourishment in the world too!"

The food was ready and waiting to feed the voracious appetites we'd worked up after a lovely morning in the park. It was light, delicious, and right on time. We cleaned ourselves up, finished eating, and packed the car to drive to the airport.

I dropped him at the departure gate and headed home to bathe and get ready for work the next day. I felt like I was glowing from both the inside and outside, and I didn't want that feeling to leave me. I savored the moment as long as I could. Just thinking about him made me excited.

The Shelter: Ashtley

I returned to work and even though I was ambivalent about taking the assignment, Lauren immediately assigned me to work on Ashtley's case. I felt like I had never gotten the opportunity to properly help Saturn and didn't want to be subjected to the same fate for Ashtley. But this time Evelyn assured me that she'd trust my decisions and back me up as necessary, so I agreed.

The ultimate goal was to counsel and prepare Ashtley for reunification with her mother. Disappointed that I didn't get the opportunity to help Saturn more, I really wanted to be able to help Ashtley. Early on it became clear to me that it wasn't going to be easy, but I convinced myself, whenever the going gets tough, to reminisce about the amazing birthday weekend and how fortunate I am. Reminiscing about things I enjoyed helped me to deal more effectively with the stress. It also aided in my attempt to avoid burnout so early in my career.

After further investigation into Ashtley's files, it turned out that her black father had abducted her from her white mother thirteen years earlier. Her father testified that he took her because he claimed he couldn't get a fair custody hearing and the courts wanted him to relinquish all of his parental rights without rationale. He took Ashtley and moved to Cleveland where he raised her unfettered until he remarried when she was eleven years old. She didn't like the new wife and started acting out and running away.

He divorced the wife a short time later but by then Ashtley had already met the boyfriend, Paul. When her father started censoring her activities, she ran away with Paul and that's how the whole move to Pittsburgh occurred. It was essentially an attempt by her father to get Ashtley away from the danger Paul presented after he finally found her.

The alleged abduction by her father was discovered as a result of Pennsylvania's recent linkage to the FBI's new missing person's database. This helped the police identify Ashtley when the other states failed to do so. As excited as we all were to have found one of the thousands of missing children alive, I knew the reunification with her mother wouldn't be easy for any of us.

According to the information I gleaned from Ashtley's file, her mother was a young, lower-middle-class white woman from a trailer park in southern Missouri, who got involved with her father, a middle-class black man. It was well documented that these types of relationships were frowned upon in the mother's family as well as the community.

Her father had relocated to Missouri from Pittsburgh to work as a production manager in the food company where her mother worked. They apparently got involved in a relationship, bore a child, and when they wanted to get married, her family forbade it and forced her to end the relationship.

As a baby, Ashtley apparently looked white enough to pass as a Caucasian baby according to her mother's testimony. Her mother's parents agreed to adopt and raise Ashtley as their child. But the contingency was that her mother had to get rid of the black father by any means necessary.

In contrast, Ashtley's father testified that he tried to get a fair hearing in court but shortly realized that the judge was the employer of the mother's father (Ashtley's grandfather). He soon realized that he couldn't get a fair trial in a white southern town. During the initial custody hearing, he quickly caught on to what they were trying to do. Shortly afterward, Ashtley's father took the baby and moved to Cleveland before they could relieve him of his rights to custody.

While reviewing the case files, I was surprised to learn that Ashtley's mother testified that although she reported the abduction to the police, she never searched for father or child and went on about her life as if they no longer existed. Again I found myself up against one of the worst societal illnesses that's pervaded American society and destroyed life and liberty for hundreds of years—prejudice. It had reared its ugly head again to destroy the love potentially shared between Ashtley's parents, and ultimately led to her becoming an innocent victim of its hideous circumstance. It became even clearer that I was fighting an uphill battle, but the situation somehow rang a familiar bell in my mind.

When it was confirmed that she'd been abducted, Ashtley was astonished. Her father had always told her that her mother was black and had died in childbirth. The most difficult task now was attempting to reunite her with a mother that she'd never known, or expected, and Ashtley didn't make it easy.

After Ashtley first introduced herself during the roundtable discussion many of the girls cried when they heard Ashtley's story. Regina and I were both touched and almost couldn't believe it until we read her file and discovered everything was true. As a result of her experiences Ashtley came to the shelter with scars. She was very feisty and oftentimes just plain mean, not only to the other girls and the counselors, but to her mother, too.

When the courts finally began to try to reunite Ashtley with her mother, the team of psychologists assigned to her case felt that gradual integration would be the best approach. But Ashtley rejected her mother first for not looking for her sooner and then for being white.

Frustrated by what one psychologist determined was her oft-cited cultural confusion, Ashtley yelled and chastised her mother in one of the face-to-face counseling sessions. She said she often couldn't figure out why the rest of the family was so dark and she looked like she was white. She'd taken a lot of criticism from her family and the public for being what she thought was an unexplainable difference and blamed her mother for the pain and rejection she'd suffered.

Although much of that confusion seemed to be clearing up for Ashtley, she was still having a difficult time communicating with, and accepting, her mother. In response, the court set up biweekly face-to-face visits, paid to fly her mother to Pittsburgh twice a month, and mandated video conference calls three times a week for three months. The objective was to allow Ashtley to get to know her mother better before returning custody and sending her back to Missouri. I had my work cut out for me.

After weeks of counseling while trying to keep up with the other girls in the shelter so they didn't feel neglected, we finally got a breakthrough when the judge allowed Ashtley to visit her father at the jail after my fifth request. Ashtley was confused about why her father was incarcerated but the judge obliged us to allow her father to explain the situation so she'd hear the reason directly from him.

We were instructed to have Ashtley at the Allegheny County jail for an 8:00 a.m. visit with her father to avoid the regular visitors. The goal was to avoid the media and the notoriety that followed the case.

Ashtley had become sort of a celebrity and her father a villain. After initially forbidding her to see her father, the judge finally realized there was another side to the story based on the father's testimony. In the meantime, Ashtley was begging to see him. After the family therapist and I pleaded for Ashtley to have the opportunity to talk to her father, the judge finally agreed but wanted to avoid the ongoing scrutiny the case was receiving from the local media.

I arrived to work at 6:00 a.m. on the morning of the visit to pick Ashtley up for the visit to the jail. She was still a bit feisty but compliant because she was getting what she wanted. The judge's order also mandated that the social worker was to stay in the room during the visit. My job was to collect additional information on the case and again I was shocked and awed by what I witnessed.

Her father reiterated the story of how he was in love and wanted to marry her mother but the mother's family was very racist and forbade it. He confessed that he'd taken Ashtley from the mother to protect her because he knew they were trying to erase him from her and her mother's life. He didn't believe they'd treat her right, nor allow him to visit his child.

He went further to say that the pain was too much for him to bear. The outright rejection of his love for her mother had sent him into a deep depression. To end his suffering and reduce the chances of Ashtley suffering, he told her that her mother died so she would never want to look for her. He and Ashtley both began to weep inconsolably. It struck a heavy chord with me and I now understood why it rang a familiar bell in my mind. All I could think about was how I could have possibly faced the same situation if I'd gotten pregnant by Chris and he and his family rejected the baby and me. "But for the grace of God!" I thought to myself. I felt like I had potentially dodged a bullet, and I was seeing the potential consequences right before my eyes. It was a daunting moment of revelation for me. But there was a more rewarding side to the story

At that moment, Ashtley's father got to hold his child for the first time in three months. It was akin to watching the father of a newborn nurture a crying baby. Ashtley kept apologizing for running away and causing her father to go to jail. She said she'd been asked to do some horrible things and knew he didn't raise her like that. So she was very relieved when he rescued her this last time.

He asked what happened to her when she was on the run and she began to elaborate. "The first few times I went out with my boyfriend, Paul, he was so cool. We always went to eat and he paid for everything. We went to the movies and the beach and to all kinds of places—he made me feel so special." She began recounting her experience with elation.

"After you married Godzilla" she said with angst about her former stepmother, "I felt like you didn't have time for me. He did. But he turned into a different person after I ran away with him," she said while rolling her eyes. I sat quietly in the corner and waited for her to drop the bomb. It was almost like I knew what was coming. I had already heard a similar story from Saturn and many other girls.

"Paul kept telling me I'd have to carry my own weight, whatever that means. I didn't know what he meant until one day we were down at the pier and I saw a guy hand him some drugs. Then the jerk kept gawking at me like I was a piece of meat. Paul assured me it would be okay to take a walk with him, but when I refused, Paul forced me to go with him," she lamented.

"Here it comes!" I thought to myself. It was an established pattern with most of the girls that came to the shelter from the streets—sex trafficking.

"First he grabbed my ass and I told him to get the fuck off me. But he just shoved me to the ground, put his knees on my arms, and shoved his dick in my mouth. I bit him! When he screamed, Paul came running and told me again that I had to pull my own weight … to just suck his dick. But I refused!" Her eyes were glassy and began to tear up again.

"Then the jerk pulled out a gun. He said he still needed me to make good on his payment. Paul forced me to suck his dick and threatened that he'd let him fuck me in the ass if I didn't. I was scared to death. I did what he said and prayed to be rescued. But nobody came," she said as she started weeping. In the meantime her father was seething mad. But she wasn't finished.

"That's when I wanted to come home, but Paul told me you didn't want me anymore. He said you had a new family and that's why you didn't come looking for me. Then he really scared me when he said I was a runaway and prostitute now, and if the police caught up with me, they would lock me up." Now she was weeping inconsolably.

Painfully weeping with her, her father could barely get his words out. "I took you from your mother because I wanted to protect you. I'm so sorry—I failed," he said. Deeply in angst from his inability to ultimately protect his child, his tears flowed relentlessly.

"I was so confused. I didn't know what to do!" she shouted with disgust. "I didn't have any money, I had run away from home, and I trusted Paul," she said with remorse.

"It's okay honey. You're gonna be fine now!" her father said as he tried to reassure her that she was safe now. "I'm so sorry I couldn't protect you. You have always been the center of my world and I let you down," he said as he continued to weep with apologetic sorrow.

"But it gets worse!" Ashtley exclaimed. "Paul threatened to kill me if I didn't agree to repay him all the money he supposedly spent on me. Then he forced me to have sex with men for drugs and money. When I told him you'd eventually look for me, he threatened to kill you!" she painfully recounted.

Her face was fraught with pain. Tears streamed endlessly. Her dress and the table were drenched with the tears of both Ashtley and her father. I had to wipe my eyes several times while trying to keep my composure.

I was not only lamenting their situation but the fact that her parents were unable to truly share their love as a result of other people's prejudices—I internally recognized it as a manifestation of the tumultuous relationship I had with Chris. It was daunting to watch the consequences continue to play out.

On the other hand, the reunion confirmed my premonition that the only person who could get Ashtley to behave was her father. I also knew from reading the file and interviewing all the parties that her father was a victim too—and I had every intention of sharing my entire finding with the judge. However there was another more pressing issue revealed during the visit and I had to notify my boss and the judge immediately.

Her father's life was now being threatened because Paul was in the same jail. Ashtley's confession wasn't over yet and she continued to tell everything.

"When you finally found me, Paul was trying to convince me to do a porn video with some other prostitutes. He gave me weed and bought me new clothes to try and persuade me. But I'm not goin' lie, I was scared to death! I was praying for God to send anyone to help me. When you found me and brought me to Pittsburgh, I was afraid he'd either kill you or both of us. Then when he found us again, I decided to act like I didn't want to stay with you. But believe me, I was sooooo relieved he crashed the car and I got away again," she said as she exhaled with relief, as if she felt assured the situation was nearly over.

After the visit with her father, Ashtley was more cooperative in her counseling sessions and her family began to fall in place. Kidnapping charges were dropped against her father and he was promptly released from jail without harm. Her mother refused to press charges and the judge hadn't formally executed the custody agreement. So technically Ashtley's father still maintained custody and his lawyers successfully argued that there was no real violation.

Her parents finally talked after thirteen long years and agreed to legally share custody of Ashtley. Because her father raised her, the custody arrangement was made for her to spend the school year in Pittsburgh with him and the summers and alternating holidays with her mother in Missouri.

Ashtley's case was one for the record books. The media attention kept her story in the news for weeks. It was truly miraculous that we managed to successfully reunite her with both her parents and to bring reconciliation to the entire family. I also learned a great deal about the profound effects of prejudice and how succumbing to other people's expectations for your personal happiness can devastate and often destroy lives.

I received commendations from both the judge and my agency for my methodology to reunify the family, and the courts later decided to use Ashtley's case as a model for best practices. In line with my methodology, they hypothesized that whenever possible, it's in the best interest of the children to try and reunite them with both parents through counseling and a parental safety net system like the one put in place by my agency.

"Case closed and job well done!" I said to myself. Then I gave myself a gentle pat on the back.

On the way home from the awards ceremony, I began to think more about my tumultuous relationship with Chris and the impending situation. I decided to give him a call. After I shared the details, he congratulated me on my accomplishments and insisted on taking me to lunch. At first I didn't respond because I couldn't let him get away with what he'd done to me so easily.

He quickly realized why I was giving him the silent treatment and then apologized for his outburst at my birthday party. He also promised to behave himself, so I agreed to meet him for lunch soon.

Menu

Join Us for a Romantic Picnic for Two
featuring

LUNCH

Marinated Chicken Kebabs
with a seasoned vegetable assortment

Fresh Herb & Garlic Chickpea Salad
topped with black beans, feta cheese, and wild rice

Pita Bread

BEVERAGE

Moscato Wine

DESSERT

Mandarin Chocolate Cake Pops
with crunchy almond topping

Fresh Mandarin Orange Slices

25

The College Crew: Chris

I t was a fancy free, tepid Saturday in the early fall, and I was scheduled to meet Chris for lunch. I put on a cute little burgundy print jumpsuit, grabbed a light sweater, and met him at my favorite Thai restaurant. He tried to kiss me but I abruptly reminded him of his promise to behave himself. He apologized and pulled the seat out for me to sit down.

I subsequently apologized for kicking him in the ass as he left my party. Then I forcefully reminded him that I took no shit from guys who feel it's okay to hit or even push girls.

"Now Chris, you've known me for a long time. By now I would think you also know that I don't tolerate men putting their hands on me," I said as I playfully, but firmly, punched him in the arm.

"You're right, Anais. I do know that you take no shit! So first, please let me apologize for inadvertently pushing you. I have too much respect for you to ever put my hands on you, except when I'm making love to you that is," he smiled, looked me directly in the eyes, and licked his lips.

I didn't want to provoke him, so I didn't respond verbally. Instead, I put one hand on my chin while resting one finger on my lips to indicate that I wouldn't respond to his provocation, and continued to listen.

"I pushed you by mistake, and for that I am truly sorry. But I've got to say, I was impressed with the asshole's efforts to protect you. I realized he really admires and respects you. So please express my apologies to him as well," he quipped with sincerity.

I chastised him for calling Tariq an asshole again, and agreed to pass on his apology. We talked in depth about our extremely sensual but torrid two-year love affair while dining on a delicious and authentic Thai soup, appetizers, rice noodles, and an incredible dessert.

We started with appetizers—for Chris, chicken satay, marinated and grilled skewers of pounded chicken served with a delicious peanut dipping sauce and cucumber salad. I chose *tom kha gai* soup—a creamy coconut, lime, and galangal (mild ginger) chicken soup with fresh vegetables and sliced chicken. For the main course, Chris enjoyed pad Thai—a traditional Thai rice noodle dish made with a sweet and tangy sauce, shrimp, chicken and topped with chopped peanuts and fresh bean sprouts. I ordered my favorite, *pad see ew*—a rice noodle dish stir-fried with roast pork, vegetables, and a tamarind chili sauce. We both sipped on a fragrant and fruity dragon pearl green tea and shared coconut sticky rice with fresh mangoes for dessert.

The meal was relaxing and delicious, which allowed us time to go back and forth about why the relationship was only successful in the bedroom. I took this time as an opportunity to tell him what I'd experienced throughout Ashtley's case. We both sat silent while processing it for several minutes. It was as if we'd both been slapped in the face with what could have been a daunting reality. Then he broke the silence by sliding in the fact that he'd recently started dating one of his sister's friends. Even though I felt like he was still letting his family control his life, I told him I was happy for him. I didn't ever want to feel like I'd relinquished my happiness to someone else's prejudice, but I was growing my relationship with Tariq and wanted to move on with my life.

By the time the warm, coconut sticky rice with fresh mango slices arrived for dessert, we had come to a consensus that we were both probably better off with other people. Before leaving the restaurant we agreed to maintain our relationship solely as friends and to share the decision with our crew at the next SNL scheduled for the following Saturday.

Menu

Join Us for an Exotic Thai Lunch

featuring

APPETIZERS

CHICKEN SATAY
grilled chicken strips with peanut dipping sauce

TOM KHA GAI SOUP
coconut, ginger, and lime chicken soup

LUNCH

PAD THAI
shrimp and chicken rice noodle stir-fry

PAD SEE EW
rice noodles in a tamarind chili sauce with vegetables and roast pork

BEVERAGE

DRAGON PEARL GREEN TEA

DESSERT

COCONUT STICKY RICE
with fresh mango

Saturday Night Live: Halloween Edition

Mark B was hosting the SNL celebration and I agreed to cook as usual. It was late in October and we always hosted a Halloween party—this year would be no different. The crew agreed that it should be a masquerade. Therefore everyone was obliged to wear a unique face mask and then unmask something new about themselves during the traditional roundtable discussion.

"This is going to be interesting," I thought.

Mark B's two-bedroom apartment wasn't very large, but it was big enough for us to move a few things around. My philosophy is that we can party anywhere at any time. After all, it's the people that truly make the party and the food that brings the love.

With that in mind, we set up an elegant small-plate buffet on one round table, a drink buffet on another round table, and created a spacious dance floor in the living room. The deck in the backyard comfortably facilitated seating for at least twenty people, so we utilized it to serve dessert and to close out the evening with a griot storytelling time.

I created a finger-licking small plates buffet to make it easier for everyone to eat without destroying the costumes. The dinner menu was hardy, flavorful, and well suited for the occasion: Crispy Cabbage Rolls—a slight twist on the traditional dish by steaming the ground beef and rice mixture in cabbage leaves and then wrapping and frying them in spring roll skins; my famous wild and crazy buffalo chicken wings with three different sauces; creamy risotto shots with portobello mushrooms; grilled asparagus, fried zucchini noodles and lemon pepper shrimp pops served with lemon butter sauce; and cheesy bruschetta bites topped with heirloom tomatoes and garlicky greens.

I used heavy-duty, clear plastic hors d'oeuvre plates and filled them with three to four pieces of each menu item to be sure everyone got to taste everything. I made extra of each dish and left these in the kitchen so anyone could go back for seconds or continue noshing throughout the evening.

Dancing was the unanimous choice for the first of the evening's entertainment. Mark B and Rafi created an upbeat, sometimes creepy, playlist filled with line dances, booty shaking, and even square dances so everyone could enjoy the night without having to know how to dance well. They even streamed an overhead projection onto a wall to accompany the music so everyone could follow the line dances from the videos. It was really cool!

We glided to the Electric Slide, some of us not so gracefully, jokingly shot arrows at each other's missed steps during the Cupid Shuffle, and went ghoulishly crazy when Michael Jackson's "Thriller" video played. After a few Jell-O shots, everybody lost their rhythm. We had an amazing time.

The small plates buffet allowed everyone to nibble and indulge at their own leisure throughout the evening. After we danced off the delicious morsels, we wound the night down with dessert, hot toddies, and warm wine on the deck, which led into our customary roundtable discussion and griot storytelling session.

In keeping with the spirit of Halloween, I made three ghoulishly delicious desserts and placed one of each on each plate. First up, ghoulish chocolate, banana, and raspberry parfaits topped with whipped cream, and bleeding chocolate eyeballs made with the raspberry coulis. The second dessert was red velvet ladybug treats coated with fondant and filled with blackened cream cheese. The third ghoulish dessert was carrot cake earthworms—a tasty combination of smashed and coated carrot cake rolled in cream cheese frosting and covered with chopped walnuts and orange sprinkles.

After virtually inhaling his dessert and gulping down three cups of hot wine, Mark B's best friend Greg was quite comfortable and decided to start the conversation. The rules suggest that each person has to reveal something new about his or her life through the storytelling. Greg suggested we roll dice and the person with the lowest number should go first, then each progressive number should proceed from there.

He threw a two on the dice. It was the lowest number. He pulled off his mask and just blurted it out.

"I like men! I'm *gayyyyy!*" he exclaimed in an inebriated slur. Mark B turned twelve shades of red but it appeared that nobody else was surprised.

In fact, most people already suspected it. Rafi, however, was gobsmacked. His jaw dropped. They'd been friends for five years and apparently he didn't have a clue. After he finally closed his mouth, he pulled off his mask. With his deepest cockney accent, he seemed to chastise Greg.

"I really don't understand what that means. Why have you made that choice," he said to Greg in a puzzled voice. "Have you ever tasted the alluring heat and molten sweet chocolate of a woman? Experienced the tinkling sensation that engulfs your body from her velvety touch when the apex of her legs are wrapped around your body?! ... My brother! Have you ever felt that soft, warm, and juicy secret garden that drives a man freakin crazy?" he quipped as he got louder and more boisterous.

"No!" Greg quietly responded.

"Well I'll tell you what, after you've stuck your fuckin dick in that amazing place, talk to me!" he shouted. "If after that you don't feel different, I'll believe you're gay," Rafi exclaimed and challenged Greg. I was taken aback by Rafi's response, but everyone else started with the oohs and awhs and laughed hysterically.

Greg, however, was very attentive to Rafi's concerns but he would not be so easily shaken. He calmly responded to Rafi's request with one of his own. "Okay my brother, I'll try a woman … if you try a man," he quipped.

A roar of disbelief and laughter overtook the place again. Rafi got just what he was asking for. He fell out laughing too and quickly responded. "Not a chance in fucking hell my brother! You've cured me," he exclaimed in laughter. "I will never, I repeat, never bother you again. But either way, I will always love and respect you like my brother as usual," he humbly followed.

It was a hilarious, but an important bonding moment. Rafi made it clear that Greg's sexuality didn't define their friendship and broke down a secretive wall. One that Greg had apparently cloaked himself in for quite some time. It almost seemed like everyone else felt like the mood had lightened up and it was safe to say anything you wanted, including me.

I went next. I announced the decision for Chris and me to officially end our nearly two-year torrid love affair. I prefaced it by sharing my experience with Ashtley's parents, and my fear of potentially being subject to the same fate. Even though they empathized with me, everyone was skeptical as expected but respected our decision. In response to their skepticism, I felt compelled to further justify my decision.

"I've always been taught to love fiercely, forgive quickly, and to let go of what doesn't make me happy. But I've clearly had a problem with letting go of something that wasn't making me happy for nearly two years. After falling deeply in love and then being continually disappointed and heartbroken, I realized that you can't force a person to respect you. However, you can refuse to be disrespected. That's how I realized I had to let go of the relationship to be true to who I am. Because there's no way I would risk bringing a child into a world of prejudice that I already know exists in their own family. It just would not be fair to the child," I said with resolve.

Chris was disappointed that I'd put our business out like that but clearly resolved with the reality of what he feared all along about the rejection of our relationship by his family. He was itching to say something, so I gave the floor to him.

"Everyone says love hurts, but that's not true. I've learned that loneliness hurts, rejection hurts, and in this case losing someone I love and trust very much really hurts. I truly love you Anais. But I'm willing to admit that circumstances beyond my control won't allow me to love you the way you need to be loved," he said as he looked at me and began to tear up.

Greg, who rarely attends SNL, and wasn't privy to the inner workings of our relationship, was now raring to talk and challenged Chris.

"If you truly love this woman, I don't understand the problem. True love may only come around once in a lifetime, and if you don't seize it while you've got it, it may never visit you again," he said in an emotional rant.

Greg seemed to be trying to make a point not only to Chris but to the whole crew. Everyone picked up on it and affirmed his statement by shaking their heads in agreement.

Chris was on the hot seat again. Somehow I think I was, too. But I couldn't nor didn't want to save him, and neither did anyone else. We all eagerly awaited his response.

It finally came with a controversial confession that opened a Pandora's box. Although I had already known the reason, he reluctantly revealed to the group that his family's expectation for him was to marry within his culture or at the very least, a white girl. He defended his decision to comply by citing their threat of disowning him, and he said he could never think about bringing his wife and children into such a hostile environment. He didn't want to be alienated from his family and said he just couldn't imagine himself in that situation. Rafi challenged his decision and called it preposterous and insulting.

"It's amazing to me how a family of immigrants can come to a country for change, yet discriminate against anyone who isn't like them. It also amazes me how anything that may take them the slightest bit out of their comfort zones is unacceptable. It's a shame and almost embarrassing," Rafi lamented.

As usual Chris fell silent. Greg, however, wouldn't let it go.

"Love, is Love, is Love!" he exclaimed. "And if your family loves you, they should be willing to allow you to be happy … to be with the person you truly love," Greg said as his emotions began to get the best of him. He started crying.

Everyone agreed with Greg. But Chris didn't know how to respond and simply sat in silence.

Again I said nothing. I had already decided the relationship was over and didn't want to revisit the situation. But I was extremely happy Chris was getting a tongue-lashing. Secretly I'd hoped that one of his siblings would end up marrying someone from another culture or race and he would have to watch their happiness with envy. But that was the not so nice side of my persona; I just had to force myself to chalk the whole relationship up to experience and move on.

The whole room got silent. Everyone seemed to stop in time to digest what had just happened … to think about their own lives. I, however, was exhausted with talking about the relationship. I was sure it was time to move on, so I abruptly shouted, "Next confession please!"

My cries seemed to awaken everyone from a drunken stupor. Even though the drama-filled relationship between Chris and me seemed to always take center stage at SNL, coming out of the closet seemed to be the theme of this particular evening.

Regina picked up on my desire to squash the conversation about the relationship and winked at me in agreement before taking over. I winked back to indicate my gratitude. However, I had a visceral feeling that there was something she was going to surprise us with.

I began to think about her strange response when Greg made his initial confession. Although she eventually laughed with everyone else, I inadvertently noticed that she seemed a bit taken aback at first. I didn't really process it until she started her confession.

She introduced Evelyn again, but this time as her girlfriend. Mark B didn't get it initially and questioned her. "Isn't she everybody's girlfriend? What do you mean by 'Girlfriend!?'" He quipped sarcastically.

"I mean we're lovers!" Regina blurted out. Then she passionately kissed Evelyn in front of everyone.

I was flabbergasted. I sensed that Regina had begun to talk more and more affectionately about Evelyn, but I didn't really see the intimacy coming. Besides, she was always chasing Mark B and everyone else's men. Just like Rafi, I was clueless.

Mark B, however, seemed not only confounded, but angry. He abruptly took over the conversation and left everyone wondering when and how Regina made this new discovery about herself.

He started out by talking about how politics makes for strange bedfellows. Initially no one understood what he meant, but he began to elaborate on his family's staunch conservative values and how he couldn't just make controversial decisions that would hurt them.

Greg abruptly interrupted and let him know that he's no different than Chris, which seemed to give Chris a little comfort. But we were all still confused about where he was going with the conversation.

He continued with a long-winded discussion about how he had been fortunate during his teenage years thanks to his parents' political connections and if it weren't for them he probably would be in jail.

When everyone began to question what he meant, he gave an example of how his parents' political connections have kept him out of trouble on more than one occasion. He talked about how certain people have their own way of communicating by donating to support their own politicians and then cashing in on favors when they need help around the law.

"For example, I used to get tickets for driving under the influence when I was in high school. The first thing my dad would do is research to see which judge was assigned to the case and somehow get this person to fix the tickets. I never got points or lost my license when I probably shouldn't have even been driving," he said.

Everyone began to ask him why he'd gotten so many tickets. He said he didn't know, but what he did know was that he just wasn't happy with who he was.

Then Sheila decided to chime in and make things even more confusing. First she concurred with Mark B's philosophy that politics make strange bedfellows. Then she began to talk about her parents, who own a construction sign company and are also staunch conservatives. She said her parents keep a line item in their budgets to donate to specific politicians so they can get help with winning contracts to provide road signs for the state roads.

Mark B protested, "Damn Sheila! My parents don't buy politicians! They just know how to work the system." He said it like her family's infractions were worse than his. The truth was that they were both breaking the law.

By this time Chantelle was livid. She lashed out and was almost in tears as she spoke about how her grandmother continually fought against discrimination and favoritism in the city's politics. Her grandmother owned a small catering company and fed hungry children in summer and afterschool programs.

Chantelle's grandmother was also a community activist who not only represented the people but also took care of their needs as best she could. Chantelle recalled numerous instances of how her grandmother was just trying to feed kids in poor communities throughout the city and hit brick walls when she tried to get help from the city government.

According to her, an enormous number of children were going hungry in the state of Pennsylvania. The city and state governments offered grants to feed the kids but there was still a hunger crisis. It was unclear to everyone why the government would budget monies for feeding children and then make it difficult for people to help feed them.

To help mitigate the hunger crisis, her grandmother attempted to tap in to the funds available to help with feeding the kids. She said that when she contacted the city to help her access the funds, they'd encourage her to submit bids to help them win the state contracts and then never reward her any of the funds. So they'd essentially "steal" her proposals and never give her the contracts. Instead of getting much needed help from the powers that be, they'd try to stop her.

Chantelle's grandmother eventually decided to submit her proposal directly to the state department of education to become a food vendor. When she finally got a contract, the state workers were so punitive and corrupt that she almost lost everything. They obliged her to sign a contract to provide the food for the kids and then found every reason not to reimburse her company for the funds they'd spent.

Chantelle said the straw that broke the camel's back was during a summer feeding program when her grandmother's company was in the second year of a service contract from the state to feed nearly two thousand kids a day. After she signed the contract, the state workers refused to give them an advance payment, which was the standard operating procedure. As a result, they were forced to use their company's personal funds to honor the contract and to ensure the kids were fed. The contract was also designed to provide monthly reimbursements for the meals fed to allow the company to replenish the funds and continue the feeding program. To further deter them, instead of honoring the contract as they did throughout the previous operating year, the state workers found every reason to refuse release of the payments and held their funds for nearly six months. That nearly caused her to shut down and stop feeding the kids.

In order to avoid paying her the reimbursements, the city and the state workers sent out monitors who harassed her workers throughout the entire program. Then they refused to pay nearly twenty-thousand dollars in reimbursements for feeding the kids. She had to abandon the program and take out loans to repay the debts incurred from feeding the kids under the state program. She didn't have the political connections like Mark B and Sheila's parents had and as a result the kids continued to go hungry while she fought bankruptcy.

Chantelle was heartbroken. She said the discrimination that she and her grandma experienced while just trying to feed starving kids was profound and still exists today. She recognized Mark B and Sheila's confessions as a manifestation of how corrupt the government is—it now became clearer to her why her grandmother wasn't getting the contracts. She considered Mark B and Sheila's families' motives as an example of how the system worked against the needy to satisfy the whims of the greedy and well connected. She wasn't a happy camper.

Rafi loved Chantelle and couldn't bear to see her suffering. A heated discussion ensued about corruption in government and the political system. It climaxed with Rafi's denigration of the American legal system, which became quite controversial.

"Wow! These people are full of shit if what everyone is saying is true. Every country has problems with hunger, but the fact that the people who profess to want to eradicate it are the same ones that are perpetuating it should be criminal. It's just plain wrong and when it's discovered, they should be held accountable and put in jail by the very people they starved. As regards pay for play in politics, like in the situation with Mark B and Sheila's parents, all I can say to that is that my father is a barrister in the British court system, and he'd never even think of fixing a ticket or cashing in on a political favor for a donation for anyone. I believe the system is too damn sophisticated to let anyone get away with something so elementary," he chided.

The conversation became an almost embarrassing situation for everyone because no one really wanted to confront the reality of how our political system worked, or not. Everyone just fell silent, again.

Mark B, however, took the silence as an opportunity to continue his confession. "Yeah, I love my country, but it does have significant faults. I know this might seem harsh and I don't necessarily agree with it, but it is what it is," he said.

Then he completely changed the subject and began talking about growing up and being confused about his relationships. This confusion would lead to him drinking and ultimately getting into trouble with drunk driving and crashing cars.

"For some reason, whenever a girl tried to get close to me, I'd usually pull away or just stop talking to her altogether. I lost a lot of friends," he said.

He didn't know why, but said he never allowed himself to get too emotionally invested in anyone. Even though he always played the role of a popular athlete, prom king, and scholar, something didn't seem right. I began to get that visceral feeling again. I felt like he was hiding something. I was right.

He concluded his long confession by telling us that when he came to college he found himself at home. Then he reached across the table, passionately kissed Greg, and said he's been in love with Greg for three years. He was too afraid to come out for fear of ruining his relationship with his parents, his siblings, and anyone else who had expectations of him.

When he almost lost his life in a drunk driving accident at sixteen, he knew he couldn't continue drinking to suppress his emotions. Becoming an overachiever was his way of compensating for suppressing his emotions. He later found comfort in working with kids to try and help them with similar issues.

Again everyone fell silent. All of a sudden Regina stood up and slapped the shit out of Mark B. She began shouting, "You mother fucker! I knew you and Greg were a little too close when we were together. I'll bet you fucked him better than you fucked me!" she screamed.

Mark B said nothing. He was extremely embarrassed.

Greg, however, had finally received the long-awaited commitment from his lover. He quickly moved to the rescue of Mark B. "Grow up! And stop acting like a fucking bitch!" he yelled at Regina as he jumped out of his seat.

Everyone was stunned but still a bit confused. We weren't sure what Regina meant by the three of them being together. She quickly cleared it up though. The confessions were being rattled off like shit hitting the fan. Regina confessed that she'd inadvertently had a threesome with Mark B and Greg after a long night of drinking after work.

Unbeknownst to me or anyone else in the room, except Mark B and Greg that is, Regina initially worked at the boys' shelter where she met Mark B before transferring to the girls' shelter. One thing led to another and she ended up in a tryst with Mark B and Greg, and she was still attracted to Mark B. However she didn't realize he was really intimately involved with Greg until his confession.

Mark B said he finally felt comfortable enough to come out and tell the crew after Greg and Regina's confessions. "After all, what the hell do I have to lose now?!" he exclaimed.

The evening turned out to be a true manifestation of how prejudice and discrimination have a profound impact on the happiness and livelihoods of the most vulnerable people. Even though the conversation diverted a bit, it became a clear demonstration of how those same prejudices can and did lead to the degradation of society as a whole.

I was startled the most by Chantelle's family experience and how the resultant discrimination, i.e. prejudice, was so profound that children were left hungry as a result of people playing on their power while supposedly working for the government. My faith in the very government that I worked for was now shaken by that poisonous concept. I came to the conclusion that prejudice is a revelatory poison that impacted Ashtley and her family, Chris and me, and even the hungry children who didn't have the political connections and weren't able to pay for play with the government workers or politicians. I think we all began to think about some kind of revolt and a desire for change after all the confessions.

Menu

*Join Us for a Masked Halloween Howling
and Noshing Soiree*

featuring

HORS D'OEUVRES

CRISPY CABBAGE ROLLS
*ground beef and rice wrapped in cabbage leaves and fried in spring
roll skins*

WILD & CRAZY WINGS THREE WAYS
*traditional buffalo; bubblin' brown sugar mustard; and spicy
Thai peanut*

CREAMY RISOTTO SHOTS
with caramelized onions and portobello mushrooms

LEMON PEPPER SHRIMP TREE
with crispy zucchini noodles

CHEESY BRUSCHETTA BITES
with roasted heirloom tomatoes

ASPARAGUS POPS

menu continues ...

Menu

BEVERAGES

ASSORTED RED & WHITE WINES

MICRO-BREWERY BEER COLLECTION

JELL-O SHOTS

ASSORTED HOT TODDIES
including hot wine and buttered apple cider

STILL & SPARKLING WATER

DESSERT

GHOULISH BANANA, CHOCOLATE, &
RASPBERRY PARFAITS

RED VELVET LADYBUGS

CARROT CAKE EARTHWORMS

ENTERTAINMENT

Dancing and the Griot: storytelling.

26

Thanksgiving Preparations

Despite the undeniable tension after a rather interesting and revealing evening, we ended it by finalizing plans for our first annual Thanksgiving Give Back at the shelter. Mark B and I had previously suggested we host a special collaborative Thanksgiving SNL celebration for the youth and staff at both of our shelters this year. Everyone agreed with our decision and donated funds for the food, activities, and special gifts to honor the shelters' staffs.

Mark B and Leila were designated coordinators for the boys' shelter, and Regina and I took responsibilities for the girls' shelter. Leila, however, was due to give birth at any moment so we were all on baby watch and tried to lighten her load.

The shelters' directors had already given us permission to sponsor the party and to engage the kids in the preparations for hosting the event. Since we'd received the green light, we moved forward with planning.

The executive director of the shelters allowed us to choose the venue from their collection of community-based group homes as long as we included all of the residents. The choice was easy. We only planned for both of our respective shelters to participate. Therefore everyone agreed it was best to host it at the girls' shelter because it was nicer and large enough to hold everyone. Also, the land surrounding the shelter was filled with apple and pear trees ripe for picking and the outdoor accommodations were beautifully appointed with rustic seating areas and an oversize fire pit.

Lauren, our supervisor, was very excited and appreciative of our decision to sponsor the event at the girls' shelter. She allowed Regina and me to adjust our schedules to accommodate preparations on-site, which was very instrumental to getting all of the logistics to work well. Preparations started in the beginning of November, and we planned for an exciting celebration of delicious food, exciting games, beautiful decorations, and gifts created by and for the kids.

We also planned for lots of entertainment to keep the kids busy and out of trouble. Karaoke, a talent show and rap/poetry contest, and a barn fire and marshmallow roast were strategically programmed throughout the evening. I also included a game of "Jive Turkey"—a spin-off of dirty bingo and one of my family's favorite holiday games. It would allow everyone to win a gift to take home at the end of the evening. It was even more exciting because the game dictated that the overall winner would get to take whatever this person wanted from anyone else's collection, including the food.

The kids made decorations and a variety of treats for gifts during their daily free time in the evenings. It kept them occupied and was great for engaging them as active participants in the Thanksgiving Give Back celebration. The goal was to get buy-in from the kids and it worked well.

Regina and I worked the overnight shifts on the Thursday and Friday before the celebration in order to prepare the food on-site with the permission and blessings of Ms. Nellie. We anticipated at least fifty people and had a very large menu to prepare. We prepped all of the meats in advance, prepared the side dishes with the kids' help during their downtime, and planned to make the desserts on the Saturday morning of the event.

When the boys came to help with set up on Friday evening, the shelter seemed like a dichotomy of two worlds. On the one hand, we had a group of what could have been wayward young girls and guys who seemed to have been abandoned by their families. On the other hand, everyone was working harmoniously to decorate the shelter and prepare for the celebration and that made the atmosphere feel like one big happy family setting up for a typical holiday party. Just the idea of the party seemed to inspire the kids to move beyond their circumstances, and they had a great time doing it.

After a quick bento box dinner of assorted sandwiches, coleslaw, and chips Evelyn helped the kids gather apples from the trees on the shelter's property. They used them to make a variety of red and green candied and caramel apples dipped in an assortment of nuts, nonpareils, and small candies. We planned to give them out as thank-you gifts at the end of the celebration.

They wrapped the apples in cellophane, tied beautiful ribbons with handwritten thank-you notes around the sticks, and made beautiful centerpieces for the tables by sticking the apples into foam balls covered in green foil. It was a great feeling to see the kids in a joyful environment without anyone bickering and everyone enjoying the celebration like one big family.

While they made the candied apples, Evelyn took the opportunity to ask the kids to talk about what they were most thankful for. After all, it was a celebration. Most of the kids said they were thankful that someone cared enough to make sure they had a great meal for the holiday. A couple of the kids really poured their hearts out.

Many of them knew Corry and Darlese from their extensive residencies in the shelter system and they gossiped relentlessly about the situation. One of Mark B's boys spoke very profoundly about how thankful he was that he wasn't out on the streets like Corry. He also talked about how sorry he was for Darlese because her baby's father was nowhere to be found.

That comment stirred up the whole group. They went back and forth about whether or not Corry fathered the baby. But Evelyn quickly squashed the conversation with her offer of everyone enjoying Ms. Nellie's special ice cream sandwiches for dessert before the boys had to return to their shelter for the evening.

Ms. Nellie used her favorite Just Add Water Happy Cake kits to create a variety of delicious frozen cake-based ice cream sandwich desserts. They were decadent, beautifully wrapped in cellophane bags, and appeared to have taken a lot of time to make. She assured us that they were very simple and everything but the fillings were part of the cake mix kits. They were delicious.

She used the chocolate mandarin cake mix to make round sandwiches filled with an orange sherbet and vanilla ice cream mixture and coated some of them with chopped almonds. The walnut toffee banana bread mix was used to create rectangular sandwiches filled with vanilla ice cream, and half were dipped in dark chocolate and coated with a crushed walnut toffee. The red velvet cake mix was used to create round sandwiches filled with chocolate ice cream and coated with crushed pecans. And finally she used the Amazon Lemon Crunch cake mix to create delicate rectangular lemon bars filled with a mixture of lemon sherbet and vanilla ice cream, and coated them with a roasted Brazil nut brittle.

They weren't your average ice cream sandwiches, but they were pretty and delicious. We all shared and enjoyed the variety of different flavors before the evening's sendoff. Even though the flavors were unusual, the kids really seemed to enjoy them and we all appreciated Ms. Nellie's surprise.

Menu

Join Us for Quick Fix Bento Box Dining
featuring

DINNER

Bento Box Sandwiches

Maple Ham and Cheddar

Provolone and Turkey

Roasted Portobellos with Mozzarella and Red Pepper Sauce

Hummus and Feta Wraps with Chickpea Salad

Assorted Chips
Sweet-and-Tangy Slaw

BEVERAGES

Milk, Water, & Fruit Juice

DESSERT

Happy Cake Ice Cream Sandwiches

Mandarin Chocolate Cake – filled with an orange sherbet and vanilla
ice cream swirl, some coated with chopped almonds

Banana Bread – filled with vanilla ice cream, half of these dipped in
dark chocolate and coated with crushed walnut toffee

Red Velvet Cake – filled with chocolate ice cream and coated
with crushed pecans

Amazon Lemon Crunch Bars – filled with a mixture of lemon sherbet
and vanilla ice cream and coated with roasted Brazil nut brittle

ACTIVITIES

Apple picking; making candied apples and decorations.

Thanksgiving Give Back

After a marathon night of cooking and setting up the serving stations for the Thanksgiving SNL celebration, Saturday arrived with a vengeance. Although we had most of the food finished by five in the morning, Regina and I still needed to go home, get dressed, and make sure all of the crew made it to the shelter on time. However we still had to make sure the morning counselors had cooked food to serve the girls for breakfast.

We'd already prepared two hams and a huge smoked salmon for the event. We used some of them to make two mini platters layered with sliced ham, smoked salmon, flavored cream cheeses, bagels, and a variety of fixings for the morning staff to serve the girls breakfast. After a quick bite with the girls, Regina and I finally left the shelter at eight in the morning.

I was exhausted when I got home. I knew I'd really have to pamper myself if I was going to have a good evening celebration. I determined that I needed an intense relaxation treatment followed by a good nap.

The gift Tariq brought me for my birthday had a sample of Bodacious Body's Intense Muscle Relaxation Bath and Body Treatment kit, which included an interesting vibrating massage ball. It was just a small sample so I had wanted to wait for the right time to try it—this was perfect.

I dropped two capfuls of the deep detox salts in the bath water, and they scented the entire bathroom with the spa-like aromas of eucalyptus, black pepper, cedar, and rosemary essential oils. The treatment started with a warm detoxification bath while I sipped the relaxing orange and hibiscus flavored yoni teatox love elixir.

The warming sensation of the black pepper oil infused through the magnesium chloride bath salts melted the tense muscles in my legs and feet like butter. I could feel the knots loosen and the dirt gently dissolving off my skin as I immersed myself in the fragrant waters and soaked in total relaxation.

At the end of my bath, I slathered myself with the creamy sulfate-free body wash, rinsed with warm water, spritzed my entire body with the cooling body toner, and patted my skin dry. My skin felt soft and smelled wonderful. I began to truly feel a sense of calm relaxation.

I didn't want that feeling to leave me, so as suggested from the pamphlet, I sealed the deal by putting the finishing touches on with a self-healing massage. I poured a small amount of the scintillating black pepper relaxation oil into the massage ball and went to work on every part of my body that was within reach. Just as predicted, it was an absolutely mind stimulating experience. I slept like a baby for six straight hours.

I woke up feeling refreshed and smelling magnificent. After quickly coiffing my hair and slipping into my catering uniform, I drove directly to the shelter and finalized setup before everyone arrived.

Lauren informed Regina and I that she was prohibiting any outside communications during the party and would only allow one senior counselor to field calls during the evening's festivities. She didn't want the party being overshadowed by the typical wheels of drama that turned at the shelter every day. I thought it was a good call and everything went off pretty much without a hitch.

The group arrived from the boys' shelter and the party began. Leila didn't accompany them because she had already passed her due date and didn't want to take a chance at going into labor during the event.

There were a few crushes and girls' chatter about liking the same guy from Mark B's shelter, but those were quickly squashed. Mark B informed everyone as soon as they walked into the living room that if there were any altercations or hanky-panky, they would all pay because we would end the party immediately and go back to our respective shelters. We kept them so busy they didn't have time to act up—just like we planned it.

The evening started with Pierre initiating a very loud drum call, prompting everyone to run into the living room. After the drum call, he implored everyone to introduce themselves with their own personal dances to the drum beating. This proved to be very exciting for the kids, and often very funny. We quickly learned who was comfortable dancing and who just didn't have what it takes to keep the rhythm. It was a lot of fun to watch.

Afterward we invited everyone to enjoy drinks and the talent show. It too was amusing and very revealing. Two of the standouts included a last-minute entry from one of the shelter's girls, who introduced the world to an amazing soon to be opera singer. The other standout was a very entertaining member from the boys' shelter who was a really funny up-and-coming comedian. He joked about his family's chronic homelessness while thanking the shelter staff for rescuing him from the streets in between every joke. All in all, it was a very rewarding and fun-filled experience for the staff and children from both shelters. I hoped to somehow make it an annual event.

During the talent show, we also had several kids take us up on the poetry/ rap challenge. Although it wasn't very successful, we had one shining star—it just so happened to be Darlese's little sister, Corrine. I didn't realize it at the time, but she was one of the little girls I'd picked up from the intake center when we replaced the runaways.

A newly crowned teenager at the age of thirteen, she wrote a sultry poem about her "tumultuous life in the hood, and fighting against the devastation caused by drugs and violence was for what she stood." It was worthy of a standing ovation from everyone in the room. Tears streamed endlessly down just about everyone's face and the standing ovation helped us to invite everyone to prayer and formation of the line for dinner.

We set up an absolutely bodacious and beautifully appointed buffet. The typically bleak dinner tables were draped in holiday finery and filled with generously sliced turkey, assorted meats, fish, and individual servings of bubbly hot casseroles and side dishes. The smells alone lured the crowd to the dining room like a pied piper.

Dinner was absolutely amazing! It looked fabulous, smelled and tasted delicious, and the reviews on how everyone felt afterward sealed our success. But we wanted everyone to work off some of the calories before dessert on the deck. We started with a little karaoke hosted by Penny and JB.

Everyone had a blast singing their favorite old and new songs—the most popular by far was Michael Jackson's "Thriller." Mark B recapitulated his Halloween performance and sang while all the kids joined in to dance with him. It was beautiful.

Then Chris, of all people, challenged everyone to a limbo contest. I think he was having the most fun—it was a very humbling experience for him. It was inspiring to see him interact with people outside of his comfort zone. I thought it was important for all of us to be able to see and understand the real plight of people from backgrounds unlike ours.

Chris danced, sang karaoke with the kids, and tried very unsuccessfully to get himself under the limbo pole again. After Rafi facetiously joked and explained to Chris that the objective of the limbo dance was to get his whole body under the pole, he was strategically outsmarted by Darlese's little sister who took the prize by dancing herself under the stick while it was only one-foot high. She even beat Tariq's record.

During the high-profile limbo contest, Regina and I carefully moved all of the candied apples and gifts we'd wrapped overnight into the living room to prepare for the Jive Turkey game. It's always the highlight of my family's Thanksgiving celebration and I was happy to see if the kids enjoyed the game.

The rules suggest that each person must pull three numbers from the box—everyone gets at least three chances to get a gift from the gift table. Matching numbers are thrown into a raffle box for the facilitator to call out and everyone gets three shots at the prizes on the table to take home as keepsakes or to eat. However, there's a caveat. There are at least one third fewer gifts than numbers. Although everyone gets three shots at winning one or more prizes, if there are no more gifts on the prize table, those who still have numbers called later in the game can take prizes from anyone who already has one. However, for those who are lucky enough to have gotten the golden turkeys, once their numbers are called at any point in the game, even if there are prizes still on the table, they can take whatever gift they want, from whomever they want. But, they can only cash in the golden turkey swap once.

Usually, the prizes run out in the first two rounds, but in the end everyone gets a delicious gift, which can sometimes be a gag gift, or a nice keepsake.

Those who select the numbers with the golden turkeys are considered Jive Turkeys because they get to take and/or trade whatever food or prizes they want from anyone. It's customary to ensure there are enough gifts so that everyone has a gift at the end of the game.

We weren't sure if the kids would go along with the golden turkey swaps, but they enjoyed it very much. Some tried to pretend they didn't have the prettiest or tastiest gifts only to be busted by another player. Others kept us laughing by making hilarious excuses about why they needed to keep the items. Overall, the game was a big hit and left everyone in sidesplitting laughter.

Chris and JB both turned out to be the highlight of the Jive Turkey game. They both received golden turkeys but used them very differently. Chris was so excited about his fortune that he didn't hear me say there were at least four golden turkeys. He thought he was the sole recipient. He also didn't realize that anyone with a golden turkey card could take gifts from others who have already used their golden turkey cards. This made for a lot of laughter.

He decided to stick his golden turkey card to his forehead with a piece of gum to intimidate everyone throughout the first two rounds. Every time one of the kids chose a beautifully packaged candied apple, he jokingly threatened to take it and eat it right away when his number was called. But the real kicker was when the adults picked the beautifully wrapped gift baskets—he really had his eyes on them. He finally succeeded in taking the biggest one from Lauren after all her numbers had been called. However he was in for a big surprise.

After everyone evened out the gifts toward the end, Chris had a nice collection of two candied apples and the gift basket he'd bullied out of Lauren with his golden turkey. What he didn't realize was that JB still had his golden turkey. At the very end, he used it to take the biggest basket from Chris and handed it to Lauren. Everyone laughed at Chris and applauded JB for his generosity. But Chris assured everyone that he was going to do the same thing before shouting, "Let's roast some marshmallows! Barn fire everyone!"

The crowd made their way outside to the deck where Ms. Nellie had set up individually boxed s'mores kits and long pitchforks for roasting marshmallows. Mr. Doug, the shelter's maintenance man, was in charge of the fire pit and had a roaring fire burning and ready to keep everyone nice and cozy while chatting and making s'mores. Although the kids overindulged in the s'mores, the fire along with Mark B's scary storytelling was mesmerizing. It seemed to really relax everyone. I nearly fell asleep in JB's lap.

We finished making s'mores and after Mark B's final story, Chris and Rafi presented the entire staff of both shelters with gift baskets. They were filled with an assortment of body treatments from Chris's brother's spa and gift certificates for free massages and a gourmet lunch. The staff was honored, including me.

Even though I'd experienced the best massage of my life at his brother's place, I hadn't planned on taking Chris up on the offer after getting sucked into his trap the last time. But I did champion how wonderful the products are. I even offered to do a workshop on skincare and relaxation with the products for the kids at both shelters.

The evening ended on a high note. We'd successfully executed our first Thanksgiving Give Back event and I couldn't have been more proud of our College Crew as a group. Everyone helped to ensure that all of the kids felt valued, the staff felt appreciated, and a great time was had by all.

Our goal of alleviating some of the sadness and loneliness the kids felt from missing their families had been accomplished. Lauren and Evelyn very graciously thanked the crew on behalf of the company, the staff, and the kids. It made us all proud.

I was on a natural high, and despite being exhausted from the prep and evening's activities, I set out on my journey to float home on a cloud of joy. I walked out the door and to my surprise, JB met me at my car.

He kindly opened the door for me and said he'd hitched a ride with Penny but would love it if I'd take him back to his car. I agreed and he jumped in the car with me. We laughed and joked about the wonderful evening all the way to his car.

During the ride, he invited me to celebrate the New Year with him and a few friends at his gig on Mt. Washington. He said he was thinking about inviting everyone from the College Crew to use it as his opportunity to host an SNL celebration. I told him I'd think about it because I already knew I'd have to work on January first. Since I had to be in Pittsburgh anyway, it sounded like a good opportunity. We said our goodnights and I went home and slept like a baby.

Menu

Join Us for Our Thanksgiving Extravaganza
featuring

DINNER

HERB-INFUSED ROASTED TURKEY
with savory stuffing

PRIME RIB ROAST

DRESSED MAPLEWOOD-SMOKED HAM

LEMON & HONEY SMOKED SALMON

SIDES

BAKED MACARONI & CHEESE CASSEROLE

SAUTÉED FRENCH GREEN BEANS
with crispy onion straws

SOUTHERN STEWED COLLARD GREENS
with smoked pork or smoked turkey

SWEET POTATO CASSEROLE

CORN PUDDING
with bacon and scallions

SAN FRANCISCO–STYLE WILD RICE PILAF

DRESSED POTATO SALAD • FRESH GREEN SALAD

CRANBERRY SAUCE

Menu

BEVERAGES

APPLE CIDER • EGGNOG • CHAI TEA LATTES

STILL & SPARKLING WATER

ASSORTED SOFT DRINKS & FRUIT JUICES

DESSERT

SWEET POTATO PUMPKIN PIE

SWEET POTATO CAKE
with cream cheese and salted pecan topping

LEMON COCONUT POUND CAKE

MOCHA & MANDARIN CHOCOLATE MOUSSE CAKE

S'MORES

FRESH FRUIT

GIFT PACKS

Candy and caramel apples. Bodacious Body and BB's Fresh Face gift pack, gift certificates for free massages and a gourmet lunch, for the staff. A workshop on how to take good care of your skin and make yourself feel luxurious anywhere, for the kids in the shelters.

ENTERTAINMENT

Talent show; rap/poetry contest; karaoke; limbo contest; Jive Turkey game; barn fire and marshmallow roast.

27

The phone rang at 9:30 early Sunday morning and awakened me from a deep sleep. After the marathon activities for the Thanksgiving celebration at the shelter, I had every intention of sleeping in. But after about the fifteenth ring, I thought it could be Pierre or Leila's sister calling to tell me the baby was on the way, so I was obliged to answer. To my surprise, it was Rafi, and he was very upset.

Apparently after Chris left the Thanksgiving celebration he'd gotten into an accident while driving home. His younger brother called Rafi from the hospital and told him the state police found Chris's car on its side and he was inside and unconscious. No one was sure what happened but apparently the impact was so hard it turned his Jaguar over. The policeman said he was sure Chris had been hit by another car but the person didn't stop. Fortunately, Chris's Jaguar was equipped with a distress system that sent an emergency alert via satellite. It led to the police finding Chris unconscious in his car on the side of the road.

Rafi immediately picked up Sheila and me, and we all went to the hospital. I was overcome with feelings of guilt because the accident occured when he was leaving my event. I was even more afraid of what I might encounter when we got to the hospital.

When we arrived Chris's entire family was in the room. He was no longer unconscious but he was a little banged up. The doctor insisted that he remain in the hospital a couple days so they could finish running tests while monitoring him. Other than a couple of minor cuts to his face, he was in good spirits and lit up when we walked in the room.

He nearly jumped out of the bed and obliged his family to go into the waiting room so we could visit. I had tried to contain my emotions when Rafi called, but when I saw Chris in the hospital bed I could no longer hold back my tears. I unexpectedly busted out in tears as soon as his family left the room. He pulled me on the bed, hugged me, and touted how much he loved me and was so happy to see me. I told him I felt a little guilty because he got hurt after leaving the celebration. But he assured me that whoever hit him came out of nowhere. He was just happy to be alive.

Strong enough to pull me into him, he gently kissed my tears as I cried with joy that he was okay and sadness that he'd been hurt. While he was holding me, two of his sisters abruptly pushed the door open, rushed into the room, and pulled him from my arms while insisting that he needed to rest. Chris relented like a weak puppy and simply allowed them to pull me out of his arms without saying a word.

I knew it was a touchy situation, however I again felt betrayed. As usual Rafi tried to clean up Chris's mess. He attempted to come to the rescue and quickly hugged me and tried to take over where Chris left off to make it seem like I shouldn't be offended. It was at that point I realized why Chris was afraid to do anything his family didn't approve of.

He was like a finger puppet on their hands. Anything they said to do, he just did. It was also clear by his reactions that it was a natural response and had very little to do with the accident.

Even worse, they started doting over him like he was some kind of a god. I couldn't believe it. After about twenty minutes of watching them wash his face, rub his feet, and kiss him on the lips, I'd had enough. I said my goodbyes and went to the car. Rafi and Sheila quickly followed and dropped me off at home.

I not only realized I'd made the right decision to end things permanently with Chris, but I seriously began to think about leaving Pittsburgh for a new life. I knew that my tolerance for working in the shelter's tumultuous environment wouldn't last much longer. I was also ready to get away from all of the drama that surrounded my relationship with Chris.

I started thinking more seriously about the best ways to move toward doing something different with my life—something that would hopefully lead to my dream of opening a successful restaurant or working with food.

As soon as I got home, the phone rang again. It was Leila's sister informing me that she was on the way to the hospital, but Pierre was nowhere to be found. I tried to call him but didn't get an answer either. So I drove right over to the hospital. Leila had a beautiful baby girl!

"I'm an auntie!" I said with elation. She was five pounds, eleven ounces, and twenty-one inches long with cold black hair, chestnut brown eyes, and silky dark chocolate skin. She looked like a precious doll baby and I immediately fell in love with her.

The Shelter: Corry

About a week and a half after the Thanksgiving event, the news aired a report about a house fire in Corry's mother's neighborhood. His mother and sister were pictured on the news distraught and in distress because they couldn't figure out how the house caught fire. Shortly after the fire was extinguished things got worse.

It was well known to everyone, including Darlese and her father, that Corry was somewhat estranged from his mother and sister. But the shelter's therapist decided it would be a good idea if he began to rebuild his familiar relationships. He was about to turn eighteen and the hope was that he would feel better about aging out of the system. At age eighteen he would no longer be eligible to take advantage of resources provided by Child Protective Services as he would now be considered an adult. He agreed with the therapist and began to meet monthly with his mother at the intake shelter.

Later, when he no longer felt safe at the shelter, he apparently decided the safest thing to do would be to sneak into his mom's house and to hide in the attic without her knowledge, according to her. He thought no one would be the wiser and that he could hide until things calmed down.

But someone figured it out. After Corry had been hiding in his mom's attic for two months, allegedly unnoticed by his mother or sister, Darlese's father made good on his promise.

He sent two of Darlese's brothers to deliver that promise to Corry. They broke into his mother's house, beat Corry to death with a baseball bat, dragged him from the attic, through the house and down the stairs into the basement while leaving a trail of his blood as proof of their deed. Then they set his body on fire with gasoline. According to Mark B, it wasn't until the fire was extinguished that investigators found his body and put the whole story together: Nearly a year after he was sentenced to life in prison for the murder in the Strip District, Eastman apparently sent two of his sons on a quest to teach Corry a lesson. They delivered the message in the most gruesome manner possible. They, too, were convicted and sentenced to life in prison.

It turned out Eastman was truly a "man of his word." He'd warned Corry that if he told anyone about murdering the man in the strip, he would kill him and his family. Coupled with his dispute with Darlese, Corry unfortunately was a sitting duck.

Girls' Night Out

Girls' night out didn't come for two long weeks and I was anxious to discuss with my friends my thoughts about moving away to do something different. I was in a kind of doldrums from the situation with Chris, and Corry's death, and my visit with Tariq in San Francisco really got me thinking about the possibilities of living in another city.

I'd already run it past Tariq, but I decided to wait to break the news to my friends. To keep myself uplifted, I occupied myself with making gift baskets for the College Crew's Christmas presents, a few catering gigs, and explicit conversations and phone sex with Tariq after work at the shelter.

When it was finally time to hook up with my girls, I was ready and excited. It was the Christmas season and we were all participating in the gift exchange. In order to facilitate our annual gift exchange, everyone agreed to meet at the Savoy for dinner and then walk across the street to CJ's for dancing and after dinner drinks.

The most notable moment came when Chantelle decided to hand out sex toys shaped like food. They were beautifully wrapped and very unassuming. Sheila opened her gift before everyone and, after unfolding layers upon layers of paper, she pulled out a cucumber-shaped silicone vibrator. She didn't quite understand what it was. In the meantime, everyone else laughed hysterically at her naïveté and refused to open any more of Chantelle's gifts at the table.

Now laughing hysterically herself, Chantelle said they were gag gifts to get us through the lonely nights when necessary. Then she wowed us with an invitation for the whole crew to join her and her friend at the Bedford Springs spa for a pampering weekend. January was her month to host SNL, so she decided to take everyone on a weekend spa escape paid for by her newest boy toy.

In the meantime, Sheila was not comfortable being the focus of everyone's attention and sought to refocus the attention away from the cucumber shaped dildo sitting in front of her. She quickly put it back into the box and attempted to break up the laughter by telling us that the police had caught the guy who hit Chris's car.

It turned out to be a disgruntled customer. The guy allegedly told the police that he'd lost more than a hundred thousand dollars from insurance and investments in Chris's brother's company. He clearly wanted revenge.

He'd found out where Chris lived, waited for him on the road to his house, and intentionally ran him off the road to send a warning. We were all shocked, however I found myself a bit confounded.

First of all, I was relieved that it had nothing to do with him being tired after attending my event. Second, I was scared for Chris's life. And finally I was pissed off with the man's accusation because, at the behest of Chris, I had also invested in his brother's company and thought there was a chance that I might have lost my money, too. But I was ashamed to admit it, so I didn't comment.

Charise quickly changed the subject and announced that not only was she starting a new internship with a prominent law firm in the fall but she had found love at the Thanksgiving celebration at the shelter. We congratulated her on the internship but no one could figure out exactly who she was referring to as her supposed love interest.

She went on to explain that she and Henri—the Congolese drummer—had begun dating shortly after the last SNL at Mark B's house, and now she was really getting into the relationship. We were all happy for her and wished her the best.

Although she'd committed to help, Chantelle didn't show up for the Thanksgiving event and was completely in the dark. I asked her why she wasn't at the Thanksgiving Give Back and she said she wasn't able to attend because she had to fly to New York to meet her new boyfriend, Damon, at the last minute.

After updating Chantelle about how successful the event was, she apologized for not being able to participate. She said she'd been flying back and forth to New York on the weekends to deliver legal documents for Damon. It seemed strange to everyone. I was confused and asked why he couldn't use a courier service. She said the documents had to be signed and hand delivered. According to her, each time she went she was paid $500 and put up in a nice hotel where she'd spend the weekends with him wining and dining her.

According to her, he's a New York businessman whose attorneys' offices are located in Pittsburgh. They were working on an international trade deal that required the hand delivery of the signed documents. Unbeknownst to everyone, she'd been traveling to New York with the sealed documents every weekend for the past two months.

She said he'd meet her at the airport in a limousine, take her to dinner or the spa of her choice, and they'd stay at a new five-star hotel every other weekend. According to her, she was living the good life. Just about everyone congratulated her and seemed to be excited for her newfound fortune. That's when I affectionately started to refer to him as "Diamond Damon." I, however, had another one of those visceral moments and began to get an awkward feeling about the situation. Regina noticeably didn't say a word either.

Regina was present but didn't seem to be herself. When Chantelle asked her about the Thanksgiving Give Back, she seemed to dote on Evelyn's role and downplayed the countless hours she spent working on the event. The most awkward moment of the evening occurred when Regina finally spoke about the relationship between she, Mark B, and Greg. Then she alluded to the growing intimacy between her and Evelyn. Chantelle nearly choked on her drink and went on a rant.

"What the hell happened to you Regina!" she exclaimed. "I couldn't have possibly missed that much. By the way, what happened with you and Mark B and Greg at the last SNL? I thought all hell was gonna break loose!" she quipped.

It became an open invitation for Regina to pour out her heart and she took great advantage. We were all dumbfounded after listening to her rant for fifteen uninterrupted minutes. She loved to go on like that.

She began by elaborating on all of the time she and Evelyn had been spending together and how she had grown to love her not only as a friend but something more. Then she dropped the bombshell about her tryst with Mark B and Greg. But this time she went into vivid detail.

"I really liked Mark B when I first met him and we hit it off. In fact, we hit it off so well that we would go out for drinks after work almost every night," she said.

"One night, Greg met us at TGI Fridays. Shortly after he arrived, the bar was closing. But it was Friday night and we wanted to party some more. Mark B suggested we go to his house to listen to music and drink some beer to continue the party, and I agreed," she said with an air of resentment. The pain in her voice was quite evident now.

"We got to his house and everything was cool. We played a few drinking games and all of a sudden, Greg went to the bathroom and Mark B started kissing me. I was so turned on that one thing led to another and we ended up in his bedroom." She was talking in a monotone now but everyone began to wake up.

"His gaze made me feel like a goddess. He looked straight into my eyes and told me I was irresistible." She purred like she'd fallen in love for the first time. "Pulling me into him, he started gently kissing me on the collarbone. My love juices started flowing like crazy. I quietly purred from the pleasure of his lips caressing my tender skin. But I wasn't quite sure if we should be doing what we were doing and began to pull back," she recalled while staring away from everyone.

"Suddenly his warm, tender lips met mine. 'I need you!' he quietly whispered to me. He tenderly kissed my face and then my lips. He stuck his tongue in my ears ... and drove me crazy! I kept thinking that maybe I'd had a few too many beers, but my body began to crave him. My love juices were gushing down my legs now and he quickly sensed it." She started getting excited. By this time everyone was on the edge of their seats.

"I helped him take my shirt off while he strategically removed his clothes and sucked my throbbing breasts. My nipples were hard as a rock. They were so tender to the touch that I quivered with every brush of his tongue. Then that magnificent tongue worked its way into my pants and he went in for the kill." Her voice grew progressively louder.

"Your skin is like silky, delicious dark chocolate. I can't get enough of it, he proclaimed as he dove into my lovejoy with that magnificent tongue." She quivered.

"Warm, juicy thrusts of mind-blowing licks sent shockwaves of pleasure sizzling all over my body. I was completely under his control. He pushed my legs over his head and teased my ass with his finger. I was quivering. I'd never had anyone do that to me before. But it made me feel so good that he could have done whatever he wanted," she said with resolve.

"Then he stuck his tongue deep into my sex and masterfully finger fucked me while he licked my clit. Let me tell you, my body jolted uncontrollably. I had an unbelievable desire to feel his cock in my ass. But I was afraid." She seemed to be gauging our reactions to see if anyone would judge her. By this time we were all so intrigued with the story, we just let her talk.

"I had never done that before. But he masterfully broke down that wall when he stuck his tongue into my asshole. I lost it!" she quipped with a joyful resolve.

"In the meantime, I was so immersed in pleasure, I didn't even realize Greg had entered the room. I'd completely forgotten he was even around." She shook her head as if to indicate that she was not acting like her normal self.

"I opened my eyes and he started licking my pussy while Mark B fucked my asshole with his tongue. I thought about resisting. I had never been with two guys before, and my conscience picked at me. But my body betrayed my entire thought process. Every part of my body tingled joyfully. It was as if someone had stimulated every pleasure nerve in my body. ... The feeling was amazing! But I knew somehow it wasn't right." A somewhat embarrassed haze came over her face. Nobody said anything and just seemed to absorb everything she was putting out.

"I thought about stopping them. But Mark B pulled me to the bottom of the bed and stuck his big dick in my pussy while Greg continued licking my clit. I was paralyzed with pleasure. I moaned with unrelenting joy. *Aht!*" She made a weird noise while licking her lips as if to indicate the feeling was intense. We were all hooked on her every word.

"Greg took my moaning as an opportunity to indulge in my pleasure and stuck his dick in my mouth. I wasn't quite prepared for that. But I was enjoying myself so much that I really wanted to reciprocate the feeling. I played with his balls while nibbling on the tip of his dick to tease him. I guess I was teasing him too much. It kind of pissed him off and all of a sudden he yelled, 'Suck my dick bitch!' real loud. And I did!" Seemingly shocked with herself, Regina appeared to be somewhat dismayed as she mimicked Greg's voice in a shouting whisper. We all laughed at her attempts to quietly tell the story in the restaurant with other people around. But she continued.

"I was filled with intense pleasure. Mark B skillfully maneuvered his cock in places I didn't even know I had. But Greg's command somehow made me feel empowered. Like I was somewhat in control, even though Mark B was fucking the shit out of me. I took on the challenge and began devouring Greg." She roared like a lion tearing into his prey while mimicking herself sucking his dick and choking.

"I shoved his entire dick in my mouth and slid it as far down my throat as possible. I completely enveloped him. 'That's it! ... Yeah! Suck it bitch!' he shouted with moaning pleasure. He rammed his dick in and out of my mouth so hard I choked. I spit it out. Then I stroked and sucked his dick to the rhythm of Mark B fucking me until I knew he was about to climax." She was even more excited now.

"I was in a crazy mood. I wanted to torture him. So I refused to let him cum. I took his dick out of my mouth and said, 'Not time to cum yet!' Then Mark B grabbed me and pulled me into him. He kissed me and flipped me on top of him. I began to lower myself onto his cock when I suddenly felt Greg positioning himself behind me. I didn't realize what they were doing until Mark B said, 'We're gonna take you all the way up!'" she recounted.

"I wasn't sure what he meant, but I was already mesmerized and feeling high with scintillating pleasure. I kissed him while he slowly lowered me onto his bulging cock. Suddenly the potency of Greg's presence became more prevalent as the head of his penis knocked at the door of my ass. With each thrust onto Mark B's cock, he began to penetrate me. I vividly recall the sensuous sloshing sounds of my ass slapping down on his lap as my juices lubricated every part of my sex. All of a sudden, I felt Greg slipping his whole dick into my ass," she said with agony on her face. We were all sitting in a state of shock. I couldn't believe that she first of all had a threesome with Mark B of all people. And second, she'd let Greg, who's gay, fuck her in the ass. I didn't feel good about the situation and quickly realized that Greg had lied to Rafi about never having been with a woman. She continued.

"I begged and pleaded for him to stop, but the more he penetrated my ass, the more aroused I became. The intense feeling of having dicks in my ass and my sex was an empowering mix of pleasure and pain. But Mark B's tender kisses comforted any anxiety caused by the pain." She licked her lips as if she really enjoyed the experience. But she still wasn't finished telling the story. I wasn't sure I wanted to hear anymore.

"I was full. The pain from Greg's penis in my ass was intermittently superseded by the overwhelming pleasure from Mark B gently fucking me while biting my neck and caressing me with his warm, tender lips. The feeling was so intense, I lost control after only a few strokes ... I exploded ... Greg exploded ... then Mark B pulled out and shoved his dick in my mouth," she exclaimed. Sheila's face turned beet red. She was dumbfounded.

"You fucked Mark B and Greg? And at the same time?!" she inquired of Regina with disbelief.

"Yep! After that I sucked his dick while Greg played with his balls until he came. I didn't think much of it at the time, but now I kind of feel foolish knowing that he and Greg were probably doing each other then. My head was pretty fucked up when he said he was gay and had the audacity to tell Rafi that he'd never been with a woman. But now I understand things a lot more clearly," she finished.

"Damn Girl! You took it up the ass!? That's a hard act for me to follow," Chantelle exclaimed with surprise and dismay. "But what the hell do you understand better? What does that mean?" she followed.

"Like I shared with Anais, I was sexually abused as a kid and I had never sought counseling. My friend Evelyn is a psychologist and she's been helping me get through Mark B's rejection and the issues I faced in my childhood. I'm really starting to like her more and she clearly likes me," Regina said with a bit of resolve.

I was just as surprised as everyone else to hear about her tryst with Mark B and Greg. I couldn't even venture a guess about what she would say next.

Chantelle, however, was awestruck. Not about the tryst, but how vividly Regina shared the details of it. She couldn't hold back her true feelings.

"Girllll, you are something else! I can't believe you felt comfortable enough to share ALL the details. I started getting a little wet between the legs myself," she joked. "And I thought I was going through a little something with my new boo's foot fetish. I think you've got me beat," Chantelle followed.

"Foot fetish!" I exclaimed. "Y'all are both hanging with nuts!" I joked.

"I need a drink!" I said as I led the way from the Savoy to CJ's to more appropriately digest what we'd just heard before closing out the evening.

28

The Shelter

It was the beginning of what would become a particularly bitter, cold winter and the euphoria of the Thanksgiving celebration quickly diminished from the minds of everyone at the shelter. The tragedy of Corry's demise haunted all of us and we were all back to the grind of dealing with the terrible attitudes, senseless fights, and constant disappointments of the kids. It appeared to be caused by what they voiced as their inability to participate in Black Friday shopping and other celebratory events that precede the Christmas holiday season.

Keeping the morale high for the kids and the staff was a constant battle—another reason I began thinking more and more about a career change. But my heart broke each time the girls complained about not being able to spend the holidays with their families.

It was clear to everyone. The time had come for some kind of a cheer-me-up for the kids. The staff was charged with putting their heads together to come up with a unique and cheap event.

After a bit of creative thinking, we came up with a plan to recreate Black Friday. We utilized the donations of clothes and shoes we had on hand and all kinds of food and trinkets we received from many of the local stores. They were stored in the attic for use in emergencies or when we'd receive children who had no belongings. The donations were regularly delivered every Tuesday and the attic was filled to capacity. This would be the perfect occasion to put its contents to good use.

Most of the items were new, overstocks, or had minor imperfections. Many still had the price tags on them. Not only would we get an opportunity to make good use of the items, but to do early spring-cleaning for a good cause. It was also an opportunity to use the event to make our jobs easier.

The girls had two weeks to earn points by being kind to each other, completing their chores without prompting from the staff, and volunteering. Access to the gift shopping was granted at the end of the two weeks. Whoever had the highest number of points was allowed to access it first. This would continue from the highest to the lowest points. The girls would also use the points to purchase gift wrapping to mail to and/or prepare the items for their friends and loved ones.

We had it all figured out. A small room on the side of the kitchen was set up like a shopping boutique—we lined up all the shoes with the original price tags on shoe racks stacked three layers high; all of the clothes and coats were hung on clothing racks with the tags facing out so the girls could see the value and truly feel like they were in a boutique; and we dressed a long table with a red velvet tablecloth to place the trinkets, jewelry, and miscellaneous items with price tags visible.

Lauren had already approved the use of petty cash to purchase miscellaneous items that we used to get an assortment of gift wrapping essentials for the four respective holidays. Patty Jo and Evelyn served as the free gift wrappers. They would not only personalize the gifts for Christmas, Hanukkah, Ramadan, and/or Kwanzaa based upon the girl's preferences, but make them look very festive and beautiful.

During the planning meeting with the counselors, we decided to make the journey a cross-cultural experience and celebrate Ramadan, Hanukkah, Christmas, and Kwanzaa. The holidays ran concurrently during this season and we had a Muslim girl, Khady, as a resident, which was the first time this had happened during my tenure at the shelter.

Khady was in the shelter because her mother needed in-patient mental health therapy after being persecuted during the war in Rwanda. She'd escaped with Khady after her husband was killed in the war and later received asylum to settle in Pittsburgh after a five-year waiting period in Senegal, West Africa. Shortly after the Thanksgiving celebration she began observing Ramadan with a thirty-day fasting period, which coincidentally would end around Christmas.

Evelyn, the psychologist, is Jewish. She felt it would also be a great opportunity to teach the girls about the eight days and nights of Hanukkah. This particular year, the eight days of Hanukkah were being celebrated during Christmas week. It was a perfect time for celebrating all three cultures and religious traditions through food, gift giving, and fun.

Fourteen-year-old Khady was placed in the shelter exactly one week before the Thanksgiving celebration and appeared to be somewhat of a mystery to the other girls. Evelyn placed her in the room with the oldest girl in the house, Zee, because at eighteen years old, Zee was a little more mature. Zee had already aged out of the system. We were just waiting for a suitable resettlement place to move her into so she wouldn't be alone and/or homeless.

During one of the daily group sessions, Khady voiced a concern that the other girls may be feeling like she was ignoring them when she'd leave the group for prayer. They'd also question why she covered her head. After being in the shelter for more than a month, she finally muscled up the courage to explain her culture.

She shared with the group that she's a practicing Muslim and as a practicing young lady, she is required to cover her head. However, they were also in the midst of Ramadan—the most important month of the year for Muslims. For them it commemorates when God gave the first few verses of the Quran to the Prophet Muhammad.

"In addition to praying five times a day—which is why I often leave the class—we fast and pray from early morning until dinner time for the thirty days. It's a month of spiritual dedication and personal growth. Most important, it's intended to strengthen our relationships with God. At the end of Ramadan, we celebrate with a mighty feast!" she said.

"It's like Yom Kippur—the holiest holiday of the year in Judaism. We are also required to fast as a necessary component of seeking God's forgiveness," Evelyn said. She had been standing in the corner observing and decided to chime in. "It means Day of Atonement—we ask for God's forgiveness and we fast for twenty-five hours," she added.

I thought I should share a little about Christianity at that point. I chimed in, too. "As Christians, we're allowed to fast at any time. Whenever we feel like we need to get closer to God or need guidance in any part of our lives, we fast. The funny thing is, I didn't know why my parents made me do it at least twice a year when I was growing up. That was until I got to college," I said.

"Sometimes I couldn't understand why my courses were so difficult and why some of my professors were so mean. My mom taught me to fast for clarity, and it worked. And the food tasted so good after the fast. Seems like all of our religions practice the same traditions for the same outcomes," I said.

Then Zee chimed in. "I like it. I think I'm gonna try fasting with Khady to find clarity on where I'm going after I leave here," she said with worry.

Evelyn assured her we'd make sure she was safe wherever she went. I prayed for truth in that statement given the devastating outcomes I'd already seen with Corry and Saturn.

Girls' Night Out

It was a dreary Monday very early in December, I hadn't talked to Tariq for a couple of days, and I began missing him. He was scheduled to fly in right before leaving for Paris for the holidays, but it seemed like forever to wait. I was missing him so much that I decided I would take him up on the offer to spend Christmas in Paris with him and his family. The caveat was that he'd have to visit my family first. I wanted to run it by the girls to see what they thought about my decision.

Girls' Night Out was still a couple of days away and I needed to get my mind off work and missing Tariq. I couldn't wait until Friday and decided to stop by Leila's to chat and see the baby. I went to visit after work that Tuesday and she wasn't very happy.

She had just found out that the same day she had the baby Pierre had boarded a plane for South Africa to visit Penny. He said he was going on tour and wouldn't be returning to Pittsburgh until Christmas—five weeks later. Although he left Leila alone with the newborn baby, he'd purchased all kinds of gifts and necessities for the baby and asked his roommate to deliver them with the message. She was torn up all over again.

It was another visceral experience for me—almost like someone had punched me in the stomach. I couldn't help but to reminisce about the time Pierre told Leila he didn't love her like that. I knew she was vulnerable and I didn't want to hurt her or stir things up. I just played with the baby, said nothing, and allowed her to vent like a good friend would do until it was time to leave. There really wasn't anything I could say to make the situation better, so I just said nothing.

Friday finally came and I wanted to look and feel good for my big Christmas announcement. This time, along with my usual beauty ritual, I tried some of the BB's Fresh Face makeup I picked up at the spa in San Francisco. I started with the mildly scented lye-free facial cleanser, followed it with a Korean rubber collagen mask, and finished with a calming lemon verbena and cucumber toner. The mask was the most amazing part of the treatment. It extracted blackheads I didn't even know I had and wasn't very painful. My face felt smooth, plump, clean, and refreshed.

They also offered a makeup primer/serum that I could wear alone, mixed with a little of my foundation, or under a full face of makeup. I found it quite interesting. It's designed to naturally protect your skin from any harsh chemicals found in makeup while providing sheen to a fully finished face. I was impressed again with the quality of the products. It seemed like I could be a walking commercial for them.

We were only going to have dinner and listen to jazz at the James Street Gastropub because I had to work the next day due to my extended vacation, so I opted for a sheer look. It only required me to mix a tiny bit of my foundation with the serum and apply liberally. The feathery lightness of the serum looked great and smelled beautiful. I was ready for the big announcement.

We sat at the table and I immediately announced my decision to spend Christmas with Tariq in Paris. It didn't get much traction though. I think everyone was in a sort of doldrums. They really didn't want to hear about my excitement. But they did tell me it was a great choice and to bring back souvenirs.

While at James Street, again we ran into JB. He now seemed to be showing up everywhere I went. I didn't know if maybe it was the places we chose to hang out or if he was just that famous on the local jazz scene. In either case, he felt more comfortable with us, and this time ordered drinks for the entire table. Then he came over between sets and ordered a round of his favorite chicken wing dinners and sweet tea for everyone.

JB turned out to be even more interesting than I'd thought. Charise had never met him and thought he was a pro football player. She continually demanded an autograph and finally after the second or third request he just started ignoring her. He seemed to find her candor amusing. But when she tried to call him out for ignoring her request, he assured her he wasn't a pro football player. He said the closest he'd come to football was when he'd received two full scholarships to Carnegie Mellon University—one to play football and one to study classical saxophone. His football career ended from a concussion that left him in a fog for ten days.

He vividly recounted how his music advisor forced him to make a choice. "Death or your saxophone!" he said. For JB the choice was obvious, instead of football, he plays and teaches music. Charise finally relented and apologized to him.

We enjoyed another brief conversation during his break between the second set. I invited him to give me a hang-out call when he was free and we reminded him to join us for our Christmas SNL at Rafi's house on the following Saturday. We said our goodbyes before his set ended and I went home to prepare myself for work the next day. I was a little saddened by the girls' lack of enthusiasm about my upcoming trip to Paris, but I too was in a sort of the doldrums so I completely understood.

The College Crew: Saturday Night Live Christmas

Rafi was transitioning from a new condo he'd recently purchased and decided to switch months for our SNL with Chris. In turn, Chris persuaded his brother to allow him to host the event at his house because it was bigger and already decorated for Christmas.

Everyone trekked up those long hills, through two tunnels, and battled long waits in traffic. But it was certainly worth it. The house was laid out beautifully and Chris hired caterers and a DJ to spoil us. We had a blast!

This time I drove to the party in an effort to not be compromised by Chris and his antics and to avoid being at the mercy of Rafi for a ride. Chantelle, Charise, and Regina carpooled with me. It made for nice conversation and anticipation of how the evening would play out.

Chris had a few surprises. However I had to check myself on some of them before responding. He greeted everyone at the door and as soon as I came in he introduced his new girlfriend, Rebecca, to everyone. I was a little disturbed because we'd always alerted the crew before bringing anyone new to the celebrations. But I had to restrain myself for fear that he'd sense my displeasure. Besides, she was very nice and seemed to fit in well with everyone.

The ambiance and location of the party were perfect—it was like looking out the Windows on the World in New York. High atop Mt. Washington, we could see Christmas lights from near and far in the distance. The Christmas tree at Point Park met at the confluence of the three rivers that flow through Pittsburgh and its lights twinkled while simultaneously highlighting all three rivers at once. It was a dazzling light show rivaling those in Las Vegas. But the *pièce de résistance* was the buffet table.

It was a stunning display of elegance—a virtuoso of sterling silver and crystal serving dishes filled with succulent appetizers, carving stations with the finest meats and fish, and white-glove service from the catering company. We didn't have to touch a thing. The dining table was set for fifteen and it was simply amazing.

At each place setting was a menu with a feather pen for selecting as many items as you wanted. It read as follows: the appetizers—shrimp and stone crab claws with heated lemon butter, and crudités with seven seas and ranch dips; the main courses—hand-carved prime rib, sautéed or crab-stuffed portobello mushrooms, and herb roasted sea bass medallions; sides—jeweled seafood stuffing, warm coconut sticky rice with Thai sesame spinach, and steamed vegetables; the desserts—a unique collection of alcohol soaked and aged cakes including aged Jamaican rum cake, aged French chocolate Grand Marnier cake, Italian limoncello cake; and homemade pecan balls. He also hired a bartender.

Chris actually purchased the cakes from my holiday collection as a standing order and Ms. Nellie sent the pecan balls as a thank-you gift to the College Crew. I prepare the cakes in October, soak them in the alcohol, then vacuum seal and freeze them until my annual Christmas cake sales begin in November.

I always feature those three different liquor cakes during the holiday sale. The rustic Jamaican rum cake is an old family recipe my mother collected while on a missions trip in Jamaica many years ago—it's a best seller. The silky French chocolate Grand Marnier and Italian limoncello cakes are my signature cakes. Every year I sell at least one hundred of each cake.

Every year the College Crew also does a Pollyanna gift exchange with gag gifts. Each of our names is put into a box, shaken up, and then either a facilitator assigns or each member of the group pulls a name for the person he or she is to purchase gifts for. The names are kept secret until the gift exchange is made, usually at our holiday party or celebration.

The name assignments must be done in advance to allow time for acquiring the gifts, and we usually like to increase the fun factor by requiring gag gifts. The name assignments are usually part of the Thanksgiving celebration, however this year it was preempted by the SNL Give Back at the shelter. Instead, we decided to have everyone bring fifteen small gifts, one for each person in attendance. The caveats—they all had to be the same thing and they had to speak to who you are as an individual. In the meantime, Chris and Rafi had cooked up another layer to the gift exchange. They announced there was another surprise for everyone.

During dinner, Chris and Rafi announced their surprise—they requested we put together a "futures chest" and obliged everyone to participate. They explained that the futures chest is a way of monitoring how much progress we make toward our life goals in the next five, ten, and twenty years. Rafi explained it as a way of keeping up with each other once we were no longer in Pittsburgh. He said he'd been thinking about moving back to England to study medicine since he didn't get into Pitt's medical school and the program in England would only require a five year commitment. The futures box was a way to ensure that the group reconvened at least every five years to continue our friendships and check on each other.

Everyone thought it was a great idea. Chris passed out pens and paper and we all wrote our goals for the next five, ten, and fifteen years. However deciding what our goals were wasn't easy. Many of us were forced to really ponder how we wanted our lives to play out in the future and what we needed to do to accomplish the goals we'd set for ourselves. I really didn't see myself working in the shelter in five years. As I began to reflect more and more, I didn't see myself staying in Pittsburgh or the country for that matter. I just didn't yet know exactly where I wanted to go, or how I was going to get there. I prayed for God's guidance and came to terms with my lifelong goals of becoming a restaurateur or some kind of food entrepreneur.

The activity took up quite a bit of the evening. Some people worked diligently on their goals right up to the time Chris pulled out what he called The Futures Box. We all dropped the papers holding our future goals into the wooden box with a promise from Chris that he'd store it in a safety deposit box at the bank. We ate, danced, and wondered about our futures for the remainder of the evening.

When I got home, I called Tariq to accept his invitation to spend Christmas with his family in Paris. I insisted that he first had to visit my family. He was elated. He couldn't wait to meet them and suggested that we stop in New York to spend a couple days with my family before leaving for Paris. It would give him the opportunity to meet my family and visit New York at Christmastime.

The love and respect I felt for him took on a whole new meaning. His quiet sensuality ignited my hunger to spend more time with him ... to get closer with him. I felt a deepening level of security and trust. I had finally shaken the doldrums and replaced them with a newfound excitement.

Menu

*Join Us for the College Crew's
Annual Christmas Celebration*

featuring

APPETIZERS

STEAMED SHRIMP & STONE CRAB CLAWS
with lemon butter

CRUDITÉS
with seven seas and ranch dips

DINNER

PRIME RIB

CRAB-STUFFED OR SAUTÉED
PORTOBELLO MUSHROOMS

HERB-STUFFED SEA BASS

*jeweled seafood stuffing; coconut sticky rice with Thai sesame spinach;
steamed vegetables*

DESSERT

AGED JAMAICAN RUM CAKE

AGED FRENCH CHOCOLATE GRAND MARNIER CAKE

AGED ITALIAN LIMONCELLO CAKE

PECAN BALLS

ENTERTAINMENT

*Dancing; storytelling; Pollyanna gift exchange: gag gifts;
The Futures Box.*

C H A P T E R

29

A Taste of New York

liked to spoil Tariq just as much as he spoiled me, so on the way to the airport I kept trying to figure out what we were going to eat for dinner. I'd just gotten off work, didn't have time to shop, and it was the Thursday evening just before we were to leave for New York and Paris. When I picked him up from the airport, he was waiting with a big red shopping bag stamped with the words *San Francisco Fish Company* on the outside, and a large gift box wrapped in scarlet red paper and tied with a giant hot pink bow sticking out of the inside. He handed it to me and wished me a Merry Christmas. I couldn't wait to open it. I pulled over to the curb and tore into the paper.

It was a box full of my favorite gifts and this time there were more special surprises. The company that sold the delicious Alaskan salmon we tried to buy while I was visiting had set up a special kiosk in the airport for Christmas, and Tariq surprised me with a vacuum-sealed pack. My brain quickly went to work and the dinner dilemma was solved. I immediately capitalized on the fortune and decided to pair the smoked salmon with a fresh green salad dressed with mustard vinaigrette and French bread croutons. My immediate thought was that the meal wouldn't be too heavy for our traveling stomachs and I would immediately get a chance to taste the delicious fish again.

The perfectly wrapped red box was filled with another fabulous collection of the Bodacious Body and BB's Fresh Face products and a few more surprises. In addition to the shelf- and travel-size jars of the cleansers, oils, and scrubs, the kit included special makeup removal clothes, sisal scrub brushes, a Korean rubber mask hydrating powder, and a touch-activated finger massager. It was really cool and I loved the fact that Tariq always brings me gifts to relax me and make me feel good. That's why I like to spoil him, too.

On the way home from the airport, I stopped by the grocery store to buy fresh salad greens, French bread, and a crisp bottle of white wine to pair with the smoked salmon. Tariq got settled in with a movie after a shower, and I prepared dinner. The sumptuous loins of the flaky smoked salmon were as tender and tasty as I'd remembered.

We woke up early Friday morning, indulged in a quick bite of the smoked salmon with fresh bagels, cream cheese smears, capers, and onions for breakfast and caught an early flight from Pittsburgh to New York. I wasn't at all nervous about introducing Tariq to my parents—I felt almost like they'd have kindred spirits. In fact, I knew they'd love him as much as I did, and I was very excited about spending the weekend with my family before leaving to celebrate Christmas week with his family in Paris.

We landed at noon and my dad and stepmother picked us up from Kennedy airport and whisked us off to brunch at the famous Katz's deli in lower Manhattan—one of my and my dad's favorite restaurants. It was also a great place for introductions and having intimate conversations.

Katz's deli is famous for some of New York's best bagels, pastrami, corned beef, and my absolute favorite, chocolate babka. We love the rush of the crowds and the fresh and delicious food, and we always purchase extra to take home—this day was no exception. It's become somewhat of a tradition for my dad and I whenever I come home.

Brunch always starts with an obligatory warming bowl of matzo ball soup and egg creams to drink for everyone—the matzo balls are moist and fluffy, and the broth is light, aromatic, and scented with just a touch of chopped onions and carrot strips for flavoring. I often order extra to take home and add chopped chicken to make a complete meal. The egg creams are a quintessential New York staple and I obliged Tariq to try one as part of his New York experience.

"They're just chocolate milkshakes with soda water," he said.

"Yep! But that's how we know if people are true New Yorkers or just tourists," my dad said with a chuckle. "If you see it as just chocolate soda water, you probably aren't aware that there really aren't any eggs or cream in the drink. The name is the result of the creamy foam produced," he said. Then my dad went on to discuss the history behind a number of New York's favorite culinary treasures. Tariq was quite impressed with his historical culinary acumen. Just as he started to voice his approval, the waitress came to the table to take our orders.

For the main course, we ordered a bakers' dozen of assorted mini bagels with a variety of cream cheese smears for the table. I ordered corned beef hash with fried eggs for me and eggs over light for Tariq, and my dad ordered pastrami and cheese omelets with home fries for him and my stepmom. I also ordered two chocolate babkas—one for the table and the other to take to Tariq's family in Paris as a thank-you gift.

Before ordering the babka, I told Tariq I wanted to give one to his mother. His first response was "You know you're going to the pastry capital of the world, right?"

"Yes, but wait until you taste this babka, it's loaded with delicious chunks of sultry chocolate beautifully layered between about a thousand sheets of tender pastry. It's a perfectly balanced presentation of a smooth, tender, and buttery chocolate pastry with a lightly sweetened and crispy crust. I think everyone will enjoy a little piece of New York through the babka," I said. He tasted it and strongly agreed.

Basking in the afterglow of the delicious and filling brunch, Tariq had lots of energy and wanted to visit Rockefeller Center to see the famed Christmas tree. My stepmom and I made a quick trip to the bathroom and returned to find Tariq and my dad in an intense conversation about religion and spirituality. I knew it was a touchy subject for Tariq, so I surreptitiously interrupted by asking my dad to join us for ice skating. He refused my offer but did agree to drop us off and to take our luggage to my mom's house.

A quick trip uptown for the ice skating, shopping at Macy's, and then to B. Smith's restaurant for dinner. We ended up passing on the ice skating because there were too many people but the shopping at Macy's was a great substitute. We walked, did quite a bit of window-watching of the holiday scenery, and enjoyed the true spirit of the Christmas season in New York. Then the hunger pains started to hit us.

B. Smith is from Pittsburgh and Tariq had been hearing lots of good things about her food and wanted to try it. However it was closed when we got there. Without missing a beat, we jumped in a taxi and went to Sylvia's in Harlem instead. We had a delicious but rather pricey soul food dinner—crisp buttermilk fried chicken, savory collard greens with smoked pork, candied yams, and buttery corn bread.

After dinner, we took another taxi to my mom's house in the North Bronx and played Spades all evening with my sisters while my mom prepared an early holiday family dinner. Playing Spades or any kind of games for the first time with my family is like a rite of passage—you have to inoculate yourself to either ignore or join in the trash talking. Especially from my older sister Laverne, the queen of trash talking, who is a music teacher but clearly missed her calling to become a comedian.

Laverne is very warm and welcoming. Her quick wit and extensive vocabulary always keep you on your toes when playing cards or making music. She, however, never bites her tongue when it comes to telling the truth, and she tends to tell it like it is all the time—even when it may not be at the most appropriate of times. She alone can keep the laughter going for hours. This time was no different. We all had a great time and Tariq learned a bunch of new tricks we'd hoped would improve his Spades game.

Menus

Join Us for a Traditional Jewish-Style New York Brunch
featuring

BRUNCH

Chicken Matzo Ball Soup

Assorted Bagels & Cream Cheese Smears

Eggs Over Light

Corned Beef Hash with Fried Eggs

Pastrami & Provolone Omelets
with home-fried potatoes

BEVERAGE

Chocolate Egg Creams

DESSERT

Chocolate Babka

Join Us for a New York–Style Soul Food Dinner
featuring

Southern Fried Chicken

Collard Greens with Smoked Pork

Candied Yams • Corn Bread

Blessed Assurance

Sunday morning and we attended church with my whole family before returning home for an early dinner and more games. My mom sang as usual, and Tariq seemed to thoroughly enjoy the music at church. I thought he wasn't paying attention to the sermon, but I would later learn I was clearly mistaken.

Dinner was quintessentially mom—simply amazing! As usual, she set out to impress everyone and she did not disappoint. She served a most impeccable selection of herb-roasted turkey with a silky, flavor-packed gravy, a brown sugar Virginia ham, her signature corn bread stuffing with water chestnuts and smoked oysters, sweet and creamy baked corn pudding, sautéed collard greens, creamy baked macaroni and cheese, silky potato salad, homemade dinner rolls, and fresh cranberry relish. Tariq had at least four servings and munched throughout the evening's festivities—he really enjoyed it.

Mom's sweet potato pies had earned a stellar reputation in the community and each holiday she'd take orders for at least two hundred—as a result she'd gotten a head start on the pies for our dessert. In addition to the silky smooth and creamy sweet potato pies, she made a lemon-coconut pound cake with a chopped Brazil nut and limoncello glaze topping—me and my sister's favorite cake. My family treasures them as rare delicacies and usually devours them as soon as they hit the table. Just as soon as they cooled down in the kitchen I hid a few slices of the cake and an entire pie to take with me to Paris along with the chocolate babka.

We almost never eat dessert immediately after dinner, as we need time for the amazing meal to digest first. Instead, we usually have dessert while playing games and snacking on whatever we want. We paired up and jumped right into our traditional fight or flight after-dinner games—Spades, bid whist, and backgammon. Winners kept their seats and continued to play, but losers had to give their seats up to the next team.

While playing Spades, Tariq insisted on being Laverne's partner again, and again he kept making mistakes, which would eventually cause them to lose the game and their seats to the next two players. She hated to lose and jokingly hammered him over and over again while everyone laughed hysterically. Every time he made a silly mistake, Laverne would comically call him out and we'd all break into laughter, including him—I was beginning to think he liked the attention. But he eventually figured out her game. To get her off his back, he told her she should be nice and love him in spite of his faults—reiterating the minister's opening and closing statements from the church sermon earlier in the day. We all broke into laughter once again and Laverne conceded.

In between losing hands, Laverne started playing the piano to calm herself down. Wanting to stay in her good graces, Tariq made his way onto the piano bench and told her he loved the song "Precious Lord" that my mom sang during the church service. Laverne decided to try and teach him the song, but his accent and lack of tonality was funny and made everyone laugh—even him. Of course Laverne jokingly gave him a hard time about it, too. It was hysterical and made for a refreshing and wonderful addition to our family celebration.

After we finished cleaning up and the rest of the family went home, mom called Tariq and me into the kitchen to chat and have a cup of chamomile tea to help digest all the food we ate before bedtime. Tariq couldn't help himself, he had to indulge in more of the leftover food and sweet potato pie. He'd never tasted it before and seemed to become somewhat obsessed with it.

He'd already polished off almost two whole pies alone. In the meantime, mom had decided to give me an early Christmas present. She presented us with two business class flight upgrades to Paris. Tariq humbly refused, but I refused to let him refuse.

"Okay, you sit in the back. I'll sit in business class and torment you all the way to Paris!" I said jokingly. He quickly relented and thanked my mom over and over again before retiring for the evening.

We had a 6:00 a.m. flight to Paris on Monday morning. After a great weekend with my family, the time to leave came very quickly. Mom and Laverne drove us to the airport, where we checked in at the curb, received our flight upgrades, and boarded our luxurious business class flight to Paris. I'd also persuaded my mom to lend me her full-length mink coat to properly play the high society role. I looked and felt fabulous.

The Mile High Club

The flight began with a light continental breakfast. Later we were served a nice baked halibut, mixed vegetables, and rice pilaf dinner on real plates and all the drinks we could stomach. We enjoyed the large cushy seats with built-in TV sets that set the stage for a very comfortable and sensual flight across the Atlantic Ocean. The food was nothing special so I was very happy I'd brought the sweet potato pie and lemon-coconut cake from mom's house for Tariq and me to munch on for dessert.

Three hours into the flight, Tariq got fidgety while we were watching movies and he started playing with me. He started tickling my feet, then my underarms and then he abruptly started kissing me and biting my neck. We were both covered by my mom's coat and took full advantage of the coziness. He slid his hand under my dress, into my lace panties, and started rubbing my sex—I lost it!

Chills ran up and down my whole body. Showers of moisture began to slowly stream down my sex. I jumped up and immediately went to the bathroom to get myself together. I had to check my underwear that was now soaked with my juices. I entered the bathroom and before I could close the door, Tariq slipped in right behind me.

"Can I help?" he said while closing the door.

"With what? I just came in to clean up a bit," I responded.

"Okay, I can do that," he responded as he sat on the toilet and started kissing my sex. I fell right into his trap. I ripped off my panties and shoved his head further into my hot, juicy sex.

Soft, gentle strokes from his tender, warm tongue blanketed my now throbbing love bud. He bathed himself in my deliciously perfumed juices. I held onto the sink and the wall for dear life as my body churned with every stroke of his tongue. The airplane hit a little turbulence and I unexpectedly fell onto his lap. I was horny as hell.

He opened his pants and out popped his big, beautiful, fully erect giant cock. I needed to taste him ... I wanted to feel him inside me. We were both on cloud nine and I wanted him to remember the feeling as much as I would.

I surrounded his hot steely cock with my juicy lips ... inch by inch it filled my mouth as I stroked and sucked with long, deep thrusts, up and down. I needed to satiate my wanton desire to please him.

"Oh! Oh! Umh Anais! ... It feels incredible!" he said as he moaned with intense pleasure.

His beautiful cock was so big I had to come up for air. I also had to remind him we were on an airplane where people might hear us.

At this point my love canal was dripping with desire to feel his steely cock inside of me. I attempted to shift myself up and he abruptly lifted me up by my behind, turned me to face him, and lowered me onto his huge love muscle. Gently lowering me down, he initially took his time to allow my body to adjust. But as soon as he got half way inside me, he impaled me.

"Oh God! It's so big Tariq! You feel amazing! Ummmmmh!" I purred—it felt so good. "But we have to keep the noise down," I said while trying to whisper. But he was riding me so fast I couldn't suppress the joy.

"Oh baby! Yeah! Right there, right there! Fuck me baby! Fuck me good!" I said as my mews got louder and louder. It was mind-blowing.

He shifted his hips, slapped my ass, and I went crazy. Joyful spasms of pleasure enveloped my entire body as he plunged deep into my psyche ... faster and faster. I went crazy. I tried to suppress my cries by kissing him to mute the sound. But he wasn't quite as savvy. He ripped his tongue out of my mouth and cried in a whispering shout, "I'm cumming baby, I'm cumming!" Then he ripped his penis out of my sex and came all over my stomach.

"Round Two?" he said as he attempted to turn me over and go into me from behind.

But I didn't have a chance to respond because someone knocked on the door. It scared the hell out of me. I quickly turned on the water and we proceeded to clean ourselves up.

"I'll take a rain check," I whispered as we both chuckled joyfully. I was a bit disheveled but felt great.

We finished cleaning up and Tariq opened the door so we could discreetly sneak back to our seats. I slid out in front of him in hopes that no one would see the two of us exiting together. It was dark in the cabin so we felt pretty safe. We slipped back into our seats, wrapped up in the coat, and fell asleep in each other's arms until we landed at Charles de Gaulle airport in Paris.

Menu

Join Us for a New York Christmas Dinner Celebration
featuring

DINNER

HERB-ROASTED TURKEY
Momma B's signature corn bread stuffing with water chestnuts and smoked oysters

BROWN SUGAR VIRGINIA HAM

BAKED CORN PUDDING

SAUTÉED COLLARD GREENS

BAKED MACARONI & CHEESE

CREAMY POTATO SALAD

FRESH CRANBERRY RELISH

DESSERT

SILKY SWEET POTATO PIE

LEMON-COCONUT POUND CAKE
with Brazil nut and limoncello glaze topping

ENTERTAINMENT

Spades; bid whist; backgammon.

30

An Introduction to Paris

After clearing customs, we grabbed our luggage and exited to the final baggage claim area where a gentleman was holding a sign with Tariq's name on it. Apparently Tariq's mom told him before we left Pittsburgh that she'd send a car to pick us up from the airport and it was right on time.

The driver collected our luggage and off we went to delve into my long awaited visit to the city of my dreams. My anxiousness preceded me, and as we exited the airport, Paris didn't immediately look quite like I'd envisioned. There were industrial parks and nondescript buildings on either side of the road. I didn't even see trees or land like I was accustomed to when leaving our airports in New York and Pittsburgh. In fact, it wasn't until about twenty-five minutes into the ride that the lights of the more urban areas began to appear, as the traffic got heavier.

After about forty minutes on the nondescript highway, we went into a small tunnel, then up a little hill while exiting the tunnel, and out of the blue this magical city appeared. It was illuminating—emotionally and visually. The romance of the city immediately began to shape itself in my mind. The picturesque and historic buildings, brilliant lights draped on the massive trees that were perfectly manicured and lined the extra-wide streets and boulevards, and the unique boutiques and bakeries that showcased their goods in the windows hypnotized me.

As we traveled deeper into the city, I caught a quick glimpse of the original Statue of Liberty—it was much smaller than the one in New York. Then we breezed past the Louvre museum with the new pyramid recently added, and off in the distance I got a glimpse of the Eiffel Tower before going up a small hill where cars were coming from all directions and merging onto a main street covered by a huge arch.

"Where are we Tariq?" I asked. He decided to be a smart ass.

"Paris!" he answered. We both laughed.

"No shit Sherlock! I mean what part of Paris are we in and what's that big arch?" I quipped while laughing.

He explained that the arch is called the Arc de Triomphe, the largest arch in the world, which was commissioned by Napoleon Bonaparte in the 1800s to celebrate a war victory. Located in the eighth district of Paris, the Arc de Triomphe overlooks the entrance to the Champs-Elysées—the most famous shopping street in the world. I couldn't wait to get out and go shopping. My curiosity was at an all-time high and I felt like I was dreaming. But I wasn't, and my exciting adventure in Paris had only just begun.

Home Sweet Home

It was late afternoon and we'd finally arrived at Tariq's house. It was just three blocks from the Champs-Elysées—I started planning my shopping adventure immediately. Two blocks down and a couple of right turns down small alley-like streets and we were there—88 bis, Rue du Colisée. In the middle of the small street, the driver stopped in front of two huge black doors that sat in between two retail shops and very discreetly served as entrance gates to a courtyard. Tariq got out to open the gate with a code and we pulled into a rather large courtyard that housed several different apartment buildings. The driver took us to the very last building, got out of the car, and put our bags in front of a small elevator. Tariq signed the driver's slip and he was on his way.

We took the elevator up to the third floor, and the doors opened into a private hallway that led directly to the apartment. Tariq and I walked in the front door and the apartment was stunning—like nothing I'd ever seen before. His mom and brother greeted us at the door with warm embraces and traditional French kisses, took my bags, and escorted me to my living quarters.

I'd never formally met Tariq's mother, however she was just as warm and welcoming as mine. A beautiful fifty-something Lebanese woman, it was clear that she was the consummate parachute mom. In fact, Tariq confessed that her only job was to travel the world and take care of her family. She was very kind and made sure I felt at home in her home, and I did.

Unfortunately, I didn't get the opportunity to meet his father as he was still on location working in Morocco. Shortly before our arrival, he called to inform Tariq's mom that he'd had an emergency at one of the construction sites he supervised and couldn't leave. Therefore he wouldn't make it home for Christmas.

In an effort to more equitably share the holidays with her family, his mother decided to stay in Paris to spend Christmas with us. Then she made arrangements for her and his younger brother, Jacque, to leave the day after Christmas to bring in the New Year with his father.

Jacque had flown in earlier in the week from Pittsburgh and greeted us upon our arrival. I'd spent quite a bit of time with him in Pittsburgh and was happy to be greeted by a familiar face. Jacque is very kind and just as handsome as Tariq; he is also quite an interesting character.

We'd often have dinner with him whenever Tariq was in Pittsburgh, and I invited him to join us in New York, but he declined. He flew home ahead of us because his girlfriend refused to join him for Christmas in New York and then broke up with him one week before the semester ended. My guess was that he needed to be with his mother to help heal his wounded heart.

Jacque's a computer genius and often revered for his creative acumen. However his genius was sometimes a blessing and a curse—for anyone that got in his way, that is. He was one of only three undergraduate students accepted into one of Pittsburgh's new and innovative artificial intelligence programs, and at the time was one of an elite few who knew how to hack into just about any computer system. He took my bags to the guest room, showed me where everything was, and warmly welcomed me to make their home my home.

It was my first time visiting Paris, and although I didn't have anything to compare it to, it was clear that the apartment was something very special that was either designed or inspired by an eclectic but modernist interior designer. It boasted four very large bedrooms, three bathrooms, an expansive eat-in kitchen, and generous living and dining rooms large enough for at least twenty diners seated comfortably. The expansive quarters took up more than three thousand square feet of living space and were beautifully appointed, chic yet quaint. Although the structure of the building was quintessentially Parisian, with Juliet balconies in just about every room that overlooked the fragrant bakeries and shops at the street level, the architecture was a brilliant bridge between traditional French and modernist design.

The interior decor was an eclectic mixture of French provincial furniture and antique Middle Eastern art and artifacts. It was stunning! However Tariq's mom's culinary reputation preceded her, and I was very much looking forward to lunch. It was already set up on the dining table and his mom insisted that we nourish ourselves before taking on the day.

She made some of Tariq's favorite items to welcome him home: fresh hummus with homemade pita bread, olives, and za'atar—a thyme and sesame seed dried spice blend; *fattoush*—a Mediterranean-style bread salad made with fried pita bread, assorted fresh vegetables, feta cheese, and romaine lettuce all dressed in a tangy lemon garlic dressing; and fried kibbe, the national dish of Lebanon. I thought kibbe was served raw, but Tariq's mom told me she prefers to fry it. Everything was simply delicious. While we indulged in the fresh, flavor-packed meal, I jumped at the opportunity to discuss preparation techniques with her. But shortly into the conversation, jet lag quickly began to set in and the bed was calling my name.

I took a nice hot bath and jumped in the very cozy down-stuffed bed with the intention of waking up and going sightseeing at 6:00 p.m. However it became apparent that Tariq and I both were very exhausted. Although we were in bedrooms on complete opposite sides of the apartment, we both slept well past 8:00 p.m. At that point some of the monuments recommended in the travel guide were already closed. Instead Tariq suggested we use the first day to go sightseeing and shopping on the Champs-Elysées—my shopping dream came sooner than I thought it would. Off we went to explore.

Living the Dream

Many of the buildings in Paris are cloaked behind electronic security doors that lead to a courtyard before entering the actual apartment complex. If you're a guest, the resident has to give you the access code or you'll never get anywhere near the apartment. It's the first thing Tariq gave me as we exited the building.

We sauntered along the small, slate stone sidewalks of the side streets and passed an assortment of scintillating bakeries, chocolate shops, and French restaurants. I ogled at the variety of merchant's shops that fill in between the entry doors of courtyards leading to buildings that house a variety of resident apartments, houses, and businesses. After walking for about fifteen minutes, we landed right in the middle of the famed avenue Champs Elysées—beautiful, glamorous, and legendary.

The bright evening lights reminded me of Times Square in New York, but the area is ten times bigger and much more ornate. The pristine sidewalks were clearly designed to handle the masses of tourists that visit daily. Separated by eight lanes of traffic, each walkway spans about 100 feet on both sides and the streets were fully lined with those perfectly manicured trees dripping with brightly lit Christmas lights.

We visited a variety of unique shops and a multitude of venues similar to indoor malls. Tariq obliged me to visit the mall with the spy store, as it was very unique. There were all types of electronics and clandestine items like writing instruments that doubled as knives when opened, hundreds of small microphones for bugging and listening to people's conversations virtually undetected, and all kinds of neat things I'd never be able to get through customs. There was also a little sex toy shop in the mall. Unbeknownst to Tariq, I secretly purchased a small gift for him as a Christmas present and I couldn't wait to surprise him.

To my amusement, the world's largest Virgin Atlantic flagship store was prominently positioned right in the middle of the popular avenue. It housed a wonderful café on the first floor, a huge bookstore in the basement, and an amazing collection of world music for testing and purchasing on the second floor. I was enthralled with the varieties of music offered for purchase. There were hoards of CDs and downloads—from the unique and artsy Argentine tango musicians to the sultry rhythmic singers and drummers from Mozambique. I was in musical paradise and ended up purchasing music from mainland Africa, Cape Verde, and even lesser known American musicians I wasn't able to find at home. It was a treasure trove of culture that I planned to use to augment the themes and ambiance of my romantic catering events and even the SNL celebrations.

Menu

Join Us for a Traditional Lebanese Parisian
Welcoming Lunch

featuring

LUNCH

Fresh Hummus
with homemade pita bread, olives, and za'atar, a thyme and
sesame seed dried spice blend

Fattoush
a Mediterranean-style bread salad made with fried pita
bread, assorted fresh vegetables, feta cheese, and romaine
lettuce dressed in a lemon garlic dressing

Fried Kibbe

Parisian Culinary Adventures

As we continued walking, we passed showroom after showroom with giant glass windows displaying the latest in housewares, clothing, and some of the world's fanciest automobiles that were clearly designed to capture the attention of the world's elite—the famous and infamous people dining in the multitude of cafés and five-star restaurants that lined the expansive sidewalk. After two hours of walking and shopping along the more than one-mile street, Tariq and I were hungry, and settled on having dinner at one of his favorite Italian restaurants.

Fully decked out like a Tuscan villa and loaded with doting patrons, the restaurant specialized in handmade pizzas baked in a wood-fired brick oven, topped with handmade cheese and roasted vegetables. They were exquisite! This was a major compliment coming from someone who believed New York has the best pizza in the world hands down—until that day.

The crust was crunchy yet soft and chewy, and the perfectly seasoned sauce was crafted from fragrant tomatoes, pungent garlic, and the freshest Italian parsley. The wood-fire smoked eggplant, zucchini, and mushroom medley was simply seasoned with olive oil and a hint of salt, and all those lovely morsels perfectly complemented the handmade mozzarella cheese and fresh basil layered atop the pizza. The ingredients were fresh, perfectly balanced, and hit every note on the scale of culinary perfection. I now felt obliged to share the prize for top honors in pizza with Paris. There were no leftovers. With our tummies full and our pockets a little lighter, we went back to the apartment and retired for the evening.

The next day was Christmas Eve. Tariq and Jacque agreed to take me to the Quartier Asiatique, aka Chinatown, for lunch, and I was on an all-time high. I had really enjoyed our last adventure in San Francisco's Chinatown and was looking forward to the Parisian experience.

We walked to the Métro, took two trains, and after nearly a forty-five minute ride, exited at the Maison Blanche in the thirteenth district of Paris. Unlike the picturesque Métro stations in the more affluent districts, the escalator ride up to the street was pretty nebulous. When we got to the street level it became clear that we were further out in the suburbs of Paris.

"Awwwh! Now this feels more like the concrete jungles of New York," I said with chuckling pride.

Multiple storied high-rise residential buildings, Asian-themed grocery stores proudly displaying their names in Mandarin and French, and small bodega-like stores lined every available inch of real estate. The streets bustled with vendors hawking fresh fruit and vegetables for tasting and a multitude of Asian restaurants proudly showcasing rows and rows of Peking duck and roasted chicken with lacquered finishes. Tariq recognized his favorite Vietnamese restaurant by the stacks and stacks of layered spring rolls that prominently decorated the window right next to the chefs who boldly showcased artistically strewn giant woks filled with ready-made foods. My mouth watered with anticipation.

I'd never eaten Vietnamese food, but the tantalizing appearance and aromatic scents dragged me into the restaurant by the nose and commanded my attention. I couldn't read anything on the menu, however I pretty much love all kinds of spring rolls. So I found us a seat and, as usual, asked Tariq to order for me as long as he included the obligatory spring rolls.

My nose did not forsake me in that very important culinary moment. The food was outstanding! We all had a bowl of pho—a fragrant soup broth filled with a vermicelli rice noodle salad and topped with an assortment of fresh herbs and vegetables and your choice of protein—grilled pork and shrimp for me, barbecued beef for Tariq, and grilled chicken and shrimp for Jacque. Tariq ordered one dozen spring rolls, aka *nem,* for the table, with a sweet and tangy rice wine dipping sauce, and fried shrimp for appetizers. Everything was so delicious and fresh, we all ate until we couldn't stuff another morsel in our mouths.

During lunch, Jacque decided that confession is apparently good for the soul and decided to tell on himself. He was heartbroken when his girlfriend unexpectedly broke up with him, so he decided to retaliate. Then he went into details and it was scandalous.

Right before finals, he was so angry with his now ex-girlfriend, that he hacked into the school's computer mainframe and posted a nude photo of her on the main landing page. Every time someone logged into the school's computer system, the first thing to pop up on the screen was a full-frontal naked photo of her whole body—face included. The whole fifteen thousand plus university community was buzzing with shock and disbelief, including her.

According to him, nobody, including his ex-girlfriend knew who did it, or even how they did it. Only Jacque and one of his closest friends knew. After the photo was posted for about two hours, the chancellor sent out a university-wide e-mail warning that if the photo wasn't taken down within twenty-four hours, he'd launch an investigation and expel whoever was responsible for posting the photo. Needless to say, Jacque quickly removed it. He said that even though he got revenge, he still wasn't happy because he was still all alone for Christmas, hence his decision to join his mother and father in Morocco since he knew Tariq would be with me.

Although Jacque never got caught, Tariq chastised him about hacking into the university's system but laughed hysterically. On the other hand, I tried to console him about his broken heart. I also told Jacque I'd bust his knees if he ever did that to me. Again we all laughed hysterically.

We left the restaurant and I insisted on visiting one of the Asian grocery stores to pick up a bottle of that delicious dipping sauce we used for the spring rolls as a souvenir. I fully intended to experiment with the flavors once I got back home. We did a little more Christmas and souvenir shopping and headed home to prepare for Christmas Day.

Menus

*Join Us for a Handmade Italian
Wood-Fired Pizza Parisian Style*

featuring

BRICK OVEN PIZZA
with roasted eggplant, zucchini, and portobello mushrooms

Join Us for a Vietnamese Brunch Parisian Style

featuring

SPRING ROLLS

PHO
*vermicelli rice noodle salad with grilled pork and shrimp,
barbecued beef, or chicken and shrimp and an assortment of
fresh herbs and vegetables*

Christmas in Paris

Tariq's mother went all out just like my mom, but in a different way—it was just as exciting. Awakened early Christmas morning by the fragrant calling of the fresh pita bread she was baking on clay stones in the oven, my nose led me to the kitchen before Tariq or Jacque woke up. When I walked in the dining room, she had the table beautifully dressed and each individual place setting sported gift boxes with each of our names, including hers. It was a beautiful and very thoughtful surprise. However it wasn't the gifts that caught my eye first, it was the amazing presentation of the foods. They were artistically plated and smelled absolutely delicious.

Each dish had its own spotlight, but together all shined with a harmonious symphony of smells and colors. The dishes included savory *fatayas*—spinach pies with crumbled feta cheese and pickled pearl onions; a colorful chickpea and tabbouleh (bulgur wheat and vegetable) salad playfully surrounded by segmented boiled eggs; the fresh baked flatbread; and for a touch of sweet, labneh—thick yogurt cheese, scented with orange flower water and Madagascar cinnamon and topped with chopped pistachios, pomegranate seeds, and silky raw honey. She skillfully sliced the chocolate babka and presented it in a beautiful swirl on an ornate platter. Freshly brewed mint tea and Turkish coffee served in traditional silver dispensers with long spouts for cooling were an added complement. The table looked like a piece of royal culinary art and the scrumptious food made for a delicious Christmas breakfast.

While sitting at the table, she implored us to open our gifts and suggested I start first. I was happy to oblige. I opened the top of the delicately wrapped box and inside was a beautiful green and white silk toiletry bag embroidered with gold cord. Inside the ornate bag was a ticket to attend Christmas dinner and a show at the famous Moulin Rouge. Everyone else had tickets and personalized gifts, but I was the only one to receive the beautiful keepsake bag. We were all delighted with the treats and couldn't wait to see the show. I was especially honored that she was so kind and thoughtful to me even though it was our first time meeting each other.

Christmas breakfast was filling, fragrant, and crafted with love. Tariq and I offered to do cleanup while his mom and Jacque excused themselves to pack for their early morning flight to Marrakech, Morocco. We played a few rounds of backgammon, got dressed, and hailed a taxi to take us across town to the Moulin Rouge for dinner and the show.

Dinner at the Moulin Rouge was a patchwork of delicious eye candy, and the venue and the show were simply awe striking. It started when we pulled up to the front door. After waiting in a long queue, our taxi pulled past the iconic red windmill that sits parallel to the entrance and dropped us at the front door. The vivacious receiving area proudly welcomes you with colorful photos and exciting video presentations of past shows framed in jewel boxes hanging from the walls on either side. After we presented our tickets at the box office, a host led us down a red velvet carpet into the main dining and show hall.

The intimate yet brazen showroom immediately dazzles you with quintessential Parisian nostalgia as soon as you hit the door. A grand hall, it hosts seating for nearly seven hundred people and is encased in red velvet walls bejeweled with sparkling gold leaf and crystal chandeliers. Red carpets and gold and red velvet chairs complement the well-staged petite dining tables that are lit with the smallest of matching chandelier lamps. The obvious focal point of the room was the stage—a harmonious amalgamation of the Broadway-like structures you'd see in old vaudeville movies. It was flanked with multicolored lights and cameras operated by remote control. The most amazing part of the showroom was a clandestine glass floor that cached a fifty-foot wide, fully stocked, retractable aquarium in front of the main stage. We were seated at a table for four that sat right in the middle of the room—about two hundred feet from the front of the aquarium.

Although I peaked at the video presentations of past shows that greeted us at the entrance, I was pretty much in the dark and had no idea of what to expect. I'm a pretty laid-back person and I don't like to spoil the party as long as it doesn't endanger me, so I was open for whatever we were going to see.

The waitress came and took our drink and dinner orders before the show began. With a few minutes until show time, I began to scope out the place—I wanted to see who was around me. Scores of Chinese and Japanese tourists dressed in elegant traditional kimonos filled the majority of the seats and quietly chatted while enjoying their meals and drinks. Anxious with anticipation, I wasn't sure of what to expect. Then the music started playing and everyone fell silent as if it were a rehearsed response.

Not long after we finished eating the appetizers of smoked salmon terrines served with artisanal breadsticks and gherkin pickles, the show started with a vaudeville number and two French singers entertaining us during the main course—crown rack of lamb with tamarind sauce, *haricots verts* (green beans), and panfried pearl potatoes. The singers were a bit boring, but the food was tender and tasty. Tariq's mom didn't really like the lamb. She said it didn't quite measure up to her flavor profile.

Shortly before dessert arrived—a Christmas cake called *bûche de Noël*—and coffee, an entourage of beautifully costumed dancers paraded onto the stage and performed several iconic cancan dances for about thirty minutes. All of a sudden we heard a loud roar from the Japanese tourists sitting closest to the stage.

We looked over to see what the commotion was to discover the giant aquarium was rising up from the floor in front of the stage. It was filled with what looked like a thousand little snakes swimming all around the water. As if that wasn't startling enough, a bikini-clad dancer ran onto the stage with a huge yellow snake wrapped around her entire body. She started dirty dancing with the snake like it was her lover—dipping the snake's tail in and out of her sex and putting its head up to her mouth like she was going to suck it. I was a little embarrassed and tried my best not to look at Tariq or his mom. But I really wanted to gauge their reaction, so I took a quick glance. I got nothing but a stoic stare from both of them.

When the snake lady finished getting the audience all riled up, she jumped into the huge aquarium and started swimming provocatively with the huge snake in the midst of little ones. I do not like snakes, in fact I'm deathly afraid of them. But we were far back enough that I didn't feel threatened or get scared. It was actually an amazing and beautiful display of Mother Nature fraternizing with her animals—a fun, exciting, and certainly different way to spend Christmas.

Our soiree at the Moulin Rouge took up the majority of the evening so we headed back to the apartment after the show. We had a quick nightcap and I thanked his mom and Jacque for hosting me and for the wonderful Christmas gift before going to bed.

Menu

Join Us for Christmas Dinner at the Moulin Rouge

featuring

APPETIZERS

SMOKED SALMON TERRINES

with breadsticks and gherkin pickles

DINNER

CROWN RACK OF LAMB

with tamarind sauce, panfried pearl potatoes, and haricots verts
(French green beans)

DESSERT

BÛCHE DE NOËL

The Raincheck

Tariq's mom and brother left very early the next morning. I was asleep in the guest room on the side where his parents' room is, and he was asleep in his room on the other side of the apartment. I woke up before he did and when I noticed we were the only ones in the house, I decided it was time to give him the Christmas present I picked up from the sex toy shop.

I'd purchased a little vibrating Ben Wa butt bead with a remote control called a Bum Bead, and it was a perfect time to cash in on the raincheck I promised him on the airplane. I slipped into his bed, and after a few tender strokes, put his cock in my mouth to wake him up with a joyous ejaculation. It was pretty easy because he loved to sleep in the nude, as did I.

I had the bum bead in my hand and the remote on the bed. He began moving his hips with each thrust of my mouth. As he moved quicker and quicker, I rubbed his asshole with the lubricant and just as his undulating movements began to climax, I slid the vibrating bum bead into his ass.

"Ohhh! ... Oh! ... Oh my goodness Anais! That's different. Oh God! ... THIS FEELS AMAZING!!!" he shouted as I sucked and slurped. Trembling with intense pleasure, he squeezed his ass cheeks as hard as he could and within five minutes he ejaculated all over my face.

He tried to grab me into him and I immediately hit the button. The beads vibrated and stopped him dead in his tracks. He went crazy, again—his body spasmed with extreme pleasure. It was like I had total control of him, and I didn't even need the handcuffs to restrain him.

"This is gonna be a fun day right Nuli Ana Tariq?" I said. I wanted to bring his memory back to the fantasy of the first night we made love.

"Yes Mistress!" he responded with intrigue and excitement. As I'd hoped, he picked right back up where we'd left off.

"Now, I gonna need you to get up now, make me a delicious French breakfast, and then take me sightseeing, okay?" I said as I hit the button one more time.

"Oh God! Please! Just sit on me. My dick is rock-hard and I can't move," he lamented. I started laughing hysterically. I enjoyed being in control of his uncontrollable desire for me.

"But I promised, so I'll obey Mistress," he said.

I was having fun with him. I decided to torment him a little more before I allowed him to take the bum bead out. I did, however, promise to make the wait worth it later on, but only if he agreed to get up.

Now fully inspired by my promise, he jumped out of the bed and rushed into the kitchen to make breakfast. It only took him about fifteen minutes. He prepared a proper French pressed coffee and a traditional French sandwich—the croque madame. It's similar to an American grilled ham and cheese sandwich, but with a little twist. The difference is that its prepared open faced on a slice of crusty French sandwich bread that's buttered with a béchamel cheese sauce (which came in a jar and looked similar to a white cheese sauce), layered with tender slices of ham and Gruyère cheese, and then topped with a fried egg after toasting the cheese in the broiler. The meal was light and delicious—just what we needed to start the full day of sightseeing we'd planned.

During breakfast, Tariq's best friend called to welcome him home for the holidays, and asked to take us to dinner. He wanted to meet me and catch up with Tariq's life in America. Although it would require us to cut our plans short, I was now not only excited about going sightseeing but also about being able to meet some of his friends. I couldn't wait to see what lay ahead. Besides, I already knew Tariq didn't like being a tour guide. While getting dressed, I joked and told him that it was pretty evident that he only agreed to take me sightseeing today because he knew I had the remote to the bum bead and wouldn't entertain his objections. He'd consistently voiced his displeasure with sightseeing and it was no different that day.

"Parisians despise being mistaken as tourists and honestly most aren't very fond of tourists because we get so many every day, of every week, of every year!" he griped jokingly. "But you know I'd do anything for my sweet Anais," he followed with a big hug and a kiss on my forehead.

At that moment I searched for the remote to the bum bead. But he grabbed it before I could get it.

"I already took it out. I'll be happy to replace it this evening," he said with a snicker while confessing with what appeared to be a bit of remorse. He seemed to be enjoying the power I had over him with the bum bead but said it was difficult to keep it in while going outside.

"I would never expect you to go outside with that thing!" I quipped with laughter. "I'd be buzzing you all over the place and people would think you had epilepsy or something," I said as we both laughed hysterically. We put on our coats, jumped on the elevator, and walked out the door to catch the bus.

We boarded a city tour bus that allowed us to pay one price and get on and off at the most popular monuments and tourist sites. The first stop, Notre-Dame cathedral where mass was being held—a definite plus for me. Although the Mass was in French, I was still able to partake in Holy Communion.

The Christmas decorations at the Notre-Dame cathedral were unlike any I'd ever seen before—rows of huge red velvet wreaths lit with thousands of micro lights were strategically suspended from the ceilings throughout the church; green, white, and red Christmas trees of all sizes sporting the same colored lights paraded throughout the corridors; and a collage of spotlights showcased a dark bronze statue of the baby Jesus that proudly hung above the sanctuary. It was a regal salute to a celebration of the Savior's birth.

After mass we teased our way over to the Latin Quarter—it was relatively close. The shopping was eclectic and reasonably priced, so I purchased another batch of obligatory souvenirs for my family, friends, and of course the people at the shelter while visiting a variety of monuments. Before boarding the tour bus again, we made a quick visit to the oldest university in Paris—the Sorbonne. There weren't a lot of people around and everything was locked up for the holidays, but it was nice to see. It made a great staging area for a variety of photographic memories.

The next bus stop landed us in the Montmartre district to visit the Sacré-Coeur basilica located at the highest point in Paris, to see the sites where notable artists lived and worked, and to have a light lunch. There I began to fall in love with Paris and the food scene all over again.

We were hungry and decided to start with lunch. Tariq ordered sandwiches called shawarmas at a little shop where they cooked delicately spiced chicken, beef, and lamb on a vertical spit. Then they sliced it off the spit with electric knives, layered it onto warm, cushiony pillows of fresh French bread, and topped it with a variety of fresh vegetables and a cucumber yogurt sauce. I'd found another piece of food paradise and now had enough energy to climb the hill to visit the basilica of the Sacred Heart of Paris.

Destiny's Calling

After the long walk and the underwhelming visit to the basilica, we skipped the bus and hailed a taxi to go back to Tariq's house and to get ready for dinner with his friends. But we were exhausted. We took a long nap, got in a quickie while getting dressed, and hailed another taxi.

Tariq wanted to surprise me, so he withheld the location for dinner. After an enchanting evening taxi ride across the City of Light, we ended up at the Eiffel Tower for dinner at the Jules Verne restaurant. I was ecstatic. Although it was the very first thing on my sightseeing list, we had not yet gotten to visit the Eiffel Tower. I'd almost forgotten about it because you can almost always see it from most parts of the city, especially when the clock strikes the top of the hour and the entire structure lights up. It was absolutely magical.

The designated entrance to the restaurant portal is somewhat private, and located in a small enclave away from the main tourist area. A doorman/security guard dressed in evening formals greeted us at the door, asked our names, and radioed up to the main floor before inviting us into a small, nondescript foyer to wait for the sole elevator to return and pick us up. We waited for what seemed like ten long minutes before boarding the glass elevator. As it ascended, more and more of the beauty of Paris revealed itself. After about a three-minute ride, it stopped, the doors opened, and we were instantly thrust into the opulent dining space known to the world as the Jules Verne restaurant.

The maître d' was waiting by the elevator and escorted us directly to the table where Tariq's friends awaited our arrival. They were introduced to me as his best friend, Ben, and Ben's American girlfriend Abby. We greeted each other, pondered what to order for dinner, and they started a long conversation in French. I didn't understand anything they were saying, so I politely asked Tariq to order for me and excused myself to take a walk around the restaurant to see Paris at night from the Eiffel Tower.

I could see a plethora of the monuments beaming and outlined with lights from every side of the dining room. To make it easy for tourists, the windows were outlined with information placards that described which monuments to look for while viewing, and their history was summed up in several different languages. The newly dedicated pyramid marked the Louvre, the Arc de Triomphe sat off in the distance, and I even spotted the basilica we'd visited earlier. The view was breathtaking.

While reading the placard describing the addition of the pyramid to the Louvre museum, the clock struck the top of the hour and the entire tower lit up from the outside. The sparkle of the lights illuminated the entire interior of the dining space. I felt like I was in a movie—it was simply magical!

At that point Tariq came to search for me and informed me that the appetizers were being served. Again I was happy to have asked him to order for me, and again the food was perfect, well almost. For starters, *foie gras à la plancha*—a delicate grilled goose liver pâté served with fresh fruit and whole grain crackers; the main course—creamy risotto with wild mushrooms, garlic prawns, and sautéed asparagus for me and Abby, and steak with fries and salad for Tariq and Ben.

Each dish was a wonderful showcase of high-class cuisine, aka haute cuisine, presented in a cornucopia of artsy serving dishes. The foil gras arrived first. I'd had it from a jar before, but this time it was served in a sliced loaf beautifully decorated with micro greens on a hand-blown glass plate. It was fresh and still bleeding—I couldn't bring myself to eat it. I don't like rare meat and after a few chuckles from everyone, Tariq asked for a well-done slice and I indulged—it was smooth, creamy, savory, and simply delicious.

The main course arrived with the same grandeur as the appetizer—beautifully packaged eye candy presented on exclusively designed porcelain china. The risotto was creamy and al dente, the garlic shrimp succulent with a slightly sweet char from the grill, and the sautéed wild mushroom medley and grilled asparagus perfectly complemented the dish—it became my all-time favorite meal.

The presentation was breathtaking! The dishes that the food was served in were unlike those I'd ever seen before—they were unique pieces of art clearly designed exclusively for the restaurant and boasted its signature on the bottom. I was even more impressed by the way they served the risotto and arranged the vegetables and grilled shrimp. It resembled a fine piece of artwork worthy of display in one of those famous museums. I was so inspired that I began taking photos and quickly drew Abby's attention.

She too was impressed and explained that she'd moved to Paris two years prior to start a food blog and had been traveling throughout Europe to write about food. I couldn't believe what I was hearing. I shared my dream with her to become a food writer and restaurateur. Then she told me she sells her photos to numerous magazines that use them to write about the food for tourists. I was amazed to learn that she made enough money to support her living expenses in Paris.

Then she offered to pay me for my photos if I'd send them to her and she pulled out a small album of food photos with some of her work. Not only was I thrilled by what I was hearing, but truly impressed by her audacity to take the risk of living in another country as a freelance photographer. My wheels of hope began churning like crazy. Then the food began to draw me in when my stomach started sending blatantly loud reminders that I was hungry.

Tariq and Ben's steaks didn't impress me much because they were almost pink on the outside and served extremely rare. In the culinary and foodie world, the beef in France is revered, and has a stellar reputation for being very flavorful, tender, and juicy. When the steaks arrived, Tariq dove right in—it was prepared perfectly for him. Ben, however, was completely turned off by the extremely rare steak still bleeding on the plate. He promptly requested a redo. He couldn't believe that Tariq was basically eating raw meat and joked with him in clear English.

"You should just bite the cow if you're going to eat meat that rare brother!" he quipped. We all laughed hysterically while Tariq continued to thoroughly enjoy his meal.

When the waiter returned with Ben's steak, he explained that the chefs prepare the meat to temperature, and that if they initially cook it too much, it's impossible to use the meat again. Therefore they err on the side of cooking the meat rare and if the diner wants it cooked longer they can do it without having to waste the expensive meat. He offered us dessert on the house as compensation for having to send items back twice.

After dinner we all shared chocolate and strawberry filled crêpes with Chantilly cream, and coffee for dessert. I was already tremendously high on life, so the delicious and delicate dessert just elevated that amazing feeling. I really enjoyed the meal, the company, and the restaurant.

While saying our goodbyes, Abby gave me her business card and said if I were interested in selling my food photos she'd pay from $200 to $500 per photo. She also said if I wrote a review of the food items and it was published, she could give me up to $1,500 and more if I could get them translated into other languages. I assured her I'd follow up with her once I got home and printed the photos. I felt like I had potentially hit the jackpot.

Farewell to a Dream

I'd received an enviable introduction to the incredible tastes and tours of Paris, spent an enchanting Christmas evening at the famed Moulin Rouge for dinner and a show, and closed out my storybook vacation with an invitation to make money doing the very thing I dreamed of—all during my first visit to the magical city of my dreams. Even though it was coming to an emotional ending, I was on an all-time natural high. I'd enjoyed myself so much that I wasn't quite ready to leave and I was determined to savor every final moment of my awesome vacation in Paris.

I was a little disappointed that Tariq would be staying until the middle of January and I had to travel back to Pittsburgh alone. I also knew that I had to mentally prepare myself for the return home and decided to focus on the beautiful memories as well as the opportunity that I'd just been afforded, which alleviated my angst.

We returned to the apartment very late that evening. My flight didn't leave until 4:00 p.m. the next day so we slept in a little bit and relaxed before going to a small café downstairs for a quick bite to eat. Afterward, Tariq drove me to the airport, I checked in around 1:00 p.m., and we had plenty of time to sit, have another coffee, and get our last smooches in.

I was overly excited about the entire trip and how I had quickly fallen in love with Paris, more and more each day. I also couldn't believe that I'd met Abby on the very last evening—she made me feel increasingly optimistic about my dreams of becoming a food writer and restaurateur coming to fruition. It was like God was answering my prayers and clearly ordering my steps.

I thought about it a little too long and started to question fate. I began to tell myself that it seemed too good to be true. But then again, meeting someone like Tariq while driving down the street was too good to be true, too. "Clearly that turned out pretty good," I thought. So I was sure God was blessing me with a great deal of favor and was certainly ordering my steps—which is my daily prayer.

Tariq and I finished our last coffee before heading to the security area where I had to say my final goodbyes. When we got into the secured area, I walked away from him to go up to the desk and give the gate agent my ticket. In the meantime I could see an armed guard immediately making his way over to Tariq where he started saying something to him in French.

He seemed angry. But Tariq quickly calmed him down with his response. When I finished with the gate agent, I went to give Tariq a final kiss goodbye and asked what happened. He said the guards like to harass Arabs and started to interrogate him, but he quickly shut him down.

I couldn't believe it. I'd had an amazing time and hoped it wouldn't be spoiled at the last minute. Then he said I shouldn't worry, the guard was just being nosy and asked him if I was his wife.

"What did you say?" I asked. He really took me off guard.

"Not yet," he said and snickered. I just laughed with him and gave him a very intimate kiss goodbye before I boarded my wonderful business class seat and headed back to Pittsburgh.

Menus

Join Us for a Traditional French Breakfast

featuring

CROQUE MADAME

FRENCH PRESS COFFEE

*Join Us for Parisian-Style Lebanese
Shawarma Sandwiches*

featuring

SHAWARMAS ON FRENCH BREAD

*chicken, beef, or lamb topped with fresh vegetables
and cucumber yogurt sauce*

*Join Us for Dinner at Le Jules Verne
in the Eiffel Tower*

featuring

APPETIZERS

FOIE GRAS

with fresh fruit and crackers

DINNER

STEAK FRITES

with traditional salad

WILD MUSHROOM RISOTTO

with garlic shrimp and asparagus

DESSERT

STRAWBERRY-FILLED CHOCOLATE CRÊPES

with Chantilly cream

31

The flight seemed extra long since I didn't have Tariq to entertain me. It's rare for me to have a lot of downtime so I started planning my schedule for the remainder of the year. It was also three days until the New Year, and I began to think about JB's invitation to his gig at LeMont restaurant to celebrate. I couldn't stop thinking about how it would have been really nice to bring the new year in with Tariq—I'd begun missing him already.

I started reminiscing about the amazing time I had in Paris and how I could stay there forever. The beautiful lights, the wonderful ambiance of the Parisian flair, and the sophisticated language made me feel like everywhere I went, love was in the air.

"I love Paris!" I said to myself as I drifted off to sleep for the remainder of the long eight-hour flight.

Twelve hours later—after a flight change in New York, it was a chilly Saturday afternoon and I was more than ready to get home and settle in before returning to the shelter on Monday morning. As soon as the plane landed in Pittsburgh, I grabbed my bags and jumped on the shuttle to the extended-parking lot.

Christmas had come and gone but the weather vividly reminded me that we were in the throes of a Pittsburgh winter. I had to clean off the nearly seven inches of snow that had made itself comfortable on my car over the week I was gone. I didn't make it home until around 6:15 p.m.—nearly two and a half hours after I'd landed.

I was exhausted. But I had to call my parents to let them know that I'd arrived home safe after an amazing trip. I finished talking, turned off the phone, and went straight to bed.

Jet lag hit with a vengeance. After about six hours of glorious sleep, I woke up around 1:15 a.m. Sunday. I tried everything to go back to sleep with no luck. I was bright-eyed and bushy-tailed like it was a regular work day.

"Oh well! Time to get a few things done," I lamented.

My body was accustomed to my daily routine of waking up at 7:00 a.m. It had apparently adjusted to the six-hour difference between Paris and Pittsburgh just that quickly. I decided to get up and personalize the gifts for the shelter girls, the College Crew, and my family.

As I packaged each gift from New York and Paris, I thought more and more about how difficult the job at the shelter is and how I didn't want to get stuck in that situation for the duration of my career. I loved working with children, but my passion is truly working with food, and I began to ponder the true reality of the situation.

Every time I went to the shelter, my heart broke for the children who seemed to be forgotten, given away, or just struggling with who they were at the most vulnerable times in their fragile lives. Although I have a passion for nurturing children, I believed my true calling was to work with food.

I'd been working diligently toward my long-term goal of becoming a restaurateur through my catering and taking professional cooking classes. However it was becoming more evident to me that the two career paths were becoming more divergent, and I'd soon have to make a choice.

Remaining at the shelter became increasingly difficult to justify mentally, emotionally, and most importantly, financially. The pay sucked, and the work is extremely difficult and time-consuming. Even worse, I was using the catering income to supplement my daily expenses. Therefore I couldn't even save for my restaurant if I wanted to. I knew I needed a change.

I began to brainstorm about how I could afford to leave the shelter while still supporting myself. I really wanted to become a food writer and I thought if I could get enough catering gigs while selling my photos and stories to Abby, there would be a possibility to grow. But the bigger question became how would I be able to afford to travel and eat at the fancier places, or anywhere, to be able to take the photos and sell them.

I was only grossing $1,150 a month from the shelter job, and after some initial calculations, I discovered that I could make the same amount if I sold only two or three photos a month. If I wrote the reviews and they were accepted, I could make a lot more.

"It could work!" I convincingly said to myself.

However I knew my parents would give me a hard time if I didn't have a stable source of income. But I had that figured out too, so I made a plan.

I would initially stay at the shelter for three months while working to sell the photos to Abby. I planned to hire students from the university's French department to tutor me in French and help me with the translations to test the waters. Their fees were $15 an hour to tutor and only about $20 per page to translate. Therefore, I could make a substantial profit if the reviews were accepted.

"Work could start immediately!" I thought. I already had a plethora of existing photos of my food and the events I'd catered. Using them and the university students to translate the stories would initially save me a lot of money and time.

Once I was able to confirm that Abby's offer was legitimate—and I prayed hard that it was—I could earn at least $5,000 from the photos I had on hand, and I'd be ready to make a move. It equated to a year's worth of rent payments and would allow me to give my two-weeks notice at the shelter.

The Shelter

Monday morning came quick, but I didn't have to be at the shelter until 4:00 p.m. for the evening shift, so I had time to unwind before jumping back into the fray. I woke up very early due to having a little jet lag, but it allowed me to have a very productive morning. I made myself a nice breakfast, took a steam shower, and made my way to work with the collection of gifts in tow. I signed in promptly at 4:00 p.m, and as usual, the place was in disarray. Zee was up for today's wheel of drama. The screaming was at full tilt as soon as I opened the door.

Zee had been in a good place before I left for vacation. She prayed with Khady during Ramadan, started working on plans to attend community college, and seemed to have been making good decisions for her future. But she was one of the kids who'd been abandoned to the system all of her life. As a result, she was very self-conscious and very insecure with herself.

Not wanting to jump in the middle of a situation that I knew nothing about, I immediately read the files to catch up and it appeared that she'd gotten into an altercation during a game of Pictionary with the group. Unfortunately the altercation was with the only remaining male counselor, Dwayne. The two got into a bitter dispute, started calling each other inappropriate names, and he made the mistake of calling her ugly. All the girls laughed hysterically and mocked her while using his comments against her. She flipped out, went to her room, and wouldn't come out for two days—Zee didn't take rejection well. There would be no hero's welcome upon my return on that day. In fact, it was clear that I had my work cut out for me.

The Shelter—Dwayne

Dwayne and I started at the shelter together. We'd graduated from college in the same year but from different schools. He went to Point Park College and majored in criminal justice to pursue a career as a probation officer. He was already working as a part-time probation officer but couldn't get a full-time position due to lack of funding. He took the job at the shelter to gain experience working with youth in the justice system and to save money for his upcoming wedding the following summer.

However he sometimes appeared to be just as insecure as many of the girls.

Although he was somewhat of a comedian, he was also a bit of a hot head. His temper was as quick as his wit. He had an even sharper tongue, which often led to unnecessary altercations. I didn't particularly care to work with him because he would often get the girls riled up for something stupid that they may have said or done, especially Zee.

He and Regina became pretty close—in fact too close, too fast. Even though he was engaged to be married, Regina got swept up by him and set her claws out to reel him in to her, and away from his fiancé. After about two months of flirting and secretly meeting each other outside of work, they finally slept together.

Afterwards, it was a wrap. She abandoned him like he had the plague. I asked her what happened and boy did she give me a mouth full.

"Girllllll ... he talked a good game. I was looking forward to him fuckin' my brains out. He got me all worked up, licked my pussy until I went crazy, and then he said, 'I'm goin' fuck your brains out!'" she recalled.

"When he got on top of me, I kept reaching for his dick to put in my pussy, but there wasn't much there to put in. When he finally got it in, I DIDN'T FEEL A THING!" she shouted. I was roaring with laughter at this point.

"That shit was so fuckin' little, he had not a damn thing to work with. I kept thinkin' to myself, what the fuck did I get myself into. Meanwhile, he was steady pumpin' and sayin' 'come on baby, cum for me!'" She started demonstrating his movements while talking. I was laughing my ass off. But she wasn't finished.

"By this time I was almost asleep," she said with humorous regret.

"You knew he was engaged to be married, so that's what you get!" I said while crying with laughter.

"Girl! ... His shit wasn't even as big as my fuckin pinky. I'm telling you ... it's a wrap! That ship has sailed!" she said as she raised her very little pinky finger to imitate the size of his penis.

I was on the floor roaring with laughter now. I knew I could never look at him the same way again after hearing that.

Despite her disappointment with his sexual prowess, they remained good friends. But after that encounter she did everything she could to avoid him. She was in charge of helping the supervisor make the work schedules and made sure she kept him off of as many of her shifts as possible. As a result I got stuck working with him more often, including this day.

Regina was leaving after working the morning shift, and Dwayne and I were signing in at the same time. She went behind his back, waved at me to get my attention without him noticing, and started wiggling her little pinky finger while shaking her head in despair—she was making fun of the size of his penis. I fell out laughing, again. Then she whispered in my ear to keep him and Zee away from each other.

The evening went like clockwork and I managed to keep the two of them away from each other for most of it. The girls did their chores, had dinner, and we had a great group session. I shared my photos and talked to them about the beauty of Paris while distributing the gifts from New York and Paris I'd purchased for them.

After having already spent most of the evening in her room, Zee started making her way downstairs shortly after the group session ended. As soon as he spotted her descending the stairs, Dwayne started yelling at her in front of everyone, and telling her to get her behind in the living room with the other girls. All hell broke loose!

Zee was about five feet tall with a stocky build, weighed 175 pounds, and she was very strong. It took her about thirty seconds to process what Dwayne said. Out of the blue, she ran the rest of the way down the stairs like a Tasmanian devil and leaped right onto Dwayne's head. While digging her nails deep into his face, she clawed her way straight down the middle and in so doing left a trail of blood and scratches straight down his face.

Completely taken by surprise—as were we all—he unsuccessfully made numerous attempts to restrain her, but she knew every trick in the book on how to get out of the restraint holds and refused to get off of him. The more he tried to get her off, the more she dug in. She even started biting him.

I ran from the other side of the room and tried to get her off of him. When I finally managed to pull her teeth and fingernails from his skin, we fell on the floor and she started scratching me and digging her nails into my thumb. I finally screamed at her to stop scratching me and she did. It was almost like she was possessed.

The lead counselor, Patty Jo, and I finally got her separated from him, sent her to the office, and sent Dwayne to the hospital. While he was leaving, Patty Jo also instructed him to write up an incident report. The other girls were traumatized and we had to calm them down before finally getting them settled in bed.

I had to write an incident report, too, so I went into the office to talk with Zee to get her side of the story. When I asked Zee what happened her responses were just as shocking as they were disturbing.

She said she'd planned the whole thing as a result of his ridiculing her too many times. According to her, when Dwayne started working at the shelter, she found him funny and attractive and said she initially liked him. She thought he liked her, too. But then he started making fun of her glasses, and she'd overheard him making fun of her to the other girls. She decided that if he humiliated her one more time in front of everyone, she was going to beat him up. He unwittingly complied, and she snapped.

When he started yelling at her in front of everyone, she said she couldn't take anymore. She went on to tell me that she knew how to get out of every restraint hold from her experience with being restrained at other foster homes and shelters throughout her life.

Still shocked by what happened and her sheer honesty, I explained to her that she should have told Patty Jo or me so we could have properly handled the situation before it escalated. I also informed her that Dwayne could potentially press charges against her because she was now considered an adult. Her response was so disturbing that it became clear to me that she was in serious need of mental and emotional health counseling.

"I don't care! I've been in this system my entire life. Nobody cares about me anyway. It'll just be another system. Who cares, it's nothing new," she chided. My heart sunk. I was speechless.

She went on to apologize to me for scratching me and offered to put a bandage on the wound. During her apology, Patty Jo walked in the office with two policemen who went on to escort her to the Western Psychiatric institute for further evaluation. Although it seemed harsh, it was the shelter's protocol to initially avoid having to send her to the juvenile detention center in hopes that she'd get the counseling she needed.

My decision to leave the shelter was confirmed with that incident. I wrote myself a reminder to call the French department and hire a tutor the next day. When I got home after work, I immediately started gathering my photos to send to Abby in Paris. I was more determined than ever to press forward with my goals. I went to bed with a whole new outlook for my future that night.

Girls' Night Out

It was the day before New Year's Eve and I'd worked the late shift. I was exhausted. But I wanted to give my girls their gifts and finalize plans for the crews' New Year's Eve celebration being hosted by JB at LeMont on Mt. Washington.

Just about everyone had already finalized their transportation plans to the restaurant except me. Chantelle said she was coming with Diamond Damon, and Charise was meeting Henri after he, Pierre, and Penny finished performing for Pittsburgh's First Night Celebration downtown. Quite a few people couldn't make it—Rafi was still in London celebrating the holidays with his family, Leila was staying home with the baby, Sheila never responded to the invitation, and Regina was scheduled to work overnight at the shelter with Evelyn. I was sure Chris was coming and would probably bring Rebecca, so I decided to ask Mark B to pick me up and take me with him.

We confirmed everyone's arrival plans and Chantelle was itching to talk. I really wanted to give everyone their gifts but instead turned over the floor to her.

"I think I'm in love y'all!" she quipped with excitement.

Apparently her love affair with the guy we all affectionately referred to as "Diamond Damon" was burgeoning. She'd met him at the Balcony during a lunch date and suddenly started working as a courier for him on the weekends.

He wined and dined her, flew her back and forth to New York on the weekends for deliveries and pampering, and she was enthralled.

Although she had been a little depressed lately, Leila was always in counselor mode. She wasn't quite comfortable with Chantelle's relationship and set out to warn her about Damon.

"Please be careful Chantelle," she started. "Many of the African men are looking for Americans to marry them to obtain their green cards. After they get them, they abandon the Americans and bring their real wives or girlfriends from home to marry and live here," she said. Then she inadvertently dropped a bomb about Henri to Charise.

"Charise, you should be careful with Henri too! I understand he took a fifteen-year-old girl from Canada with him to South Africa when he accompanied Pierre on the tour last month," she said with reproach.

Chantelle was highly insulted by Leila's warning and didn't hesitate to make her disapproval known to everyone. She said Damon's different. At that point it became clear to most of us that her naïveté and greed would lead her right into his trap, and she wasn't going to listen to us anyway. She went on to tell Leila that he's royalty and has diplomatic immunity, so he doesn't need to marry anyone to stay in the country. She was emphatic in her belief that he could do whatever he wanted, and she wanted to be an integral part of his life.

"I just know he's falling in love with me and I really like how he makes me feel," she stubbornly responded while rolling her eyes.

The truth was that she believed he was loaded, so she really liked what he had to offer her financially. The conversation started to get a bit heated so I tried to break up the tension by interjecting and telling everyone about my fabulous trip to Paris and pulling out the gifts.

I gave everyone their gifts, but Chantelle decided to surprise us with something special too. She gave everyone small samples of an expensive perfume with instructions to be careful of the side effects. Her gifts seemed to always come with a warning label.

"What side effects?" I asked. Her explanation was rather interesting.

"This perfume is from the world-famous designer Tom Ford and his scents are known to send a special message." She purred with the excitement of its potential.

"What kind of message?" I asked with a heightened curiosity.

"Chantelle, what the hell are you talkin' about now?" Sheila exclaimed. "Don't tell me you're giving us some more of your crazy sex shit," she followed.

"Well hell, I'll take all the help I can get," Charise said jokingly.

"Well ... word on the street is that this particular line of colognes are affectionately called the 'Fuck me' perfumes. The secret is that they were developed and tested with both men and women using some type of pheromones that advance erotic stimulation. In other words, 'the fuck me chemical,'" she said with true excitement. "So if there's anyone you really want to get your groove on with, spray away!" she joked. I was laughing hysterically by this time.

"Chantelle do you really think any of us need pheromones to make these men come on to us?" I asked.

"No, but if you want somebody to take care of you for the rest of your life, you might." She said as a matter of fact.

"Wouldn't you want somebody that's got money and resources?" she said. Everyone shook their heads in agreement. But my suspicion about why she was so quickly falling in love with Diamond Damon was just about confirmed.

"See! I'm doing y'all a favor, and you're doubting me? How do you think I got Diamond Damon to agree to sponsor our trip to the spa and spend New Year's with us!" she pompously touted as we all laughed.

"Just as I suspected," I thought to myself.

When I got home I thought more about what Chantelle said about the allure of the perfume. Tariq was in Paris and I was done with Chris, so there was nobody to test the theory with—but it did mix wonderfully with my body chemistry.

New Year's Eve at LeMont

I'd traded shifts with Regina so I could have the evening off to prepare for the dinner party at LeMont. I had already worked the evening shift when Zee flipped out, so coming back the next morning at 8:00 a.m. made for a quick and exhausting turnaround.

The morning shifts were typically easier. The girls would have all kinds of appointments, or we'd just have to take them to the alternative school after making sure they got dressed and had breakfast. There were no school or appointments during the holidays, so we let them sleep until 9:00 a.m.

The girls finally dragged themselves out of bed, got dressed, and finished breakfast around eleven. Then we took them down to the PPG center to go ice-skating for the day and used petty cash to buy them lunch. By the time we got back to the shelter it was almost quitting time. I was thankful for a busy, but fun-filled drama-free day. I finished my paperwork and left at 4:00 p.m. on the nose.

When I got home there was a message on my answering machine from Tariq. He had something important to tell me and said he'd be calling me back at 5:00 p.m. He was six hours ahead of me in Paris but called at 5:00 p.m. on the dot. He wanted to wish me an early Happy New Year before going out with friends. Then he delivered what he thought was disturbing news.

As a French citizen, everyone has to either do military service or serve in the civil service overseas in some capacity. He'd applied to become a civil service volunteer upon the advice of his wealthy college friends, who used their parents' political connections to get civil service jobs abroad. Tariq, however, didn't have such connections and tried to get in through the luck of the draw based on his skills.

Working as a civil service volunteer would have allowed him to serve as a diplomatic liaison in one of the many French territories throughout the world. They were prized positions that were supposedly reserved for those with advanced skills. However, more often than not, they were reserved for the lucky and those who were well connected politically.

Neither skills nor luck came through for Tariq. He received a letter on New Year's Eve stating that his civil service application had been rejected. One full year of military service was therefore obligatory and he was to mandatorily report for duty on July 15th. If not, he risked losing his French citizenship. He was not happy.

His initial message made me a little nervous. But when he delivered the news on the phone, I was relieved it wasn't worse. I'd already convinced myself I was going in a different direction with my life. Therefore it was somewhat comforting to me that I wasn't the only one at a crossroads. But things quickly began to get more complicated.

Before ending the conversation, he told me he was falling in love with me. My heart was pounding a hundred miles a minute, and the butterflies in my stomach began to flutter like crazy.

I was very fond of him, but I wasn't sure if it was love yet and didn't want to rush my feelings. I casually told him that I loved him too, and tried to reassure him that we'd be just fine. We could visit each other on his breaks.

I finished my conversation with him, showered off, and got dressed. I wore a gold and white sequined bustier under a black velvet pantsuit with two-inch red velvet mules. Then I topped it off with my mom's full-length black mink coat. I felt and looked gorgeous. I was perfectly coiffed for JB's boogie New Year's invitation. Then I thought about the Tom Ford perfume Chantelle had given me, and wondered whether or not to wear it.

After a quick sniff, I loved the smell and decided to go with it. If nothing else, I thought it would give me an opportunity to test Chantelle's theory. However the question I had to ask myself was with whom did I expect it to work since Tariq wasn't going to be there.

LeMont

Mark B picked me up at 10:30 p.m. and we headed up to Mt. Washington. Traffic was still light so we arrived in about twenty-five minutes. The valet took the car keys and Mark B opened the door and escorted me into the restaurant. When I walked through the door, the waitress looked both Mark B and me up and down and seemed to turn her nose up at us—as if she disapproved of us being together. Mark B immediately noticed what appeared to be her reticent prejudice, and the other side of his personality quietly took over.

"What you looking at bitch?! You better stay in your lane!" he said quietly so only she and I could hear him.

I laughed hysterically as she quickly buried her face in the book and asked if we had reservations. Just then JB walked over to welcome and retrieve us. She starred us down as we walked away and Mark B facetiously put my arm around his waist and gently kissed me on the cheek to give her a show.

"Bye bitch!" Mark B whispered.

"Be good Mark B," I said. He laughed too and we followed JB on the long walk to the downstairs dining room and finally to our table.

LeMont is a well-appointed restaurant built on the cliffs of Mt. Washington. It's one of the upscale go-to destinations for special occasions in Pittsburgh, and is close to Walter's house with the same view, just not as intimate.

When we finally got to the table, everyone else had already arrived, so JB made his welcome announcement and said he was happy to be hosting everyone. He described it as his turn to finally host a celebration, and said he was grateful that we'd agreed to come for New Year's Eve. We were invited to order whatever we wanted and then he went to work with the band.

The table was almost full with the exception of three chairs left empty for Pierre, Henri, and Penny. Chantelle was with Diamond Damon—who was tall, dark, and not very attractive, but he was very polished. Charise was saving the chair for Henri and sitting next to Chris and Rebecca. Mark B and I ended up sitting across from them, and the piano player's girlfriend sat at the end of the table. He'd introduced her as his girlfriend, but he was wearing a wedding ring. I initially thought she was his wife but would later learn that I was sorely mistaken.

Dinner featured a mélange of freshly butchered meats and fresh seafood flown in overnight just for the holiday celebration. The obligatory shrimp cocktail, jumbo crab cakes, tomahawk steaks, triple-thick grilled pork chops with apricot sesame glaze, and a variety of sides stood out on the menu and eventually perfumed the table.

During dinner, JB introduced everyone to the band on a set break. I noticed Chris seemed to get really nervous while shaking hands with the piano player and equipment manager, Andy. After dinner I asked Chris why he seemed so nervous. He said he'd recognized Andy from work and didn't like him. He also seemed to wrestle with the idea that he might have been the one who'd ran him off the road after the Thanksgiving celebration at the shelter. Although he wasn't certain about the incident, he said he knew Andy in passing from working in his building and visiting his brother sometimes. However it was very clear to me that Chris wasn't comfortable and didn't trust Andy.

Now my curiosity was elevated. I pulled JB aside during another break and asked him about Andy. According to JB, Andy worked as a stockbroker during the day, and freelanced as a piano player with JB and other bands in the evenings. He said Andy was often the designated equipment manager. While I was talking to JB, Chris and Rebecca struck up a conversation with Andy's girlfriend. In the meantime, the clock was quickly approaching midnight.

At about 11:45 p.m. Mark B started handing out his own confetti poppers and everyone put on the New Year's hats that sat at each place setting. At midnight we pulled the strings to the poppers and scared the hell out of everyone in the place. It was hilarious! We were all sitting there with long strings of confetti all over our heads laughing hysterically. JB tried to kiss me at midnight, but I wasn't comfortable. I didn't want him to get the wrong idea, so I only allowed him to kiss me on the cheek. I was missing Tariq and didn't want to betray him. Andy's girlfriend, however, let it all hang out.

She was about five feet four inches tall and a 175-pound dirty blond. As soon as the clock struck midnight, she jumped on Andy's lap while he was still playing the piano, grabbed his face, and planted a big, sloppy kiss on his lips. Then she shoved his head into her bosom and tried to smother him with her boobs. I don't usually give a crap about how people express their affection for each other, but I couldn't believe how tacky they were. They were in the middle of the dance floor licking and rubbing on each other for a good fifteen minutes straight.

Pierre, Henri, and Penny arrived at 12:30 a.m. and the party really started at our table. While finishing dessert, JB asked if anyone had made New Year's resolutions. I was happy to start and it set off a parade of resolutions that turned into revelations—some of which came out of left field.

We continued to drink, eat, and talk the evening away. I shared intimate details about the beautiful city of Paris and confirmed everyone's participation in Julio's upcoming Valentines fundraiser. My resolution came in the form of my decision to leave the shelter, study French, and pursue my dreams of becoming a food writer and restaurateur. I told them about Abby's offer and everyone was happy for me, even Chris to my surprise.

"I'm very happy for you, Anais. I admire you and truly hope you find your happiness without compromise," he said. I was pleasantly surprised. I didn't think Chris would support my decision to leave the shelter.

Out of nowhere, Chantelle and Diamond Damon abruptly announced their pending nuptials. Everyone was taken off guard. All we could think about was how Rafi was going to react when he found out. Diamond Damon had apparently popped the question at midnight and she said yes. I wasn't convinced that she was truly on board with it and neither was anyone else. When they announced it everyone at the table just sort of fell silent. Then JB broke the tension with a quick word of congratulations.

Still startled by Chantelle and Damon's announcement, Charise shared her decision to move to New York and to accept the internship at the District Attorney's office for the summer. She'd made a resolution to always be true to herself. Henri wasn't happy but reluctantly said he supported her decision. She made it quite clear that she no longer trusted him and didn't care what he thought.

"It's okay, I don't need your support," she said.

He was clearly taken aback and didn't know what to say. In fact, nobody said a word for about two long minutes. We were all in shock at her response. However Chantelle and I knew why she was so candid with her response.

After the resolutions began to turn into revelations, Pierre sought to lighten up the situation as usual, and called everyone to the dance floor. He and Henri joined JB's band and started drumming.

That's when the party really began—it was a bit boring before that. The place was a bit too reserved for us. JB said the band was only allowed to play light jazz, oldies, and a few R&B songs until midnight. After midnight, the band played their final set and a DJ took over to play dance music.

At one point, I was slow dancing with JB and Chris decided to cut in. He doesn't even like to dance, so I didn't quite understand why he'd left Rebecca sitting at the table. But I agreed to dance with him.

He said he just wanted a dance for old time's sake and to properly wish me Happy New Year. I was a bit skeptical, but we had agreed to remain friends and I still enjoyed his friendship. But then he got a little too close. He pulled me into him and started rubbing his nose on the back of my neck while trying to kiss it.

"You smell so fuckin' good I could just rip your clothes off and fuck you right here!" he quipped.

"Go fuck Becky, Chris!" I quipped. "Why are you being so disrespectful to her?" I said as I playfully pushed him away from me. He pulled me back into him while we continued to dance and apologized for getting out of hand.

My mind went right back to the perfume and whether Chantelle's theory about it was actually true. I just laughed and told him about it. It didn't matter though. I had just got back from an amazing time in Paris with Tariq and couldn't help thinking about him. I told Chris I was really falling for Tariq and he gave me the silent treatment. We finished our dance and returned to the table.

As was customary with the College Crew, we danced and sang into the wee hours of the morning. I wasn't quite sure, but it seemed like JB may have been hiding a secret of his own. Every now and then he'd disappear without a word. Then Mark B said when he went to the bathroom, he saw JB in a compromising position with a waitress who'd been hanging around him all night. I didn't really care, but I did feel like he was being disingenuous at that point and found it kind of strange that he'd try to kiss me at midnight if his love interest was there the whole time. I inadvertently got my answer.

At the end of the evening we all got up to leave the restaurant together, but JB stayed behind. While waiting for the valet to bring the car, Mark B said he had to go to the bathroom again. We were standing outside and it was cold. But he didn't want to go back inside. Instead, he walked up the street a bit to relieve himself in an alley. On the way back, he passed a car that seemed to be rocking—it was very dark and nearly three in the morning. It startled him. As he got closer he could see the bass player sitting in the back of the car rolling his head around and moaning with pleasure. He was comfortably couched in the back seat of the car and getting his dick sucked by the girl who was bartending. Mark B quickly ran back to where I was standing and told me what he'd seen.

"Looks like JB and his band have a pretty strong fan base here huh!" I joked with Mark B.

"Yep! I'd say so," he responded.

The valet finally arrived with the car and when we drove by the rocking car the bass player was on top of the girl with her legs straddling the seat and he was humping like crazy. We laughed hysterically.

"I guess the bass player had to blow off a little steam," Mark B said while laughing.

"Yep!" I responded. But I couldn't help thinking that JB was probably somewhere doing the same thing.

32

The holidays were over and work seemed to become increasingly arduous. I had to force myself to do things I enjoyed to distract me from getting the doldrums again so on my days off from work I immersed myself into working with Julio to coordinate the Valentine's fundraiser and things were looking great. We had all of the events solidified by early January, including the food, lodging, games, and entertainment. In addition, we'd convinced the Omni hotel to give us a huge discount on the venue and the sleeping rooms.

The invitation-only event was affectionately titled Six Degrees of Separation—A Love Celebration for Singles and Couples. Julio's philanthropic team at Doctors Working Borders had sent out the invitations and had more than three hundred people registered to participate by mid-January. It quickly became evident to us that we had our work cut out for us. I dedicated all my free time to the planning and coordination of the event.

The Shelter

I was also inspired by the prospect of becoming a paid food writer and immediately got to work on preparations to leave the shelter. I sent a few photos to Abby and began writing draft articles about some of the most exciting foods I'd prepared for catering, and from photos of meals I'd eaten at restaurants. It took about three weeks, but I also managed to register for a French writing class at the University of Pittsburgh and to hire a French tutor. I was making progress and excited about moving toward my goals.

Armed with that confidence, I began to go to work every day at the shelter with a new attitude. Zee was gone, Dwayne wasn't on the morning shift with me, and when I arrived the girls were just getting up. Initially things were looking positive, but as usual the wheels of drama reared their ugly head, albeit briefly.

Shortly after Ed's arrest, Regina had been subpoenaed to provide a deposition about the encounter between Ed and Saturn. Ed's trial had come up and he was being formally charged with child endangerment and statutory rape. He was facing eight to ten years in prison and everyone was in shock. Even though we knew he would serve some jail time, we all began to feel vulnerable.

The kids craved attention, were often from dysfunctional homes, and regularly used threats of reporting the staff to Childline as a tool to get what they wanted. It was also clear that they would even lie if they felt trapped into a corner or just didn't like a counselor.

Childline is an anonymous child abuse reporting hotline and the kids' caseworkers mandate the shelter's counselors to provide the kids with twenty-four-hour access to call on demand. According to the training we received, if one of the kids reports you, you're considered guilty until proven innocent, which could take months of investigation. You're placed on an unpaid leave and even if the claim turns out as unfounded, in most cases you're assigned to a different location.

The worst part is that your life could be detrimentally affected on the whim of a disgruntled kid who's in a shelter where they clearly don't want to be. While under investigation you receive no pay and you can't look for another job working with children because the state mandates you to have the child abuse and criminal history clearances. To make matters worse, if you're innocent, you will most likely have a difficult time recovering financially because they don't pay you while you're under investigation. I was sure my decision to leave was appropriate and began to voice it with the other counselors. They too lamented about feeling vulnerable and clandestine talk began about changing jobs on just about every shift.

SNL Spa Weekend

It was mid-January, I already needed a break from work so I was looking forward to the upcoming spa weekend. The weather was a bit contemptuous, but Chantelle had already anticipated it and surprised us by renting a private party van to transport us to Omni's Bedford Springs Resort and spa—about two and a half hours east of Pittsburgh. There were a total of eight of us—Chantelle, Diamond Damon, Charise, Chris, Rafi, Sheila, Regina, and me, and the ride to the resort was a blast.

The cushy party van was decked out with plush seats, disco lights, dance music, and even a stripper pole. To get the party started early, Chantelle had arranged to have a variety of alcoholic and nonalcoholic beverages and snacks for noshing, which came in handy. We drank, sang, and partied all the way to Bedford Springs.

Upon our arrival, Chantelle checked everyone into their rooms and handed out the keys with the weekend's itinerary attached. She'd had the whole weekend planned to perfection—it was designed to be fun, luxurious, and wonderfully relaxing, just what I needed.

While we were all standing in the lobby, she read the entire itinerary out loud to ensure we were okay with each of the planned activities, and it was a good thing that she did. She'd initially planned to start the activities with a paintball game outside, but it was snowing heavily and we were in the mountains. There was already about eight inches of snow on the ground.

Before anyone else could voice their opinion, Regina abruptly shouted her dissent. "I don't know about anyone else, but my idea of a spa weekend doesn't include freezing my tits off while being hunted like a runaway slave!" She quipped.

"I agree!" Charise said while everyone else laughed.

"Well Regina, we all know you don't have a lot of tits, so you need to keep all you have!" Chantelle joked.

"I have a plan B," she said.

She suggested and we all agreed to play laser tag at the indoor arcade and disbursed to our rooms with the agreement to meet in the arcade in an hour.

When we got to our rooms it felt like we were almost having a huge slumber party. Not only were all the rooms on the same floor, they were also connecting rooms. Charise and I agreed to share a room and when we opened the door, it was a beautiful haven for relaxation.

The first thing I spotted were the two large gift boxes that sat at the foot of each queen-size poster bed. They were beautifully wrapped in clear cellophane and complemented by delicate lavender and purple origami butterflies attached by souvenir keychains from the resort. Charise's curiosity got the best of her and she immediately opened one while I continued to tour the room.

The boxes were elegant superfood gift boxes labeled Super Fun Snack Boxes and had a card on each of them welcoming us to the resort. They were filled with a variety of gourmet snacks and drinks presented in six different half-pound cellophane bags and included jumbo cashews, mixed popcorn, savory chocolate-covered fruit and almonds, dried and seasoned vegetable chips, crunchy vanilla granola, and an interesting dark chocolate chunk trail mix. Underneath the snacks were a variety of canned drinks. Charise was enamored with the boxes. I, however, was very impressed with the room and about how much Chantelle and Damon spent on it.

The well-appointed room boasted a variety of luxurious touches that took the relaxation to another level. The focal point was the two matching queen-size cherrywood poster beds topped with silky soft sheets and triple-thick goose down comforters, flanked by matching cherrywood benches at the foot of each bed. A fully stocked drink bar and mini refrigerator filled with a variety of fresh fruit, more snacks, and drinks was comfortably couched next to the marble clad bathroom.

The bathroom was absolutely beautiful. Intricate marble with blue and amber veins covered the floors, walls, and the Jacuzzi tub surround. The shower sat enclosed next to the tub and bordered the double vanities, which were separated by a gift basket filled with a variety of bath products.

"Wow! If this is how she's been spending her weekends away, Chantelle's been living it up with Diamond Damon!" I quipped.

"I don't know, but I'm gonna live it up this weekend!" Charise responded. We changed into our jeans and T-shirts and went downstairs.

Everyone met in the arcade. Most of us had never played laser tag before, but we were very excited about trying something new.

The attendant met us in a receiving room that sat in the back center of the arcade. He explained how the game and laser tag vests worked, and handed them out while dividing the girls and guys up into red and blue teams. We chose blue vests in an attempt to throw the guys off a bit—we thought the blue would be less visible.

After everyone was suited up, the attendant checked each person's vest and showed us how to use the recharging cords. He explained that you only get three lives out of each charge. Once the laser tag from the other team hits you three times, you have to recharge at a station to get back into the game. Then he invited us to enter the laser tag arena.

He opened the door to a huge, dark combat-style room fitted with a variety of fake buildings covered with ropes, nets, army-style fatigue fabrications, and bull's-eye targets all lined with neon lights. He pointed out each of the charging stations, the scoreboard, and the time clock.

After sending each team to opposite sides of the room, he suggested we huddle up to make a plan. The attendant returned to his booth and suddenly yelled "Four, three, two, one. Game on! Attack!"

Loud rock music poured from speakers surrounding the entire room. Everyone scattered to find a suitable hiding place and the shooting began.

It was so much fun! We played like we were under attack from enemy soldiers. As soon as we saw a red vest, we shot like crazy. I didn't know how they kept getting me because I missed at least ninety percent of my shots. I had to recharge nine times in the first ten minutes of the game. It was apparent that one of the guys had stalked me, but I couldn't see who it was.

We played three rounds in total because the guys won the first round by a substantial margin. The girls came back in the second round after we made a plan to lure the guys by sneaking up behind them and kissing their necks to throw them off. Then we prompted the other three team members to drain all of their points at once. We cheated a little. But we had to do something to address how they hammered us in the first round.

We paid for it though. Round three was a bust. The guys hammered the girls again. I was no help to the girls because after I'd kissed Chris's neck, he wouldn't leave me alone. To be honest, I'd begun missing his scent and touch. I had difficulty resisting him and he took full advantage of my vulnerability.

He cornered me while threatening to zap me with the laser. I pleaded for him to give me the point. Instead, he grabbed my face and passionately kissed me. I melted and completely forgot about the game. Then he zapped me anyway.

To make matters worse, while he was kissing me, it later became apparent that he was flagging Rafi and Diamond Damon to come and zap me of my last two lives. The clock ran out shortly after that and they won the game by one point. We couldn't even dispute their tactics because we had done the same thing to win round two. It really didn't matter though. We had a great time and vowed to get back at them.

To recover from our unusual defeat, we played a few more games in the arcade. Chris and I got into a heated game of air hockey and everyone teamed up again. This time I won by three points.

Afterward we all retreated to our rooms to freshen up for dinner. Charise jumped in the shower while my bath was running. When she finished I spent thirty luxurious minutes in the bath steaming with a mixture of warming mandarin and magnesium bath salts.

The citrusy smell of the mandarin oil permeated the entire bathroom. I used a sisal brush and the body shampoo to scrub every inch of my body. It seemed to remove every ounce of dirt leaving an unsightly ring around the rim of the tub. I drained the tub, quickly rinsed off my body and the ring of dirt before slathering myself with a palm full of the juicy mandarin body oil, and doubling up with a light spritz of the matching cologne.

"Umh! Umh! Umh! I smell good enough to eat!" I said to myself.

We got dressed and met everyone in front of the 1796 Room for what the itinerary described as the Signature Menu Tasting Dinner. The executive chef was hosting it—it was an elegant, well-portioned, five-course meal composed of the most requested items on the menu. There were a series of palate cleansers in between each set serving, which allowed us to savor the distinct flavor of each dish.

It was astounding! We even gave the chef a standing ovation.

It started with the chef instructing us to start with a couple sips of water before diving into the meal service. He also noted that a small dollop of lemon sorbet to cleanse our palates would precede each course. Doing so would allow us to fully enjoy the experience of each individual dish without it being distorted by the taste from the previous dish.

Then he pointed us to the itemized menus at each place setting and walked us through each course of what was labeled the Surf and Turf Signature Collection. First up, smoked bluefish pâté with micro greens and toast points. Next, colossal shrimp spring rolls served with a sweet and tangy chili sauce, followed by succulent sea bass medallions steamed in banana leaves with a sweet chili soy sauce and a side of sesame sticky rice.

The portions were perfect, but I was already getting full. Still, each item was so delicious that I couldn't wait to see what was up next. It did not disappoint.

The meat servings followed the seafood. Next up, triple-thick slices of marinated and grilled pork chops surrounded a heap of dressed kale and cabbage slaw and roasted fingerling potatoes. It was an elegantly articulated work of art and drew me right in. The pork melted in my mouth like butter, the slaw was unlike any one I'd ever tasted—citrusy, tangy, and nutty—and the smooth and buttery fingerling potatoes brought everything full circle.

Although most of us were fully satiated after the first four courses, dessert was also exquisite, and it came with an interesting twist. The waiter delivered well-portioned petite black and white raspberry tarts atop a swirl of raspberry coulis and topped with toasted almonds and shaved chocolate. To everyone's surprise, Diamond Damon said he had a special announcement and asked everyone to partake in a Champagne toast.

"First I'd like to thank everyone for joining us and to propose a toast. I know you are all special to my lovely Chantelle, and I'd like us to toast to officially declaring my true love for her to all of you who mean so much to her," he said before passionately kissing her.

It was a beautiful display of affection, however I wasn't quite sure it was the right time to do it. We were all still a little suspicious, especially Rafi who wasn't privy to their announcement at the New Year's dinner at LeMont. Chantelle had only known Diamond Damon for a couple of months, and we were unsure of what she was really doing when she would transport the packages back and forth to New York for him. But everyone politely smiled and raised their glasses to join in the toast.

After dinner and nightcaps, we were all exhausted from the day's activities and retreated to our rooms. But I got restless and decided to explore the mineral springs pool. I changed into my bathing suit and on the way to the elevator, I conveniently ran into Chris. He too wanted to soak in the mineral springs and grabbed his bathing suit to join me.

We entered the indoor solarium that housed the swimming pool and it was completely empty. Although it's a twenty-four-hour retreat, it's located in a secluded corner of the hotel right off the spa, and it was well after 10:00 p.m., which was probably why it was empty. I was a bit scared and decided to scope the place out a little more to feel safe.

It's closed in on both sides with a wall of windows facing the outside and the inside entrances from the hallway. Inside, the pool area is suited with twenty lounge chairs on either side and a bunch of table sets for eating. There are also two small enclaves with fully stocked lounges that lead to men's and women's dressing rooms. The lounges were filled with snacks and had mini bars, too.

Chris and I grabbed towels, laid them on the chairs and jumped right into the heated pool. The minerals from the nearby spring served as an all-natural muscle relaxant, making for an amazing evening swim. The best part was that it was the middle of a cold and snowy January in Pennsylvania and I was swimming in a wonderful open solarium that made it feel surreal. We had the entire pool to ourselves and it made for a very playful and relaxing swim. After forty-five minutes, I was floating on a lapboard and Chris started to get frisky again and cornered me in between one of my laps. I tried to resist him, but then he challenged me, and the foreplay began.

"I'll race you to the end of the pool and whoever wins, gets to do whatever they want," he said.

I was cool with that. I was already craving him when he took his shirt off and jumped in the pool. He started the countdown and I made a feeble attempt at racing him.

He won! And I was now at his mercy. But we both took full advantage. He cornered me again and asked if he could kiss me. I kissed him. He lifted me out of the pool and led me into the secluded lounge area. He had hypnotized me once again.

I bent over to place a towel on the lounger and he buried his face in my ass and peeled my bikini bottom off with his teeth. I was horny as shit. I laid down on the lounger and wrapped my legs around his head as he devoured me.

"Oh baby! I've missed you so much!" I said as I purred with desire.

He stuck his finger in my ass and ate my pussy like he was a hungry lion. The convulsions triggered from his finger in my ass increased my desire to feel him inside me. I just wanted him to fuck my brains out.

"You want me baby?" he whispered.

"Fuck me baby! Fuck me please!" I pleaded. I was in heat. I needed to feel his rock-hard steely cock inside my sex.

Then he took his finger out of my ass, licked it, and impaled my sex with two fingers. He finger fucked me and licked my pussy until I climaxed.

"Oh! Oh God Chris! I'm cumming," I shouted.

He pulled his fingers out and stood up to take his bathing trunks off.

"Hello! Is anyone in here?" someone shouted from the pool area.

I guess I'd gotten a little too animated. Someone apparently heard my cries and came searching to see where the sound was coming from. We were so embarrassed that we quickly scurried to get out of there. I grabbed my bikini bottoms, Chris pulled his trunks back up, and we slid out the men's locker room to avoid being seen by whoever was talking. We laughed all the way back to the room and agreed to meet up early for breakfast. I slept like a baby.

Saturday's itinerary was even more exciting. I woke up before Charise and went downstairs to meet Chris for breakfast. We got a chance to talk about our latest rendezvous and it was like we had a little secret that no one else knew about. It made the weekend even more fun.

After a visit to the delectable breakfast buffet in The Crystal Room, individually scheduled spa treatments for everyone were the order of the day. On tap were warm caramel apple cider and Mediterranean mud body wraps, followed by hydrotherapy shower massages for the ladies, and hot stone sports massages followed by milk and honey body polishes for the men. Everyone was also treated to aromatherapy facials, manicures, and pedicures. We didn't finish the day at the spa until late in the afternoon.

A light lunch inside the spa lounge followed the spa treatments. We had the rest of the afternoon to relax, sleep, or do whatever we wanted before meeting everyone for dinner at 8:00 p.m. A few people went hiking, but I chose to enjoy a few good hours of sleeping in my extremely comfortable cherrywood bed.

The ladies corralled in front of the Frontier Tavern and lounged in the luxurious leather wing-backed chairs while waiting for the guys to arrive for dinner. They'd gone on a short hike after their spa treatments and went back to their rooms to freshen up a bit.

Dinner was more laid-back on Saturday—traditional American cuisine, craft beers, and a sensuous bourbon tasting. Most of us ordered craft burgers, steaks, and barbecued rib meals from the grill. The selections paired well with the smooth bourbons.

The bourbon tasting was an interesting party unto itself. The bartender set up three elegant petite whiskey glasses called Glencairns in front of each of us. He filled the glasses with three different types of bourbon and covered each glass with a playing card. He said the cards are used for two purposes, including helping to avoid the alcohol from evaporating. Then he pulled out a bourbon flavor wheel and challenged us to identify the flavors in each one we tasted.

The wheel contained a variety of characteristics and flavor profiles instrumental to determining which were your favorite bourbons. After we identified our favorites, he told us to add up the cards that covered each glass. The person with cards closest to twenty-one would win a bottle of their choice. In this case it was Rafi, and it was a perfect outcome. He really loved the idea of the bourbon tasting and couldn't get enough. Now he was able to take some home to cherish and enjoy.

I, however, was high as heck. I'm a lightweight when it comes to alcohol, and between the bourbon tasting and the craft beer, I was beyond my limit.

After dinner, the sleep monster attacked everyone. I think those comfy beds were calling us, while the bourbon tasting and craft beers lent a helping hand. Everyone retreated to their rooms and agreed to meet in the pool after taking a nap.

I had already slept all afternoon and wanted to go to the mineral springs pool and soak a little before going back to bed. So I left the dinner table shortly after dessert, went to my room, changed into my bathing suit, and made my way back to the pool. When I opened the door, it was empty again. I started singing and enjoyed being alone—it was a remarkably peaceful experience. The acoustics in the pool area were amazing.

I went into the lounge area to get a bottle of water, and just as I reached into the mini refrigerator someone gently caressed my waist. I screamed and nearly jumped out of my skin. When I turned around to see who it was, Chris was holding onto me. He'd scared the hell out of me.

"Shish! Be quiet Anais! You're gonna spoil our peaceful time alone," he said as he kissed me relentlessly.

I couldn't resist him. His gentle caresses ... that musky smell I missed so much ... the kiss that always sent me into a tailspin ... he had reeled me in again. I was already a little high from drinking bourbon at dinner, and his kissing took me over the top.

He picked me up and I wrapped my legs around him. We tore into each other. The tension had been mounting all night. I was missing Tariq, but I was horny as hell.

I told myself not to think about Tariq. He was going to the military and I wasn't sure if I'd ever see him again.

I knew Chris wasn't for me, but unfortunately I didn't know nor care what Rebecca or anyone else thought. I was in the moment and the flame reignited again. It was as if he'd looked into my eyes and put a spell on me.

He slid my bikini bottom over and impaled me with his fingers while we kissed. Then he gently laid me onto a lounge chair. My sex was dripping with my juices.

"Damn! I missed you so much Anais!" he quipped as he licked his fingers.

"Umh! I miss you too baby. I want to feel your big cock inside me," I said. "Fuck me baby!" I purred.

We pulled our bathing suit bottoms off and I laid down on the lounger. He tenderly caressed my body while gently kissing my neck ... then my breast ... then he kissed my sex. He licked my pearl and my body quivered with anticipation.

He flipped me over, stuck his finger in my sex and licked my asshole. I couldn't take it anymore. I was about to erupt like a volcano ... I wanted to feel his cock inside of me. Then he did it. He mounted me. But he mistakenly shoved his dick in my ass. I screamed to the top of my lungs and pushed him off me.

"What the fuck are you doing Chris?!" I shouted.

He tried to apologize, but it hurt so bad I refused to let him touch me again. I was pissed off, and he was standing there with a rock-hard cock. So he was pissed off, too.

He continued to apologize and begged for another chance. But my high from the bourbon had worn off and somehow triggered my memory. I came to my senses and realized he was the same ole asshole. I refused to entertain him anymore.

I grabbed my bathing suit and left his ass standing there. I went back to my room, showered, and went to bed. Thankfully Charise was already in the bed snoring so I didn't have to explain myself.

Sunday morning came early. Chantelle ordered a limousine to shuttle us back to Pittsburgh—our beautiful weekend had come to an end. Breakfast was pretty quiet. I intentionally showed up late so I didn't have to see Chris, grabbed a bagel and coffee to go, and jumped right into the limousine. Then I insisted on sitting in the front seat so I wouldn't have to talk to him. He said nothing to me either. The ride back to Pittsburgh was peaceful but eerily quiet.

Menus

Join Us for a Spa Weekend to Retreat, Relax, and Release.

Friday: Signature Menu Tasting Dinner

featuring

PALATE CLEANSER

Cooling Lemon Sorbet

FIRST COURSE

Petite Smoked Bluefish Timbales

served with micro greens and toast points

SECOND COURSE

Colossal Shrimp Spring Roll Wraps

with sweet and tangy chili sauce

THIRD COURSE

Sea Bass Medallions

*steamed in banana leaves, topped with sweet chili soy sauce,
and served with sesame sticky rice*

FOURTH COURSE

Grilled Glazed Pork Chops

with citrus kale and cabbage slaw and roasted fingerling potatoes

FIFTH COURSE

Black & White Raspberry Tarts

topped with shaved chocolate and toasted almonds

BEAUTY RITUAL

Mandarin and magnesium soaking bath and body oil treatment.

menus continue ...

Menus

Saturday: Traditional Tavern Meal à la Carte

featuring

DINNER

Craft Burgers

with caramelized onions, sautéed mushrooms, and artisanal cheese

Grilled Seasoned Rib Eye

served with a grilled vegetable medley

Smoked Ribs

with a bourbon barbecue sauce

BEVERAGES

Craft Beers

Bourbon

ENTERTAINMENT

Bourbon tasting; laser tag; swimming; hiking.

SPA TREATMENTS

*Caramel apple cider body wraps; Mediterranean mud body wraps;
milk and honey body polishes; hydrotherapy massages; hot stone massages;
aromatherapy facials, manicures, and pedicures.*

33

The spa weekend ended a little crazy but it was a wonderful treat. It was now time to finish preparations for the upcoming Valentine's fundraiser. I called Julio to finalize the guest list, confirm the planned activities, and update the budgets. We were well positioned to host the party at the Omni hotel and had made major strides toward our goals.

The event featured lots of games, an open cash bar, five international food and drink stations, a cakes and cocktails fundraiser, and a variety of fun love items, potions, and aphrodisiacs for sale. I outlined a number of interesting games for singles and couples, food sales, and a host of activities to raise funds for his organization's volunteer trip to Africa with Doctors Working Borders aka DWB. After my third briefing with him, he was very impressed with the amount of work I'd put into the event. He surprised and complimented me.

"I've been volunteering and hosting fundraisers with DWB for the past fifteen years and I've never worked with anyone so dedicated. We could use someone like you to manage our new traveling food program in Africa, Anais," he said.

Then he surprised me again. I'd previously told him about my work at the shelter with the girls and how we had a difficult time getting them resettled after they aged out of the foster care system. He suggested we share the proceeds from the cakes and cocktails fundraiser and use them to start an endowment fund to support the shelter girls. I was elated.

However I'd now have an even bigger stake in the outcome of the fundraiser. I had to make certain that the College Crew and my workers were fully aware. It was imperative that we made sure everything was top-notch.

After I finalized the details with Julio, I immediately called each of my crew members to outline our staffing needs and duties. I couldn't afford any no-shows. In addition to his offer to share proceeds with the shelter, I also came to the realization that it would be the only time I'd get an opportunity to show Julio and his colleagues my events coordination skills if I wanted to accept his offer to work with them. Hence, the event would also be a kind of off-the-record audition.

The fundraiser was an invitation only event. Most of the invitees were single, unmarried volunteer staff and donors to Doctors Working Borders. Julio also asked me to invite a few people from the shelter and gave me complimentary tickets for anyone who wanted to attend. I was excited because this was also an opportunity to earn brownie points with the shelter's management.

DWB linked the fundraiser to their website and sent out invitations nationwide. Those who accepted the invitation could register online with a secured code matched to their invitation. Once they opened the registration page, they could book rooms, upload photos, and complete a series of questionnaires to ultimately be set up in a tribe. The tribes were groups of players who had complementary profiles that we matched up to play the games. They had the option to share their profiles with other attendees if they were single and ready to mingle, or just be set up in a group with a coregistered partner.

The theme of the event was Six Degrees of Separation—A Love Celebration of the Heart, Body, Mind, and Soul. Julio and I had set up games for each category—Games of the Heart, Games of the Body, Games of the Mind, and Games of the Soul.

The attendees would be divided into groups or tribes based on four to eight common characteristics identified through their registration forms. Then they'd be rotated throughout the evening so they could intermingle. Each participant would receive a tribal T-shirt, food and drink tickets, and a badge to wear on the day of the event. At the end of the evening each member of the winning tribe would receive one of the beautifully wrapped gift baskets on display filled with a variety of adult toys and Bodacious Body and Fresh Face products donated by that company.

The Games of the Heart and the Games of the Mind events were orchestrated throughout the week before the event as well as upon registration. The first was titled Unlock My Heart with the Golden Key. Guests were allowed to preregister for a fee, or register at the party. A pair of lanyards would be assigned—one with a lock with a number, and one with a golden key that would unlock that lock. If a guest found a person whose profile they felt especially attracted to and/or may have invited to the party because they wanted a stronger chance of making a love connection, they could select that person by preregistration and we would send an invitation saying a lanyard with a key reserved for them would be waiting when they got to the party.

In advance of the event, the person could also send a special invite via e-mail and/or a gift of beautifully boxed dark and white chocolate candy lips inviting that person to celebrate the event as their special guest. We'd already sold and mailed nearly two hundred in advance and received orders for another fifty-five to be delivered on-site.

We also received more than two hundred orders for the premade Valentine's cupcakes for delivery at the party, and another three hundred for Just Add Water Happy Cake kits. I only had to order them directly from the company with a one-week notice. They were prepackaged and allowed us to offer a large variety including coconut carrot cake, banana walnut "love muffins" with chocolate-covered walnut toffee, luscious Amazon lemon crunch cake, chocolate mandarin almond silk cake, and sweet potato cake with maple pecan praline. Specialty martini kits were crafted from complementary ingredients to pair perfectly with the cakes so that anyone could host a party. We had everything working in our favor.

The Shelter

It seemed like whenever I got back to the shelter on Monday mornings, all hell would be breaking loose. I was on a relaxation high from the great spa weekend and didn't feel like engaging in the typical drama. Fortunately I'd been assigned to do an off-site placement.

I spent the entire day taking two of the younger girls to their new placement in a long-term shelter twenty miles away. If all went well, they would live there with six other girls until they turned eighteen years old and aged out of the foster care system. Although I was going to miss them, it was good for them. It would provide the stability they craved and needed.

This time I was spared from the daily drama on Monday. However this week, the drama wheel reared its ugly head on Tuesday. I worked the evening shift, and when I entered the office to sign in all of the counselors and staff were distraught. I asked what was going on and Dwayne abruptly blurted it out.

Ed had pleaded guilty to the corruption of minors and statutory rape charges. He'd been sentenced to nine years in jail. Even worse, he'd be serving time in the same jail as Saturn's stepfather.

"That doesn't seem like a good combination," I said.

"Where's Saturn now?" I asked.

Evelyn reluctantly responded, "I believe Saturn is still in the girls' home and reunifying with her daughter. But I've heard rumors that she's back on the street prostituting."

If anyone were thinking like I was, they would have been thinking that Evelyn's efforts at protecting the kids had failed again. I was certain Lauren was feeling the same way. However it was clear that she didn't want to offend Evelyn, so she decided to do something to cheer everyone up.

"How about a Valentine's Dance with the boys' shelter?" she suggested. "The kids would really enjoy it and it'll help us get our minds off Ed and Saturn."

Everyone agreed. Dwayne and Patty Jo were working the evening shift with me and we were charged with starting the plans in the evening's group session with the kids.

I was stuck working with Dwayne again and he wasn't happy. Ed had helped him get the job and was a good friend to him. He seemed to think Ed had been set up and was not ashamed of blaming Evelyn for Ed's demise. Shortly after the morning staff left, he decided to pull me into the office and voice his dismay. He started flipping out.

"I'm so fuckin' pissed off and sick of this shit. Evelyn always thinks she's the big cheese and her decisions are the best. But she is so wrong. She escorts these girls in and out of here like they're commodities, inadvertently led Corry to his death, and now she's gotten Ed caught up in the trap. That's fucked up!" he shouted.

"I agree with the first two, but she didn't put Ed's dick in Saturn's mouth," I said jokingly. We both laughed and it seemed to calm him down a bit.

"Now let's go get this off our chests by spending their money on this party. We only have a week to pull this off," I said.

"Yeah, but I've got to get out of here. It's worse than working with people on probation," he followed.

The average amount of time for the girls to reside in the shelter was six months, which was the same amount of time that had passed since the incident happened with Saturn and Ed. So most of the girls didn't know Ed or what happened to him, nor did they pick up on our angst. During the evening group session, we told the girls that we were going to have a cheer-me-up Valentines party to help everyone heal from all the bad things that happened over the past few months. They were excited about having a Valentine's soiree with the boys' shelter. I wanted to test some of my games for the DWB fundraiser, so I started by proposing to use them with the kids as icebreakers.

First we'd play Gotcha Number—a game that splits everyone into tribes and forces them to work as a team. Each team member is given a clue card with information about the opposing team members and must figure out which team member fits the clue. Whichever team fills in all clues on the game board wins the game and the prize. The game is an attempt to get the groups to mingle. It forces players to interact and ask questions of people in the other groups to figure out the clues. I thought it would also give the kids an opportunity to learn more about each other.

Next we'd play The Bobbling Apples—a relay game played in teams with apples. The apples are passed back and forth using a spandex cloth to catch and launch the apples to and from your teammate while running from end to end of the room to drop the apples in a basket. The first team to fill the baskets on either side wins a prize.

We'd serve dinner and then end the night with a dance party and, as Patty Jo suggested, parting gifts for everyone. The girls asked if we could ask Ms. Nellie to make heart-shaped mini cakes from her favorite Just Add Water red velvet and chocolate mandarin cake mixes as parting gifts. I suggested we could cover them with red fondant and chocolate ganache, and then gift wrap them with beautiful ribbons. Everyone agreed and the party planning was complete.

It made for an easy night of getting the girls to bed before the shift change, despite the rocky beginning. Dwayne, however, was still pissed off and vowed to start planning his exit strategy.

After completing all of the planning and coordinating the events, I didn't realize it at the time but the shelter's Valentine's dance was on the same night as Julio's fundraiser, so I didn't get to enjoy it with the girls. I didn't even get to test in real time the new games I'd designed before introducing them at the fundraiser. But when I returned to work after the event, Lauren assured me that, although they missed me as the facilitator, everyone seemed to enjoy themselves and the games.

The College Crew: Planning for Change

I was getting tired of the drama wheels of the shelter being continually front and center of my thoughts. My mom always says that when you get tired of being tired, you'll seek change. It was with this thought in mind that Julio's offer to work in Africa started to sprout and became more and more tempting. I wanted and needed a change.

Traveling to Africa would allow me to check off a lot of items on my bucket list, especially if my expenses were going to be paid. I could also be on my way to saving for my classes in France and ultimately owning a restaurant. I began to get excited.

I was almost sure it'd be a great opportunity and just what I needed to move my career goals forward. Although I was convinced, I knew I had to run it by my family to see what they thought. I couldn't tell them until I was officially offered the job, so again I shifted my focus to the fundraiser.

I'd only had a week left to finish all of the details. Given the stakes, I was determined to perfectly demonstrate my events coordination and catering skills to Julio and his colleagues. I'd decided that I really wanted the job with his organization. Impressing them would give me the greatest opportunity to get it. I was geeked!

The Valentine's Shindig: It's Showtime!

It was showtime and Julio and the crew arrived at the hotel at 8:00 a.m sharp with bells and whistles on and ready to work. We were all excited and the College Crew agreed to use the Valentine's fundraiser as February's SNL give back.

The event was scheduled to start at 5:00 p.m. Although the hotel staff had already decorated, we had a lot of training and setup to complete.

Each person was assigned a hosting role and given specific stations to monitor. I was sure to be keeping an eye on everyone. I couldn't afford any slipups.

Julio had been in charge of having the T-shirts made and surprised us with personalized T-shirts for the College Crew. Our shirts were the reverse of the others and we were the only ones with blue and gold shirts—to honor us as University of Pittsburgh alumni.

The front of the shirts were embroidered with our names on the right side and The Cool Crew on the left side. The back was a virtual advertisement for the event and its many sponsors. They were a beautiful surprise and helped us stand out in the crowd.

Chantelle showed up with Diamond Damon, who also booked a room and agreed to help her welcome the guests. Rafi and Sheila were responsible for registration and on-site ticket sales. Mark B and Regina helped the bartender with serving, and with selling the cakes and cocktail tickets throughout the evening. It was a key part of the fundraiser for us.

Chris and his so-called girlfriend Rebecca arrived a little late. Honestly, I wasn't even sure if he was going to show up after I'd rejected him at the spa. But he kept his word. They both agreed to assist Leila, Regina, and Charise with facilitating the group games, orchestrating dinner seating, and promoting food purchases.

Then JB surprised everyone and showed up with Andy, the piano player, to play music with Pierre and Henri as the masters of ceremonies. They were also responsible for promoting the cocktails and cakes sales, facilitating the raffles, making gaming announcements, and directing the silent auction.

Julio's fundraising goal was to net $50,000 in donations. We'd already sold 315 tickets and raised more than $48,000. Our goal was to raise the remaining funds from donations and sales during the event. Therefore the MCs also had a vital role to play in promoting why DWB needed the funds for the African Relief tour.

Given that the Valentine's fundraiser was an invitation only event, most of the attendees were single, unmarried volunteer staff and donors to DWB. Dwayne, Regina, Mark B, and Leila were the only representatives from the shelters. Everyone else was at the shelters' Valentine's Day party.

After their registration packets were collected, the attendees were divided into groups or tribes, based on the four to eight common characteristics identified through their registration forms. Then they were rotated throughout the evening so they could intermingle. Each tribal member was identifiable by his or her tribe's T-shirt and badge.

The Games of the Heart and the Games of the Mind events were orchestrated upon registration and some had started throughout the week before the main event. The first Game of the Heart was Unlock My Heart with the Golden Key. Guests who had been selected during preregistration received a lanyard with the key to their suitor's lock as part of the on-site registration packet. There seemed to be a significant number of affectionate crushes and interesting reveals among the hospital staff, especially directed toward Julio. He'd received five golden keys but he was too shy to look for the matching numbers.

The evening-long Game of the Mind event was titled Bodacious Badge Wear. It was designed to encourage conversation among the attendees while breaking the ice. Upon registration, attendees had an option to choose which badge they'd like to wear for the game. The badges were prefilled in with the registrant's name and a fill-in-the-blank statement for others to finish. If the person wearing the badge liked the words or statement filled in by another person, they could grant the person a token. The person with the most tokens won a prize and a point for their tribe. However this game was somewhat challenging. A lot of people forgot they were wearing the badges and we had to constantly make reminder announcements to keep it moving.

We offered ten different Flirtatious Name Badges. For fundraising they served a dual purpose. The first was to have fun, and the second was to get the attendees to purchase more food and drinks. The most popular badges were:

"Hi, my name is ....   Will ... for food."

"Hi, my name is ....   For one night only I'll ...."

"Hi, my name is ....   Meet me! I'm ...."

"Hi, my name is ....   Will flirt for ...."

"Hi, my name is ....   Will kiss you for ...."

"Hi, my name is ....   Will ... for a kiss."

"Hi, my name is ....   Will ... for a drink."

"Hi, my name is ....   I'm sweet, sexy, and ...."

"Hi, my name is ....   Always ready, willing, and ...."

"Hi, my name is ....   My favorite exotic drink is ...."

Julio and I were both in agreement that the spirit of competition always draws people in, so the second Game of the Heart event was called Lip-Smackers—a game where trivia cards are exchanged from lip to lip, similar to a game of musical chairs. We were sure to match people with their tribe members to reduce the awkward factor.

Each person had to moisturize their lips to pass the cards and once the music stopped, the person who ended up with the card was obliged to attempt to answer the trivia question on it. If their answer was correct, that person could potentially steal a kiss from their favorite flirt in the group. It was like a game of musical chairs with your lips doing the walking. It was a lot of fun and provocative. There were a lot of love connections made that led to after party hookups.

Following the Lip-Smackers game, we built in time for the groups to mingle, purchase items, and prepare for the Games of the Body event. This was the same Bobbling Apples relay game I'd proposed for the shelter but with an intimate twist.

The Games of the Body event, a couples game, was titled Don't Drop the Bobbling Apples. Again the assigned tribes designated the teams. Singles were paired in couples by pulling names from the on-site registration lists. The objective of the game was to figure out how to get five apples from a table into two buckets located on alternating sides of the room with your hands tied behind your back. The apples must stay in the front of the couple and they must walk the apples together without dropping them.

This was one of the most hilarious events of the evening, especially after most people had finished a few drinks. Some of the couples tried moving the apples back and forth with their breasts, and some with their hips. The winners eventually sank their teeth into the apples and walked them to the bucket. It resulted in quite a bit of kissing while trying to hold on to a little four-inch apple.

Dinner followed and I'd designed playful and sexy food for the soul menu. In conjunction with the hotel's executive chef and four of his sous chefs, I also arranged for an intimate dining setup.

I didn't want the food to weigh the guests down, so I planned a delicious but light collection of bowls and handheld items that people could eat quickly. In keeping with the love theme, each collection of food included specially crafted Libido Lifting Love Shooters. These were also a big hit.

We set up the dinner room with serving stations in each of the four corners and a single cakes and cocktails station in the middle of the room. Each station was fashioned with giant signs notating the station's name and menu items on offer. All five of the stations offered a distinct collection of dishes, with a sous chef and bartender to serve guests on demand.

Station One was labeled Mexican Hot Tamales. I'd selected a variety of handmade tamales filled with roasted pork, chipotle chicken, and sweet corn, wrapped and steamed in corn husks. The servings were accompanied by a choice of several savory sauces and a condiments bar. Dessert was vanilla spice tres leches cupcakes, and the featured Libido Lifting Love Shooter was watermelon and lime juice with or without vodka. Watermelon is often referred to as a "natural Viagra," and is known to heighten sexual pleasure, hence the choice.

Station Two was labeled Sassy Sexy Soul Bowls. I'd selected a triad of feisty mild and spicy buttermilk-fried chicken poppers, smoky barbecued riblets, and sassy Southern-fried catfish bowls filled with garlic mashed potatoes and fried corn or savory collard greens. Each meal included corn bread madeleines and a visit to the macaroni and cheese bar, which was stocked with a variety of toppings and add-ins. We served heart-shaped sweet potato–pumpkin pies for dessert. The featured Libido Lifting Love Shooters were iced green tea and ginseng melon balls made with Midori—a melon-flavored liqueur—sweet ghost pepper syrup, and sour mix. Green tea and ginseng are known to augment the release of oxytocin, also known as the love hormone, and the ghost pepper syrup adds an extra kick to get the blood pumping. We sold out of these very quickly because there was a lot of oxytocin being released during the entire evening.

Station Three was labeled Audacious Asian Hot Pots. It served a variety of on-demand noodle bowls filled with a choice of Japanese udon, vermicelli rice, or ramen noodles, a protein choice of Korean barbecued roast pork belly, thin-sliced beef round, or marinated and fried tempeh, and a plethora of fresh herbs and vegetables immersed in a steaming hot savory broth. Dessert was a small plate of steamed sweet sticky rice topped with sweetened coconut milk and fresh mango and papaya slices. The featured Libido Lifting Love Shooter was a Fun Love—yoni teatox love elixir with or without a shot of gin—the tea is a combination of aphrodisiacs and a relaxant.

Station Four was labeled Juicy Jamaican Jerk Bowls. The menu featured traditional jerk chicken served in bowls filled with red peas and rice, sautéed collard greens, and a fried dumpling. The dessert was three petite coconut macaroons, and the featured Libido Lifting Love Shooter was Blue Mountain Coffee and amaretto creams. Coffee boosts the love hormone for women, and the almonds in the amaretto liquor boosts it for men.

Station Five was labeled Happy Cakes and Cocktails and featured The Erotic and Exotic Martini Bar. It was set up to make at least twenty-five varieties of sweet, savory, and dirty martinis. Joe, my bartender, made a list of very interesting and provocative aphrodisiac cocktails, some of which I'd never heard of. They were perfect for the occasion—a Screaming Orgasm, a Blowjob, Sit on my Face, a Creamy Pussy, and a Royal Fuck were just a few on the list. To avoid the puke fest that tends to happen when most people forget to eat while drinking alcohol, we also set up a variety of relish trays, crackers, dips, and cheeses for those who chose to skip dinner but still wanted to drink. All the setups worked wonderfully, and the hosts did an excellent job of moving all the tribes through the feeding lines and preparing them for their next events.

We built in dinner breaks between each of the games. Quickly realizing that people could get easily distracted and miss out on some of the items for sale, we made reminder announcements every twenty minutes for people to collect their coins from the Bodacious Badge Wear game, bidding on items from the silent auction and purchasing cakes and cocktails. Although it was a necessary evil, it kept each of the mini fundraisers at the forefront of the evening, which helped us surpass the $50,000 goal.

The Game of the Soul event was the Gotcha Number Game—a team activity designed to challenge the guests' ability to socialize with as many people attending the event as possible, and to document one characteristic about each of these on their tribe's game board. Each tribe was provided with a large game board set up with twenty boxes labeled with the names of the opposing tribes and given twenty clue cards with brief descriptions of a participating team member's personal characteristics taken from the registration forms. Once a tribe identified a member of an opposing team, they had to get that person to fill in their name before the competing team could post the completed card on their game board.

The teams were only given fifteen minutes to complete the search for all twenty people in the opposing tribe; therefore they had to work quickly. The winning tribe(s) would have the most names completed on the game board once the time was up. At the end of this game, the two winning tribes actually strategized—they divided the cards into four per member, and each one targeted the other tribes directly. They filled the board up pretty quickly, but they didn't get to mingle a lot. However the game was very informative and lots of fun, especially for the College Crew hosts.

The hosts were given a matching group of character clue cards for each tribe and charged with reading them out loud to determine if they were placed on the master identification game boards correctly. Things seemed to get a bit puzzling at one point—there were a few fakes and a couple of times some people had the same characteristics written about themselves. But it wasn't difficult to figure it all out based on the tribal assignments and the matching cards.

The last event of the evening was the dance party and it was all the rage. We'd hired Pierre and Henri to serve as MCs and set up portable poles for pole dancing. A male and female pole dancing contest, a twerking contest, a variety of line dances, and a soul train line were the featured events. Pierre and Henri also did a drum spotlight where they invited attendees to participate in the African drumming and then asked the guests to choose winners by applause. It was another wonderful way of keeping everyone involved in the fun.

In the middle of the dance party, Julio announced that they had surpassed the $50,000 goal and had raised $25,000 to help the shelter kids. After discussing the generous gift, the entire College Crew suggested that the fund be named after me. I was so honored and humbled to be able to leave a legacy and to hopefully make a lasting and positive impact on the children I so dearly loved.

The remaining time allowed guests to dance, purchase more items, and enjoy each other's company. The event ended at midnight, however the hotel's lounge was open until 2:00 a.m. The concierge invited the booked guests to the lounge for more drinks and mingling at the end.

After all the guests left the event space, I got a chance to debrief about the event with Julio. I really wanted to know how we earned the $25,000 for the shelter so quickly. To my surprise, he told me that Javier donated the money but wanted to remain anonymous. He also said the DWB group was leaving for Africa in June and would be honored if I would join the tour as the culinary emissary. I was speechless.

"It's a year-long tour, but we'll pay you a handsome salary, a few perks, and pay for all of your expenses," he said.

I just stared at him. I was in awe. All I could do was think about how it would allow me to save the money to go to Paris to study cooking. I could also hone my skills as a food writer and eventually open my restaurant. I didn't even want to think about it for too long for fear he might change his mind.

"I'm in! I accept!" I responded with sheer disbelief.

I couldn't believe I was getting an opportunity to further showcase my culinary and catering skills. Even better, I'd get the chance to travel and become a real food writer. It was definitely a changing point in my life. I just had to convince my parents that I was making a good choice.

Menu

*Join Us for a Valentines Love Celebration
of the Heart, Body, Mind, and Soul*

featuring International Food Buffets

STATION ONE

Mexican Hot Tamales

*A variety of handmade roast pork, chipotle chicken, and sweet corn
tamales wrapped and steamed in corn husks, accompanied by a choice of
savory sauces and condiments.*

DESSERT

Vanilla Spice Tres Leches Cupcakes

BEVERAGE

Watermelon & Lime Juice Shooters

with or without vodka

Menu

STATION TWO

Sassy Sexy Soul Bowls

A triad of mild and spicy buttermilk-fried chicken poppers, barbecued riblets, and Southern-fried catfish soul bowls filled with garlic mashed potatoes and fried corn or savory collard greens; corn bread madeleines; and a macaroni and cheese and condiment bar.

DESSERT

Heart-Shaped Sweet Potato–Pumpkin Pies

BEVERAGE

Iced Green Tea & Ginseng Midori Melts

melon balls with sweet ghost pepper syrup and sour mix

STATION THREE

Audacious Asian Hot Pots

A variety of on-demand noodle bowls filled with Japanese udon, vermicelli rice, or ramen noodles; Korean barbecued pork belly, thin-sliced beef, or fried tempeh; fresh herbs and vegetables immersed in a steaming hot savory broth.

DESSERT

Steamed Sweet Sticky Rice

with sweetened coconut milk and fresh mango and papaya slices

BEVERAGE

Fun Love Elixirs

yoni teatox love elixir with or without a shot of gin

menu continues ...

Menu

STATION FOUR

Juicy Jamaican Jerk Bowls

Jerk chicken served with red peas and rice, sautéed collard greens, and a traditional fried dumpling.

DESSERT

Petite Coconut Macaroons

BEVERAGE

Blue Mountain Coffee & Amaretto Creams

STATION FIVE

Happier Happy Cakes

an assortment of heart- and phallic-shaped cupcakes

The Erotic & Exotic Martini Bar

*at least 25 varieties of sweet, savory, and dirty martinis, including:
Screaming Orgasm, Blowjob, Sit on my Face,
Creamy Pussy, and Royal Fuck*

accompanied by relish trays, crackers, dips, and cheeses

ENTERTAINMENT

Games of Love & Attraction

*Games of the Heart, Games of the Body,
Games of the Mind, and Games of the Soul.*

was on an all-time high and extremely optimistic about being able to pursue my dreams. I was even more excited about being able to leave an endowment fund at the shelter with the $25,000 donation. The fund would help girls like Zee and Saturn get settled and have mentorship once they aged out of the foster care system. Most of all, I was riding on cloud nine after Julio offered me the job with DWB.

On a less positive note, I was a little sad that I'd have to give the shelter my notice of resignation. But that sadness quickly dissipated. Every night I'd prayed and asked the Lord to order my steps. Now, he was leading me just where I wanted to be—and that certainly wasn't working in the shelter. But I had a little surprise I thought would lighten the blow a bit.

We'd brought twenty-five cases of the Just Add Water Happy Cake mixes to sell at the fundraiser. After Julio announced that the Cakes and Cocktails fundraiser would benefit the shelter kids, Javier purchased the whole lot for a twenty-five thousand dollar donation. He took a case home with him, gave a few boxes to his colleagues, and gave me ten cases to take to the shelter for the kids to enjoy. I was extremely grateful for the gift and the financial donation.

Sunday was just a blur for me—I slept the entire day. When I arrived for work at the shelter on Monday morning, Dwayne and Regina had signed in before me. They had already spread the news about the endowment. When I walked in the office everyone broke out in an overwhelming applause and congratulated me for raising the money to help the kids. Lauren, Patty Jo, and Evelyn apologized for not being able to attend the event, but promised to honor me at the upcoming awards ceremony.

I left the office and went into the kitchen to surprise Ms. Nellie with the cases of Happy Cakes. I also shared my good news about the success of the fundraiser, and the not so good news of my departure.

Without failing, her reaction surprised me again. Ms. Nellie's a profoundly wise woman who always applauded my efforts. Not only did she encourage me to make the world my oyster—her favorite food—she assured me that this was God's plan for my life.

"People like you are the salt of the earth ... the kind who possess the truth, the courage, and the resilience to get things done," she said.

I started crying. She always touched my heart in a special kind of way, but this was different.

"You have God's seeds of greatness to sow on fertile soil, and nobody will stop that. I truly admire you and will always be praying for you and your journeys," she finished.

Tears of joy filled both of our faces. Ms. Nellie was always like another mother to me, and a prayer warrior. I gave her a big hug and cleaned up my face so I wouldn't alarm the girls.

After I left Ms. Nellie, I realized I'd forgotten to tell Lauren about my departure and went back into the office. Dwayne was sitting in the corner and seemed upset. He wasn't shouting or being rude so I didn't think anything of it. I told Lauren that I had gotten the job with DWB and would be leaving the shelter at the end of April.

Lauren is also a wonderful person and applauded my decision to take the opportunity to work overseas. She stood up to face me, placed both of her hands on my shoulders, and thanked me.

"If only for a season, I thank God, and I know he sent you to us for a reason. It appears that season has come to an end, and I want to thank you for following his direction. It's quite clear that you are a special gift, and He now wants to share that gift with the rest of the world. God bless you on your journey and we will always be with you," she said.

I was taken aback. I started to tear up, again. But Dwayne quickly burst my bubble.

"I want to get out of this shit hole too!" he complained.

Apparently he was in the office talking with Lauren about the amount of stress he was under. He had taken three big emotional hits in the past week and had become depressed. After rather rudely interjecting in my conversation with Lauren, he apologized and felt obligated to explain his reaction to me.

First his fiancée had broken off the engagement after finding out he'd cheated on her. Then he'd asked Regina to attend the Valentine's fundraiser with him and she refused, so he felt rejected. Third, and the biggest problem, was with his other job as a probation officer. Although he only worked the job part-time, he was responsible for monitoring his clients around the clock to keep them in compliance with their probation rules. He lived in the same community and was friends with many of his clients, which wasn't regarded well by his bosses. It unfortunately came back to bite him as feared.

He'd gotten into an argument with one of his clients, who just so happened to be a friend. The guy was in a bar drinking illegally. The owner and bartender, who was also a friend, called Dwayne to pick him up. When Dwayne confronted the client, he pulled out a knife. Dwayne said he was attempting to take the knife from him so he wouldn't go to jail if the cops came, but during the scuffle Dwayne accidentally cut him on the thigh.

Then Dwayne tried to get the guy to go to the hospital for treatment, but the guy was afraid he'd be arrested and refused. Dwayne left the guy with the agreement that he'd go home and take care of the wound. But he was now haunted by what happened and afraid he'd lose the job if his bosses found out they were all friends.

Lauren had already left the office after Dwayne's initial comment, so I asked him if I could pray with him, but he resisted. I told him I'd pray for him anyway and with that I left him and went to check on the girls.

The College Crew: Rafi

It was three weeks after the Valentine's fundraiser and I began making preparations to leave the shelter. But I felt obligated to get things set up for what would be one of my last SNL celebrations until I returned to Pittsburgh.

Rafi was hosting the much-anticipated African Fusion Saturday Night Live celebration at his newly acquired condo. Renovation of his condo was finally finished and he couldn't wait to welcome the crew.

The week before the SNL celebration, I stopped by Rafi's new condo to lay out the plan and finalize the menu. Rafi's a trust fund baby and he received his inheritance when he turned twenty-three years old over the Christmas holiday. The first thing he did was to purchase and renovate a condo, and he was excited about everyone visiting for the first time during the upcoming SNL celebration.

He'd just moved into the beautiful two-bedroom condo located fifteen minutes northwest of downtown Pittsburgh in suburban and photogenic Ross-lyn Farms. It's a very quiet and picturesque community set in the woods and surrounded by the Allegheny Mountains—a perfect setting for a quaint and more subdued celebration.

During breakfast at the spa retreat, Rafi said he wanted to do an upscale but more toned down celebration of his homeland—he wanted to focus more on dinner and conversation as opposed to dancing. He'd suffered a major hip injury while playing rugby in high school, which left him with a pronounced limp, and as a result he wasn't much of a dancer. In addition, he wasn't certain about how his new neighbors would respond to the noise. Even though dancing was always at the top of our activities list, everyone respected his request.

We planned to prepare a traditional African fusion–themed dinner, to play Taboo, a good word game to keep the conversation moving, and to chat about our plans for the summer. We also wanted to set up the dining area to reflect a traditional mealtime in Africa.

Upon my suggestion, Rafi agreed to position the dining area in the middle of the living room floor. It would be similar to the setup we'd used for the Latin Fusion dinner, but we would change the tablescape and planned to add padded stools instead of the pouf pillows for seating.

Rafi was very proud and excited to be celebrating his culture with the group. He was adamant about the dinner being very upscale but traditional. Hence selecting the appropriate dishes was very important. However I did throw a little twist in the menu. It started with two appetizers: First, delicate East African fried samosas filled with curried potatoes, shrimp, and sweet peas—a typical street food served in Tanzania that arrived with the Arabs and East Indians during colonization; second, shrimp farci—jumbo shrimp filled with a tender crab stuffing, breaded, and deep fried. The dish hails from Senegal, West Africa, and is often served in high-end hotels.

The second course was more intense. Rafi's family is from Ghana, West Africa, and he insisted that we serve his country's national dish—Gold Coast groundnut stew. It's a very sensual dish made with a whole chicken that's cut into pieces, seasoned, and stewed in a delicate peanut sauce. It's traditionally served with aromatic steamed rice or *fufu*—a whipped and boiled soft dumpling that can be made from a variety of starches including wheat flour, plantains, or cassava root.

A second, and one of my favorites to make and to eat at African restaurants, is *chioff* or *ceebu-jen*—the national dish of Senegal. It's a savory fish stew made with hake or grouper and short-grain rice sautéed and stewed in a creamy tomato, vegetable, and herb sauce.

The third and final part of the main course would be a popular dish from the country of Nigeria, in mid-Western Africa—okra and dried fish stew with *fufu*. Made with fresh okra and a variety of dried fish and broth, it's a light and savory stew served with the *fufu*. I'm fond of all three variations of *fufu*, however the pounded cassava or yucca version is very light and has a nutty flavor and a texture that goes particularly well with the okra.

In an effort to cover more regions in Africa, we decided to pay tribute to Southern Africa with one of the two dessert selections. The first dessert, sweet potato and banana galettes from South Africa, were soft and flavor-filled tea cakes that we planned to serve with fresh mint tea, which is traditional in Morocco, North Africa.

The second dessert called *thiakry* is native to Senegal, West Africa. It's a creamy toasted millet custard flavored with vanilla and orange flower water, and topped with sweet and creamy yogurt, fresh mangoes or papaya, grated coconut, and chopped cashews. *Thiakry* custard is a triple threat—it's creamy, fresh, and nutty.

In keeping with the theme, we chose a nice variety of beverages including a collection of craft beers, wine, soda, and a few traditional drinks. We would also set up a complementary iced vodka bar, and I planned to make a batch of Senegalese *bissap* punch—a traditional drink made with hibiscus, pineapple, and guava juices. It would be placed in the middle of an ice bowl filled with the flavored vodka shots. This would allow people to choose from a variety of flavored vodka shots and mix it up a bit if they wanted to add a flavor boost to the punch.

Rafi had also brought back a case of Ghanaian stout beer from his Christmas trip. He always bragged about how much better the beer was at home and was excited for everyone to taste it.

In a valiant attempt to avoid the hangovers we all knew would likely occur after drinking the beer and vodka, I also decided to make Senegalese *kenkiliba* with fresh mint tea. It's a warm, nutty, and sweet herbal tea used as a digestive and cure-all throughout West Africa.

Our celebrations usually included up to fifteen people, but I decided to invite Julio to join us. I thought it would be a sort of preamble to some of the culinary experiences we'd possibly encounter while in Africa. I also wanted him to further explain what my job would entail and to convince the crew and me that I'd be making a good career choice.

In the midst of planning my mind began to drift. I couldn't stop thinking about my encounter with Chris at the spa. Eventually my curiosity got the best of me and I needed to find out what was going on with Chris and Rebecca. I knew Rafi would have the inside scoop so I just went for it.

"So what's going on with Chris and Rebecca?" I asked.

"It won't last! He's clearly still in love with you. He said her pussy's like a dark hole. Anytime he tries to have sex with her, that shit just swallows him up," he said while laughing hysterically.

"That's probably why he tried to fuck me in my ass!" I shouted.

"Oh shit!" Rafi exclaimed while still laughing hysterically. "He should know black girls don't typically go for that shit! He probably goes in her ass cause her pussy's so fuckin' big he can't feel anything. You know what *that* means Anais?" he questioned while prompting me for a response.

Initially I wasn't quite sure how I was supposed to respond. But then after I thought about it for a minute, the answer came quickly.

"She's a hoe!" I exclaimed. "She's either been fucking a whole lot, or she's been fucking somebody with a big dick! Worse, if he's fucking her in the ass, he's really looking for trouble," I responded.

I began to regret my inquiry. I was disturbed by the thought of him fucking her in the ass and then trying to fuck me. All I could think about were the horror stories of women whose men were doing sexual things on the downlow and then infecting their women with incurable diseases. It was like I had an epiphany. At that moment I promised myself not to ever trust Chris again.

"Just stop fuckin' him and you won't have to worry Anais," Rafi followed.

"That used to be easier said than done," I said with regret. "But not anymore. I'm truly done," I replied.

I couldn't stop thinking about the possibility of being exposed to some crazy incurable disease. I was so happy I hadn't fully engaged with him at the spa retreat. He used to be able to take me just about anywhere sexually, but not when there's someone else involved, and certainly not in that way. However I still worried about what he was getting himself into with Rebecca. But Rafi quickly interrupted my thoughts.

"We'd best hurry and finish the setup so you can get back to the food, Anais. Otherwise neither of us will get our work done. And you know I really want this SNL celebration to be a special representation of the beauty of my homeland," he said.

"No problem! I'll make sure it's an elegant and tasty celebration," I said.

I forced myself to put those thoughts behind me. I did, however, make a vow to myself that if I were ever again in a compromising position with Chris, I'd remember the feeling of potentially being exposed to something egregious and readily reject his advances.

The Shelter

I was three days away from finishing my final two weeks of work at the shelter. I worked the morning shift with Regina and was assigned to take Ms. Nellie grocery shopping after dropping the girls off at school. My cherished conversations about food with Ms. Nellie were one of the most refreshing parts of the job. It was one of the things I'd miss the most, along with her unwavering grace.

Upon our return from shopping, the house was unusually quiet again. The girls were still at school, but something seemed a bit off. I helped bring the groceries in from the van and promptly headed to the office.

The office was tucked in a back corner away from the main living room and kitchen. As I was walking toward it I could hear what seemed to be moaning. It scared me. I was afraid to open the door.

I slowly pushed the door open to find Lauren, Evelyn, and Regina crying.

"What's going on? Don't tell me you all are going to miss me that much!" I quipped jokingly.

They lightly giggled and assured me they'd miss me. But what they followed with broke my heart.

"I just got a call from headquarters, Anais. Apparently Dwayne committed suicide," Lauren said with regret.

I was shocked. It was like something had punched me in the chest. I dropped into a chair and began crying, too.

"What in the world happened?" I inquired.

Lauren explained that she had just given him time off to get his head together. Apparently the altercation with Zee wasn't the only incident at the shelter. She became concerned about his mental health and the safety of the girls, so she asked him to take a break.

When she received the call from headquarters, she wasn't sure if she'd made the right decision. However after calling his mother to express her condolences, she learned more about what had really been going on with him.

He was completely overwhelmed with the two jobs and the recent breakup with his fiancée. His fiancée had broken up with him after finding out he was unfaithful. Shortly after the breakup, he found out that his friend and client, who he'd accidentally stabbed, had died. His mother told Lauren that even though the guy promised to go home and wrap his leg, he didn't. Instead, he went back to the bar and continued drinking. Two days later the guy died from exsanguination—he bled to death in his sleep.

During the investigation into his death, the bartender told the cops about the altercation, and Dwayne was held liable for the death. Not only did he lose his job as a parole officer, but he'd never be able to work in his chosen field again.

In summary, he was essentially laid off by Lauren, dumped by his fiancée, and had just found out that he'd be held liable for the death of his friend. It was sad, but clear—he simply gave up on life. Ironically he shot himself with the service weapon he was given to protect himself as a probation officer.

I was numb. I couldn't wait to finish those last couple of days before the shelter tried to consume me like it did Dwayne and Ed. It appeared Regina and Evelyn were beginning to experience the pangs of burn out, too.

Celebrating the First Signs of Spring

I finally finished my last official week at the shelter. Before leaving I promised Lauren I'd fill in until she found replacements for both Dwayne and me. She was extremely short-staffed but promised she'd only call me if it was urgent.

In the meantime, I set out to finish packing up my apartment and to work full-time on my language translation training. I wanted to improve my chances of selling articles along with the photos I sent to Abby. I was confident it would improve my chances of becoming a full-fledged food writer, and I wanted to take full advantage of the downtime I'd been afforded.

I also decided to take JB up on an earlier offer to help with moving. I called him the week after I left the shelter, and he came over and worked like a dog. I was truly honored. I didn't want to inconvenience any of the crew, but he'd offered at the Valentine's event right after Julio offered me the job.

After we finished moving the boxes to storage, we were starving. The only thing I had in the kitchen were the dehydrated superfood meals I'd prepared to take with me to Africa. I felt like I needed to thank him for all of his help.

In an effort to take a little piece of home with me overseas, I'd made a variety of dehydrated superfood meal kits, including collard greens with smoked pork, smoked turkey, and curried chicken with sides of rice and corn bread. I even made dehydrated sweet potato casserole kits for dessert. He was enthralled with how I made them and insisted on having a couple of them for dinner and dessert.

All we needed to do was add hot water and dive in. I designed them to be quick and easy because I wasn't sure what kinds of foods or cooking facilities would be available to me. I had a battery-operated hot water cup, and all I had to do was heat the water to rehydrate the food and eat. We both really enjoyed the meal kits. They were not only delicious, but also very convenient and nutritious. JB helped to reassure me that I'd at least have a little taste of home with me on my trip. But I also wanted to give him a real thank you gift for helping me move my things.

I offered him a facial and hand massage with some of the Bodacious Body products I was taking with me. He chose the lotus flower bomb facial kit and a calming calendula hand mask. It was another love connection made with the Bodacious Body products. The skin cream was clean, smooth, and smelled delicious. He was most excited about how soft and relaxed his hands and face were after the treatments. It was a perfect thank you to end a very productive day.

"Mission Accomplished!" I said and I wished him goodnight.

SNL African Fusion: Party Time!

Tariq called me early Friday morning to inform me that his flight would be arriving very early in the morning from San Francisco on SNL Saturday. It meant that he'd arrive in time to join the celebration and I was very excited. I hadn't seen him since I'd left him in Paris, and really missed him—especially after the brain fart I'd had with Chris at the spa. The airport is only ten minutes away from Rafi's condo, so I picked Tariq up first and we went straight to Rafi's to have breakfast and set up early.

Our ultimate goal was to create the facade of a traditional African dining experience with the cool and earthy elements from the forest. With Tariq and Rafi's help, the dining table came out even more amazing than I'd imagined. We covered the long makeshift table with a black table liner and topped it with a double-wide piece of traditional green and yellow kente cloth, accented with a masterful color blend of early spring-like greens and bark from the backyard trees. For seating, Rafi purchased a bunch of inexpensive stools from Ikea and we wrapped them with pieces of the kente cloth to match the dining table. The matching stools provided the perfect contrast to the overall tablescape. Then we went to work on the place settings.

Each place setting was prepared to host an individual feast for each person—marked by a black placemat that complimented the kente cloth, the placemats hosted an accoutrement of beverage glasses, serving utensils, and plates. Three individual servings of small covered clay pots filled with steamed rice, fluffy cassava *fufu*, and the okra and fish stew would sit at the top of each placemat. Complementary oval plates for holding the food were topped with cloth napkins that were wrapped with handy wipes and gold spoons tied with floral branches and magnolia flowers.

The middle of the table resembled a colorful Garden of Eden hidden in a vibrant and flourishing forest. Six large, colorful Moroccan clay pots (tagines) would be strategically stationed with serving utensils between every three place settings for sharing; three natural-edge wooden platters topped with mini Tanzanian samosas, Senegalese stuffed shrimp, and crushed chili pepper sauce would separate each tagine; and crystal glass decanters filled with still and sparkling water and *bissap* punch would divide every other place setting. To bring the tablescape together, we outlined the center of the table with a cornucopia of dried bark, branches, and flowers from Rafi's back yard.

The dessert and extra drinks were set up on the formal dining room table. Additional bottles of *bissap* punch, Ghanaian stout, wine, and vodka sat on ice in a giant beverage bucket.

We worked throughout the day to make certain that everything was as perfect as Rafi wanted. Shortly before everyone arrived, Rafi cranked up a mix of West African music, and I lit an essential oil diffuser filled with the warm scents of frankincense and myrrh to set the mood—it made for a calm, relaxed, and seductive atmosphere. The room looked and felt wonderful, and the aromas were celestial. It set the stage for a classy and tasty celebration of a multidimensional African-inspired feast.

A Welcoming Salute

I guess the crew was very eager to see Rafi's new place. In a not so ordinary fashion, everyone arrived on time, and around the same time. Most people carpooled, which also made it easy for parking and planning.

As for the guests, Julio came alone and luckily found the place with no problem. Penny had temporarily returned from her internship in South Africa and carpooled with JB, Pierre, and Henri. I was in the kitchen when everyone else arrived so I wasn't quite sure exactly who drove together. However all of the guests were present and ready to start the festivities on time.

Rafi greeted everyone who walked in the door with a traditional *bissap* drink and welcomed them to make themselves at home. When everyone got settled in, he informed them that akin to the African tradition, they'd have to eat with their hands. Even though some people thought it was a joke, there wasn't a lot of pushback. Most people were even excited to try.

Rafi went on to demonstrate how to properly pick the food up. For support, he asked his fellow Africans to chip in on the explanation of the culinary traditions behind eating only with the right hand, except in the case where it's prohibitive. The eating tutorial was very brief and dismissive. I wasn't quite sure how it was going to play out.

A traditional African dinner service, especially in the village, always starts with everyone washing their hands at the table in a bucket or large bowl. We replicated it at our table to ensure that everyone had clean hands. I also included handy wipes with the napkin and spoon packets to allow everyone to clean their hands between dishes if necessary. It proved to be a very valuable addition to the utensil pack.

When hosting culturally inspired events, I always attempt to design menus that include authentic yet familial dishes. I'd apparently done a pretty good job in this case—every featured dish received five stars for taste and authenticity.

During the meal, we learned that when totaled, all sixteen of us represented twenty-seven countries and ethnically diverse culinary backgrounds. The funny thing was that everyone was able to relate most of the dishes being served to similar ones served by their families. Although some people struggled with remembering the preparation techniques, they almost always reminisced on the love that was shared from the memories of their relatives preparing the dishes. Dinner turned out to be a touching and heartwarming celebration of food, family memories, and fellowship.

Meal service started with a prayer by Rafi, and then we dove right into the tantalizing appetizers—Senegalese shrimp farci and Tanzanian samosas. I wanted to serve them piping hot, so I fried them just before everyone arrived and placed them on the table right after the prayer.

The tender crab meat lightly mixed and coated with eggs and breadcrumbs perfectly complemented the sweet, juicy jumbo shrimp. The nicely flavored samosas were crunchy and creamy, and perfectly complimented those stuffed shrimp—everyone relished them as African culinary treasures.

The main courses were just as exquisite. But I was very happy with the choice to have everyone eat out of individual plates as opposed to traditionally eating from a single familial bowl. The way everyone initially struggled to get the food in their mouths was hilarious and disturbing.

First of all, they were all very hungry, so patience was absent. They put the bowls up to their faces and slopped the food in the best way they could. After everyone broke into roaring laughter, Rafi decided to do another demonstration on how to pick the food up with your hands before serving the sizzling hot fish and rice and the peanut chicken stew from the tagines.

I'm not sure if his demonstrations worked, but the flavor-packed dishes quickly disappeared, and there was very little conversation going on. Tariq commended me for bringing back the delicious and heartwarming memories of his summers spent in the Ivory Coast with his uncle's cooks. All of the Africans agreed with Tariq's compliment, but a few people were a bit taken aback by the okra and cod stew. It made for some of the most hysterically funny and interesting moments during dinner.

Okra is very flavorful and loaded with a plethora of nutritional benefits when prepared properly. However it's mucilaginous, which means it's very slimy when cooked, especially with fish. It tastes and smells wonderful in the stew, but the traditional way to eat it is to grab a small amount of stew with a dollop of *fufu.*

Due to the slimy nature of the okra, there were a lot of jokes and laughter about its texture resembling body excrements. It was all in good fun and clearly didn't prohibit anyone from finishing their servings—all of the small clay pots were empty. Some people were even searching for additional servings. Okra stew is slimy, but very delicious. Even the most skeptical cleaned the plates.

After dinner we moved to the other side of the living room for more drinks and to play Taboo. I'd set up a beautiful vodka bar on the drinks and dessert table. I selected the flavors from my personal collection of flavored vodkas I'd made three years earlier by adding a variety of fruits and spices to good-quality vodka. It included twenty different flavors in half-ounce beakers that were immersed in ice to keep them chilled.

Whoever chose to drink vodka could either add it to their *bissap* for a kick of additional flavor, or drink it straight up as a shot. A lot of the guys drank the vodka straight up, including Rafi. It made for a very interesting game of Taboo.

Taboo: It's Game Time

The game starts by everyone throwing a dice and being assigned to teams by odd and even numbers. The rules of the game are pretty simple—each team is assigned a stack of Taboo cards, each of which contains a keyword for the active player to describe, and for his or her team members to identify, followed by a list of forbidden words. Team members take turns pulling and describing cards from the Taboo deck and the winning team is the one with the most correct words described, or points. At the start of each round a timer is set and the player has sixty seconds to get as many words described as they can. Each word successfully identified without the active player using one of the forbidden words before the timer runs out earns a point for the team.

I was on the even team with Rafi and we didn't even make it through the second round before he preempted the game. It was only his second time pulling a card. The keyword was *race.* That's when the vodka kicked in. It sparked something in him and he insisted that we should talk about what it meant.

"What the hell does the word *race* mean anyway?" he exclaimed.

I looked at his card and the taboo words were *color, running, ethnicity,* and *culture.* The entire card took him in a totally different direction. He boldly stated, "Let's talk about race and relationships," with a drunken slur.

"I've been watching my best friends wrestle with their love for each other for the past three years because of racial and stupid cultural differences. And to be honest, I don't quite understand it," he pontificated with a deep cockney accent. He was on his pedestal and clearly intended to speak his mind.

"Chantelle, with whom I've been in lust with since we were juniors in college, won't give me the time of day and keeps telling me that we're just too different. But now she's all huddled up with Diamond Damon, the so-called African Prince. Well I'm African too! Just because I grew up in London doesn't change the fact that I, too, am African. So why doesn't she like me?" he said.

Chantelle's eyes were as wide as saucers. And it seemed like her boyfriend, Diamond Damon was clueless. Rafi, however, wasn't done.

"Sheila, on the other hand, has been close to me for years, but if she took me home, I don't think her mom and dad would even let me in the house. I really don't get that shit. In England, nobody tells you who you can and can't love based on their race or culture," he lamented.

"Finally, the cream of the crop falls with my dear friends Chris and Anais. They've had my mind fucked up for a couple of years now. It's clear to everyone that Chris is obsessed with Anais. But he refuses to commit himself to her because of his family's so-called cultural expectation for his choice of a mate. Along comes Tariq, who's the same race and culture as Chris, and sweeps Anais off her feet. You know, I think Americans use race as an excuse to oppress people and make some feel more superior than others," he said in disgust.

Everyone was taken aback by his boldness. It was as if he opened a Pandora's box. I was startled and somewhat embarrassed that Tariq and Julio had to hear it, but glad that he'd finally really called Chris out.

"What the fuck Rafi!" Chris yelled. "Why are you calling me out like that?" he questioned.

"The shit's fucked up Chris! You know it's fucked up, I know it's fucked up! Everybody here knows it's fucked up!" he said with a cockney slur.

The drinks had clearly taken over Rafi's ability to practice restraint. He slurred his speech a bit, but as the saying goes, a drunken mind speaks a sober tongue. He was telling it all. Secretly, I was laughing my ass off.

Chantelle, however, was pissed off. She was very cool though and politely responded. "I'm just not that into you Rafi!" she said with a smug grin.

Nobody knew whether to laugh or feel sorry for him. After a very long, pregnant pause, she tried to clean up her statement and walked over to hug him.

"Seriously Rafi, I love you dearly. But I've always seen you as my brother. It has nothing to do with race or culture," she said.

Charise, who seemed to concur with Rafi's feelings, finally broke her silence.

"I don't understand the culture thing either. I'm afro-Caribbean and Henri's from the Congo." Out of the blue she started speaking with a heavy Trinidadian accent.

"I thought we had a beautiful relationship, but he finally admitted that we couldn't get married because he'd be ostracized by his community if he didn't marry a Congolese woman," she lamented. Then she lashed out at Henri.

"I was falling in love with you Henri. But you betrayed me!" She stared him down like she wanted to cut his penis off. I was scared for Henri.

"Is that a part of your culture too?" she chided him with vengeance in her voice.

He was in shock. But after he thought about it for a few minutes, he surprisingly responded. It wasn't quite what we all expected.

"Actually it is!" he quickly responded. It shocked everyone. "Just about every Congolese man in my family has a concubine. As long as they're discrete and the wife is confident that he's not going to leave her, it's quietly tolerated," he said.

His answer blew everyone away. I thought he was not only crazy for admitting it, but I knew she wasn't going to let it go. And she didn't. She dug in harder.

"So are they also pedophiles who date underage girls like you?" she snarked. "I know about your travels and relationship with the fifteen year old girl in Canada," she followed.

The room got completely silent. It was like an asteroid had dropped in the room and stunned everyone. Even the beautiful music had stopped playing.

Not only were we all in shock that *all* the dirty laundry was being aired, but it was like a herd of elephants had burst into the room to get all the dirt off their backs. We were just in the way.

I, however, couldn't even look at Chris. But I felt like I'd owed Julio and Tariq an apology. I couldn't imagine what they were thinking. I had already spoken to Tariq about my relationship with Chris, so that didn't bother me as much. It was the fact that I was attempting to get a job with Julio's organization, and I didn't like that our dirty laundry was being exposed in front of him.

"Dessert anyone?" I quickly interjected.

"Of course! It looks so yummy," JB responded.

"I need a drink!" Henri said with regret. "Me too!" Pierre followed.

Fortunately the dessert spoke for itself. It seemed to cheer everyone up—at least for a short period.

The light and creamy *thiakry*, a Senegalese millet pudding, topped with a thick creamy yogurt sauce, tender mango and papaya cubes, and chopped cashews, hit the spot after all the drinking. I had gift wrapped the sweet potato and banana galettes so if anyone wanted to take them home they could. However they turned out to be a perfect accompaniment to the vodka shots, and most people enjoyed them during the conversation, including JB who relished them and asked for seconds.

Thank God for JB. He'd been like a fly on the wall during many of the conversations over the past nine months, and had witnessed a lot of the impending drama. After everyone got their drinks and dessert, he decided to chime in.

"You know, I've watched a lot of things happen with you guys and girls during these parties, and there's something I'd like to say in hopes that it'll make all of you feel better. I hope it will also give you more clarity on these ideologies of culture and race," he said.

Rafi immediately interjected. "I'm not quite sure I'll ever understand this shit JB. Honestly, I apologize if this is offensive to anyone, but it's been clear to many of us for years that Anais and Chris clearly belonged together. However *he* allowed his bullshit excuses about fear of societal rejection to tear them apart because she's not white or Lebanese like him. Now she's with another Lebanese man and there are no such problems," he said with frustration and continued, "Clearly that's who she belongs with."

"Charise just told us about the bullshit with Henri. I'm African and I've never heard any shit like that. Then again I grew up in London. But as for me, I have to swallow the fact that Chantelle just doesn't like my ass, so that's neither here nor there," he quipped and we all laughed cautiously.

"Honestly, I really believe that lives are destroyed due to the racial and cultural intolerability of Americans. I know that nowhere is perfect, but one thing I can say with confidence is that most of the British and Europeans have pretty much surpassed the idea of racial superiority when it comes to personal relationships." He finished with another shot of vodka.

JB agreed with him and shared his personal battles with his family about dating a white girl. His mother and sisters wouldn't support him dating a white girl because they felt he'd be betraying his race. To steer him toward black girls, they'd often set him up with dates from his church, and use biblical scriptures to convince him of their choices being correct.

"You should be equally yoked!" he quipped as he recalled his mother's rants from interpreting what she translated from the bible to mean that his suitors should be from the same background as him. Therefore the only women they'd endorse were black women like them.

He's the youngest boy of seven children, and they consider him the golden child because of his musical gift. But he'd never been able to get married and settle down because he said somehow his family would sabotage all of his relationships. They felt that if he didn't marry someone they approved of, he risked being betrayed by someone from another race or culture.

Charise agreed that there could be some truth to that given how she was treated by Henri. Although I didn't agree, I did somewhat understand her response, and I believe everyone empathized with her pain.

Chantelle too empathized with Charise's situation, but she poignantly reminded us that anyone could betray you from any race or culture. She emphatically insisted that betrayal is not exclusive to one race or culture. At that point, Diamond Damon decided to add his two cents to the conversation, but it wasn't at all inspiring.

He said many of the Nigerians refer to African Americans as *oyinbo* or *dudu* and that's probably why Henri didn't want to marry Charise—everyone was confused and didn't understand where Diamond Damon was leading the conversation. Then Penny chimed in and said the cultural significance of the word *dudu* roughly translates to the idea of African Americans being impure because they were subjected to slavery and the mixing of the races. Then Diamond Damon came out and said exactly what was on his mind. He said that culturally the Nigerians feel they're better than the Americans and other Africans because they were never enslaved. I was insulted as were just about everyone else, including Chantelle. Then he tried to convince us that he didn't feel the same way about Chantelle because he really likes her. But he wasn't very convincing. In fact, he angered most of us.

Again, Chantelle was really pissed off. She started telling him off and things really started getting out of control. She confronted him about everything she didn't like about his culture including his roving eye with many of her girlfriends. She even cussed him out about Henri betraying Charise. I was laughing hysterically. The problem was, Henri isn't Nigerian and even though they're from the same continent, Diamond Damon didn't even know Henri before meeting him at our celebrations. Diamond Damon's only defense was that she was the only one for him and out of the blue he asked Chantelle to marry him again.

It was completely ridiculous and spontaneous. However, since he'd already declared his undying love for her in front of everyone at the spa, it wasn't a surprise. We simply congratulated them. But we all knew he was just trying to get her off his back and didn't take him seriously about the proposal.

By this time Mark B had knocked back quite a few shots of vodka. He finally broke his silence.

"All my life I was afraid to love the way I felt comfortable for fear of rejection," he said.

"By who?" Regina said as she quickly honed in and questioned him.

"Rejection from my family, my friends, and ultimately myself. I feel like in some ways I actually betrayed myself. But, for the first time I finally feel free to be who I was born to be. And I really don't care about what anyone else thinks," he replied.

"Umh! I really don't give a shit what anyone thinks about my choice of who to love ... and you shouldn't either," Regina followed. "Life is too short! Dwayne was the same age as us and he took his own life. Clearly he didn't think he measured up to what somebody else thought he should," she said, and started weeping heavily.

I started to cry, too. A bunch of us jumped up and gave Regina a group hug to console her. In the meantime, Tariq decided it was his time to get in the conversation.

He talked about being discriminated against while growing up in France because he's Arabic, and the arguments he'd get into with other students at Carnegie Mellon about religion, culture, and politics. They didn't often end well for him. Therefore, early in his college career, he decided it was in his best interest to stray away from those types of discussions, even though he had a burning desire to learn and talk about them. As a result, he loves when these types of conversations pop up and was very happy for the opportunity to engage with us.

Tariq's family escaped the war in Lebanon in the early 1980's after his father won a scholarship to go to college in Paris where he and his parents settled when he was twelve years old. In an effort to distance themselves from the atrocities of the war and the politics that accompanied it, his parents became agnostics—in other words, spiritually noncommitted. As a result, they never taught their children to pray or practice any spiritual rituals. According to Tariq, they believed it was a safety issue for their Arab children in a prejudiced country.

However Tariq was older than his brother and had already learned about prayer from his grandparents and extended Christian family in Lebanon as a child. Therefore he grew up with what he described as the burden of wanting to understand more about God, religion, and creation.

In an effort to bridge his curiosity with his parents' desires, when he got to college he began to study, and eventually associated himself with scientology. He had a strong desire to belong to something bigger than himself, but had a difficult time really explaining his theoretical connection to religion. When I questioned him about it, he would only state that he believes everything comes from science.

Although JB attempted to make everyone feel better about the prejudices and pressures they felt to conform to other peoples' expectations for their lives, after Tariq's statements, the room was still pretty heavy. Instead of the cool, toned down celebration we'd planned, it seemed like it was beginning to feel like the party had turned into a bitching session. I knew I had to bring the conversation back to something more congenial.

"Hey everyone, I'd like you to hear about the opportunity I have from Julio," I announced. "You all know that I've already left the shelter, and in addition to the opportunity I have to make money with Abby in Paris, Julio has presented me with an opportunity to work for Doctors Working Borders, also known as DWB, as a culinary emissary. But I'm going to allow him to explain more about the opportunity to you to garner your thoughts," I followed.

Julio started by saying this would be his second time going on the West

African tour. He noted that many of the outposts they service don't have proper nutrition programs. Therefore, my job would be that of a culinary emissary with duties as a nutrition logistics specialist. He warned that the work would be challenging, but given my background he believed I was well qualified and could handle it.

He said I'd first have to complete a six-week nutrition and cultural protocol training program in Paris, France. Then I'd travel with him and the other volunteers to Dakar, Senegal, to implement the nutrition plan for the four West African countries we'd be working in throughout the year.

He explained that the programs are administered through mobile hospitals and the medical teams travel to three villages in each country and stay in each one for a month. As the culinary emissary, I'd eventually travel ahead of the medical team to set up the nutrition programs, stock the mobile units, and train the staff. The other countries we'd be working in throughout the year would be Ghana, the Gambia, and the Ivory Coast.

The most exciting part of my main duties included setting up the menus in collaboration with the headquarters in Paris, shopping for and ordering the food, and training the local cooks on how to prepare some of the food. I'd also be responsible for training the local staff and coordinating set up of the food trailers to feed the volunteer staff working in the hospital trailers. He went into a good amount of detail and the opportunity was very enticing.

"During the yearlong tour, we're tackling global poverty and the dearth of healthcare through our vaccination program, eradication of parasites, and performing minimal OB/GYN services. We'll be working in remote villages in each country. During previous tours, we had too many problems with our staff returning home early due to contracting painful parasitic infections that were mainly caused from the food being prepared improperly. The new culinary emissary program was developed to address the problem more effectively and hopefully eradicate it. Our ultimate goal is to attract and maintain more of our volunteers to participate in the mission trips," he finished.

"Is this a volunteer or paid position?" Rafi quipped.

"Anais will be paid a pretty hefty salary as well as receive a stipend for all of her travel and living expenses. Plus she told me about her arrangement with the food blogger in Paris, so she'll be able to continue writing stories about the food she procures," he responded.

I was extremely excited at that point. My dreams were finally coming together. I hoped that the wonderful announcement would pull everyone back up to the joyous side of our celebration, so I decided to make another announcement. To my amazement, Chris preempted me.

"Anais, I know I've been very quiet. I'm going through a lot right now, but I really want everyone to know how sorry I am for not committing to you the way that I should have. I mean no disrespect to anyone here. But I want everyone to know that I'll always love you and want the best for you. I'm so excited for you and will miss you terribly. And I know you'll knock their socks off," he followed and then asked for everyone to make a toast to my success.

I hugged him. Neither of us wanted to let go of each other. Suddenly a flash of sadness came over me. My whole relationship with him was flashing before my eyes and at that point I realized it was really coming to an end. At that very moment I finally felt like it was okay to let go of him and the torrential relationship.

Confession is surely good for the soul, cause shortly after the toast Henri suddenly jumped up and decided to apologize for his dishonesty to Charise. Although she was cordial, she wanted nothing to do with him anymore and made it perfectly clear.

"I appreciate your apology and hope you'll be happy with your choices," she responded. Then she went on to chastise him. "I know my worth and it's certainly not to play second fiddle to someone who's too immature to love me the way I'm supposed to be loved. Besides, I'm moving to New York to work in the Manhattan DA's office for the summer," she finished while shaking his hand. He tried to pull her into him, but she refused to allow him to hug or kiss her. She simply walked away.

I didn't need Julio exposed to any more drama at that point, so I tried to change the subject. I asked Rafi if it was okay to turn the music up and invited everyone to close the night out with a little dancing before we said our goodbyes.

My Boudoir: A Special Treat

On the way home, Tariq and I talked about visiting each other in Paris and Africa throughout the year. He was just as excited as I was about Julio's offer. However he was a bit intimidated by being forced to enter the military to maintain his French citizenship.

I was excited, but unsure of what to expect, and a bit intimidated by the unknown. But I trusted that it was God's answer to my prayers, and how He was ordering my steps.

Tariq, however, thought of it as good karma—in other words we somehow willed it to happen and it did. In any case, we both were happy that we could look forward to spending time together throughout the year.

When Julio mentioned that I'd be sent to DWB's headquarters in Paris for a six-week training before going to Africa, we checked the dates and the timing worked out almost perfectly. Tariq wouldn't be leaving for his military service until July 15th. I was scheduled to attend the training program in Paris from June 4 through July 16th. Therefore we had nearly six weeks to enjoy each other in Paris before we both had to report for our duties.

I was very excited and began to crave the excitement of being able to travel, sell my photos to Abby, and visit him. It would also give me more time to work with Abby on how to write articles. Just knowing I'd be doing what I loved aroused me.

Tariq was happy to see me so excited and took full advantage of it. He reached down and kissed my inner thigh while we were at a stoplight. "Swish!" A rush of heat overwhelmed my sex.

Now I was horny as hell—my underwear were quickly soaked with my juices. At that point I only wanted and needed to feel his body touching mine. But I knew he was exhausted from packing, traveling, and all of the stress of moving back to France. He needed to relax and I knew just what to do.

We pulled into my garage and he began to voraciously delight in my joy. I had to restrain myself for both of us. I decided to take it slow and relax him first by luring him out of the car and into the living room. Then I told him to strip. He quickly obliged.

While he was undressing, I turned on some light jazz to relax our minds. Then I added a few drops of rose, amber wood, and myrrh essential oils to a cup of sea salt with a little unscented liquid soap to make a sensuous body polish and bath treatment.

Rose oil is very soft and warm, and helps with anxiety. Amber wood calms the mind and stimulates the libido. And the ancient oil of myrrh promotes relaxation and strengthens muscles. Together all three create a soft and sensuous scent that screams "Fuck Me!" I jokingly call it "The F*** Me Blend."

With the bathwater running, I put in a few scoops of the body polish before calling Tariq into the bathroom. The warm and relaxing smell filled the entire room. It made for a delicious aphrodisiac.

I couldn't help it. I started kissing him. He began rubbing my sex and attempted to kiss it. While gently guiding his head away, I shared my plan to relax and promised I'd treat him to something very special if he complied.

We slipped into the tub, I sat between his legs, and we relaxed for nearly thirty minutes. The fatigue from his travels and my preparation for the party began to melt away into the warm, softened water. Soothing bursts of aromatic roses from an English garden and subtle hints of amber wood calmed our minds. We nearly fell asleep.

Then the oil of myrrh kicked in and his lovejoy kept springing up every time I touched him. He started to bite my neck ... I was overcome with light, tender waves of warmth all over my body. But I didn't want to spoil my surprise, so I suggested we take a quick shower.

After lathering my hands with a scoop of the body polish, I began delivering the surprise. Inch by inch I rubbed and massaged the polish into every one of his muscles. His beautiful butterscotch skin glistened like sparkling gold, and the smell was orgasmic! From then on it would always be The F*** Me Blend.

He reciprocated and gently polished every inch of my body. I resisted when he got to my sex for fear of irritation. His response was tempting.

"No problem, I'll do that with my tongue," he said,

His soft and warm tongue gently embraced my sex with long, luscious, swirling strokes. Another rush of heat and chills sparked throughout my body.

"Ummmmh! You feel soooo good!" I quipped. Gentle waves of pleasure rippled through my body. But I didn't want to have an orgasm yet—so I stopped him, and it.

We finished the body polishing and rinsed off. I led him to the bed and prepared a massage oil by adding some of The F*** Me Blend to a cup of almond oil.

In preparation for giving him a skin-to-skin massage, I ladled the massage oil all over my body while he watched. Extremely titillated and throbbing with anticipation, he couldn't help himself. He was so horny he started masturbating.

I couldn't allow that. I wanted to take him all the way up without him taking the edge off before I touched him. I kissed his hand and stopped him by pulling him to the bottom of the bed. I wanted to take my time ... to feel his skin touching mine ... every last bit of it.

I poured some of the massage oil on his chest and massaged him with deep, penetrating strokes. Moving down each arm, I pressed and kneaded each muscle. While rolling and stretching his fingers, I put each one in my mouth and provocatively sucked it.

Then I mounted myself onto his stomach and rubbed the oil on his lovejoy with my sex while gently massaging his chest. Turning around, I continued to slowly rub his sex with my bottom while massaging each leg, inch by inch.

Now it was time to increase the stimulation. Positioning myself between his legs, I poured the remaining massage oil directly onto his sex. Stroke, after long, twisting stroke, I rubbed and he purred with intense pleasure.

With one hand stroking his sex, I took the other hand and massaged right under his balls before slipping the tip of my finger in his ass. Apprehensive at first, he began trembling with extreme pleasure. But I wanted to take him over the top.

As soon as he calmed down a bit, I enveloped the tip of his sex with my mouth and began stroking it. His body quivered with violent pleasure until he nearly exploded. He screamed!

"OH GOD ANAIS! I'MMMM ... AH! AH! I'M ... I'M CUMMING!" he shouted in a desperate whisper.

He pulled his sex out of my mouth and shot his load all over his stomach. I was super horny now.

I wiped him off, and massaged my way back up to his face, and gently kneaded his cheeks, his jaws, and his sinuses with my thumbs. After working my way onto the back of his neck, I massaged his entire head with both hands, paying close attention to grazing his scalp and ears.

The tingling sensation from stimulating his scalp and ears sent his lovejoy right back up. The F*** Me Blend was doing it's job very well. In the meantime, I started nibbling his ear to intensify the stimulation.

"I want you to make love to me!" I whispered in his ear.

His gentle kiss … his tender touch as he held me by the small of my back … the warm, moist sensation of his breath while lightly nibbling my breasts … I was captivated.

He put on a condom, peered deep into my eyes, and pulled me into him. With each bit of penetration I began to feel closer and closer to him. I deeply trusted him now.

With every move of our bodies, I craved him more. The emotional connection at that moment indelibly imprinted itself in my mind and heart.

His thrusts got faster and faster—he felt so good … I felt so good. Love became lust.

"Oh baby! Fuck me please … fuck me hard baby," I whimpered … I pleaded.

The more he gave, the more I wanted. "Come on baby, slap my ass! I love it when you fuck me hard and slap my ass!" I said with a whimpering whisper.

The deeper and harder he fucked me, the higher the pitch of my whimpering got. He turned me over, lifted my hips up, and plunged into me from behind.

"Yes baby! I like it like that!" I shouted.

"Oh! … Oh yeah! … YES BABY! … I LOVE IT!" I cried.

Shifting his hips, he lifted my ass cheeks up and fucked the hell out of me. I was consumed by an amazing wave of invigorating warmth and pleasure. Scintillating chills enveloped my entire being.

"I'M CUMMING BABY!" I shouted as he fucked me so hard my entire body convulsed with overwhelming joy!

I fell on top of him. We laid still for so long that he started to snore. I knew he was tired, but I at least wanted to know how he liked my surprise, so I gently bit his chin and he nearly jumped off the bed.

"I'm sorry! I'm worn out," he said. "But I'm a little hungry," he slurred as he dropped back onto the bed.

"I'll bet you are," I quipped. "How'd you like my surprise?" I asked.

"Will you marry me!?" he responded as he drifted off to sleep again.

I laughed. My guess was that he really enjoyed it from that reaction.

After pulling myself together and covering him up, I went to the kitchen and grabbed the leftover sweet potato and banana galettes and two glasses of milk. I woke him up and we ate them before falling into a deep and relaxed slumber.

Menu

Join Us for a Celebration of
Traditional and African Fusion Cuisine
featuring

APPETIZERS

Samosas from Tanzania

fried hand pies filled with curried potatoes, shrimp, and sweet peas

Shrimp Farci

crab-stuffed fried jumbo shrimp

DINNER

Ghanaian Groundnut Stew

chicken stewed in a fragrant peanut sauce

Senegalese Chioff aka Ceebu-Jen

hake fish and rice in a tomato, vegetable, and herb sauce

Nigerian Okra & Dried Cod Stew

with fufu–pounded cassava dumplings

BEVERAGES

Iced Flavored Vodka

Senegalese Bissap Punch

made with pineapple, guava, and hibiscus juice, served with or without vodka

Ghanaian Stout Beer • Wine • Craft Beers • Soda

Mint Kenkiliba Herbal Tea

DESSERT

Sweet Potato & Banana Galettes

Thiakry

toasted millet custard flavored with vanilla and orange flower water, topped
with yogurt, mangoes and papaya, coconut, and cashews

ENTERTAINMENT

Game of Taboo.

C H A P T E R

35

Preparing for the Journey

To help me finish packing up my apartment Tariq stayed in Pittsburgh a couple of extra days before leaving for Paris. When he left, my emotions were all over the place.

He's kind, gentle, and rocks my socks off in the bedroom. I truly grew to love him a lot. I'd been dating him for nearly a year, but I didn't know if I was truly in love with him. I don't think I even understood what that meant.

I wasn't sure if it was love, lust, or some combination thereof. What I did know was that he taught me how I'm really supposed to be treated as a woman, and I resolved myself not to ever settle for anything less than the love and respect he showed me.

Even though Chris was a gentleman, it was clearer than ever that he couldn't give me what I needed, and didn't respect me for who I am. Tariq made it clear that I didn't have to settle for being treated without the respect I deserved. For that, I will always love him.

I was also trying to process the fact that I wouldn't be seeing him again for another three months. I didn't know whether to cry or be happy for our blooming, albeit long distance relationship.

"Would there still be butterflies, or will they have flown away? Will we still have the same euphoric feelings as when we'd made love before he left?" I asked myself.

"What if he finds someone else once he returns to Paris? After all, it is the city of love," I wondered.

I was so confounded. I was afraid.

My mind started playing tricks on me. I'd carried too much baggage from my relationship with Chris. Although I had no problems with physically committing to Tariq, I realized that I was not yet able to truly commit to him emotionally. Good or bad, deep down inside I knew that's what was going on.

I still wasn't ready to let my guard down. I tried to convince myself that I wouldn't be disappointed if he moved on.

In the meantime, I decided to focus my attention on preparing for my new job and new life. After finishing my class at Pitt, I registered for French writing and spoken French classes at the Alliance Français, and increased the time I studied with the French tutor to two-hour sessions, four days a week. In an effort to more expeditiously prepare myself to start writing the food articles alone, I also began writing more detailed practice articles in French and English about some of the food photos I'd taken during the last nine SNL catering events.

About a week and a half after Tariq returned to Paris, I received a letter in the mail postmarked from France. I assumed it was from him, but we'd spoken on the phone at least three times and he'd never mentioned a letter. I was running out the door so I tossed it on the dining table with the other mail and went to my French class.

When I got back to my apartment, I found a message on my answering machine from Julio. He was touching base with me to find out if I'd received my employment packet from DWB headquarters. "Mystery solved!" I thought.

I immediately returned the call to Julio. After a few pleasantries, he gave me another in-depth overview of the culinary emissary program. With more extensive details this time, he discussed the same job duties he'd discussed briefly at the party. I'd be in charge of setting up the culinary commissaries at each location. He also wanted to ensure that I'd make the connection with DWB's worldwide nutrition coordinator. Her name was Gabriela and I'd be working under her supervision.

After a series of questions and answers about the duties and expectations of the appointment, I asked if he could further elaborate on what kind of working conditions to expect. That's where things began to get a little intimidating for me.

He explained that many of the outposts they'd been working at had poor sanitary conditions, and even worse, the local cooks weren't trained in serve-safe protocols. Therefore, in addition to teaching menu preparation, I'd also be responsible for serve-safe sanitary training of the local staff. Other duties included menu testing, nutrition program development, and scheduling to ensure feeding times and nutritional requirements were being met. I started thinking about whether I'd be safe and if I was truly prepared for the job.

I tried not to allow him to hear the angst in my voice, but he clearly sensed my fear. Then he tried to comfort me by informing me that he would be the medical director leading the tour, so I shouldn't worry because he'd make sure I was safe and happy. I was thankful for the reassurance—but still a little nervous.

Although he talked a little about the pay and perks at the party, his next instructions really perked me up—I completely forgot about being nervous.

He instructed me to be on the lookout for my travel itinerary, airline tickets, and a call from Gabriela. My first duty was to fly to Paris to work with the nutrition team for the initial training, menu planning, and conducting preliminary tastings for the tours in Senegal, The Gambia, Ghana, and the Ivory Coast.

"Bingo!" I thought to myself with elation.

He really had my attention now. The opportunity to work in Paris had already drawn me in. The additional travel was even more alluring. Visiting those countries was already on my lifelong bucket list.

Julio went on to say that throughout the one-year appointment, we'd be stationed in three locations per country for one-month stints. Gabriela and I would travel with him ahead of the volunteer doctors to do the trainings, taste the local foods, and finalize the menus with photos and nutrition descriptions, including common allergens, etc.

I'd been approved to receive a salary equivalent to $40,800 US plus paid travel and living allowances. I'd also been cleared to receive an expense account for incidentals.

There were even more perks. The program would pay for all of my meals, I could take photos for both DWB and Abby's articles, and if Abby could use them for the magazine, I could make more money.

DWB also offered to pay for me to enroll in an intensive cooking class while training in Paris. It was one of the most attractive perks. Not only would that increase my culinary training record, it would provide more preparation for me to open my restaurant.

"When God answers prayers, He shows out! What a blessing!" I shouted after hanging the phone up.

I quickly reached for that envelope from France and ripped it open. There was a perfectly creased and folded letter inside. I unfolded it and a check fell out. It wasn't from Gabriela nor DWB. It was from Abby.

My despair had turned into dollars! When I came home frustrated from all of the chaos during my first day back at the shelter after returning from Paris, I'd sent a bunch of photos to Abby with the articles written in English. Apparently she'd sold three of the photos and an article to a Dutch magazine. The check was for $3,500.

"Now this is affirmation that I'm on the right track!" I shouted with joy. It was another unexpected blessing!

The Shelter: A Promising Farewell

About two weeks after my last scheduled day of work at the shelter, Lauren called and asked if I could fill in for an evening shift. She said they were extremely shorthanded after having to replace shifts once occupied by Dwayne and me, and someone had called off.

I was determined to be well prepared for my new duties, so I forced myself to be very disciplined with my French studies. I had isolated myself from just about everyone for several weeks and didn't want to be disturbed. However it was a short shift, only from four to eight in the evening. So I did not know whether or not to work it.

Although I was ambivalent, I knew they were short-handed and had told her to call me if she needed me to cover a shift until they found a replacement for Dwayne. With that promise in mind, I agreed to take the shift.

Before leaving my apartment, I called Regina to see if she'd be working with me, but I was unable to get in touch with her. I became a bit leery about not knowing who I'd be working with—thoughts of canceling briefly crossed my mind several times. I didn't feel like enduring any extra drama besides that which I'd already anticipated.

"Oh well!" I thought. "I'll just have to wing it. If it gets crazy I just won't fill in again," I said to myself.

When I pulled into the shelter's parking lot, there were cars parked everywhere. I was aggravated because I had to park on the side of the road. The first thing I thought was that something awful must have happened. I started getting frustrated. I was trying to deprogram myself from all the stress I'd endured while working there, and really wanted to fully move on. But it seemed like they were trying to pull me right back into the shelter's drama.

I actually considered turning around. But again, I'm a woman of my word. I couldn't just leave them hanging without coverage. So I fixed my attitude and got out of the car, walked to the porch, and slowly crept in the door.

"Surprise! Surprise! Surprise!" people shouted from everywhere. All of the staff, the girls, and even the administration from headquarters broke out in song.

"For she's a jolly good counsel-OR, for she's a jolly good counsel-OR, for she's a jolly good counsel-ORRRRR, that we, we all ad-ORE, that we, we all ad-ORE, that we, we all ad-ORE. For she's a jolly good counsel-ORRRR, the world will love for SURRRRE!"

I was gobsmacked! I thought I was walking into another crazy day at the shelter. In the meantime, they had planned a beautiful farewell party. They even wrote a song for me. It was kind of cute, too!

"They couldn't just let me leave and fade away into the sunset," I thought facetiously to myself. They were determined to drain every last tear out of my body, and it was an absolutely beautiful and heartwarming experience.

One at a time, each of the girls thanked me and presented me with beautiful and touching thank-you cards. After the presentations, they walked me into the living room where the executive director presented me with a plaque and showed me where they had mounted another one that honored the establishment of the Anais Alexandre Foster Care Endowment Fund. I was so touched. My tears took on a mind of their own.

I finally found Regina, too. She was already at the shelter helping with setup for the party. After they presented me with the plaque, Regina said they'd contacted the foundation that manages the fund to request a grant to help get Zee settled into an independent living facility for young adults. The best part of that news was that Regina applied to serve as her settlement mentor and Zee agreed to accept her help.

I later asked Regina and Lauren if it was possible to reach out to Saturn in hopes of helping her as well. I kept thinking about her plight the entire evening.

"We kinda knew you'd be asking about her. We put an application in for her, too. We're just waiting for her caseworker to get back to us," they replied.

I was so happy. It was a farewell befitting a queen. I didn't even end up working that evening. After the presentation of the plaque, our noses led us to the amazing smells coming out of the kitchen.

They had set up a beautiful buffet and dessert table. Ms. Nellie made a delicious macaroni and cheese bar filled with all kinds of accompaniments. A cornucopia of crunchy fried popcorn chicken and shrimp, steamed broccoli, Buffalo chicken bites, and even sautéed mushrooms tickled my nose. I dumped a spoonful of everything over the macaroni and ladled a heap of cheese sauce on top. It was heavenly!

For dessert, she humored me with an amazing ice cream cake made with my favorite chocolate mandarin Just Add Water Happy Cake mix. Each layer was filled with chocolate ice cream topped with candied orange bits and chopped almonds—it was creamy, moist, and simply delicious. I ate like a pig and talked to everyone throughout the entire shift.

Before leaving, I finally shared my good fortune with the girls. There'd been so much drama going on before I left that I'd forgotten to tell them why I would no longer be working at the shelter. After giving them a brief rundown of where I was going and what type of work I'd be doing, there was complete silence. They all just looked at me like I was crazy.

"Any questions?" I asked. Not a peep came out of anyone for about two long minutes. Then they laid it on me.

"*Africa*!?" exclaimed the new girl Trina.

"Are you ever going to come back?" Alona questioned. She was one of my favorites.

"She's not coming back! She's going to get eaten by an elephant!" Trina exclaimed.

Everyone started laughing hysterically, including me. It was almost like I'd told them I was going to another planet—but it became a great teachable moment.

I assured them I would not be working where I could get eaten, and that elephants don't eat people anyway. I also promised to visit and prove it to them when I returned to Pittsburgh.

After lamenting about not being able to see me for a long time, Alona asked if she could come with me. I explained that although it wasn't possible this time, it might be in the future. I concluded by asking each of them to promise to take care of each other and the staff while I'm overseas. With that I said my goodbyes to everyone, and it was my last time at the shelter.

Menu

Join Us for the Farewell Party

featuring

HELP YOURSELF

MACARONI & CHEESE BAR

accompaniments:

crunchy fried popcorn chicken, shrimp, steamed
broccoli, Buffalo chicken bites, and sautéed mushrooms

DESSERT

CHOCOLATE MANDARIN
ICE CREAM CAKE

The College Crew: A Farewell to Remember

Two weeks later, my farewell fortune continued with my College Crew. Pierre and Charise planned a going away party at his friends' club over the Memorial Day weekend, which was two weeks before I was scheduled to leave for Paris.

Chantelle called to warn me about how to prepare myself for the celebration. "Saturate yourself with layers of your most relaxing Bodacious Body and bobby socks. It's gonna be a long night of drinking and dancing," she quipped. I laughed with anticipation.

"Those Trinis party long and hard!" she finished.

Charise's family is from Trinidad. She collaborated with Pierre to have an Afro-Trini celebration with both djembe and steel drums, and carnival-style soca dancing. We had so much fun. They really pulled out all the stops for this party.

Taking advantage of the heads up given by Chantelle, I decided it was an appropriate time to dive into my collection of Bodacious Body's intense lotus flower bomb—it was one of the gifts Tariq brought on his last trip. Boasting the warm and fragrant scents of lotus blossom and black pepper essential oils, it was the most expensive of the collection but offered the most intense relaxation and was completely designed to relax the mind, body, and mood. It was just the touch I needed to get ready for a long evening of dancing.

I finished my beauty ritual, pulled my hair up in a bun, put on a taunt teal and cream–colored linen jumpsuit and matching leather sandals, and I was ready for action. The doorbell rang and when I looked out the window, Chantelle, Regina, Sheila, Mark B, and Rafi were outside waiting for me in a stretch limousine. My jaw dropped. Again they had taken me by surprise.

A bunch of my neighbors were gawking and gossiping about us, so I rushed into the limo and we took off for a tour of the city. When I got inside, the limo was stocked with snacks, Champagne, and chocolate-covered strawberries—my favorite.

We rode all around the city, and then stopped to take a bunch of photos on Mt. Washington. After a forty-five minute tour, we finally arrived at Serene Café—an African fusion dining and dance club.

I walked into the room and Pierre, Henri, Penny, and Leila were accompanied by a steel drum player and playing traditional Congolese ceremonial music. There were about fifty of my closest friends seated at the tables. Rafi ceremoniously escorted me to a seat in the middle of the dance floor. After I was seated, a group of eight dancers came from behind a small stage, surrounded me while locking hands, and began to serenade me. I felt like a queen—again.

As soon as the singing ended, out pops Charise. She was the mistress of ceremony. I was totally surprised. She was always so laid-back that I didn't even think she had it in her to be an MC. But she handled it really well.

"We want to welcome everyone to a send-off celebration for our sister …

our chef … and our inspiration—Anais Alexandre," she started.

"Anais has taken us all over the world with her amazing, and simply delicious, culinary genius. So tonight, we have a special celebration prepared in her honor," she followed.

"I've invited my mother and my aunt to prepare traditional Trini-style food from my family's native Trinidad. So tonight's celebration will be called Kickin' It Live Afro-Trini style. In addition to the Afro-Trini band, we invite you to also enjoy the casino games and dance your hearts out," she finished, and the Afro-Calypso music took over the dance floor. It was truly something special.

They had set up a whole section with a variety of casino games including roulette, blackjack, Pitty Pat, and poker. Most impressive was that all monies betted were donated to the DWB vaccination fund for Julio and me to take on our trip to West Africa. Participants were given vouchers when they'd win, which they could trade in for gifts. It was truly another unexpected blessing.

I'd never had the privilege of participating in a Trinidadian carnival celebration. And, I can now attest to the fact that they party hard! And the food—*amazing*!

My parents are from Mississippi and when the food is really good they have a colloquial expression they use. The saying goes: They put their foot in it! It was the most appropriate way to describe the Afro-Trini food. The sweet, aromatic, and sophisticated layers of flavors were worthy of praise and deserved an award of their own. Each dish represented an amalgamation of the rich culinary resources that migrated from Africa, India, and South America to culminate into the amazing Afro-Trini cuisine.

I couldn't believe how many selections they prepared. The food was set up buffet style and there were at least ten different food, drink, and dessert selections.

Dinner selections included a mildly spiced and fragrant sweet curried chicken served with a buttery flatbread called buss up shot; oxtails stewed with root vegetables and spices then finished with fragrant herbs—they were melt in your mouth tender; an aromatic rice pilaf called pelau; fry bake—a yeast bread that's fried in small patties and served with a salted cod sauté—it reminded me of the Nigerian okra and fish stew without the okra; roti, an unleavened flatbread served with dal puri—seasoned chickpeas that offered a huge dose of umami; pigeon peas and rice—flavor-rich and tender rice and peas that served as a foundation for all of the side dishes; and a traditional condiment known as chow or mango chutney—a sweet-and-sour salsa. They even offered a tasting of a dish I'd heard so much about called souse—or pickled pig parts. It was akin to a snack I'd often enjoyed when visiting my family in Mississippi.

Along with the variety of staples, they made alcoholic and nonalcoholic traditional beverages. Presented in shot glasses for tasting, they were strategically labeled for self-service and included: sorrel—a cold drink very similar to

Senegalese *bissap*; peanut punch—made with fresh peanut butter blended with condensed milk and fresh milk, nutmeg, and cinnamon—a sweet and nutty but somewhat thick drink; and mauby—an obligatory digestive tea made from the bark of a tree; this is an acquired taste. I didn't quite like it but the benefits far outweighed the taste.

For dessert, Charise's aunt made a colorful coconut fudge candy—which was my all-time favorite, and sweet potato and oatmeal crunch cakes—they were tender, tasty, and delicious. The whole meal was just heavenly.

Many of the staples in Trinidadian cooking and beverages are akin to African dishes, but are simply given local names. For example, the sorrel is a drink made from the hibiscus flower. In Senegal, West Africa, it's called *bissap* and in Nigeria, Central West Africa, it's called zobo. However in the Caribbean, which includes Jamaica and Trinidad, it's called sorrel.

The Afro-Trini celebration was a cultural clash between the traditional rhythmic nuances of African dancing, augmented by the super hyper jumping and waist wining of Caribbean calypso dancing. It was pure, unadulterated fun—and funny. The calypso dances are very charismatic and often tell amusing stories just by their nonverbal demonstrations, and the addition of the African talking drum brought the rhythm to a whole other level. We ate, gambled for charity, and partied until three o'clock in the morning. The entire celebration was a profound manifestation of fun love with food.

A Still, Small Voice: My Farewell to the College Crew

A few days later, I decided to invite everyone to one final night out to chat and thank them for the amazing celebration. I also needed to catch up with everyone's lives. I'd been so busy trying to finish the language training and packing that we hadn't scheduled Girls Night Out, nor time to just talk with everyone. Strangely enough, that still, small voice that guides me through life quietly informed me that I was in for a rude awakening!

We all agreed to meet at Dave and Buster's to have drinks and dinner while enjoying a few games and catching up. Everyone showed up except Chris. I initially discounted it to his inability to deal with the situation. But Rafi had another story.

I started the conversation by thanking everyone for the amazing send off. Then Charise asked if I was having any second thoughts.

"No! I'm really excited. But I do have some concerns," I responded.

"About what?" Leila questioned.

"Just about fitting in socially with all the doctors. Although I'm excited about being able to immerse myself in the culture, I'm sure I'll get homesick for my people, places, and maybe even my food," I responded.

Leila took this time as an opportunity to reassure me that I was on the right track. "First of all, you're a social worker. The work doesn't stop once you leave the border. The need for support is worldwide, especially in Africa," she said as a matter of fact.

"As regards you having the misconception that you won't fit in, it's just that—a misconception. You've created one of the most multicultural groups of friends that adore and worship you—especially your cooking. I'm sure you won't have any problems fitting in," she said

"Finally, you've been cooking up all kinds of things in the kitchen forever. I'm sure you can figure out a way to take a little piece of home with you. Besides, you'll make new types of dishes your favorites and share some of your culinary art skills with others. You'll be just fine," she finished.

"Thanks for the encouragement Leila. I really love and appreciate all of you. I'm going to miss our monthly celebrations. But as far as the food goes, that won't be too far from me. I figured out how to dehydrate some of my staples and I'm looking forward to taking them with me. Julio challenged me to figure it out and I did," I said.

Just as I finished speaking, Penny walked in with Pierre and Henri. "Why are you guys always together?" I quipped. "Are you like the three stooges or something?"

"No, they're the three heartbreaks!" Leila chided. "Yep!" Charise lamented.

Everyone greeted them with hugs except Charise and Leila. At that point I knew there was some drama going on. "What's up y'all? What's going on? Fill me in!" I questioned.

Leila pulled me to the side and told me she was pissed off with Pierre because at the farewell party, Penny was bragging about him and Henri joining her in South Africa for a summer tour. Then she started talking about Henri bringing his new bride.

"What!?" I said with confusion.

Nobody trusted Penny. But Leila had confronted Henri at the farewell party, and he apparently confessed that his claim for asylum as a refugee had been approved and he no longer needed to marry for his citizenship. Therefore, he'd made plans to wed the young Congolese girl in Canada. Apparently, she was a virgin gift to him from her family before he left the Congo. He said he wanted to marry before leaving for South Africa so she could join him on the trip.

Leila told Charise at the party and she said she didn't care anymore. But it was very clear from her initial reaction to his presence that she was heartbroken.

We went back to the table and Rafi couldn't help himself. He'd had a few drinks and was clearly pissed.

"Anais, I want to be honest with you about why Chris isn't here," he shouted with a sense of disgust. "Chris and his fucked up brother were both arrested. Evidently, his brother had been cooking the books and the whole firm was under investigation for securities fraud. Chris is ashamed and doesn't want to confront the group because many of us purchased insurance from him," Rafi followed.

"How do you know that Rafi?" Sheila asked.

"Because I paid the bail to get Chris out." Rafi had lost a lot of money. "By the way, why were you and Diamond Damon at the courthouse Chantelle?" he asked facetiously.

She hesitated for a moment. Growled at Rafi. Then reluctantly went on to shock the hell out of everyone.

"I married Damon last week!" she said.

I didn't see a ring, nor had she said anything to me.

"When and why?" I said in dismay.

"He convinced me to elope on Monday with a beautiful diamond ring. I must admit—I was smitten. We went to the courthouse on my lunch break the next day, and I took the leap," she said with a somewhat remorseful tone.

"Well why didn't you share it with us Chantelle? We would have at least celebrated your union," Charise quipped.

Chantelle went on to tell us that two days after they eloped, the police showed up and arrested both of them. He apparently was a diamond smuggler and got her caught up due to not declaring the diamonds while traveling internationally. Rafi just so happened to be at the courthouse with Chris. As fate would have it, he spotted Chantelle behind a glass wall with handcuffs on, and ended up posting bail for her, too. I was flabbergasted.

None of us ever really trusted Diamond Damon, especially Rafi. I could only hope and pray that Chantelle had learned a lesson.

It seemed like all I was hearing was how people were either making or getting into trouble. But there was a bit of refreshing news, too.

Regina and Evelyn announced their plans to take the summer off to go on a motorcycle ride across the country. It was an orchestrated bike ride with nineteen hundred women tag teaming across the world to bring awareness to mental health issues, suicide prevention, and ending gun violence. They dedicated their portion of the journey in honor of Dwayne. I was happy that at least somebody else was doing something productive.

I followed by asking Regina if they'd been able to locate Saturn to get her off the streets. She said they'd found her and offered to help her get an apartment with the baby. But she rejected their offer because they'd kicked her out of the shelter, and she couldn't find forgiveness in her heart for them.

Saturn said Regina, Evelyn, and the system betrayed her, and she'd rather stay where people who cared for her were genuine. It was a bit heart-wrenching. But Regina promised to continue watching her in hopes of at least convincing her to stop prostituting.

I couldn't take any more bad news. "That still, small voice is never wrong," I thought. At that point I was confident that it would take care of me throughout my journey. I began to feel more secure with my choices.

We played a few more air hockey and basketball games before saying our good-byes, and again JB offered to walk me to my car. Although he didn't have much to add to the conversation with the crew, he ended up getting the last word that night.

"Ms. Anais," he said with a stumbling voice. "Am I going to have to keep sending you drinks, help you move again, or do I have to take you out to dinner alone to get in another good conversation before you leave?" he followed.

Even though I was flattered by his request, I was swamped with preparations to leave in the next eight days. But I didn't want to be rude and ended up inviting him to come to my place. Again I didn't have anything to prepare a full meal for him, so I offered him another shot at testing a new variety of dehydrated meals I intended to take overseas with me. I wanted someone else to test them and he agreed to be a guinea pig. With that in mind, we agreed to meet at my place the following evening.

Prelude to a Kiss

It was a crisp, late spring evening. The flowers were in early bloom and perfectly scented the evening air after baking in the morning sun. I was sitting on the porch practicing with my French tapes and spotted JB's car pulling in the driveway. When I greeted him at the door, his hands were full with a bottle of wine, two paper cups, and a small gift.

"What's the gift for?" I inquired.

"It's a special gift to welcome you to the Citizen of the World Club," he responded with excitement.

"Oh! Okay!" I said. "Let's eat! I'm eager for feedback," I quipped.

I added water to the burrito and pasta bowls before placing them in the microwave. After five minutes of heating and five minutes of rest, everything was ready to eat. Even I couldn't believe how quick it was.

Again he was impressed by how easy they were to prepare. But he seemed to be a bit skeptical.

"Are you sure it's real food?" he jokingly questioned me with apprehension.

"I assure you it's real food. I did all of the real work when I was cooking and dehydrating them," I said, trying to reassure him.

"Here are the choices," I exclaimed. "I love, love, love collard greens, and my doctor says they're a cure all. But since you've already tried them, I've prepared two burrito bowls—one with chicken and one with beef; a cheddar macaroni and cheese with beef and broccoli bowl; and beef and bean chili. They each have separate seasoning packets included, so all I have to do is add as much seasoning as I want, then fill the cup with hot water to the line and voilà! It's done," I explained.

He seemed to be rather impressed. I took some of the pasta and some of the rice from a burrito bowl and fed them to him.

"Wow! They're delicious!" he said in amazement. "And it's real food. You've got a winner here!" he touted.

I gave him a taste of each dish and he chose to have some of each for his dinner. He was in heaven.

His enthusiasm aroused me. I enjoyed them just as much as he did, and I was so happy that I could successfully utilize them on my trip.

We were sharing the bowls and when I went in to put a spoonful of the chicken burrito bowl in his mouth to taste, out of the blue he kissed me. I was awestruck. I wasn't expecting it nor was I ready for it.

Chills ran up and down my spine. My heart began to flutter. All kinds of thoughts raced through my mind.

I was already resolved to the fact that I was leaving in less than a week. To avoid getting into a compromising situation with him, I quickly kissed him on the cheek in an effort to suppress his approach, and tried to blow it off.

"Thanks for tasting my new inventions," I said. Would you like to crack open the wine? We can sit on the porch and enjoy this beautiful evening while eating and chatting?" I asked.

"Sure," he replied.

We brought the food out to the porch. As I walked back into the kitchen to get the wine, the doorbell rang. I asked who it was through the intercom, but there was no answer.

Halfway into our instant dinner, the doorbell started ringing again like crazy. It was akin to Chris's signature annoyance. But I didn't want to believe it was him. I walked out to answer the door this time to avoid any confrontation. But there was nobody there.

As soon I went back in, it started ringing like crazy, again. I went out one more time and decided I would just ignore whoever it was if they didn't answer. But before I closed my door, I could hear JB calling someone from the terrace.

It was Penny! She said she happened to be walking by and saw his car.

She was full of shit! I knew she was still trying to keep him on a short leash. I didn't even acknowledge her, nor let her in. I was pissed off with her antics.

Despite her attempts at thwarting JB from spending time alone with me, we really enjoyed our conversation. I opened the gift and it was a Swiss army knife. He coupled it with numerous tips on how to protect my security. Most interesting were the memories he shared with me about his playing tours in Russia and countries within the former USSR during the cold war. They were most intriguing. He said he ate only bread for fourteen days because the food was unrecognizable. It scared me a bit.

"I truly earned my resilience!" he said. Then he threw me for another loop.

"By the way, I know you're pretty busy, but I have a couple of gigs this weekend. I'd like to invite you to attend Anais," he said.

"Okay go for it!" I replied. "I think I'm mostly caught up with everything, so I may be able to slip away for a bit," I said.

He invited me to see him play at the opening of the arts festival, again. I'd promised to go the past year but actually forgot about it. I felt obliged to attend this year. He wasn't done though.

"Sure, I'll meet you there. Just give me the details," I said.

"That's what you said last year," he quipped. I laughed nervously.

"My apologies! I'll be there this time. I'm a girl of my word and I won't let you down," I replied.

"Great! I also have a gig on Sunday. It's a Steelers' celebration at the Fox Chapel Country Club, and I need a date. Will you join me for dinner and dancing?" he followed.

Again I was taken off guard, but in a good way. I love the Steelers. To be able to go to an event where we'd have dinner and dancing at a country club was nothing to sneeze at either. I jumped right on that offer.

"Of course I will. I see you're running with the high rollers," I replied.

He just chuckled. "It's no big deal. They just like my music," he responded with modesty. I was really impressed with his humility.

We closed out the beautiful evening after dinner and conversations around 11:00 p.m. I had a tutoring session scheduled early and needed to finish homework before getting some rest. So we ended the night with a light kiss on the cheek and a nice long hug.

Stunting: A Last Ditch Effort

The arts festival jumped up on me two days later. Despite my crazy schedule, I knew I had to keep my word. I met JB there just before he was scheduled to play. He greeted me with a kiss on the cheek and I sat in the audience to check out his band.

After sitting and waiting nearly fifteen minutes for the anticipatory crowd to settle down before the band was introduced, the romantic, sultry, and alluring sounds of the saxophone began to titillate my entire being. His band played two fifteen-minute sets and it became clear to me that he is a masterful musician. Not only did he play the alto saxophone, he played three different ones and the flute. I was quite impressed.

At the end of the show he thanked everyone for coming, and suddenly all these girl groupies started going crazy and throwing panties on the stage.

"What the heck is going on?" I said to myself.

He started calling me for help. Then a bunch of the girls rushed the stage and started grabbing and hugging him. They acted like he was Michael Jackson.

In the meantime, he tried to get them off of him.

"Anais! Come rescue me, please!" he shouted.

I walked over and the girls disbursed. It was the first time I'd experienced anything like that first hand.

"Phew! Thanks for rescuing me," he said. "Can I take you to dinner?"

"Sure!" I replied.

He invited me to meet him at Red Lobster—his favorite restaurant. We enjoyed a lovely steamed and fried seafood collection with Red Lobster's famous sides, and chatted more about our college careers and the de facto rivalry between CMU and the University of Pittsburgh. He finished his undergraduate degree at CMU and won the argument about the better education—after all, CMU is like a junior Ivy League school, so I relented. However I did win the argument about the University of Pittsburgh having the best public education, the best sports, and of course the best partying. We finished the conversation with more travel tips from him, and orders for him to eat better, from me.

After dinner, he confirmed a 5:00 p.m. pickup for the Steelers event, and gave me a goodbye hug—a deep, thoughtful hug that felt more entrenching this time. Again I wanted to keep him at arms length, but I felt myself being drawn to him. I knew it wasn't the right time, so I gently kissed him on the cheek and got into my car.

The Steelers event was the next evening, but I didn't have anything to wear. Everybody knows that if there's a Steelers event you must wear black and/or yellow. I didn't have a lot of clothes with me so I went to Macy's and purchased a beautiful sparkly mustard colored backless dress. It perfectly complimented my skin, hair, and the occasion.

I paired it with a black silk scarf and black-strapped sandals with a striking two-inch heel. Although the yellow was a bit loud, the sparkles muted it just enough to shine. I curled my hair, finished my makeup, and matched my jewelry for a photo finish. I felt beautiful!

JB picked me up a little late, so I was ready and waiting. He didn't say much during the car ride. It was a bit awkward and I began to think that something was wrong. But I didn't want him to confront me about not reciprocating his approaches. So I stayed quiet too.

We arrived at the country club and the valet escorted me out of the car. He grabbed his instruments and handed me over to the hostess to show me to my table.

I was feeling a little out of place. I didn't know anyone other than him, and there was no one in the room who looked like me. The only thing we had in common was that everyone was wearing black and/or yellow.

JB started by introducing the band and himself on the mic and again the women started going crazy. I couldn't believe it. He apparently had a following.

I'd remembered the faces of some of the women from the arts festival.

He started blowing that saxophone and it sent everyone into a tailspin. It was smooth, sultry, and just plain ole sexy as hell. I'm pretty sure I wasn't the only one feeling that way though.

The band started playing a song that I didn't recognize, but everyone jumped out of their seats and started dancing like crazy. Those same ladies I recognized started grabbing at him. I resigned myself to just sit back and watch the show.

Out of the blue, he played his way over to my table and started serenading me. I'm not really good with being in the spotlight. I sat there and just smiled for the cameras.

He finished playing the song, went back to the stage, and picked up the mic. I was wondering why he abruptly stopped the music when everybody was dancing and enjoying themselves.

He tapped the mic and proceeded with an announcement. "Thank you ladies and gentlemen. I hope you're all enjoying yourselves. I have a special guest here tonight by the name of Anais Alexandre, and I'm hoping she'll marry me," he said.

I was floored! I couldn't believe the words coming out of his mouth. Again, I did not want to stir him up, so I shied away with a smile. But I was completely taken aback by his boldness.

I just sat there startled with disbelief. In the meantime, he began playing another song. Suddenly someone tapped me on the shoulder.

"Would you like to join me at my table for dinner?" she said.

I looked up to see who was asking me. It was a well-coiffed, middle-aged white woman dressed in a black and gold, sequined Halston dress.

"Sure! Thanks for the invitation," I replied.

I moved to her table and sat next to her. That's when the evening got even more interesting. I'd almost forgotten all about JB's stunt.

The waiters arrived with the dinner trays and they served our table first. It was kind of strange because we were sitting in the middle of everyone. It seemed as though it would have been more appropriate to start at either end of the table instead of starting in the middle.

We made our requests and as soon as they placed the food in front of us, I bowed my head and said a blessing. We enjoyed juicy, tender rib-eye steaks with twice-baked potatoes and steamed broccoli. As the dinner service continued, I soon realized why they served our table first.

"Do you see all those women stopping by the table and vying for my attention?" she whispered.

"Okay?" I replied ambivalently. I wasn't quite sure where she was going with her statement, but there did seem to be a lot of people stopping by the table and greeting her like kiss-asses.

"They want to sit here with me, but they're all backbiting witches. I recently got saved and I don't want to be around their crap anymore. That still, small voice told me you were saved. When you prayed over your food, it was clear that the Lord led me to you," she said.

"God bless you too!" I responded. She smiled at me and said thank you.

JB came to the table shortly after her statement and joined us for dinner. After a wonderful dinner conversation, we soon discovered that she was the owner of the McCain French Fry Empire. She was very gracious and welcoming, and made me feel comfortable for the remainder of the evening.

The ride home was quiet again. I tried to make conversation about Mrs. McCain to avoid the guerilla in the room, and I refused to address his proposal because I had already told him that the timing wasn't good.

He didn't say much either. He dropped me off and asked if he could take me to the airport to say a proper goodbye. I told him it was fine but my parents were coming to send me off and he could meet them if he wanted. But I think I just added more fuel to the fire.

Becoming a Citizen of the World

It was departure day and I was excited and nervous. I had to give my keys to the landlord on the day before I was scheduled to leave, so I stayed at the hotel with my parents.

In the meantime, Julio called and asked if we wanted to have brunch before going to the airport. He wanted to share contact information and meet my parents. He said he'd meet us at the hotel downtown. Since we'd be going to the airport after brunch, I invited JB to join us too.

It was an informative brunch filled with pleasantries. My dad was emphatic about Julio protecting me from the animals. My mom said she wasn't worried, but she kept reiterating to Julio, "Please take care of my baby, please take care of my baby." She said it over and over again. When she wasn't saying it, my stepmother would reiterate the same thing. "Please take care of our baby." I think Julio got the point.

JB showed up an hour into the meal. He teaches classes on Saturdays and was delayed by a student who needed extra help. He missed brunch, but wanted to make sure he arrived in time to go to the airport with us.

I introduced him to my parents and they seemed to hit it off right away. He jumped in the car with us and we laughed and joked all the way to the airport.

We arrived at the airport and met up with Julio who was joined by three of the doctors who were volunteering on the tour. They were all substantially older than me. I felt a little intimidated, but my dad sensed my angst and began massaging my shoulders. His massages always calmed my nerves and this time was no exception.

We checked in at Delta airlines as a group—business class seats. I was impressed. "I could get used to this real easy," I thought to myself.

After we finished checking in, the rest of the group headed to the security checkpoint while I said my goodbyes to my parents. JB accompanied me to the security checkpoint and in a last ditch effort to persuade me, he dropped another bomb.

"You know Anais, it's not too late to just marry me and call this whole thing off," he said.

I was floored once again. I'd been avoiding him all this time, but he wouldn't let it go.

"I'll take care of you until you find a job if you stay with me," he followed.

I was already nervous and couldn't take any more unnecessary pressure. I went off on him.

"JB, that is so selfish of you! You know I have to do this. I told you straight up that I was leaving and the timing isn't right. Besides, I'm still in a relationship with Tariq," I said. I was honored, but upset that he'd put more unwanted pressure on me.

"I'm not worried about him," he said with a smug sense of confidence. "But I will await your return. Please accept my apologies. I just don't want to lose you," he said.

I couldn't believe what I was hearing. But he wasn't finished and for some reason thought it was the perfect time to confess his undying love for me.

"I fell in love with you the first time I saw you at the Balcony in that baby blue dress. It was the first time I'd been so awestruck by someone. I knew God sent you to me. But I do realize that you need to spread your wings," he said as he looked me in my eyes and spoke with more sincerity than just about anyone I'd ever encountered.

"You're right though. I've traveled the world and would never want to deny you the opportunity to become a citizen of the world," he said as he pulled out a card and handed it to me. On the card was a beautiful photo of the world from space and the words written in calligraphy: *You have now become a Citizen of the World. Cherish it. Spread Peace. And encourage others.*

"I was given this card after I finished my first world tour, and I couldn't be more honored than to share it with you. After all, when you get back we'll have to share some of those travel stories together," he finished.

I started tearing up and shaking in my boots. Still in disbelief that he actually proposed to me right before I was getting on the airplane, I pulled myself together. I kissed him on the cheek, gave him another big hug, and joined Julio and the others in the security line.

When I looked back, my mother was hugging JB. He was crying and she tried to console him.

I blew them a kiss and continued on to the gate. I'd finally boarded the airplane and took off to become a Citizen of the World. Although I was still in shock from JB's last-ditch effort to stop me, the nerves quickly dissipated. The still, small voice assured me that I was on the right track, and I was well on my way to continue my life's purpose of sharing fun love with food.

Menu

Join Us for a Kickin' It Live Afro-Trinidad Celebration

featuring

DINNER

MILDLY SPICED & FRAGRANT SWEET CURRIED CHICKEN
served with "buss up shot," a buttery flatbread

STEWED OXTAILS WITH ROOT VEGETABLES
with spices and fragrant herbs

PELAU
an aromatic rice pilaf

FRY BAKE
a yeast bread fried in small patties, served with a salted cod sauté

ROTI WITH DAL PURI
a tender flatbread filled with seasoned chickpeas

PIGEON PEAS & RICE

CHOW AKA MANGO CHUTNEY
a sweet-and-sour salsa

SOUSE
pickled pig parts

BEVERAGES

ICED TEA • SORREL • PEANUT PUNCH

MAUBY
a digestive tea made from a tree bark boiled with anise seeds

DESSERT

SWEET POTATO & OATMEAL CRUNCH CAKES

COCONUT FUDGE CANDY

ENTERTAINMENT

CASINO GAMES
fundraising for DWB with roulette, blackjack, Pitty Pat, and poker.
Caribbean DJ for dancing Trinidad carnival-style all evening.

ABOUT THE AUTHOR

DEDICATED TO MY CHILDREN, family, and the countless friends around the world I've cooked for, fellowshipped with, or who fed me, the *Fun Love with Food* series of novels and cookbooks are an homage to the seven evolutionary taste sensations* I aspire to capitalize on while growing into a pecuniary culinary connoisseur. In my never-ending quest to indulge in and share delicious and affordable food and fun, I set out to write the first book more than thirty years ago. Deeply rooted in my unyielding obsession with good food, the excitement of traveling to new and interesting destinations, and satiating even the most discriminating appetites with my culinary prowess, I have been able to observe and incorporate three decades of global traditions, food trends, and evolving culinary experiences into a series of books.

The series is also rooted in my lifelong quest to eradicate the systemic prejudice and racism that distorts and contradicts the ideology of loving another just as you love yourself. It seeks to reach across all races, cultures, religions, and classes to use cooking and food as a foundation to build bridges to the true meaning and manifestations of love and respect from one to another.

A *nom de plume*, the name Dominique Beriniki means "Victorious Woman of God." As such, I offer this series of novels, recipes, and titillating experiences as intimate gifts that I hope will bring everlasting joy, happiness, and bountiful blessings to my current and soon to be family, friends, and loved ones the world over. My hope is that these books will serve as living and breathing love letters that inspire you to create infinite ways to cook, eat, and have fun love with food.

Although many people recognize only four to five taste sensations, as a chef, I construct food with the goal of stimulating a more extensive palate of taste buds that represent sweet, salty, sour, bitter, astringent, pungent, and umami.

ACKNOWLEDGEMENTS

I would be remiss if I didn't give homage and my most heartfelt thanks to those closest to me that helped bring this book to fruition in the final stages:

My mother, who has ALWAYS been my inspiration and forever love of my life;

My immediate family for the wisdom, unconditional love and willingness to test and critique all of my creations and recreations;

My nieces, nephews, and dearest friends who served as the primary readers and listeners;

My amazing editor and graphic designers who are simply incredible experts at what they do; and most importantly

Almighty God who orders my steps everyday.

Thank you!